Macmillan Publishing Company

• New York •

Maxwell Macmillan Canada

• Toronto •

Maxwell Macmillan International

New York • Oxford • Singapore • Sydney

La Vera Cucina Italiana

The Fundamentals of
Classic Italian Cooking

DONALDO SOVIERO

Macmillan Publishing Company
866 Third Avenue, New York, NY 10022

Maxwell Macmillan Canada, Inc.
1200 Eglinton Avenue East, Suite 200
Don Mills, Ontario M3C 3N1

Macmillan Publishing Company is part of the Maxwell
Communication Group of Companies.

Library of Congress Catagloging-in-Publication Data
Soviero, Donaldo.
   La vera cucina italiana : the fundamentals of classic Italian
cooking / Donaldo Soviero.
      p.   cm.
   ISBN 0-02-612570-6
   1. Cookery, Italian. I. Title.
TX723.S663   1991
641.5945—dc20   91-19687   CIP

Macmillan books are available at special discounts for bulk purchases
for sales promotions, premiums, fund-raising, or educational use.
For details, contact:

Special Sales Director
Macmillan Publishing Company
866 Third Avenue
New York, NY 10022

10 9 8 7 6 5 4 3 2 1

Printed in the United States of America

Book Design by Liney Li

CONTENTS

INTRODUCTION

I 'VE been cooking, studying, and teaching *la vera cucina italiana*—the true cooking of Italy—for some thirty years now and remain fascinated with its endless variety and the "correctness" of its cooking methods. In saying "correctness," I'm really trying to translate the Italian phrase *È giusto*—it is just, appropriate, correct!

In my opinion this is perhaps one of the greatest aspects of *la vera cucina*—aside from the freshness of ingredients and cooking with love, care, and devotion—is that Italians always seem to come up with the right treatment of available ingredients at the right time. This is referred to in Italian as *stagionale,* or "seasonal." When I first came to live in Italy several years ago, it was difficult to adjust to what seemed to be a continual lack of ingredients after I had become accustomed to total year-round availability of such things as produce and game in America. As my son Dino so aptly put it, "It's a shock to come to Italy and not be able to make linguine with broccoli whenever you want it."

Of course, there is greater availability in the larger cities such as Florence, Rome, Milan, and Venice, but in the smaller towns and hilltop villages, such as Todi, where I live, people exist in a more ancient manner—waiting for artichokes, broccoli, cauliflower, cardoons, escarole, fennel, pheasant, quail, venison, wild boar, in turn, but thereby getting a fresher, more natural product; and treating each newcomer with more respect and interest than would be the case if they were available all year round.

The regions of Italy are so different in so many aspects that even the slightest consideration of them becomes an immediate delight. But in spite of these differences, and in spite of so many authoritative opinions to the contrary, I'm convinced that there is a national unity to Italian cooking—a national cuisine, so to speak—that is unmistakable, and that separates it from all others. Giuliano Bugialli, in *The Fine Art of Italian Cooking,* supports this contention this way:

Just as one speaks dialect or vernacular in the home, with the family, so home cooking tends to exaggerate regional differences. And rarely does one region restrict its cooking to those dishes which are "alla" that region. Cotoletta alla milanese is made all over Italy, as is Pizza napoletana.

It might be as simple as starting with a clove of garlic and some rich extra virgin olive oil instead of shallots and butter; or as complicated as the many different lasagnes from Sicily to Milan and all points east and west; but the taste, the feeling, and the reality are Italian. Whether it is *cucina casalinga* or *casareccia* (home cooking), *alta cucina vecchia* (ancient high cooking), *tradizionale* (traditional), *alto livello* (high level) or *novella cucina* (nouvelle cooking), there is an unmistakable taste—a quality engendered by "correctness"— that is the subject of our work. For in our opinion all Italian cooking is *veramente giusto*—truly just and appropriate—when truly Italian. Of course, that leads back to the question, "What is *la vera cucina italiana?*"

To put this into proper perspective, it will be helpful to look briefly at the history of food in Italy. As in perhaps no other country, the food of Italy has been a function of its history. But before we do that, please allow me a personal digression (the better to know me by) that will explain how and why I became so enamored of the world of Italian gastronomy: for a serious romance it has been, is, and—from all odds—now will remain, the greatest love of my life.

When I was a little fellow, eons ago, my father and I were unusually close; and although it was rather strange for someone as politically involved as he to have a child tagging along, our relationship was mature enough not to interfere with the endless appearances he had to make in further-ance of his career. For some reason, I was ac-cepted.

As it turned out, that was my gastronomic good luck. I was a second-generation Italian-American in Queens County, Long Island, during the thirties and forties, growing up with a politi-cian-lawyer-philanthropist diehard Italian fa-ther, which meant being exposed to an infinite number of weddings, funerals, rallies, balls, pic-nics, and affairs, not to mention the more serious and more intimate family exchanges of Sunday dinners.

And so I found myself standing on the side-walks outside innumerable funeral homes, look-ing up and listening to well-groomed men who seemed to have a warm affinity and respect for one another. In spite of their main preoccupation with politics, charities, and the need for Italians to join together, there weren't any conversations I can remember that didn't turn on a recent gas-tronomic adventure.

"Well, Giuseppe, it looks like Tony is gonna get the Appellate Division. He's a good boy, and you as president of the Bar ought to push the judge a little bit. The Court of Appeals makes the final decision. I know you'll do what you can. At any rate, you know the Luna out by Belmont racetrack? A bunch of us went there Monday night after the meeting. Where were you? You slipped out early? Get the boy home, eh? Well, Giorgio had a linguine with broccoli that was as good as my Maria makes . . . . They weren't afraid to crisp it—you know, that dark golden brown with the chopped garlic thrown in at the end so it don't burn."

Or perched on the edge of an ornately carved chair with red velvet backing, balancing a doilied plate with *biscotti* (biscuits) and cookies clustered with powdered sugar as the bereaved widow in-tertwined the impermanence of life with the need for sustenance . . .

"Aiutami Dio [God help me], Counsellor, Car-mine was just a boy, *sessantaquattro* [64]. Such an angel, God bless him, he took care of everybody. Such a good man. Here, let the boy have some of this anisette with the cookies. It's the best, from Palermo. Carmine saved it for special occasions. Eh, boy, why you not eatta your cookies? Better yet, comea with me—I got some meat balls and cold spaghetti you gonna like very much. I told Carmine to eat breakfast, but he's always on the run. Too much coffee and brandy. No good for you. But you eatta good all the time you be big and strong and live forever. Come on! Come with me! *Mangia!"*

No matter where we went, there was always a special cake, cookies, homemade wine, or the finest imported Marsala or anisette to be sampled, approved, raved over, and, actually looking back, treasured.

Favorite restaurant lunches, dinners, and late-night pizza or *linguine aglio olio* parties were just the icing on the cake of a life in a society that thought more about the recent crop of figs, or Aunt Giulia's manicotti, than philosophy or religion. Church on Sunday was for women, and the rest of the week was to experience one culinary delight after another. Not to imply that one didn't eat on Sundays.

Oh, those wonderful family Sundays! Never less than ten, and upward of twenty, people there for serious eating. The rest of the week was just a warmup, and now each brought his biggest and best appetite to be measured and approved by the quantity of the food ingested and the joy that one apparently experienced.

By the age of sixteen, I was not only able to enjoy, but required, a whole pound of macaroni for openers at these endless feasts. Dinner started at noon and continued until four or five in the afternoon, after which, with a few hours' recess to nap or play pool, the ritual began again at seven or eight o'clock and continued until midnight, with high-stakes poker as a further incentive.

Looking back at the menu and the quantities of food that were not only eaten but savored, it seems hardly possible that we survived.

It was an era of prodigious and good eating. Fast and frozen were unknown, and respect was given to the best and finest ingredients as if that were the only criterion for eating something. People waited for the next spring peas and ate them fine and fresh and rushed to the table, as they did with corn and beefsteak tomatoes. M.F.K. Fisher's paean to a bowl of fresh peas was more readily understood back then, and although the Italians could have been considered the "gourmets" of that society, this preoccupation with quality wasn't limited to them. No, the German side of my family (my mother was a Nordic blonde from Heidelberg) was always searching for the best knockwurst, *bockwurst, weisswurst,* and rabbits for *hassenpfeffer,* as well as the best gingersnaps to finish off a *sauerbraten.* Her father, my maternal grandfather, was a handsome giant of a man with luxurious steel-gray hair who, as a

butcher in one of the wholesale meat houses in Brooklyn, was always bringing home choice cuts of well-aged meat, sweetbreads, calves' brains, and all the sausages he could find. My mother was a born and bred eater.

I remember well and fondly her solo Saturday luncheons. This was a lady who guarded her comely figure so well that she would embrace all the latest diet fads of the time while cooking sumptuous Italian feasts for my father and his friends. She would diet on grapefruit juice and black coffee all week and then, at noon every Saturday, she would sit down, by herself, to a platter of assorted wursts in wine kraut with bay leaf and juniper berries; a bowl of homemade potato salad and the essential coffee cake—otherwise known as a butter cake with sliced almonds and sugar.

My father and brother and I were allowed to sit and watch, but it was an unbroken rule, or understanding, that it was now time for us to enjoy her pleasure, as she'd enjoyed ours, all the rest of the days, year in and year out. There was something very special in sharing this time with her. It gave us a chance to seem unselfish for a change, and trained us to appreciate and enjoy a woman's pleasure. It was these times that made me realize she was really a separate, individual, pleasurable person, and not just a mother.

My mother's being German should have removed her from the competition in cooking with the Soviero side of the family. It didn't.

"Oh, you know they like the *sauerbraten* and dumplings, and the red cabbage, sprouts, potatoes *rösti*—the whole thing. But then, they're sitting there waiting for the spaghetti. No, your mother can teach me and I'll make them Italian food they won't forget."

Of course, Grandma Soviero, who was from Vesuvio, was no slouch—and teach she did. She lived with us till she died at the age of ninety. I was only eight or nine at the time, but I can remember how guilty I felt because I was enjoying so immensely all the wonderful cakes, pastries, and cookies my Uncle Frank, a baker, kept supplying the week-long wake with. They took dying seriously in those days, but didn't forget to nourish the living.

So, to my great benefit, my mother learned to cook Italian. I can remember how proud we all were that after a while she was not only accepted, but received the highest praise of all.

"Oh, Betty, she's a bright one, all right! She wasn't going to let her in-laws beat her at the cooking game. There isn't a dish she can't do—and even better than mine. . . . She's got a special touch . . . so light . . . yet the flavor's always there." This from my Aunt Giulia.

The wonderful part of our relationship was that, although she had certain dogmatic traits, she nevertheless was a great teacher, and had the patience to explain things to me in a very relaxed and pleasurable manner. I just knew she enjoyed my interest, which I suppose is the *sine qua non* of teaching.

It was rather odd for a somewhat roistering schoolyard tough—we lived directly across from what was originally a little wooden red schoolhouse become a brick fortress, complete with a concrete schoolyard and wire fencing—to take such an interest in cooking. I was certainly affected by the intense gastronomic surroundings I was raised in, but what really hooked me was *Gourmet* magazine. (Now, if that's not a testimonial, I never heard one!) To my recollection, back in those days they featured French, Viennese, and other high European cooking, without any consideration of Italian. It was this exposure to the highest forms of these other culinary cultures that so impressed me that I had to learn more. My mother nurtured that interest to the extent that one semester, I can't remember which, although I was certainly not more than thirteen or fourteen, she actually allowed me to remain out of school to help her in the kitchen.

As usual, she had an incredibly busy fall schedule. Aside from the endless extra preparation for Thanksgiving, Christmas, and the New Year, she had two or three bridge club luncheons, several pre-theater suppers, a cocktail reception for seventy-five to a hundred people that, as president of the Red Cross, she catered herself, as well as the usual round of dinner parties that my father would give both for friends and politicians, usually both together. All told, I guess she had to entertain four or five hundred people that fall. Well, she broke her wrist by slipping on the cellar staircase. It turned out to be my good fortune, for I was not only allowed to stay out of school—which was unheard of at that time, especially since she was also president of the mothers' club—but really learned how to cook as well; not just recipes, but production—getting it all out there in proper sequence, looking pretty, on nice, warm (or cold, where needed) plates.

What a fall that was! Strangely, however, for many years I forgot it, until my mother reminded me of it on her eighty-third birthday, during a speech she made to the many guests at the party I gave her.

"This grand chef, who prepared this loving feast with such care for us all, probably doesn't remember that it was my broken wrist that started him on his career."

To this day I use her recipes for manicotti, *sugo di carne, salsa al pomodoro,* marinara, creamed spinach, walnut roll, and rum cake, among others. Yes, I guess it's fair to say my mother learned her lessons well and taught me equally as well.

What was a surprise for me was that, in the end, it was really Italian food she liked, even more than her beloved assorted wursts with wine kraut. She lived a full and happy life and was blessed with an iron constitution.

Never sick a day in her life that we knew of. But at eighty-four she was afflicted with terminal abdominal cancer, and at eighty-six she died. In the last weeks before her death I moved in with her in Florida to provide love and companionship (my father had died ten years previously), and to cook for her. Well, I began with the usual rich chicken broth, *bollito mistos* of all types, puddings, custards, tea cakes, and even went so far as to purée her vegetables and make her some lovely little soufflés I might not have otherwise tried. The surprise was, after being extremely polite for a week or so, she finally blurted out:

"Look, son . . . what's the point. There isn't a diet in the world that's going to stop what's happening to me. It's just my time to go. So why don't we stop kidding. Please don't think I don't appreciate what you're trying to do, but it won't work. I might as well eat what I want . . . what little I can."

"What do you want?"

"Marinara! Linguine with marinara. Would you believe that?"

The last thing she ate was *linguine alla marinara*.

My father, on the other hand, didn't cook. But he sure could eat. I remember well how he taught me to strip a lobster with my teeth. He'd suck every bit of meat and juice out of every corner of every piece of shell and fiber.

Friday was fish night. I learned at an early age how good fresh oysters and fresh littleneck clams on the half shell could be—just a bit of lemon and pepper on the first three-quarters, and then the indulgence of hot, spicy cocktail sauce with extra horseradish on the rest.

Yes, the Soviero clan were, and still are, from the towns of Vesuvio outside Pompeii, and from the greater Neapolitan area, but the endless intermarriages that occurred over the years on both my mother's and father's sides of the family expanded our cultural contact to include many other regions of Italy and parts of Germany as well.

And it wasn't just the Italians and the Germans that provided this life of rich treats. We were not that provincial that we weren't able to savor wonderful Yankee clam bakes and corned beef and cabbage with our Irish counterparts. Not to forget to pay tribute to the marvellous soups, cabbage dishes, sandwiches, cakes, wine, cordials and the ever-present special feast dishes of the Poles, Hungarians and Jews. Dark German beers and rich English ales were also abounding, and never tasted better than when drunk with charcoal-grilled, or griddle-browned, hot dogs. In spite of our Italian preferences, we'd spend many nights driving all the way to Coney Island (about an hour each way) for fresh little neck clams on the half shell and crisped, crunchy hot dogs from the old, well-worn griddles of Nathan's. Hamburgers weren't thought much of back then.

Every house you went to back then, regardless of its nationality, took pride in its cooking, and eager ladies were ever present to push you to sample their humble efforts. For this was still a country of immigrants who knew only how to present the best of their cuisine as a form of social grace, the charm of which seems to have been lost forever.

The most respected and sought-after experiences outside our own milieu were French. The political and social scene we knew in Queens back then was devoid of French culture, which made French cooking a remote and wonderfully mysterious thing.

We had no acquaintance with kitchens that might be making *poulet à l'estragon, tripe à la mode de Caen,* cassoulet, onion soups, *ris de veau financier, sole bonne femme,* or the supreme lobster thermidor. Nor did the Italian-American community I was brought up in seem to know that the true cooking of Italy encompassed all of these dishes and more. French was considered the *alta cucina,* haute cuisine, and was thought to be far superior to *la cucina casalinga*—the home cooking of Italy. They just didn't know the *alta cucina* of Italy nor realize its greatness or historical significance.

The American Italian restaurant scene in the late forties and early fifties, in comparison to French, simply fortified this ignorance. Whereas marvels of gastronomy were being put forth by some of the great French chefs who came to America to cook at Chambord, Le Pavillon, Le Grenouille, the Waldorf, the Plaza, and the Pierre, the great chefs of Italy stayed at home, so it was failed Neapolitan cooks and waiters who suddenly became the Italian chefs and restaurateurs of America. So what we looked for was *cucina casalinga*—home cooking—rather than the feeble attempts at international cooking formed in the phoney continental Italian restaurants.

Among restaurants, Giambelli, Romeo Salta, Barbetta, Grotta Azzurra, and Vesuvio were a few of the exceptions that produced creditable regional presentations, but neither in price, prestige, nor actual quality was the cooking on a par with the Villa d'Este at Lake Como or Pappagallo's of Bologna, which at their best, in those days, could easily be preferred to the sometimes overwrought complications of French haute cuisine. It seems a crime that Mama Leone's was to become the American ideal of Italian cooking. Fortunately, the wave of the eighties in America is Italian, and respected, established restaurateurs and chefs from Italy have chosen America in which to open a proliferation of *trattorias, cantinas,* and *ristorantes,* which have greatly improved the situation.

But back then my exposure to the cooking of Italy was mainly through the housewives, who were not trained or knowledgeable in the more complex dishes of the *alta cucina d'Italia.* When I first raved about lobster thermidor in our circle, no one countered with an *aragosta* or *astici alla parmigiana,* nor knew that béchamel and mornay were Italian inventions. It is for these reasons— this lack of knowledge and subservience to snob appeal—that later on, in my early twenties when I was becoming a chef, I put all my energies and studies into the grand cooking of the French haute cuisine.

My training in a formal sense came through Carême, Escoffier, Diat, and Fernand Point, to the total exclusion of both the Italians and the historical significance of *la vera cucina italiana.* Of course, my interest might have been different if the same caliber of chef that came from France had come from Italy. But since this was not the case, I became an idolater, a worshipper of false idols.

It was not until several years later, after a few abortive attempts at *la grande cuisine* in hotels and restaurants, that, when reading the bible of French gastronomic literature, *Larousse gastronomique,* I came across a reference to Italian cooking as a "veritable mother cuisine." This changed my culinary life. To a young, impressionable chef of that time, such an admission by the most accepted, authoritative treatise on cooking in the world was a finger pointing backward—to my roots, to the real cooking of Italy. And suddenly I wanted to know:

Who the hell are we?

Where did we come from?

How did Italian cooking start?

What was its development historically?

What is regional Italian cooking?

How do we relate to the French in the world of gastronomy?

What is the true cooking of Italy—*la vera cucina italiana*?

A whole world of enchantment was revealed to me that was to provide interest, pleasure, and an occupational challenge that would remain with me my entire life. Not only did I regain new respect for the home cooking I was brought up on, but found a truly sophisticated and most important historical cuisine that to this day remains the most honest and properly respected culinary art in the world.

And the conviction grew to a certainty that:

"I knew all along that eating all those damned peppers would lead somewhere."

And so, if I may, I'll share a little of my continuing research with you as an introduction to our endeavors in basic Italian cooking.

As I have said, the food of Italy has certainly been a function of its history. It seems that over the centuries everyone was drawn to "sunny Italy" with its rich soil, abundant game, and seemingly endless variety of fish. Since the early settlements of the Etruscans in the eighth century B.C., waves of invaders swept through Italy. Phoenicians, Illyrians, Celts, Gauls, Greeks, Longobards, Vandals, Arab-Saracens, Slavs, Austrians, Spaniards, Catalans, Hungarians, Angevins, Hohenstaufens, Aragonese, and French—all, at one time or another, sacked, raped, pillaged, and conquered the Italian peninsula. But the ones who left the greatest gastronomic mark were the Greeks and the Saracens (Arabs).

The Etruscans were a hardy and happy agricultural people who, according to the best authorities, came from the Greek islands. The Greeks knew them as Tyrrhenians or Tyrsenians, and it was the Romans at a later date who called them Barbarians or Tuscans. Tuscan also meant "Italie" to the later Romans.

Their lives were governed by a religion that saw God in everything. The cities were laid out according to religious laws based on divination, as were the crops planted and harvested. Celebrations and feasts were all part of a divine plan. They were a simple people whose spartan lives were reflected in their cuisine. Their great contribution to Italy was the cultivation of wheat, out of which they made a primitive flour and a sort of mush called *puls.* It is said that the Roman Empire was built on *puls,* for that was the standard diet of the Roman legions, just as hardtack, or biscuit, was a staple for English and American seamen in the eighteenth century. It is interesting to note that the cities and areas known as Etruria constitute Tuscany and Umbria, where the cuisines remain rustic, simple, and agrarian, as opposed to the lush prodigality of nearby Emilia Romagna.

Now picture, if you will, the introduction of oil, garlic, wine, and fish chowders or soups from Greek traders as a superimposition on this basic, simple agrarian fare. Practically every region of Italy touches the sea; only Lombardy, Piedmont, Trentino, and Umbria do not, and these areas abound with well-stocked lakes and rivers that add freshwater fish to the already multitudinous presentation of all kinds of fish from the sea. So the Greek contribution was extremely valuable and remains central to Italian cooking. Fish was,

and is, as important as pasta in the Italian diet. *Zuppa di pesce, brodetto, zuminno,* or *caciucco* (names of fish soups from different regions) probably predate bouillabaisse by centuries, contrary to French insistence. In a country where no one is more than 150 miles from the sea, "freshest" and "best" can hardly be considered euphemisms. No country has fish cookery that even vaguely rivals that of Italy, and practically every known method of eating and cooking all the varieties of fish and shellfish were known to the early Romans. One has only to browse through *De Re Coquinaria* by Apicius to realize the extent of cooking technology in early Roman times . . . poaching, braising, grilling, roasting, roux, sauces, and the marvels produced in *bagno maria*—waterbath cooking— were all prevalent.

The Arab-Saracen contributions to Italian cooking did not occur until the eighth century A.D. when the Arabs conquered Sicily, bringing with them nutmeg, mace, coriander, cardamom, fennel, anise, clove, ginger, tarragon, and cayenne—all the spices and herbs that later were to become the essence of great Renaissance cooking. They also brought with them the method for distillation that led to the development of grappa and brandy, and their expertise for making *millefoglie* or *millefeuille* (meaning "1,000 sheet" in both languages)—or puff pastry—and ice cream, which was brought by the Arabs from China through Morocco to Sicily.

To understand "Roman" cuisine one has to be careful to look at the right period in time. If we understand history correctly, all civilizations seem to grow, prosper, and thrive on the spartan lifestyle and strong will of their people. The Romans were no exception. They were an incredibly strong, spartan, and seriously accomplished people, and this "quality of life," so to speak, was translated directly into their cooking. So that as much as Carême in the nineteenth century turned up his nose at what he saw in Apicius writing in A.D. 80, nevertheless that cuisine was rich beyond belief for the world at that time. There is no doubt that the Romans from 100 B.C. to A.D. 100 created a completely sophisticated cuisine. They had developed the bain-marie, poaching, egg sauces, cream sauces, stocks, soups, roasting, basting, braising, stewing, baking, the roux, bread, and *lagane* (lasagne), as reported by Cicero. At that time the cuisine was without the vulgar excesses that were to typify the Romans "at orgy" previous to and during the fall of the Roman Empire. What happened?

Well, the great conquerors, soldiers, statesmen, lawmakers, road builders, administrators "nonpareil" grew soft and dissipated, and what had begun in or near 100 B.C. as some fifty-five religious festivals per year ended as being 550 drunken revelries staged by politicians to gain votes in the Senate and curry favor with the populace—the mob—at the time of the fall, between A.D. 250 and 300.

This degeneration was also to be found at the table. The nobles had vomitoriums, which allowed them to feast at orgies for weeks at a time, only interrupting to vomit so they could eat more. What had been an austere and technically advanced cuisine, marrying the best of simplicity to technical innovation through a wealth of ideas and money, became as vulgar and insane as their games had also become.

The corruption from within was so vast that it took very little for the so-called barbarians to turn and conquer. And when they did, they didn't bother with luxurious feasts. They hacked meat off the spit with one hand while they raped, sacked, and pillaged with the other. And so the great cooking of Rome disappeared. Fortunately, the monks and nuns in monasteries and convents preserved the basics—the best part—of Roman cuisine for its eventual return in the Renaissance some 1,100 years later.

Now that is rather interesting in itself. While there is no doubt as to claims by Luther and others of degeneracy, debauchery, simony, and lechery being prevalent among the Catholic hierarchy during the Dark and Middle Ages, nonetheless there were a great number of dedicated, so-called religious people who worked and lived a communal life of frugal simplicity. It was here that the best of Roman cooking, its technical competence, was preserved, nurtured, and practiced—handed down, in effect, to become the second greatest gastronomic wonder of the world, Italian *alta cucina* cooking in the Renaissance.

It wasn't until the Renaissance that a true understanding and respect for gastronomy re-emerged. Those same artists, poets, scientists, and thinkers who were to bring about the unparalleled glory of the Renaissance were at the same time exchanging recipes, cooking for one another, expanding ideas through gourmet societies, and working with professional chefs to bring about a culinary renaissance as well. They developed the most sophisticated cuisine in the world once again, and forever married the wondrous spices of the Levant to the indigenous cooking of Italy, to produce some of the finest taste sensations the world has ever seen. And all this without the tomatoes and peppers that came from Mexico, America, and Peru late in the sixteenth century.

They had preserved the best from the cuisine of ancient Rome and perfected its techniques while the French were still spit roasting. In fact, the first, oldest, and to this day most important French gastronomic society in the world—*les chaînes des rôtisseurs*—literally means "the spit-roasting guild." Founded in the twelfth century, this was a guild of cooks who roasted meat on a spit.

When Caterina de' Medici went to France in 1540 to marry Henry II, she was accompanied by a retinue of chefs and a complete staff of cooks, sauciers, and pastry chefs. She so dazzled the French that they were immediately converted to the higher world of gastronomy. Her daughter Maria was to continue that good influence when she came to marry Henry IV by also bringing a fully trained staff with her. Hence the recognition by *Larousse gastronomique* of Italian cooking as "the mother cuisine." This is not just historical hogwash. The debt is clear.

Of course, this in no way takes away from the brilliance and scientific amplification that the French made in creating their own haute cuisine. In fact, it is mainly this scientific approach that makes the difference between *alta cucina* and haute cuisine.

Chefs and cooks in Italy retained an autonomy that enabled them to make their own sauces and pastry, among other things, rather than to rely on the French guard system, where the work is broken down into sections, and a sauté man gets his sauce from a saucier, and so on. In Italy every chef is his own saucier, and nothing is scientifically standardized in the French manner. This accounts for the fact that bolognese sauce in Bologna will be made differently in hundreds of restaurants throughout Italy and will still be called *salsa bolognese.*

These regional variations become more understandable when you study the language and suddenly realize that there are over seven hundred dialects: Ladin in Friuli Venezia Giulia, Catalan in Sardinia, Senese in Siena, and so on.

In spite of this specific and intense regionalism, however, the country can still be realistically divided along cuisine lines into north and south. This north-south division is known as the "poverty line" or the "veal line," because in truth the wealth of Italy, industrially and commercially, is in the north and the south remains the poor country cousin with all the faults that are endemic to such connotations.

But even here there is sharp disagreement as to where one begins and the other ends. Some purists maintain that anywhere south of Florence is southern, and others accept the Via Salaria ("salt road") starting in Rome as the natural dividing line.

Gastronomically, the north luxuriates in cream, butter, truffles, egg noodles, veal, and coffee, while the south makes imaginative use of flour and water pasta *(pasta secca)* and aged cow *(vitellina),* although it is obvious they have more than compensated with a robust cuisine based on oil, garlic, and tomatoes.

Even within these divisions all is not clear cut, since the best oils come from Tuscany (Lucca), and Emilia Romagna uses three fats proficiently—butter, oil, and lard. Of course, if there is a dominant style of northern Italian cooking, it is to be found in Bologna, just as Naples and Sicily dominate the south to some extent.

But whether you have a *pasticcio di lasagne verdi alla bolognese* (made with green spinach egg noodles, bolognese sauce, truffles, cream, and parmigiano) or zita or zitoni (the long tubular spaghetti) and sardines and garlic in green olive oil from Sicily, the unmistakable unity is there, and you know you're eating Italian.

The arguments may go on endlessly about the regional variations and *alta cucina, autentica* and *genuina, la vera cucina dell'Italia*—the true cooking of Italy—but to anyone not involved directly, it is quite easy to sit back, relax, and let the battle rage as to which lasagne is the best as you sample and enjoy hundreds of unbelievable adventures in gastronomic perfection.

What is *la vera cucina italiana?* Time was when we would answer the question by saying what it was not. To wit:

1. Soggy and watery pasta smothered in tomato-paste sauce.
2. Lead-sinker meat balls poached in water on a steam table.
3. Rubbery turkey breasts substituting for veal and coated with premixed bread crumbs.
4. Greasy soups made with vegetables that were dead *ab initio* and embalmed through boiling.
5. Awful, sweet desserts laced with artificial coloring, liqueurs, rum, and so on.

Fortunately, all that has changed in America. *Trattorias* abound with wood-burning ovens, grilled veal chops, ravioli in sage butter, and *torta mascarpone* made with the real thing instead of cream cheese.

Thanks to such fine writers and teachers as Giuliano Bugialli, Marcella Hazan, and Ada Boni, the lid has been taken off the mystique of Italian cooking, and you find authentic *ragùs* and *sugos* simmering in a bit of cold-pressed extra virgin olive oil. Fresh basil, thyme, sage, marjoram, chervil, rosemary, mint, nutmeg, mace, coriander, red pepper, and juniper are not only used but understood.

Every city in America now seems to have a half dozen "fresh" pasta stores, and although the quality is not what some of us would like to see, nonetheless it is obvious that the general consciousness has been raised to admit that in reality classic Italian cooking is the mother cuisine of the world and not just a historical anachronism.

From the somewhat Frenchified and Germanic north to the Greco-Moorish south, there is a unified Italian cuisine, even though there are innumerable regional variations. This unmistakable Italian taste exists in spite of the modifications, elaborations, and endless innovations to be found as you travel from one region to another and drop from the mountains to the plains, valleys, and the ever-surrounding sea.

Antipasti, soups, breads, hundreds of different varieties of pasta with dozens of special fillings, stuffings and sauces; meat, shellfish, poultry, feathered and hooved game, variety meats; poached, boiled, grilled, broiled, sautéed, fried, wood-oven baked and roasted—it's all here, and using most of the known herbs and spices from around the world. Add to this thousands of wonderful and economical wines; hundreds of the finest cheeses; fabulous pastry, cakes, and cookies, as well as the ubiquitous *gelato*—then superimpose seasonal and festival changes, and one begins to perceive what *la vera cucina* is all about.

To us the simplest definition came about in 1958, and has been prominently displayed in every kitchen I have worked in since:

Start with the finest and freshest natural ingredients, cook with love, knowledge, and devotion, and serve everyone as if they were the most honored guest ever to come into your home.

This, in the final analysis, is perhaps the real meaning of *la vera cucina italiana*.

THE
BASICS

THE BASICS

MANY prospective students ask, "What do I have to know about cooking in general to cook Italian?" Fair question! To say "everything" or "very little" would beg the question; as would an answer that it doesn't matter, since we're going to teach you everything anyway.

What follows, I hope, is a useful reference source for unfamiliar terms and techniques you might encounter as your cooking progresses, not just the bare essentials.

Since baking bread requires special ingredients, equipment, and terminology, this subject will be treated separately in its own chapter.

GENERAL TECHNIQUES

To score or bleed (intaccare). By making incisions in an ingredient with a sharp knife, you accomplish several things. First, in the case of garlic cloves and onions, you allow their juices to "bleed" out and better flavor the dish. Then, in reverse, by scoring something such as a hot dog or sausage, you're allowing better penetration of heat. Or, if the ingredient is in a pan with wine, stock, or another liquid, scoring will permit better permeation by the liquid. This is different from larding, where the incisions are deeper and fat, aromatics, and so on are inserted (see Larding).

Fix, refresh (fissare, rinfrescare). This term describes the process of stopping the cooking of vegetables—to "fix," set, capture the color and doneness of the product. This is done by placing the vegetables in a colander or strainer and running cold water over them until they're completely cold. Preferably this is done with a spray attachment, or failing that, with very gently running water.

Marinate (marinata). Marination is a very ancient technique of preserving meat. Many centuries B.C., meat was preserved in salt. Then someone must have noticed that meat stored this way was more tender and had a better flavor than fresh meat. This recognition led to further discoveries that acids (lemon, vinegar) and alcohol preserved meat while imparting an even better flavor. It would then be a very short step indeed to add aromatics (bay, rosemary, and so on) and thereby develop savory methods of toning down the gaminess of many meats, game, poultry, and fish to go beyond preservation and contribute to the development of cooking as art. All of this was known, practiced, and written about by the Romans as early as 100 B.C.

The preservative aspect of marination has

3

been diminished in importance by such modern methods of storage as refrigerating and freezing. But the use of marination to "tame" wild flavors and to enhance other not-so-gamy meat and fish is very prevalent in most international cuisines. The Italians, of course, having started it all, continue to use marinades extensively—in fact, more than any other cuisine I know, the Italians use the marinating liquids as the main liquid in their cooking. To wit, *lepre in salmi, coniglio, cinghiale, daino, fagiano*—all the game birds and meats are first marinated and then cooked in the marination with a bit more oil and garlic to make a salmis. French and international chefs will use a few tablespoons of the marinade added to other liquids such as stock and wine. This may well be the exact point where Italian cooking differs from French and others. The Italians will cook the rabbit in the marinade and only use a bit of *brodo*, or broth, not stock, to liquify it if needed. In fact, *salmi* in Italian indicates that it is cooked in a marinade, whereas in French, *salmis* is an elaborate procedure to extract more flavor. It is also one of the reasons why the average home cook in Italy wouldn't understand the need for rich-flavored stocks—and therefore *brodo* is ubiquitous in Italy.

Be that as it may, let's take a look at a light and a dark marinade to get a better sense of what this is all about. For game birds and meat that tend to be gamy, I use the following marinade: oil, garlic, carrot, celery, onion, parsley, thyme, basil, chervil, crushed red pepper, black peppercorn, bay leaf, juniper berry, coriander seed, salt, regular pepper, and red wine, the strength of which would be determined by the gaminess of the meat.

Assuming that we're talking about *lepre* (hare) or *daino* (deer), the red wine might be a big Sagrantino, Rubesco riserva, or Barolo, and the steeping time would be from eight to twenty-four hours. To steep, partially but not fully cover the meat with liquid and aromatics. Let it stand in a cool, dry place—not the refrigerator—and turn every 2 hours or so. The recipe would change radically, however, were we to be dealing with game or birds in the middle ground, such as pheasant, quail, rabbit, capon, turkey, or grouse. In that case, the recipe looks like this: oil, garlic, celery, carrot, onion, parsley, thyme, basil, chervil, marjoram, coriander, cardamom, rough-cut lemon, a few pieces of orange (cut and squeezed), salt, pepper, and a light Grignolino, Chianti, big Chardonnay, or highly aromatic Gewürztraminer.

In both cases, wash the birds or pieces of game with lemons, Cognac, and port before adding the other ingredients.

In the case of fish, eliminate the Cognac and port wash and make the marinade lighter yet, for example: oil, garlic, carrot, celery, onion, thyme, basil, chervil (in lesser amounts), parsley, lemon, and white wine of some fruitiness such as, depending on the fish, one of the lighter Rieslings. The Italians have a particular method of marinating fish. It's called *scapece* or *in saor*. The fish is usually breaded and fried first, and then placed in a marinade of vinegar, oil, garlic, onion, white wine, lemon, bay leaf, parsley, raisins, and pine nuts.

For every recipe in this area I can give you, there are hundreds of others. Some emphasize the onions by laying the meat on a bed of them and then simply pouring oil over all. The type of onion used will affect the dish. The simplest is the salt and water solution called brine, which is used for pickling, when certain aromatics are added. Others (such as a particular Umbrian recipe) call for the meat to be placed on a bed of bay leaves before lacing with oil and a few garlic cloves.

Marinades can also be cooked and used repeatedly, if you are careful and take them out and boil them every few days, the same as can be done with stock or glazes. The important thing to understand here is that good cooking begins with the finest ingredients, and a marinade is an ingredient that is very important because it sets the tone for the later flavor of the dish.

"Anglaise"/breading, dredging (impanare, dragare). The technique of breading, where you first dredge the meat with salt- and pepper-seasoned flour, then dip it in egg wash (seasoned eggs, beaten with a bit of water, wine, or milk) and then in seasoned bread crumbs, prior to deep-fat frying, is known as "anglaise." There has been some discussion among chefs about the right way to do this. Those who have to consider production in large quantities (restaurants, caterers, and so on) will eliminate all seasoning from the bread crumbs, since salt will break down the frying fat and thereby require more frequent changing of it. But for those who don't have the problem of economics, I recommend a seasoning as mild as just salt and pepper, as opposed to one that is enriched by salt and pepper, Parmesan cheese, nutmeg, cayenne, and parsley. The flour should always be lightly seasoned with salt and pepper and the product then "dredged" or dragged through it to give it an even coating and season the meat. This coating should be done lightly so that there is no taste of flour at the end. The procedure is then to dredge the piece and shake it lightly to remove any excess.

The reason for the flour is to give the egg wash something to hang on to; otherwise, it just runs off. The egg wash then provides the moisture needed to allow the bread crumbs to adhere to the product. The seasoning of the egg wash is optional, of course. I prefer a bit of white wine, salt, pepper, cayenne, nutmeg, parsley, and parmigiano for many breaded things other than fish, where I find just salt and pepper better suited.

The crumbs themselves should be given consideration. For a very light outside effect where a delicate finish is wanted, I would recommend a combination of stale and fresh fine-crumbed white bread with crusts removed. This would be used for fish, light cheese canapés and other products. For a more robust presentation, as is found desirable with cutlets, croquettes, and larger breaded meats, I prefer a combination of fine crumbs made of half toasted crumbs (including the crusts) and half of the more delicate stale and fresh white crumbs without crusts. Regarding the consistency of the crumbs, generally the finest texture is most desirable. However, in some cases a combination of very fine and rougher crumbs works better. For toppings, rather than breadings, I always use mixtures of fine and rough and also accent further by the addition of fine croutons which are about the size of a brunoise (1/10 inch).

The procedure is to dredge the piece in the flour and shake it lightly to remove the excess. The piece should then be dipped in the egg wash. The trick here is to keep one hand dry. Use your alternate hand for handling the meat when it's wet. I find the use of a fork and a large spoon very helpful in turning the product in the egg wash to avoid getting your hand saturated. I also recommend making a well in the bread crumbs and inserting the product in the well. Then take the remaining bread crumbs from the sides, cover the product liberally with them, and press down with the palm of your dry hand at the same time as you cup the product with your fingers. Turn it over and repeat the procedure. Then pick up the product and shake lightly, removing excess crumbs, before placing it on a clean plate.

Batters (pastetta or pastella). To get a smoother, lighter finish, eliminate the bread crumbs and mix the flour and egg together with water and milk or buttermilk, beer, seltzer, and/or wine or Cognac. The addition of egg whites will make a batter lighter yet, and the addition of melted butter will make it richer. The lightest batters I've ever seen are made with rice flour and egg whites. This type of batter is usually used to fry the very delicate little eel-type fish called *bianchetti* in Italy.

Whereas with a breading you can sauté *or* deep-fry, with batters you *must* deep-fry, so the food doesn't turn out soggy.

The quality and temperature of the fat in deep frying are very important. The best deep frying is done with tasteless fats that don't interfere with the flavor of the product. For that reason I prefer sunflower oil or other light polyunsaturated vegetable oils. There are several good cooking reasons, health considerations aside, why these lighter oils are better.

To begin with, the "smoking point," the point at which an oil breaks down, is higher in vegetable oils (450°F) than in animal fats (375°F). The higher the smoking point, the more leeway you have before the oil overheats. Any oil that has started to smoke should be discarded because the flavor is changed substantially in the process. Secondly, vegetable oils are less greasy and will be more unobtrusive in the finished product. The Italians sometimes prefer to deep fry in *strutto*, which is rendered lard (pork fat) just to have that deeper, greasier flavor. Olive oil won't work well at all at high temperatures because its smoking point is even lower than animal fats. While peanut and corn oils are very usable because of their higher smoking points, nonetheless they do impart a particular flavor, which is good or bad depending on what you're after.

The procedure is quite simple. Use a tall-sided pot (the less aeration, the better) and heat the fat over a moderate flame for a few minutes. The fat should be 3 to 4 inches deep, depending on the volume of the product; also be careful that there is at least a 3 to 4 inch space from the top of the pot to allow the oil to rise as you immerse the product. I then use a small piece of bread to test the temperature. When the fat bubbles forcefully around the bread, it's ready. You can (and should) also use a thermometer to test the oil and follow the temperature guidelines in the particular recipe.

Next, make sure the food to be fried is well drained of water and patted dry with paper towels before being breaded or dipped in batter; oil and water don't mix, and the introduction of water to hot oil will result in an "explosion" of popping oil. Ready for frying, the food (potatoes, fritters, sweetbreads, zucchini) should be lowered gently into the fat in a basket. Hold the basket submerged for a few seconds and, as the fat be-

gins to bubble over, lift it up and out to let the fat settle down again. Repeat this procedure several times until the fat settles down to a steady cooking movement. Continue cooking and occasionally separate the ingredients with a long fork. Continue to cook over medium heat (adjusting it if need be) till the food has reached its desired level of doneness. Lift the basket out of the fat and let all the excess fat run off into the pot. Shake the basket a few times, then slip the food into a warm bowl lined abundantly with paper towels. Turn the food over a few times to degrease, finish as indicated in the specific recipe, and serve directly. You can keep it warm in an oven for a brief period, but you will lose that wonderful crispness fried food has coming right from the fat.

Lard (lardellare). Larding goes back to the beginnings of cooking. First man found out he could preserve, tenderize, and add flavor with acids, alcohol, and aromatics, and then he discovered that inserting pieces of fat in meat kept the meat moist and tender even when long cooked. This is particularly useful for all the leaner cuts of meat.

The simplest method of larding is to make incisions in the piece of meat with a small, sharp knife, and then insert, by pushing with your fingers, pieces of solid fat, ham, bacon, lard, fatback, and so on into these small cavities. It also contributes greatly to the flavor if you first marinate or macerate whatever you're inserting in a liquid such as wine, Cognac, port, sherry, Madeira, or Marsala, with a few aromatics, such as garlic, onion, bay leaf, parsley, thyme, basil, chervil, rosemary, marjoram, or sage. Pieces of these aromatics can also be inserted along with the fat.

The French have perfected larding by developing needles of varying sizes to insert the fat with. No bloody good using the old fingers in *those* kitchens. The term for the pieces of fat to be inserted is *lardoon,* which also refers to pieces of bacon or fat bacon that are cubed and crisped after being blanched. Nothing wrong with all this. I don't find it necessary, however.

Bard (bardare). Barding was developed to help game or poultry that has a tendency to be dry. Quail, pheasant, guinea fowl, and others do better if, after browning the meat, a strip of pork fat is placed over the breast and secured with string before the meat is roasted or braised. If you truss and bard the bird before browning, you will lose most of the fat while browning. In some cases this is desirable, as found in my own recipe for *quaglie alla perugina* (page 220). The slice of fat should be from 1/16- to 1/8-inch thick, depending on the size of the bird.

MOIST HEAT COOKING METHODS

Boil (bollire, lessare). We start by boiling water. Simple enough, one would think, but there are actually several things to consider—the first, and most important of which is cooking with love. I have learned from experience that cooking is alchemical. Your emotional approach to the stove will be transmitted to each dish—not through some esoteric permeable membrane, but directly by the way you handle a pot, place things to cook, and boil water. If it boils at full strength—"angrily hard"—as too many professional cooks are so perversely fond of, it will tear the outer edges of a vegetable or pasta before cooking the rest through. If, on the other hand, potatoes and certain other foods are cooked too slowly, and not on a brisk but gentle boil, they will become soggy, waterlogged, and unappetizing unless you're only using a bit of liquid and a cover, where slower is actually better, or making a *bollito misto* (a mixture of boiled meats), where slow cooking, even if the meat is totally submerged in liquid, is preferred.

Simmer (sobollire, pippiare). A simmer is a very gentle bubbling—less than a gentle boil. Soft boil *(gentile),* fast boil *(rapido),* medium rolling boil *(mezzo bollendo)* are all terms to describe the rapidity and intensity of the action you want to take place by cooking a food in liquid. The decision as to which is made by consideration both of the nature of the product and its size, in relation to the "doneness" factor you want in the finished dish. Simmering is slow cooking where the foods bubble gently.

Parboil, blanch (far bollire a metà, imbiancare). The terms "parboil" and "blanch" refer to methods of precooking in a gently boiling liquid. This is a very practical technique for preparing, or precooking, a particular food that is to be cooked further before being served, usually by means of a sauté. A good example of this would be the blanching, or parboiling, of green beans before a Sauté almandine. Some foods, such as potatoes, can be blanched in hot fat instead of water.

Scald (scottare). Scalding is very useful if you wish to loosen the skin from a tomato or other vegetable or the feathers from some type of fowl. To do this, plunge either into a pot of rapidly boiling water for a few seconds, then pull it out, and continue your work.

To scald milk or any other liquid for cooking or baking, heat it slowly over medium to medium-low heat just until bubbles begin to form along the edges of the saucepan; do *not* let it boil.

Poach (affogare). Poaching is more similar to simmering in that the liquid is very hot, but not boiling. Like simmering, the liquid can bubble a little. Eggs, fish, and vegetables are the foods most cooked in this fashion, although you can poach anything that is tender and doesn't require strong treatment; chicken breasts, sweetbreads, and veal come to mind most readily in this regard. By using stock, wine, or spirits instead of or in addition to water, you can infuse the dish with subtle flavor.

En papillote (in cartoccio). Cooking *en papillote* is a form of poaching, or steaming, in which the dish is baked in the oven in a paper or foil package with liquids and/or aromatics. A bit of fat is usually added (butter or bacon, for example) to enhance the flavor further.

My own favorite *in cartoccio* dish is only partially done in paper. I find this the best method for grilling or chargrilling a chicken. Lay a chicken half on a double-size piece of aluminum foil. Place a nut of unsalted butter on top of the chicken and add a few sprigs of thyme. Squeeze a quarter of an orange over the chicken, then cut the orange into pieces, surrounding and covering the chicken with the pieces. Sprinkle with white wine, salt, and pepper before sealing the package. Now roast it in a hot oven, about 400°, for 15 to 20 minutes, depending on size. Open the package (carefully, to avoid escaping steam) and place the chicken over the glowing coals of a charcoal fire to brown. Baste with the juices *in cartoccio* and cook till browned perfectly and done.

Steam (cuocere al vapore). Even though steam is created at the same temperature (212°F) as boiling water, it is far hotter, and it penetrates the food deeper and quicker. And if you use a pressure cooker, the steam builds up to 250°F. In addition to speed, steaming offers the further advantage of keeping in more vitamins.

Do I recommend, therefore, that we all rush out and buy a pressure cooker?

The answer is no, for several reasons. Food that is steamed tends to lack crispness and seems overcooked, even when it's not. The reason for this is the steam penetrates so deeply and evenly that a certain crispness that I find desirable is impossible to maintain. I wish to caution immediately that I do not endorse the recent vogue for undercooked and barely cooked vegetables. A food must be properly cooked.

My own preference with vegetables is to poach or semisteam them. The Italians call this method *soffocato* ("stifled"). By putting a cover on a pot containing just a little water, broth, or wine (about half a cup) and cooking the food over medium-low heat, a certain gentle steam descends from the cover to penetrate the vegetable, yet not as insistently as pressure-cooker steam does.

Braise (brasare). The distinguishing factors in braising are slow cooking in a covered pot (well sealed, preferably) with very little liquid and/or fat. Meat, fish, game, poultry, and vegetables all braise well either in the oven or on top of the stove. The oven provides a steadier and more even heat and requires considerably less attention. Pop it in, set your timer, and take care of other things while your braise silently and efficiently works its wonders. Lovely process! Constant attention and adjustment of the flame and diffusers is the name of the game when braising on top of the stove. It's just not worth the effort.

Some fish and vegetables are actually braised in their own juice. What happens is that, as I explained in my technique of semi-steaming, the lid on the pot (tightly closed) creates a certain amount of steam, which cooks the food from above, while the heat of the pan cooks it directly from underneath. Braised endive and other lettuces are among my favorites, along with cabbages. The Italians do a lot of braising, and usually incorporate a bit, or all, of the marinade they customarily use first, before proceeding to sauté (brown) and then braise in a covered pot. Pollo alla cacciatora (chicken "hunter" style) is a typical braise that is emulated throughout Italy, as is the wonderful Brasato al Barolo of Piedmont, and other "brasati" of Lombardy. They also can be done on top of the stove uncovered and are then referred to in Italian as cooked "in umido".

Stew (stufare, cuocere in umido). The only real difference between a braise and a stew is that more liquid is used, resulting in a sauce or gravy. They sometimes overlap, and what one chef will call a braise, another might deem a stew. It's not really very important to distinguish between them, since if they're done right the eating of either is absolutely glorious. Stews and the braises are also known as *stracotto* ("long cooked").

Fricasse (fricassea). "Fricassee" is a term used to describe a stew that is made with white meat, whether it be chicken, turkey, or veal. The meat or poultry is sautéed in a bit of fat without browning it, then liquid—stock, wine, water—is added. It is cooked in a covered pot like a braise or stew, although sometimes it's left uncovered. I usually begin with a cover to allow tenderizing, and then finish it uncovered to thicken the sauce naturally through reduction.

Clarify (chiarificare). Or, to make a liquid clear. We go a bit further than straining here. By the use of ground meat, egg whites, eggshells, and aromatics all the impurities are gathered together so they can be removed from the liquid. The stock or broth, and all the other ingredients, must be cool. We then mix the cool stock with the clarifying ingredients over a low heat, whisking all the while. As the liquid heats to just under a boil, the whisking is stopped and the solids allowed to coagulate. They will come together and form a "raft"—so called because the egg whites have now hardened and the whole thing floats in the liquid like a raft at sea. This raft must not be disturbed, and as the liquid comes to the boil (gentle now, we don't want to break up the raft) all of the impurities will leach out of the liquid and be absorbed by the raft. The clarified liquid should be strained through a wet cheesecloth set in a china cap, a conical strainer. Thus you have made consommé.

Deglaze (deglassare). This is a wonderful technique that captures all the good brown bits that stick to the bottom of the saucepan or skillet when you sear or brown something. By adding wine or some other liquid to the pan and turning up the heat, whisking and scraping all the while, the liquid will release all that good stuff stuck to the pan. This can then be used to flavor a stock or sauce. Good and brown, however, does not mean burnt, and if the pan has gone too far, don't try to salvage anything left in it.

Bain-marie (bagno maria). This method goes back to ancient Rome. There are two main uses for this "pan of hot water." The first is to cook custards, mousses, pâtés, certain soufflés or *sformati,* and other egg-type preparations that will spoil on direct heat. By placing such a preparation in one large container or several smaller ones, and setting in a larger pan with enough hot water to partially come up the sides of the container, the product will be protected, and the heat created by the oven and a certain amount of steam will cook the product.

The second use is to hold sauces that are already at a warm temperature without cooking them further. Set your hollandaise, or whatever sauce you have, in a container and put the container in a pan of hot water. This can then be kept warm over a very gentle flame or on top of the stove, or on a steam table.

Deep fry (friggere). The food is fried in a total submersion of fat, which is liquid or liquefied, by heating it to between 350° and 380°F. The trick is to end up with a totally crisp, nongreasy product, without any off flavors, and having an appealing coloration, like golden brown.

Fritto misto (mixed fry) is very popular throughout Italy and almost all regions have their own versions. These *fritti* can be breaded, or dipped in flour and egg (see Breading, p. 5) and include mostly vegetables and offal. Calves' brains, sweetbreads, livers, kidneys, in addition to cheeses and all kinds of vegetables, are the most often seen, breaded and deep fried until golden brown. Quite good actually.

DRY-HEAT COOKING METHODS

The key to flavor—savoriness—in dry-heat cooking is browning. Since man has cooked with fire, meats and other foods have been spitted and roasted in front of or on top of a fire, and because of the intense heat, they brown and form that universally desirable crisp outside crust.

The Italians pay great attention to roasting and grilling in all their forms. In fact, they're so popular in all the regions of Italy that I don't know of a town that doesn't have its local *rosticceria*. There you can buy chickens, rabbits, sausage, vegetables—all the fixings for a good dinner—while you watch the gigantic spit turning (electrically now) in front of a blazing fire.

The historical significance of this ancient method of cooking was reenacted for me personally the other night when I went to dinner at a friend's grandmother's house in the hills outside Rome. His grandmother, at ninety, was sitting next to the fire in this seven-hundred-year-old farmhouse, slowly turning by hand a spit that had two plump, freshly killed chickens on it. She did this with her right hand. In her left hand she had a brush, made of rosemary branches that had been tied together, which she would occasionally dip into a pan that, besides catching drippings, also contained garlic and oil, and then she would brush the chickens slowly, gently, but thoroughly with the liquids.

As I watched the skin on the chickens bubble and brown and inhaled deeply their perfume, it seemed as if I were transfixed in time. I felt that a Roman soldier who I had encountered in a past-life regression was going to appear and sit beside us at the fire. Of course he didn't, and just as well, too, since those two golden-brown chickens disappeared quite rapidly without outside help. Ahh . . . sweet nostalgia!

The techniques to achieve that outside browning with inner succulence will be discussed in this section, among other aspects of dry-heat cooking.

Sear (disseccare). The purpose of searing is to brown the outside of a food while retaining the juices inside. It can be done in a pan over high heat on top of the stove, or in a very hot oven (500°F). There are two main schools of thought concerning the efficacy of hot searing; there are those who believe that hot searing seals in the juices and makes a browner crust and those who believe the meat will be juicier, and better, if you cook it over low heat, and then brown it at the end by turning the heat up.

Harold McGee, in his book *On Food and Cooking,* says

You will want to sear the meat either in an initially super-hot oven, or in a large frying pan, if you prize the brown crust and its intense flavor, and don't mind if the meat is somewhat drier as a result. But if juiciness is your consideration, then skip the initial browning. . . .

After many years of experimenting with both methods, I'm convinced that you get better results by browning first. There is an unmistakable richness to the outer crust when formed initially. I've also found that you can preserve the juiciness McGee mentions will be lost, by another technique called *in salmis,* which is discussed under Roast.

Singe (bruciacchiare). Singeing has a particular use in the preparation of poultry and game birds. If you have ever plucked a chicken, you will know how difficult it is to get all the feathers out—even with tweezers. Those, and the ends that remain, can be singed on top of an open flame, thus removing them.

Bake (cuocere al forno). Baking generally applies to bread, cakes, and pastries, although you will see the term used with chicken, fish, or pasta (lasagne, manicotti, etc.). Dry air surrounds the uncovered dish in an oven (covering the dish would create steam and thus bring you to braising).

Roast (arrostire). Roasting and baking are terms that are generally interchangeable. Whereas roasting can be done in front of, or on top of, an open fire or in an oven, baking refers to radiant heat cooking in an enclosed box—an oven. An oven can be made of clay, brick, or, as is usually the case today, a combination of metals. Ovens do not cook evenly since they tend to be hotter on top and cooler in front near the door (except convection ovens, which circulate the air). One should pay attention to this factor when roasting in an oven and move the meat around accordingly. When roasting meats, it's also important to rack them so they are not steaming in their own juices. I have found the use of aromatics (onion, celery, carrot, bay leaf, etc.) under the rack to be effective in enhancing the flavor without interfering with the browning. When baking lasagne and other dishes in the oven, I usually start them out on the bottom of the oven, which creates a nice browning underneath, and then halfway through put the dish on a rack in the upper part of the oven, where the higher heat will brown the top nicely.

As I mentioned in Searing, I have found a solution to the dryness that may result from initial searing, a procedure called making something *in salmis*. Now, while to Italians this term usually means to cook something in its own marinade, the French taught me a totally different definition some thirty years ago. They roast the dish partially at very high heat, then remove it from the oven and place it in a bit of stock or broth. This holds the meat in a rare juicy state. Right before serving, removing it from the stock and finishing its browning under a broiler to recrisp it works wonders.

This technique was really developed as a method for finishing a roast tableside in a chafing dish. It was also developed to get a double concentration of juices from roasted birds to add flavor to the final sauce. The rare, but well-browned, bird is cut into serving pieces, and the back, neck, wing tips, and so on are pressed vigorously through a cheesecloth in a china cap, a conical strainer, to extract all the juices. These juices are then added to a stock that might have been made from another bird, thus intensifying the flavor. Quite good actually, and the preferred method for roasting poultry and game of all types. This is not to say that you can't be simple about the whole thing and sear the food in a hot oven (500°F) for 15 to 20 minutes (depending on the food and size) and then slow-cook it for whatever additional time is required. Just remember to allow for further cooking to take place in the 3- to 5-minute settling time you should allow before serving.

Roasting in front of a fire is another business that can be enhanced by a few tricks. Since there are no walls to contain the dry heat in this method, the food is exposed to air and will be dry if you are not careful. Occasional, but constant, basting is the name of the game here. The rosemary (or sage, or thyme, etc.) brush used to baste those chickens I mentioned in the introduction to this section is an efficient way to give the roast the oil that is needed, while imparting aromatic flavor at the same time, as is larding and barding, not just with oil, but with aromatics as well. The other "trick," so to speak, is to find the perfect wine (a Prunotto Barolo "Bussia" 1978 for beef, or a Castello di Ama Chianti Classico 1983 for rabbit, and so on) and do a supplemental basting alternately with your regular oil-based baste. Why not combine the wine and oil? Why not, indeed. I must say that the basting with wine will produce a roast that is absolutely smashing. Whatever method used, if the food as an ingredient has been properly selected, roasting in front of or on top of an open fire can't be beat—and don't worry, it's Italian!

Wood-burning oven (forno da legno). Here we find cooking alchemy at its best. Put a whole chicken in a hot, well-prepared wood-burning oven, and watch it bubble and sizzle. It looks as if the chicken is going to burst apart at any moment, or at least burn and dry up. Not a bit of it! In spite of the fact that the heat is 1200° to 1500°F in one of these ovens when properly stoked up, as against the 500°F maximum in a gas or electric oven, birds will cook through in twenty minutes, be wonderfully blistered and golden brown, and yet as juicy as if they had been steamed. Absolutely miraculous. *Pizza bianca* (plain with a little oil) is done in 45 seconds, *pizza margherita* (oil, tomatoes, and mozzarella) in a minute and a half, and speed is not the only thing. The oven itself exudes an aromatic perfume that permeates each dish with a special flavor that has built up over the years, and is now amplified by the type of wood being used.

As a matter of fact, the recipe for christening one of these ovens provides the original flavor. The old-timers in Italy will tell you that it's best to fire it the first time with olive wood, tons of bay leaf, and hundred-pound bags of sweet white onions, rosemary, sage, and thyme, sprinkled (believe it or not) with rainwater and good, green extra virgin olive oil. They claim that it's essential you keep the fire going and feed it with these aromatics over the course of at least three days.

We have a three-hundred-fifty-year-old oven here at the school that must have been broken in that way because of the wonderful flavor it imparts to everything. When I renovated this old farmhouse and made the present school, I also built a small indoor wood-burning oven in case it rained. My son Dino and I took turns for three days and nights, following those ancient instructions right down to the rainwater, which we had collected for this purpose; we must have used six sacks of onions and untold amounts of fresh herbs. The oven works well and smells good, but neither cooks nor flavors food like the one that is 350 years old. But I must say we don't regret the time and effort spent in seasoning the little one. On the contrary, it was an experience that gave us a feeling of grounding—being centered—that we'll never forget.

These ovens were originally made of clay and go as far back as the ancient Egyptian civilization in 5000 B.C. At some point, brick was discovered, and ovens have been made in Italy that way for thousands of years. Originally there was only one large oven to a village, and the people would bring their bread dough—or pigs—to be roasted by the local baker. The oven here at the school was one of these, and I'm told they would make two to three hundred loaves of bread in it three times a week.

These ovens, with their profumatic and aromatic properties, remain one of the most "sophisticated" forms of cooking that I know of. They are so simple and cheap to build that, in my opin-ion, no backyard grill setup should be without one.

Chargrill (abbrustolire). Grilling on a grate over coals from a wood fire or charcoal must be as ancient as fire itself. Reach into the fire with a stick and push out some coals. Put some kind of a grill (with openings is the key) to suspend the meat over the coals and cook. The trick is to prac-tice. Only through experience can you relate to the variables in heat that occur as the fire dies down and blazes up again.

In a canteen I had in a ski area I owned in Pittsfield, Massachusetts, from 1955 to 1969, we had an enormous charcoal grill. In the beginning, before I had experience, we would load the grill and light it. Surprise, surprise! First it was too hot to cook anything from less than three feet away, and then it was too slow to cook a hamburger in less than fifteen minutes. Three thousand skiers made us learn to adjust that fire correctly.

You must move whatever you're cooking to various hot points and cool points in your grill, turning and watching, without keeping it so busy that the food can't cook. Also don't move things on the grill until they're well set up or else they'll tear, stick to the grill and require a cleanup. After a while, you can become so sensitive to the condi-tion of "doneness" in all types of food that there will be no need for testing. You can see it and feel it.

For the home cook, chargrilling is probably the easiest of all cooking methods to master. A few mistakes at the backyard grill and you're readily an expert, as is proven in millions of backyards every day in America.

Griddle (cuocere sulla graticola). Griddling needs a solid surface, usually made of heavy stainless steel. Pancakes, eggs, bacon, waffles, sausage, hot dogs, and hamburgers are what you're most likely to find on American griddles. In Italy, and many other European countries, well-worn griddles are very popular for cooking fish. They call the dishes *alla griglia,* the same as if it's cooked on a grill. They also have a ridged griddle called a *graticola,* which leaves attractive markings on the meat, as if it were done on a grill. The heat with griddles is much lower than cooking on a grill over an open fire, but generally the same techniques are involved.

Broil (cuocere alla griglia, in salamander). The difference between broiling and grilling is that in broiling the heat comes from above, and in grilling from below. In commercial kitchens, broilers are built differently from those found in home ovens. The heat is far more intense, sometimes reaching as high as 2000°F, and normally running at 1200° to 1500°F. This intense heat gives you the ability to brown the outside for real "charred" flavor and yet have the inside remain rare. Home broilers will rarely be capable of this because the heat generally does not exceed 500°F—about the same as maximum oven temperatures. Broiling, therefore, in my opinion, is not something to be done at home unless you buy a special one with a high heat range capability.

Assuming that you have such a broiler, the same principles of handling the food apply as for grilling. The most popular, and perfectly constructed, food to broil is lobster, since the shell remains on the bottom of the sizzler and the lobster meat is open to the intense radiant heat from above. This works perfectly if your broiler is hot enough and you pay attention to the distance between the lobster and the flame.

Sauté (saltare). What is sauté? And what is all the fuss and reverence all about in professional kitchens?

Webster says it comes from the French verb *sauter,* meaning "to jump." *Saltare* in Italian also means "to jump," so in a cooking context it means to make things jump around in a pan to keep them from sticking to the bottom. A good sauté is usually done in very little fat with thin, or small, pieces of food. It's a very rapid method of cooking that does require a bit of practice. This is not to imply that it's in any way beyond the reach of beginners. Anyone can, and practically does, sauté more frequently than might be imagined. Every time you pan-fry anything, you are in the realm of sauté—the only technical difference being that you use more fat in pan frying. Pork chops, lamb chops, steak, veal, shrimp, hamburgers, sausage, and so on are all being sautéed when you step up to the stove, put them in a pan with a little fat, and fry them. So then, what is all the fuss and reverence about?

The answer is quite simple and well founded. Sauté is a direct method of cooking fresh ingredients and presenting them at table in a matter of minutes. The cooks who have talent in this are, therefore, the heroes of the restaurant kitchen, because they are under tremendous pressure to come up with dish after dish rapidly and, at the same time, perfectly executed. There's no holding oven or steam table to help the cook out where he can have twenty, thirty, forty, or fifty orders prepared and on hold. To do quantity sauté work you really have to know how to cook.

The good news for home cooks is that you don't have to do fifty, seventy-five, or a hundred sautés at a time, and the principles that a professional sauté whiz employs are quite simple and readily available to you. Our students have told us over and over, "I never knew doing all these dishes could be so easy." We will provide you with the "blow-by-blow" description in our chapter on meats. As the saying goes, there's nothing to it—as long as you don't have to do it under pressure and in large quantities.

Pan-fry (friggere in padella). Pan frying is very similar to sautéing, only there is usually more fat used because the pieces of meat, fish, chicken, and so on are larger. Also, there is not the "jumping around" that's found in sautéing; the pieces of food being larger, can remain in one place longer to brown before being turned over.

Flambée (infiammare). I'm not sure how long they've been doing this in Italy, but chefs I know here say "forever." My own association with flambé goes back many years to a night when I was making crêpes suzette for some customers in a nightclub I owned called Max's Kansas City. The waiter who was assisting me was new and lit the warming Cognac and liqueurs just as I bent over to smell them. Do you know what it feels like to be without eyebrows? . . . well, it wasn't that bad, but bad enough.

There are more important uses for flambé than to attract customer comments about the pretty blue flame. In the preparation of meats, poultry, and game of all kinds, you can add delicate flavor to the food by heating spirits (Cognac, whisky, and so on) in the sauté of the particular meat, and then lighting it. The alcohol burns off, preventing the taste from being too strong, yet leaving a very delicate trace that is quite pleasant, adding a certain complexity to a dish that cannot otherwise be reached.

Of course, "start with the finest natural ingredients . . ." Never use cheap booze to flambé! Can I be more positive than that!

Gratin (gratinare). *Au gratin* is the French and international term for browning the top of something under a broiler after it has been cooked elsewhere. It is a finishing technique that gives good visual, as well as textural, sensations. The term conjures up images of beautiful golden crusts on top of such dishes as baked fish, vegetables, pasta, and meat. The Italians call this crust *dorato* (golden), and they sprinkle parmigiano cheese on top of their gratin preparations because the cheese browns so nicely. I go one step further and whip parmigiano into cream to top dishes before finishing under the broiler. This technique is called *glassage, glassato,* or *glacé* and is absolutely foolproof; it will give the prettiest brown spots you ever saw in a matter of seconds.

Microwave (microonde). I don't use them and have removed them from several operations that I have consulted for.

The reason? I quote Harold McGee, *On Food and Cooking* (page 618):

Several disadvantages of microwave cooking should be noted. One is that, in the case of meat cookery, speedy heating can cause greater fluid loss and so a drier texture. Another problem is that microwaves cannot brown foods, since the surface gets no warmer than the interior. And our expectations for many foods, including breads, baked potatoes, and roasts, include the flavors produced by browning.

Notwithstanding newer models with convection fans that brown some, I'm afraid microwave ovens are anathema to everything I teach about basic cooking principles.

AROMATICS AND SEASONINGS

These are all the wonderful plants, bushes, roots, and essences that give man the ability to turn cooking into a very high art form. They are the smells and flavors of the fields and woods married into all of the better gastronomic creations.

Seasoning extends to every form of cooking and is the most important tool a chef has at hand. A sprig of mint, a field mushroom, a clove of garlic, a piece of onion, a touch of mustard, a drop of mandarin orange or almond extract, a grating of nutmeg . . . the list seems endless. And when celery, carrots, turnips, parsnips, and fennel are used to flavor, they change their action from vegetable to aromatic as well.

It is important to understand that aromatics are sometimes synergistic—that is, the total is not necessarily the sum of its parts. Some alchemical transformation takes place, and a use of several different herbs and/or spices, or essences, produces a different result from that normally expected.

You will see throughout the recipes in this book a call for small amounts of thyme, basil, and chervil. Their use in dried form serves as a background to particular dishes and does not eliminate special accents with fresh thyme, basil, or chervil, but not in conjunction. Therefore, a *salsa marinara* (sauté of tomatoes) will contain dried thyme, basil, and chervil as well as salt, pepper, garlic, and crushed red pepper; and then for a dominant accent, freshly torn basil leaves are thrown in at the end. Can you make this sauce without the elaboration? Of course you can, and I often do. But the dried thyme, basil, and chervil are synergistic and "color" the dish with a special flavor that is beyond their separate identities. I've experimented with combining these three herbs in a container to have them on hand for easier use, rather than keeping them separate, and found the result to be totally different and, to my taste, unpleasant. This seems to be the same with one of my other synergistic combinations, nutmeg, mace, *peperoncini* (red pepper flakes), cayenne, and black pepper. On the other hand, Renaissance cooks and present-day Milanese and Torinese cooks used, and continue to use, ground herbs and spices in combinations and prefer to store them together for use according to specific recipes: "Three parts clove, white pepper, dried bay leaf, and thyme to ten parts nutmeg and cinnamon. Shake together and store." They use these mixtures sparingly, but effectively, in their *stracotto* (long-cooking) braises and stews.

Two classic combinations are the *mirepoix,* or *battuto,* and *duxelles,* or *trifolato,* both of which deserve extended descriptions.

Mirepoix (battuto odori). is a much-used mixture of carrot, celery, and onion, diced somewhat roughly. It also contains diced prosciutto, ham, or another fatty product and provides an enhancement of flavor to a wide variety of dishes. When the ham or fat is left out it is referred to as a *brunoise.* The Italian chefs I know might say *un battuto senza grassi*—a battuto without fat—or call for *odori* instead of *brunoise. Battuto* usually means with prosciutto and/or pancetta (bacon).

This is the base, the beginning, of hundreds of dishes and sauces. The *mirepoix* or *battuto* is sau-

téed, cooked, or sweated to varying degrees of brownness in a bit of butter, oil, or lard, depending on the degree of lightness or darkness desired in the final dish. The Italians use *insaporire*—to flavor or season—to describe the use of *battuto* and aromatics. The important thing is to have excellent fresh carrots, celery, and onion and not to prepare it in quantities in advance since it loses its freshness overnight. Don't make the mistake of one student I had who said, "Well, I always buy the second-rate stuff for that. My grocer gives it to me cheaper—and hey, it's only for cooking."

Start with the finest natural ingredients, cook with love, knowledge and devotion.

Duxelles (trifolato). This is a very ancient mixture, of mushrooms, garlic, and parsley (or mushrooms, shallots, onions, and parsley in the case of French cooks) that was created as a substitute for truffles—a poor man's truffle paste, so to speak. The ingredients are finely diced and sautéed (in olive oil in Italy, in butter in France) to resemble diced truffles. As a matter of fact, many companies in Italy put out a jarred product in oil by that name and add finely diced truffle peelings to further enhance it. The French also use nutmeg in a *duxelles,* though, strangely enough, the Italians don't, in spite of the fact that nutmeg is ubiquitous in northern Italian cooking. It might well be because of their use of garlic and oil in this preparation which does not marry as well with nutmeg as do shallots and butter. *Duxelles* or *trifolato* is used for seafood dishes, particularly when they are done *en papillote* (or *in cartoccia,* in Italian). A bit of the mixture with some butter or oil and wine, perhaps a sprig of thyme or other herb, a touch of salt and perhaps white pepper and your fish in a "paper bag" will be as aromatic as is possible. The Italians use *trifolato* in a great many other dishes, such as *funghi trifolati,* artichokes, eggplant, or kidneys. In some areas, particularly Liguria, anchovies, capers, and wine are sometimes added.

Mis en place. This use of *battuto,* aromatics, and personal touches in cooking adds up to a general term that is quite common in commercial kitchens. It's known as *mis en place* (things in place). These are the aromatics or seasonings that will be lined up on a station next to where the chef cooks. Here's my own personal list:

- *Herbs:* Thyme, basil, chervil, sage, rosemary, marjoram, oregano, bay leaf, tarragon, dill, and mint (never dry—it has an awful flavor).
- *Spices:* Nutmeg, mace, cayenne, red pepper, peppercorns (black, white, and green), coriander, cardamom, paprika, fennel, ginger, clove, cinnamon, juniper berry, and anise.
- *Essences:* Vanilla extract, almond extract, lemon rind, orange rind, tangerine rind.
- *Wines and liquors:* High-fruit fragrant whites such as Gewürtztraminer or Riesling, as well as a good Pinot Grigio or Chardonnay. Reds are light Chiantis or Grignolino and some bigger taste sensations such as Rubesco riserva or a Barolo or Barbaresco. Marsala (both sweet and dry), Madeira, sherry, vin santo, port, white and red vermouths (sweet and dry), Cognac, apricot liqueur, triple sec, Cointreau, anisette, grappa, and nocino (a green walnut liqueur from Emilia Romagna).

This is backed up by an assortment of cheeses, oils, prosciuttos, bacon, fruits and nuts (including raisins), pine nuts, hazelnuts, and walnuts.

Is all this needed just to cook Italian? Of course not! But it is essential for me to have to make the variety of dishes I teach and to allow me the freedom to orchestrate my own cuisine.

Some warnings: Only use fresh ingredients. That old jar of chervil that you haven't used in a year is better thrown out. As a matter of fact, I find a great many things in the average kitchen that are more appropriate for the garbage can. Garlic salt, celery salt, dried mint, and parsley flakes are all abominations, as are "cooking sherries" and "cooking wines," margarine, process cheese products, and dozens of other unnatural products. Out! Out! Out! I say. Once and for all,

do yourself a favor and throw it all away. Don't look back! "Start with the finest natural ingredients . . ."

There is also a caution to be considered in the use of aromatics. Medieval and even Renaissance cooking was notorious for its excessive use of herbs and spices. Fortunately, modern cooks are aware of the danger and recognize that aromatics must be used so subtly as to be indistinguishable, unless you are after a dish with a pronounced accent, such as lamb with rosemary or chicken with tarragon. Even then, of course, the other aromatics must be so understated as to be the perfect backdrop for the particular accent. It requires patience and experience to learn the proper use of these things. What it adds up to is good seasoning. Start with small amounts of a limited variety and then explore further. By and by you'll come to understand the world of aromatics in such a way as to make you wonder what the fuss was all about.

Bouquet garni (odori, mazzette guarnite). One cannot have a discussion about aromatics without mentioning bouquet garni—or, as it is known in Italian, *odori* or *mazzette guarnite.* It's actually a little bundle of herbs (usually parsley, thyme, and bay leaf), called a "faggot," which is tied together and suspended in the liquid of a stew or braise and removed when the dish is finished, resulting in a more subtle infusion of the aromatics in the dish. Sometimes the French will tone down these aromatics even more by putting them in a cheesecloth sack.

Zest (aroma, gusto). The zest of a citrus fruit has tremendous potential for infusing a delicate suggestion of the fruit, most usually, orange, lemon, or lime that in their pure forms of juice or meat would otherwise be too strong. The trick is to get pieces of the outside skin without the pithy white part underneath. The pith is bitter, and the decision as to how "pithless" you want the zest to be depends on how much you do not want that odd, bitter flavor. Fortunately, there is a handy little gadget called a "zester" that will enable you to do just that. Zests are wonderful in all forms of cooking—salads, roasts, stews, baking, and of course in a variety of drinks, desserts, and sherbets. They can be blanched in wine or water to tone them down further or used directly.

Which brings me to a question. How many of you taste everything? I find it essential, particularly when you're trying to create subtle taste sensations. How do you know the number of zests to use if you haven't tasted them? Different lemons from different crops are different. Only after tasting a little snip are you prepared to use the food knowingly. This is true, of course, of most everything, and I find, when I cook, that my hands are continually reaching out and then traveling to my mouth. Seems to be a sensible part of the cooking process. Taste! Look! Feel! Smell! See! Taste!

OLIO DI OLIVE • OLIVE OIL

The most commonly used fat in Italy is olive oil. It originated with the ancient Greeks and Etruscans in approximately 3000 B.C., and has been used extensively throughout the world ever since.

Ninety-eight percent of the acreage in the world under olive cultivation is in the eastern Mediterranean—Italy, Spain, and Greece. It is also interesting to note that 90 percent of the world's olive production is turned into oil of varying grades, in spite of all the olives that are seemingly consumed in bars and at cocktail parties ad nauseam.

Olive cultivation, like grape cultivation, is more complex than it first seems. To begin with, there are many olive types, ranging from very light green through shades of brown, russet, and mahogany to black. The trees, when planted, are just like grape vines, subject to variations in soil, climate, cultivation, harvesting, handling, and pressing. It becomes immediately obvious, therefore, that those who claim the best oil comes only from Lucca or Tuscany should be asked, which crop, from which hill, in what year, and pressed by whom?

There are many years when Todi, Spoleto, and parts of Calabria or Sicily are entitled to that distinction, not to mention hundreds of others that have the potential of the "best" crop in any year. Just as with vintage wines, there are years and then there are years, and there are crops and then there are crops.

Most olive oil production is a combination of different olive types, and a master olive oil maker will skillfully blend them to produce his concept of the "best." Quality, however, is determined by the number of pressings and the amount of oleic acid remaining, not just by olive types. In fact, many oil makers will blend different extra virgin *(extra vergine)* oils to satisfy demand. While the quality is always high to qualify as extra virgin (1 percent maximum oleic acid and first cold pressing), nonetheless there is no comparison between the blends and a hand-picked, hand-pressed, first run of oil as you can buy from individual farmers.

I'm also told it's essential that the olives don't hit the ground during harvesting. Prime-quality oils are from hand-picked olives, and it is a modern innovation to use machinery to shake the olives from their trees into waiting nets. The difference is noticeable, but unfortunately you'd have to live in Italy to realize it. The extra virgin oils being exported now are costly blends, and I doubt that you'll be able to find an equivalent to some of the gorgeous rich oils available locally.

As I've indicated above, grading is government controlled and done according to the method of extraction and the amount of oleic acid remaining. We start with a cold first pressing, then a second pressing. Subsequent pressings are cooked with water to remove the bitterness and are therefore known as refined oils. There is also a little-known and hard-to-find (even in Italy) "cream" of the first pressing known as *afiorato*, where the top of the first pressing is skimmed off and bottled separately. Let me show you the grading system, which fortunately works consistently to guarantee you high-quality oils.

Type of oil	Pressing	Oleic Acid Content
Afiorato	1st pressing	1% max.
Extra virgin (*extra vergine*)	1st pressing	1% max.
Super fine (*sopraffino*)	2nd pressing	1.5% max.
Fine (*fino*)	Refined	3.3% max.
Virgin (*vergine*)	Refined	4% max.

Don't confuse the virgin with the extra virgin. As you can see, there's a big difference. Look at the label for the oleic acid content.

So-called pure olive oils are not graded and can be a combination of virgin and other residues, which are then filtered and refined (cooked). Because of this lack of control, you are subject to the honesty and ability of the producer. Sasso and Bertolli come to mind immediately as quality houses that make very good refined products called "pure olive oil."

The universally acclaimed "best"—or king of oils—is called "extra virgin" and can be filtered or unfiltered. Originally, all the best oils were unfiltered, but due to a popular preference for a milder-tasting, cleaner-looking oil, most extra virgin in Italy today is filtered. The difference between the two is one of preference, not quality, and the oleic acid content remains under 1 percent.

Olive oils are heat sensitive, light sensitive,

odor sensitive, and, in my opinion, have a shelf life of only six months after being opened, and one year if left closed in a cool, dark, dry place. Don't leave your oils next to the stove as so many people do. They'll become worthless in a week. Store in the back of a dark, dry closet and bring them out only for use. Do not refrigerate them. The best rule of thumb here is to "buy 'em as you use them" to avoid deterioration in flavor from too long a shelf life.

The best use of higher-quality extra virgin oils is for salads or to pour on vegetables, fresh and uncooked or after they're cooked. In fact it's not a waste to cook with extra virgin oils, but high heat will take away some of the subtlety of flavor. Also, since olive oil has a low smoking point, you're better off with vegetable oil for all types of frying.

Flavored oils are easily made by infusing the oil with whatever herb or aromatic you'd like—thyme, basil, chervil, rosemary, sage, red pepper flakes, garlic, onion, pepper, or even cheeses such as Romano and parmigiano. One of my Italian partners is very fond of a pecorino Romano–flavored oil that I put up for him in extra virgin oil with black peppercorns, which is left to infuse for a year before using.

Yes, there is no question that long infusion imparts more flavor. But if you were to put a dozen basil leaves in a pint of oil for a half hour, you would have noticeably affected the taste of the oil. Here at the school, I always have on hand garlic, red pepper flakes, basil, sage, rosemary, and thyme oils, and use them extensively in cooking.

Although most of the olives grown are used for oil production, nevertheless a plate of olives with oil, garlic, salt, pepper, red pepper flakes, and vinegar is a wonderful accompaniment to an antipasto. A little-known aspect of the preparation of these olives is that they are soaked in lye solution and then washed to remove the excessive bitterness indigenous to fresh olives. Anyone who has tasted an olive picked straight from the tree will understand the necessity for this procedure. This is why Greek olives are so strong tasting . . . they are cured simply by being packed in salt, or pickled, without first being treated with a lye solution.

Californian olives are first dipped in a special solution to fix their color—hence the uniform look—then treated with a lye solution and packed in brine. Since they do not have the advantage of being fermented for several weeks, they lack a good pickled flavor and are more easily subject to spoilage. They must, therefore, be sterilized and packed in a can. This accounts for the strong preference of knowledgeable people in America for European imports.

I've provided a recipe here for an olive marinade (see page 253) that is easy to make and very delicious. Once again, you can use them immediately after infusing, in spite of the fact that they will become appreciably better with age.

ACETO • VINEGAR

If ever there was a marriage made in heaven, it's vinegar and oil. But as ofttimes happens in real life, the combination needs a bit of shaking up to stay together.

The tart, acid taste of a good vinegar can be smoothed out to whatever degree you'd like by the addition of various oils in a wide range of ratios, depending on the strength of the vinegar and the richness of a particular oil. Just as with oils, vinegars can be as light as white wine or as dark as Marsala, with all the varying shades in between.

From my experience here at the school with a variety of students, there seems to be a misconception about how vinegar is made. Bad wine does not a good vinegar make. In fact, in making the justly famous *aceto balsamico* (balsamic vinegar), special Trebbiano grapes are raised and harvested just to make these incredibly dark, rich, sweet vinegars. The result is different from what people normally consider as vinegar, and many

students here at the school have been surprised by its use as a topping for strawberries, for example.

But not everyone can afford to use *aceto balsamico tradizionale,* and therefore it's necessary to approach the subject of vinegar from a different tack.

Make Your Own Wine Vinegar

Buy a good unflavored red wine vinegar (from Progresso, for example), in the medium (16-ounce) bottle, and a bottle of your favorite red wine—not the cheapest, mind you. A rich Barolo or Gaja's Barbaresco will do nicely. Now, open both bottles, drink half the wine (or reserve) and fill the wine bottle with the vinegar. Shake thoroughly and set, uncovered, in a cool, dark, dry place. Let rest for a few hours before using. You will immediately have a rich, red wine vinegar that is far superior to normal vinegars.

By leaving the vinegar exposed to the air, after two to three weeks, you will soon develop a yeasty mother, a placenta-like substance. Don't get frightened and throw this away. The mother will continue to convert new wines to vinegar as you add them. You can keep your vinegar bottle going indefinitely in this manner by adding a bit of every wine you drink to the bottle and, occasionally, more commercial wine vinegar to maintain the flavor you like best. Don't use leftover sour, spoiled wine or you'll spoil the vinegar. Of course, if you add a bit of aceto balsamico, it will improve the flavor greatly. Just a few tablespoons will make all the difference.

Then again, if you can get a vinegar barrel—

any decent small barrel with an air hole in addition to the bung hole will do—and a "mother" from some friend in the Italian community of your town, you can make better vinegar yet. The process is the same, however, in the use of commercial vinegar and wine to start it, and then continual additions. (If you can't find a "mother" in the Italian community it's simple enough to make one. Pour a bottle of good red wine in a bowl and add two cups of white bread, diced up. Let it stand, covered lightly but aerated for a day, and then put the mother in your barrel.)

In any event, remember that these vinegars are usable after only a few hours in spite of the fact that they continue to improve with age. Unlike oils, properly made vinegars are not perishable, although they should be kept away from heat and light, which will cause them to develop off-tasting flavors.

Balsamic vinegar (aceto balsamico tradizionale). It wouldn't be right to discuss the subject of vinegars without an explanation of the very specialized world of *aceto balsamico tradizionale.*

The reason I use the word *tradizionale* in referring to this vinegar is that there are a lot of ersatz vinegars on the market calling themselves *aceto balsamico. Aceto balsamico tradizionale* is the only authentic product, and it is certified by the Consorzio L'Aceto Balsamico nella Tradizione in Modena. The bottles of this vinegar bear an official seal and a traditional shape that are unmis-

takable once seen. You might ask what all the fuss is about. Believe me, once you taste this "liquid gold" you will be grateful for the extreme care and diligence that is involved in the making, bottling, and labeling of this extraordinary product.

Although most of the other labels are deceptive in that they say *aceto balsamico,* there is only one that I know of that is outright fraudulent in that it calls itself "Tradizionale di Modena." At 4,000 lire ($3) versus the controlled price of 60,000 lire ($45) for the real thing for similar quantities you are immediately put on notice that something is wrong. The company is Berni, and they are being enjoined and fined for this obvious fraudulent marketing by the authorities here in Italy. Of the others, the one with the picture of a duke, called *del duca,* and a product from Fini are both deliberately misleading but don't use the word *tradizionale.* An honest producer of a very, very good (aged in the barrel for twenty-five years) wine vinegar is Giuseppe Giusti, who has one of the most beautiful gastronomias in Italy. I say honest because his label does not say *aceto balsamico* but rather *aceto stravecchio* ("very old") and does not in any way trade on the fame of true Modenese *balsamico.*

So what is the real thing?

The traditional balsamic vinegar of Modena is one of those ancient products that go back so far in history that it's hard to say how old it is. We do know that in A.D. 1065 this precious commodity was held in such esteem that Cardinal Bonifacio di Canossa sent a barrel of it to the Emperor Henry III as a coronation gift. He had a special keg made with repoussé designs in silver that was then sent in a special carriage drawn by white horses.

But it wasn't just the nobility who took their vinegar seriously. What can be more serious than a legacy in a will? By the time of the Renaissance it was common practice for people of all walks of life to leave their barrels of *balsamico* to heirs in their wills. As an extension of this ancient practice, my wife's grandfather very proudly gave us a seasoned vinegar barrel with a "mother" as a wedding gift and measure of his extreme affection.

Rather than reach for a description myself, let me quote from a pamphlet prepared by the consortium of producers of the traditional balsamic vinegar of Modena:

The Traditional Balsamic Vinegar of Modena is made from cooked grape must matured by a long and slow vinegarization process through natural fermentation followed by progressive concentrations by ageing in a series of casks made from different types of wood and without the addition of any other spices or flavourings.

Colour: dark brown but full of warm light.
Density: with a fluid and syrup-like consistency.
Fragrance: distinct, complex, sharp and unmistakeably, but pleasantly, acid.
Flavor: traditional and inimitable sweet and sour in perfect proportion. To the taste buds it will offer a full and rich flavor with a variety of shadings and evolving bursts of new expressions as the mood or the carrier changes.

I understand all that and compliment the President, Paolo Guidotti Bentivoglio, for his carefully restrained description. But how does it get that way?

Therein lies another quite extraordinary tale. Very early on experimentation proved the sugary, white Trebbiano grape to be the best; so good in fact that the Modenese poet Alessandro Tassoni defined it as "God-given Trebbiano, sweet and biting."

It is the must (a combination of free running and pressed grape juice left to ferment when making wine) from these specially cultivated grapes that is cooked before it has fermented that begins the long process of aging that continues in a series of diminishing barrels for sometimes as long as a hundred years. A chart of this aging process might look like this—although no one is giving away the secrets of the process.

First: 50-liter oak barrel for about five years
Second: 50-liter chestnut barrel for about five years
Third: 40-liter cherry barrel for about ten years
Fourth: 30-liter ash barrel for about ten years
Fifth: 20-liter mulberry barrel for about ten years

Transferring from one barrel to the other is called "topping," and is the secret to making great *balsamico.* Recipes have been passed down from generation to generation and remain closely guarded secrets.

Finally there is the unusual control system that guarantees the quality of every bottle. There is a committee of *maestri assaggiatori* (master tasters), composed of thirty local authorities, twelve of whom have to be available at specific times to taste samples from various Modenese producers. If they don't approve, the producer is not allowed to bottle it with the official seal of the *consorzio,* and it is not *aceto balsamico.*

Because of the lengthy process, highly developed recipes, and the reduction that takes place in topping, *aceto balsamico* can truly be called a labor of love. Even at very high prices of $60 to $70 a bottle, however, it is not a major money-making proposition because the normal yield is only 200 to 300 bottles; and from what I'm told, half of that is reserved for family and friends. No, the genius of this product is not its commercial value but its unique contribution to the world of gastronomy.

Aceto balsamico tradizionale can be purchased in America at Corti Bros., 5770 Freeport Blvd., Sacramento, CA (tel. 916/391-0300). To my knowledge, this is the only vendor that has the real thing. Dean & De Luca have Giuseppe Giusti's good aged wine vinegar, I'm told, and Williams Sonoma imports the Fini product that is called *aceto balsamico di Modena,* but it is not the same thing.

ANTIPASTI

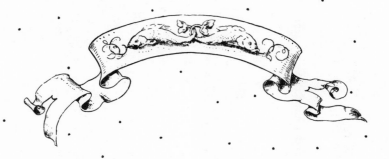

Appetizers

APPETIZERS

ANTIPASTI · APPETIZERS

Of all the fun things to do in cooking, I suppose making antipasti would be first on my list, unless it would be petits fours with their myriad shapes, fillings, and icings.

To some of the unknowing restaurateurs around the world "antipasto" is an excuse to put a piece of salami or prosciutto on a plate with some olives and a hard-cooked egg. Hardly an antipasto, when there are literally hundreds of possibilities to choose from. Here in Italy, and particularly in Umbria, the antipasti are very good but quite limited. The usual items encountered are confined to *bruschetta* and/or *crostini,* with perhaps some beans in oil, a pickled onion, mushrooms, peppers in oil, and prosciutto as the standard fare. Not very inspiring unless you seek out the better restaurants, where a proper effort is being made, or those wonderful rare exceptions like Villa Vecchia, in Fiesole above Florence, where they feature over five hundred antipasti laid out on acres of tables, or the wonderful Villa Vecchia in the *paese* ("village") of Fiumicino near

Rome Airport, where they state boldly on the menu under antipasti, *varietà infinita* ("infinite variety"). At the restaurant I had in Pittsburgh, Pennsylvania, called One Grandview, antipasti were divided into cold and hot and encompassed the following:

ANTIPASTI FREDDI · COLD APPETIZERS

Our regular *antipasti misti* included roasted peppers, anchovies, shrimp *remolata,* crab *ravigotta,* leek frittata, caponata, *pappa col pomodoro,* cold lemon broccoli, mushroom salad, olives, scallions, celery and radish salad, tuna, various salami, prosciutto, and pesto eggs (hard-cooked). In addition we featured:

Ostriche e caviale marinati (marinated oysters and caviar)

Insalata di grancevola e gamberi alla ricca con barchette di cetriolini (crab and shrimp salad with cucumber boats filled with horseradish whipped cream and topped with toasted sliced almonds)

Grancevola alla ravigotta (crabmeat with a caper mayonnaise dressing in avocado halves)

Carpaccio di pesce (thin raw slices of swordfish or salmon with an *aïoli* sauce

Cozze alla remolata (cold poached mussels in a mayonnaise dressing with diced gherkins)

Sogliole in saor (deep-fried sole in sweet and sour sauce)

Vitello tonnato (cold poached veal slices in a tuna and cream sauce)

Carpaccio di bue (thin slices of raw beef with *aïoli* sauce)

Peperoni al forno con alici (roasted peppers with anchovies)

Melanzane orientali (eggplant sandwiches with an Oriental filling)

Pappa col pomodoro (Tuscan bread soup with tomatoes and basil)

Carciofi origanati (cold artichokes with bread crumbs and oregano)

Bagna cauda (raw vegetables with a truffled anchovy dip)

Insalata di funghi crudi (raw mushroom salad in lemon and oil)

Insalata di ravanelli e sedano (radish and celery salad with a lemon oil and fennel dressing)

Insalata di pomodoro e mozzarella (tomato and mozzarella salad with fresh basil)

Antipasti caldi (hot appetizers)

Vongole o cozze in bianco (clams or mussels in white wine sauce)

Vongole o cozze Posillipo (clams or mussels in a Neapolitan tomato sauce)

Vongole o cozze origanate (clams or mussels baked with bread crumbs and oregano)

Gamberoni all griglia (jumbo shrimp in a white wine sauce)

Fritto misto di mare (mixed fish fry)

Mozzarella in carrozza (cheese in bread carriages, deep fried)

Crocchette di formaggi (various deep-fried cheese croquettes)

Ravioli nudi fritti (breaded and deep-fried spinach ricotta dumplings)

Crocchette di melanzane (eggplant croquettes)

Crocchette di carciofi (artichoke fritters)

These lists don't even include the pasta items that were often ordered as appetizers, nor the seasonal specialities, which were a regular part of extra daily offerings.

Although most of these antipasti were not the most exotic or original dishes, nonetheless they were fun, delicious, and certainly far from boring—as too many antipasti around the world can be.

The *bruschetta* and/or *crostini* mentioned earlier, which are so prevalent and sometimes dominant in Italian antipasti offerings, were a big disappointment to me when I first arrived to live in Italy. Over the years, however, I've grown to appreciate their simplicity and now find myself occasionally ordering *bruschetta all'aglio e olio* as a supplementary starter. The problem in making them in America is that you have to find that air-holed saltless bread the Italians seem to prefer, which is so normally unappealing and yet so fabulous when grilled (toasted) over coals, rubbed with garlic, laced with extra virgin oil, and salt and peppered. Ordinary toasted bread won't do!

Crostini are easier to make well, since they depend more on toppings than the particular bread used. The toppings in Umbria and generally throughout Italy are limited to diced tomatoes, *tartufata* (a mushroom and truffle paste), and bean pastes—a mixture of *ceci* (chick-peas) and fava preferred. These simple spreads are served on toast, and can be very good if you don't have to eat them more than once every three or four months.

But, as you can see from the foregoing lists, I'd prefer to be a little more adventurous. Here, then, are some of the recipes I'd like to share with you.

Ostriche e Caviale

OYSTERS AND CAVIAR

This is a classic appetizer from the days of ancient Rome. The nobility were inordinately fond of both oysters and caviar, and the marriage of the two was only natural. We've never encountered this dish on any menu in America, except for our own Grandview in Pittsburgh years ago, and surprisingly enough have yet to find it featured in Italy, although I'm sure any restaurant that has both ingredients would be glad to put it together for you. To us there is no equal to its elegance, especially when washed down with good champagne. Make sure to use the best possible caviar you can afford.

 6 *large, plump fresh oysters*
 1 *tablespoon fresh lemon juice*
  Dash Tabasco
  Scant pinch cayenne
  Pinch freshly ground white pepper
 2 *tablespoons (approximately 1 ounce) best possible caviar*
 1 *soup bowl crushed ice*
 6 *thin lemon slices*
 2 *sprigs fresh parsley*
 1 *lemon wedge, wrapped in cheesecloth*

1. Shuck the oysters carefully over a bowl to catch their liquor. Set aside the deeper half of each shell. Strain the liquor through a double thickness of cheesecloth, and then add the oysters, checking for bits of shell or other detritus. Add the lemon juice, Tabasco, cayenne, and white pepper and lightly mix with the oysters and their juice.

2. Let the oysters marinate in the refrigerator for no longer than 20 to 30 minutes.

3. Return the oysters to their reserved shells. Spoon some of the marinade over each oyster (approximately ½ to 1 teaspoon, depending on size), and then coat with caviar. Be careful not to bruise the caviar. It is best to hold each oyster in one hand and apply juice and caviar using the other for a clean, decorative finish.

4. Set each oyster, in a circular fashion, in the bed of crushed ice. Slip one fourth of each lemon slice under each oyster in a uniform manner for all six. (Although one might be tempted to use lemon slices dipped in chopped parsley and paprika, it is our considered opinion that that would be gilding the lily. So we prefer plain lemon slices decoratively placed.)

5. Garnish the bowl with parsley sprigs and a wrapped wedge of lemon.

YIELD: *1 serving*

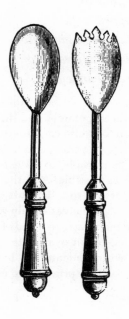

Grancevola alla Ravigotta con Avocado

CRAB SALAD RAVIGOTE WITH AVOCADO

1 cup finely diced peeled potato

4 ounces crabmeat, fresh, frozen, or canned

1 teaspoon chopped fresh chives

1 teaspoon chopped cornichons

1 tablespoon capers

2 teaspoons chopped fresh parsley

1½ cups mayonnaise

Salt to taste

¼ teaspoon freshly ground black pepper

1 ripe avocado, peeled, pitted, and cut in half lengthwise

1 cup chopped lettuce

8 strips julienned pimiento

4 pitted black olives

1 sprig fresh parsley

1. Poach the diced potatoes and drain.
2. Mix the potato, crabmeat, chives, cornichons, capers, and chopped parsley in a large bowl, tossing as lightly as possible, to leave as many large pieces of crab as possible. Add the mayonnaise, salt, and pepper and toss lightly again.
3. Stuff the avocado halves evenly with the mixture and place them each on a bed of the chopped lettuce arranged on an oval plate. Garnish each avocado half with pimiento and black olives on one side and parsley sprig on the other.

YIELD: *2 servings*

Carpaccio del Salmone

CARPACCIO

There are quite a few ways to present this rather special appetizer. The one we've chosen is something of a departure from the norm, and quite pretty. The dill garnish can be changed to fresh tarragon, thyme, or fennel leaves, if dill is unavailable.

Four or five 2- to 2½-ounce slices fresh salmon or tuna

2 tablespoons Aïoli (see page 124)

1 teaspoon red pepper puree, cold (see below)

6 sprigs fresh dill

6 lemon chips (roughly cut pieces with a bit of skin)

6 capers

1 hard-cooked quail egg, quartered (optional if unavailable)

1. Super-chill or partly freeze the salmon or tuna fillet so it will slice easily (about 20 minutes).
2. Using a clean, lemon-rubbed cutting board, slice the fish, as thinly as possible, into 4 or 5 slices.
3. Spread the *aïoli* evenly with a spatula or the back of a spoon over two thirds of a large, chilled plate.
4. Arrange the salmon slices on top of the aïoli on the plate from 1 to 5 o'clock, approximately.
5. Place the pepper puree at 10 o'clock and striate with a knife to create a star shape.
6. Garnish with the dill, lemon pieces, and capers and quail eggs in an irregular pattern.

YIELD: *1 serving*

RED PEPPER PUREE

Roast 2 large peppers, one tablespoon of extra virgin olive oil, 1 whole bled garlic clove, and salt and pepper to taste for 20 minutes in a 375°F oven. Then puree in a blender and pass through a food mill.

Zuppa di Vongole o Cozze

CLAM OR MUSSEL SOUP

The principles involved in preparing shellfish for this kind of dish allows for many variations. If left with a sufficient liquid, you have *zuppe* (soups); if the liquor is reduced to a thicker sauce, the shellfish is called *in bianco* (in white sauce). If the liquor is reduced and tomatoes are added (or better yet, a marinara is infused with some of the poaching liquid), the dish is called *vongole rosse* (red clams) or *cozze rosse* (red mussels), or the shellfish is referred to as *al pomodoro.* When various shellfish are combined, it could be a *zuppa* (or *brodetto*) *di crostacei,* or *crostacei in bianco,* and so on. If combined with other fish, it becomes, among other things, a *zuppa di pesce* or *pesce e crostacei in bianco.* If you learn the basic procedures correctly, all of these dishes are possible.

One of the "tricks" of the trade, so to speak, is to make a separate stock from some of the shellfish you are using and reduce half of it to a glaze. You then have an enriched liquid if you dry up the sauce and/or a double flavor concentrate to increase the richness of the *zuppa* or sauce you're making. So, if you wanted to make the best shellfish *in bianco* of your life, buy some extra shellfish and poach them in a covered pot with a bit of wine, herbs, and chopped onion, carrot, and celery. Add some water for volume and then reduce until you have a strong shellfish broth. Take half the shellfish broth and reduce it further, by half, till it is a double concentrate. Now you're ready to make shellfish *in bianco.*

1. Sauté garlic cloves (bled) in oil.
2. Add the shellfish.
3. Season with fresh or dried thyme, basil, or chervil and parsley, crushed red pepper, salt, and pepper.
4. Deglaze with white wine (aromatic preferred).
5. Cook, covered, for a few minutes until the mussels or clams open and release their juice.
6. Reduce the liquid slightly to concentrate the flavor, whether using for a *zuppa* or sauce.
7. If making *zuppa,* add stock and concentrated glaze made previously.
8. If making *in bianco,* add the glaze only.
9. If making *rosse* or *al pomodoro,* leave out the stock, add the tomatoes (better yet, a marinara infused with stock and glaze) and then the glaze, and cook a few minutes to amalgamate.
10. If making a *zuppa* with tomatoes, also add the stock for more liquid.
11. If making *zuppa di pesce,* proceed in the same way but add the fish beginning with the firm-fleshed fish and ending with the soft after the base broth is made with the clams and/or mussels.
12. The addition of such seasonings as orange and lemon rind, other herbs (fresh or dry), fennel, etc. does not affect this basic procedure.
13. You can also use crab instead of clams, lobster, sea urchin, etc.

I don't mean to imply that this is the only way to make these dishes, but I assure you that these principles if followed will serve you well—at least till you are convinced that there is another method that suits your preference. Anything is possible as long as you're cooking with love, knowledge, and devotion.

If you want to make pasta dishes with shellfish, there is a natural extension of these techniques. For example:

Linguine alle Cozze in Bianco

LINGUINE WITH MUSSELS

1. Make the stock and glaze as described on page 29.
2. Make mussels *in bianco* as described on page 29.
3. Cook the pasta in boiling, salted water until al dente; drain.
4. While the pasta is cooking, remove the meat from three fourths of the mussels and discard the shells.
5. Take off and discard the top halves of the shells of the remaining fourth of the mussels and reserve the mussels in shells in hot broth for garniture.
6. Take the remaining broth from making the mussels *in bianco* and place it in a sauté pan large enough to toss the pasta in. Reduce by half and add the glaze.
7. Add the shelled mussel meat.
8. Drain the "al dente" pasta and toss with the mussels in the sauté pan, coating thoroughly with reduced broth and glaze.
9. Serve in hot bowls, garnished with the remaining sauce, the mussels in their half shells, and the chopped parsley.

Vongole o Cozze Posillipo

CLAMS OR MUSSELS "POSILLIPO"

Al Posillipo indicates a style of preparation found in the Posillipo area of Naples. It's really a *rosso* or *al pomodoro* treatment, except that the marinara used is rather tight so that the dish is more *stretto*—not of the liquidy or soupy types.

The recipe therefore is the same as for mussels *in bianco* on page 29, except that you add only glaze and not stock. Make a marinara (see page 100) and infuse with a bit of fish glaze (see page 94). For 24 to 30 clams or mussels, add 2 cups of infused marinara after the deglazing with white wine and serve.

To make a pasta dish from this, toss the pasta in a bit of glaze and stock, adding the tomato sauce to the toss. The rest of the procedures are the same as for pasta *in bianco*.

Vongole Origanate

CLAMS ARREGANATA

Oregano has become arregano in America but aside from that, the herb is really only popular in Naples and the south. The treatment here is to lace bread crumbs heavily with oregano, coat the clams, mussels, and artichokes, etc. with this herbed mixture, then bake in the oven.

6 *littleneck clams*
½ *cup best available olive oil*
2 *cloves garlic, bled (scored)*
Salt and pepper to taste
⅛ *teaspoon crushed red pepper*
2 *tablespoons chopped fresh parsley*
2 *tablespoons best available white wine*
½ *cup bread crumbs*
2 *tablespoons freshly grated parmigiano*
1 *tablespoon dried oregano*
Lemon wedges to garnish
Additional chopped parsley to garnish

1. Scrub and wash the clams with cold water several times to remove sand.
2. Heat the garlic in ¼ cup of the oil in a sauté pan. Place the clams in the warm oil and stir. (Dry them off first to avoid explosions.)
3. Season with salt, pepper, and crushed red pepper and stir. Add half the chopped parsley and stir. Turn the heat up and add the wine to the natural juices from the clams. Allow the liquid to reduce by half.
4. Pry open any unopened clams and smell. Discard any that do not smell fresh and good. Remove the clams from their shells. Reserve one shell for each clam, placing a bit of the poaching liquid in the shell before returning the clam meat to the shell.
5. In a separate bowl, mix half the parmigiano with the bread crumbs and slowly add another ½ cup of the oil, mixing all the while.
6. Add the oregano and the other half of the chopped parsley and mix with some of the clam liquid. Season with salt and pepper.
7. Arrange the clams in one layer in a shallow baking pan. Coat the clams with the bread topping and drizzle the remaining oil on top of each clam. Spoon a bit of the remaining poaching liquid over each clam. Top with the remaining parmigiano cheese.

8. Bake in a 400°F oven for 5 to 10 minutes. Place under a broiler to brown the tops.
9. Serve on a warm plate and garnish with a lemon wedge and sprinkle with chopped parsley. For a formal dinner party, this dish is very attractive if placed on a good paper doily and garnished with a parsley sprig and a lemon wedge wrapped in cheesecloth.

YIELD: *1 serving*

Gamberoni alla Griglia

GRILLED JUMBO SHRIMP

Oni in Italian signifies "large," as in macaroni, meaning large pasta, or tortelloni, meaning large tortellini. *Gamberi* are shrimp, hence *gamberoni* indicates jumbo shrimp, not to be confused with that awful redundancy, shrimp scampi. Scampi is a different crustacean found only in the Mediterranean and is similar to the American crayfish. Shrimp scampi is not only redundant, therefore, but incorrect.

Be that as it may, this is not the only language confusion that lies within this dish. Grilled—or *alla griglia*—to Americans usually means chargrilled, or at least grilled on a steel grill. But here in Italy, *alla griglia* can mean grilled as Americans understand it, or sautéed in a pan—*saltato* (or *rosolato*). The distinctions are not clearly defined and the Italians seem to have a preference for saying *alla griglia* rather than *saltato*.

The reason for the explanation is that this dish, although called *alla griglia,* is a sauté of jumbo shrimp with white wine and herbs. Aside from the literal complexities, it's really quite simple.

20 to 24 *jumbo shrimp*

½ *lemon, for cleaning shrimp*

½ *cup olive oil*

4 to 6 *cloves garlic, bled (scored)*

1 *tablespoon minced garlic*

⅛ *teaspoon each dried thyme, basil, and chervil*

1 *tablespoon diced onion or shallot*

2 *tablespoons finely chopped fresh parsley*

Crushed red pepper to taste

Salt and pepper to taste

4 *fresh basil leaves, torn*

½ *cup white wine (Gerwürztraminer preferred)*

1 *teaspoon fresh lemon juice*

1 *tablespoon best available sauterne*

2 *tablespoons unsalted butter*

4 *lemon wedges, wrapped in cheesecloth*

4 *sprigs fresh parsley*

1. Peel and devein the shrimp. Rub each one with the lemon and set aside.
2. Heat oil and whole cloves garlic over medium heat in a large sauté pan or, if necessary, do the dish in two batches. Place the shrimp in the hot oil and quickly sauté, adding the minced garlic, herbs, onion, half of the chopped parsley, the crushed red pepper, salt, pepper, and basil leaves.
3. Deglaze with the white wine and mix well. Tilt the pan by lifting the handle toward you so that all the liquid flows to the front of the pan. Pull the shrimp back toward you to the top of the pan so that you can reduce the liquid in front without overcooking the shrimp.
4. Add the lemon juice, sauterne, and butter to the liquid and turn the heat up to reduce by a third. Return the pan to a flat horizontal position

and swirl the shrimp around in the sauce, coating them thoroughly.
5. Serve the shrimp on warm plates napped with the sauce and sprinkled with the rest of the chopped parsley. Garnish with the lemon wedges and parsley sprigs.

NOTE: Of course, this can also be made *rosso* by adding a cup of marinara after the deglaze. Once again, marinara infused with shrimp or fish stock would be better.

YIELD: *4 servings*

Fritto Misto di Mare

MIXED FRY FROM THE SEA

The Italians are very fond of *fritti misti,* whether it be of fish, meat, vegetable, or fruit. Breaded and deep-fried or batter-fried, the better restaurants all seem to include some versions of *fritti.* And of course, *fritti* make wonderful appetizers. Cheese, artichoke, shrimp, eggplant—whatever—fritters are delicious finger food appetite stimulants, particularly when washed down with cold champagne.

Aside from this use, however, when increased in size and quantity, *fritti* can be proper antipasti or even main entrees. The trick whether for finger food, antipasti, or entrees is to see that they're fried properly. By that I mean golden brown with the product inside cooked properly and greaseless. It's not really difficult to do this if you pay attention to the following:

1. Use fresh vegetables each time.
2. Do not let the fat smoke. Watch the heat carefully. Use a temperature gauge, if necessary.
3. When frying single unstuffed items such as French fries, shrimp, and other fish, be sure the vegetable oil retains a temperature of 370°F.
4. Fry stuffed and thicker items such as meat or rice balls with mozzarella in the center at a lower temperature (340°F) to allow the filling, etc. to cook before the outside darkens too much.
5. Drain well on an abundance of paper towels.
6. Serve immediately.

Almost any and all fish and shellfish can be deep fried. However, fat fish such as bluefish and mackerel, and tougher fish such as squid *(calamari)* and octopus *(polpi),* should be fried at a lower temperature (350°F) and coated with a whole egg (rather than an egg white) batter to allow for further cooking.

> 3 jumbo shrimp, peeled and deveined
> 2 oysters, shucked
> 4 scallops (bay preferred)
> 2 clams, shucked
> 4- ounce piece fillet of sole
> 2- to 3- ounce lobster tail (petit)
> ½ lemon, to clean seafood
> 1½ cups Beer Batter (recipe follows)
> Vegetable oil for frying
> Salt and pepper to taste
> 1 lemon wedge
> 1 sprig fresh parsley
> ¼ cup Aïoli (see page 124)

1. Clean and lemon all the seafood.
2. Dip the seafood in the batter, coating evenly.
3. Heat 4 to 5 inches of vegetable oil in a deep, heavy pan until it reaches 370°F. Beginning with the shrimp, fry the coated seafood, 2 to 3 pieces

at a time, until they are golden brown. Be sure the oil regains its temperature between batches.
4. Drain the seafood well on paper towels.
5. Season with salt and pepper.
6. Serve on a warm plate with the lemon wedge and parsley sprig.
7. Serve immediately with aïoli sauce on the side for dipping.

YIELD: *1 entree serving*

Beer Batter for Frying

> 1 cup all-purpose flour
> ½ teaspoon baking powder
> Pinch of salt
> 1 teaspoon sugar
> 1 extra large egg
> ¾ cup best available beer,
> at room temperature

1. Sift together all dry ingredients.
2. Break the egg into a large bowl. Using a wire whisk, beat in the cup of flour mixture. Add the beer little by little while whisking to avoid lumps. Add more or less depending on the absorbency of the flour.
3. Let rest, covered, at room temperature, for at least 1 hour before using. The consistency should be liquid but thick, like a well made sauce. Add more flour if needed.

NOTE: For an extra light and crispy batter, separate the egg, use the yolk only in the recipe. Whip the egg white and fold it into the batter just before using. This technique gives a tempura effect, and is especially suited for smaller, quicker cooking foods such as a mixed fry of vegetables or fish. The longer cooking required by the *mozzarella in carrozza* (next recipe), however, makes the whole-egg batter more suitable.

YIELD: *1½ cups*

Mozzarella in Carrozza

DEEP FRIED CHEESE CARRIAGES

6 ounces best whole-milk mozzarella, cut into thin (⅛-inch) slices

8 slices thin white bread, crusts removed

2 cups milk

1½ cups Beer Batter (see page 33)

8 cups vegetable oil

¼ cup Caper Butter (see page 123)

8 anchovy fillets

4 large lemon wedges

1. Distribute the mozzarella slices evenly on 4 slices of bread. Mound the cheese in the center of each slice so that none hangs over the sides. Top with remaining slices of bread to close the "carriages."
2. Pour the milk into a shallow bowl and dip all four ends of the sandwiches in it to moisten them for sealing. Press down on the sandwiches with the palm of your hand to flatten, and then seal each edge firmly with your fingers. Wrap each sandwich neatly and tightly in plastic wrap and repeat the sealing procedure.
3. Let the carriages rest in the refrigerator for at least 1 hour, but preferably not more than an afternoon.
4. When ready to serve, unwrap the *carrozza* and check for loose seals; reseal where necessary.
5. Heat the oil in a large, heavy saucepan to 340°F. Put the batter in a bowl wide enough to accommodate two sandwiches at a time and place two in it. With a long, two-tined fork, carefully turn them over to coat thoroughly.
6. Carefully lift each sandwich from the batter and let the excess run off. Lower the sandwiches into the hot oil. Avoid marring the even coating of batter when handling. Only place as many in the oil at one time as can float freely.
7. Turning occasionally, fry each sandwich for 4 to 5 minutes, adjusting the heat if the browning is too fast or slow. As the cheese melts, steam is generated and trapped inside, puffing the carriages and making them bob on the surface of the oil, signaling that they are done. If in doubt, let them cook an extra minute to guarantee a fully melted center.
8. When done, lift out with a slotted spatula and drain thoroughly over the fat. Place in a thick nest of paper towels and pat gently to absorb excess fat. Hold these first two in a warm (125°F) oven while the remaining two are cooking. Be sure the oil regains the correct temperature. When all are done, spread them evenly with half of the caper butter, mounding any remaining caper butter in the center of each. Criss-cross the anchovy fillets over the butter. Serve immediately with lemon wedges.

NOTE: All fried food suffers a dramatic loss of quality in the first minutes, even seconds, after frying. This dish especially, with its soufflélike puffiness that falls within the first minute, is by far best when eaten immediately after frying. An alternative for serving four guests at once is to use two separate fryers, though we haven't met the person yet who objects to the staggered service. Or, arrange the course to be served near the stove with the first wine of the dinner, as we do here at La Scuola. It's a wonderful way to break the ice, and it provides an entertaining demonstration.

YIELD: *4 servings*

Scamorza allo Spiedo

SCAMORZA (CHEESE) ON SKEWERS

2 *whole smoked scamorza cheeses (6 to 8 ounces each)*
4 *lemon wedges*
   Extra virgin olive oil to taste
   Salt and freshly ground black pepper to taste

1. Thread each scamorza lengthwise on 2 parallel skewers so that the cheese doesn't slip as it's turned. Cook the scamorza on top of the stove over a high flame to char it. This is the same treatment used for blistering peppers before roasting them in an oven.
2. Roast quickly in front of, or on, a wood fire, distancing the cheese so that the desired degree of crust and blistering is achieved before the cheese melts away, but is nonetheless nearly runny inside.
3. Serve on very hot plates with lemon, oil, salt, and pepper.

NOTE: This can be served as a separate first course or as part of an antipasto.

YIELD: *2 servings*

Crocchette Ofritti di 5 Formaggi

CROQUETTES WITH 5 CHEESES

¼ *cup thinly sliced and coarsely chopped Gruyère*
¼ *cup finely diced mozzarella*
2 *tablespoons crumbled gorgonzola*
2 *tablespoons freshly grated parmigiano*
2 *tablespoons freshly grated pecorino Romano*
1 *large egg, beaten*
¼ *thick Balsamella, warmed (see page 116)*
   Salt and freshly ground black pepper to taste
   Freshly grated nutmeg to taste
¼ *cup flour*
½ *cup plain bread crumbs*
1 *teaspoon milk*
2 *anchovy fillets, cut into sixths*
2 *cups vegetable oil*
1 *lemon, cut into 6 to 8 pieces*

1. Combine the cheeses in a bowl. Separately combine half the beaten egg with the *balsamella* and add to the cheeses. Mix well and season with salt, pepper, and nutmeg. Cover and refrigerate until well chilled.
2. Place the flour, remaining egg, and bread crumbs in separate bowls in front of you, adding the milk to the egg.
3. Form rounded *fritti* or larger *crocchettes* from the chilled cheese mixture using a floured spoon and a palmed hand. Make an indentation in each and

insert a piece of anchovy. Close up and fry as for *crocchette di melanzane* (see page 163).

YIELD: *12 fritti or 3 to 4 crocchettes*

Bagna Cauda

HOT OIL AND TRUFFLE DIP

This typical Piemontese antipasto dish has variations only in the ratio of oil to butter used. We like it with mostly butter. Though called for as an optional ingredient, the white truffle is really intrinsic to the dish. Though a very nice dip is made without the sophistication of its perfume, you might postpone serving it until fresh (not canned) white truffles are available to you. They're appearing more and more frequently in specialty food shops and Italian restaurants in America.

> 4 tablespoons (½ stick) unsalted butter
> ½ cup extra virgin olive oil
> 2 cloves garlic, minced
> 2 anchovy fillets, minced
> ⅛ ounce fresh white truffle or more, sliced thinly
>   Bell peppers, celery, chicory, and artichokes for dipping

1. Heat the butter and oil over low heat, gently in an earthenware crock. Add the garlic and anchovies and simmer gently while stirring until the anchovies dissolve.
2. Stir in the white truffle and serve immediately,

keeping the dip warm over a sterno in the center of the table and surrounding it with the fresh vegetables, which are then dipped into the hot dip.

YIELD: *4 servings*

Ravioli Nudi Fritti

FRIED SPINACH GNOCCHI

> 10 ounces fresh or 5 ounces frozen spinach
> 1 tablespoon unsalted butter
>   Salt and freshly ground pepper to taste
>   Freshly grated nutmeg to taste
> 1 cup fresh ricotta cheese
> 1 large egg
> ¼ cup freshly grated parmigiano
> 1 cup flour (approximately)
> ½ cup plain bread crumbs (approximately)

1. Steam the spinach with butter, salt, pepper, and nutmeg until tender. Drain and allow to cool. Squeeze it as dry as possible and chop fine.
2. Mix the ricotta, egg, and parmigiano together

in a bowl. Add the chopped spinach, mixing well and seasoning to taste. Cover and chill the mixture thoroughly.

3. Lightly knead half of the mixture on a well floured surface, adding 1 or 2 tablespoons of flour until the mixture thickens just enough to shape.

4. Roll out into a thin log, as for gnocchi, and cut into regularly sized, 1-inch pieces. Take up each piece separately and roll between the palms to shape the nudi (size of a large walnut in an almond shape). Repeat the procedure with the remaining half of the mixture. Finally, roll in the bread crumbs until evenly coated.

5. Fry as for *crocchette di melanzane* (see page 163).

YIELD: *1½ cups about 25 to 30*

INSALATE

Salads

SALADS

TALIANS raise a great variety of lettuces and salad greens and use them daily in one form or another. And, as a matter of fact, they're not all green. Bright and dark ruby reds of various types of radicchio contrast sharply with the white and yellow trimmed leaves of Belgian endive and *indivia ricciatissima* (curly endive). *Insalata mista* (mixed salad) does not mean what it sounds like—mixed lettuces. No, it refers to the addition of shredded carrots, tomato wedges, and sliced radishes, with an occasional addition of celery and/or onions. A variety of lettuces can be found in *insalata verde* (green salad), and a favorite combination of mine is a mixture of escarole and curly endive with a few arugula leaves and chicory for darker green accents. There's nothing like crisp salad greens to stimulate the appetite and simple dressings of extra virgin oil and rich homemade wine vinegar to provide an incomparable taste sensation.

I've been privy to a lot of discussions as to the proper place in a menu for the salad course. The French prefer salad at the end of the meal with cheese and perhaps fruit. The Italians will either serve it as part of the (or the only) antipasto course or in place of a vegetable accompanying the second course. My own preference is to use salads as an appetite stimulant and therefore as an antipasto.

Insalata di Pomodori e Mozzarella

TOMATO AND MOZZARELLA SALAD

Salads in Italy are as fine, if not finer, than anywhere in the world. The Italians use romaine, chicory, arugula, dandelions, and every other green available to make perfectly dressed salads. The trick is in their vinaigrette dressings; and the trick within the trick is the exquisite, full-bodied red wine vinegar used in every dressing. No one in the world treats vinegar with more reverence.

Here is a salad of thick slices of tomato and mozzarella cheese, marinated in a vinaigrette and served with fresh basil that is also a favorite of mine.

- 3 large ripe beefsteak tomatoes, sliced ½-inch thick
- ½ cup Vinaigrette Dressing (see page 47)
- 2 shallots, finely diced
- 1 teaspoon chopped fresh parsley
  Salt and freshly ground black pepper to taste
  Two ¼-inch-thick mozzarella slices
- 8 leaves fresh basil
- 4 sprigs fresh parsley

1. Marinate the tomatoes in half the vinaigrette with the shallots, chopped parsley, salt, and pepper for at least an hour.
2. Remove and place on a salad plate with the mozzarella. Pour the marinade and the remaining dressing over them. Garnish with the sprigs of basil and parsley.

YIELD: *4 portions*

Insalata Caprese

TOMATO AND MOZZARELLA SALAD FROM CAPRI

- ¾ pound ripe tomatoes
- 1 cup extra virgin olive oil
- 1 tablespoon good homemade red wine vinegar (or best available)
- 1 teaspoon balsamic vinegar
- ⅛ teaspoon each dried thyme, basil, and chervil
- 1 teaspoon snipped fresh chives
- 1 celery heart
  Salt, pepper, and cayenne pepper to taste
- 12 ounces fresh mozzarella, sliced into rounds
- 30 to 40 fresh basil leaves

1. Put all ingredients except the mozzarella and fresh basil in a blender. Add 6 to 10 basil leaves and blend all until pureed.
2. Make a lake of the sauce on chilled salad plates and place the mozzarella slices in the center of it overlapping each other. Garnish with the remaining fresh basil leaves and serve immediately or hold in the refrigerator for 1 to 2 hours.

YIELD: *4 servings*

Insalata di Endivia con Salsa Limone con Menta

BELGIAN ENDIVE SALAD WITH LEMON MINT DRESSING

6 to 8 medium-size Belgian endive, trimmed and each cut into 8 pieces

1 cup extra virgin olive oil

Juice of 2 lemons

2 tablespoons dried or 4 tablespoons fresh mint

Cayenne, salt, and pepper to taste

1 tablespoon sugar

2 tablespoons finely chopped fresh parsley

1. Arrange each endive in fan shape on a chilled platter.
2. Whisk the remaining ingredients except the parsley together for the dressing and pour it over the endive. Top with the chopped parsley and serve immediately or hold in the refrigerator for 1 to 2 hours.

YIELD: *4 servings*

Insalata val D'aosta

SALAD FROM VAL D'AOSTA

2 red bell peppers, seeded and sliced into 3- or 4-inch batons (sticks)

2 yellow bell peppers, seeded and sliced into 3- or 4-inch batons

10 to 12 ounces imported Fontina, sliced into 3- or 4-inch batons

1 cup green and black pitted olives

Salt and pepper to taste

1 cup extra virgin olive oil

1 tablespoon Dijon mustard

½ cup heavy cream

Cayenne to taste

1. Toss the peppers, cheese, and olives in a salad bowl and season with salt and pepper.
2. Make the dressing by whisking the oil, mustard, and cream together. Season to taste with salt, pepper, and cayenne.
3. Arrange the tossed salad on chilled salad plates and pour the dressing over it. Serve immediately or hold in the refrigerator for 1 to 2 hours.

YIELD: *4 servings*

Insalata Siciliana

SICILIAN VEGETABLE SALAD

6 to 8 *large ripe tomatoes*
¼ *pound sliced mushrooms, marinated in oil (enough to cover) and the juice of half of a lemon for ½ hour (at least)*
½ *cup sliced gherkins*
12 to 16 *green and black pitted olives*
¼ *pound peas (frozen acceptable), blanched*
¼ *pound canned cannelloni beans, rinsed of their juices*
  Salt and pepper to taste
½ *cup extra virgin olive oil*
¼ *cup good strong homemade wine vinegar (or best available)*
1 *cup Maionese della Casa (see pages 123–24)*

1. Toss the tomatoes, mushrooms, gherkins, olives, peas, and cannelloni in a salad bowl and season with salt and pepper. Add the oil and vinegar and toss lightly.
2. Arrange the salad equally among chilled salad plates and top each with a tablespoon of mayonnaise.

YIELD: *4 servings*

Insalata di Pollo con Vinaigrette al Tartufo alla Panna

CHICKEN SALAD WITH TRUFFLE AND CREAM VINAIGRETTE

4 *tablespoons (½ stick) unsalted butter*
2 *large boned chicken breasts (approximately 12 ounces)*
  Salt and pepper to taste
½ *cup peas (frozen acceptable), blanched*
½ *cup green beans, blanched*
¼ *pound mushrooms, thinly sliced*
1 *cup olive oil*
½ *cup red wine vinegar*
½ *cup snipped fresh chives*
1 *tablespoon dried mint*
  Cayenne to taste
10 *small Bibb lettuce leaves*
½ *cup heavy cream*
2 *tablespoons finely diced truffle*
1 *tablespoon balsamic vinegar*
1 *bunch arugula or watercress*

1. Heat the butter and sauté the breasts over medium heat, turning several times, until done. Slice the breasts into thin slices and season with salt and pepper.
2. Marinate the peas, beans, and mushrooms in a dressing made of the oil, vinegar, chives, and mint. Season with salt, pepper, and cayenne.
3. Place Bibb lettuce leaves on a platter and spoon the vegetables over them. Fan the chicken slices over the vegetables.

4. Whip the cream, truffle, and balsamic vinegar together and spoon over the chicken. Garnish with arugula or watercress.

YIELD: *4 servings*

dressing and spoon over the bed of lettuce. Drizzle with the remaining dressing and sprinkle with the shaved parmigiano. Season with the salt and pepper.

3. Drizzle a bit of olive oil over the cheese and the whole as a garnish. Serve chilled.

YIELD: *1 serving*

Insalata di Finocchi e Ravanelli con Parmigiano

FENNEL AND RADISH SALAD WITH PARMIGIANO

The use of shaved parmigiano for salads is found throughout Umbria and works particularly well in combination with radishes and fennel. The trick is to use the best possible "light" extra virgin oil.

This salad is pretty, different, and delicious and certainly can be served at the most formal parties.

⅛ head green leaf lettuce
½ small fennel bulb, sliced into thin sticks
2 jumbo radishes, if available, or 5 to 6 smaller radishes thinly sliced
¼ cup Al Limone (see page 47)
½ cup paper thin, shaved parmigiano
Salt and pepper to taste
Olive oil

1. Shred the lettuce into ⅛-inch thick strips and place on a chilled salad plate.
2. Toss the fennel and radishes with half the

Insalata di Sedano e Ravanelli

CELERY AND RADISH SALAD

Here is another interesting use of fennel. Our celery and radish salad is enhanced by fennel, cayenne, coriander, and lemon juice, which contribute to a rather piquant salad. This is used mainly as an addition to antipasto or as an interesting appetizer, along with olives and cheese.

2 ribs celery, trimmed and thinly julienned
1 bunch large radishes, thinly sliced
½ teaspoon fennel seed
Juice of 1 lemon
2 tablespoons extra virgin olive oil
Pinch of dry mustard
Pinch of ground coriander
Pinch of cayenne
Pinch of sugar
Salt and freshly ground white pepper to taste
2 tablespoons chopped fresh parsley

1. Mix the celery and radishes together in a bowl, then add the fennel seed and mix lightly.

2. In a small bowl, whisk together the lemon juice, oil, mustard, coriander, cayenne, sugar, salt, and pepper, and toss most of it with the salad. Add the parsley and toss again. Let marinate for at least 2 hours.

3. Before serving, toss with the remaining dressing.

YIELD: *4 servings*

Insalata "Festival"

SALAD WITH GRUYÈRE AND MUSHROOMS

There's probably not a more elegant salad than this wonderful combination of mushrooms, cheese, celery, olives, and truffles. And although you can certainly omit the truffles if they are not available, I feel very strongly that they're worth the expense in this situation.

The use of Gruyère, or in Italy, *groviera*, is also not essential, but once again I do recommend it highly.

If you do follow the recipe and wish to use it at its formal best, I suggest a lemon wedge wrapped in cheesecloth as a fitting final touch.

3 to 4 *tablespoons unsalted butter*

9 *ounces mushrooms, finely sliced*

½ *medium-size onion, finely diced*

1 *teaspoon each dried thyme, basil, and chervil*

Pinch of cayenne

Salt and pepper to taste

2 to 3 *ribs celery, thinly julienned*

10 *ounces Gruyère, uniformly julienned*

8 to 10 *pitted black olives*

¼ *cup fresh lemon juice*

2 *tablespoons chopped fresh parsley*

1 *truffle, finely sliced (optional)*

6 *large lettuce leaves*

Al Limone (see page 47)

6 *sprigs fresh parsley*

6 *lemon wedges, wrapped in cheesecloth*

1. Heat the butter in a skillet and sauté the mushrooms lightly. Add the onion, thyme, basil, chervil, and cayenne and cook for a few more minutes, stirring. Season with salt and pepper. Remove and chill.

2. Toss the chilled mushrooms with the celery, cheese, olives, lemon juice, and 1 tablespoon of chopped parsley. Add the sliced truffles and toss again. Cover and refrigerate for at least 1 hour to chill and to marinate.

3. When ready to serve, place the large lettuce leaves (spread open) on each plate. Divide the mushroom mixture equally among the chilled plates on top of the lettuce leaves.

4. Spoon a teaspoon of dressing over each salad and garnish with the remaining chopped parsley, parsley sprigs, and wrapped lemon wedges. Serve while still cold.

YIELD: *6 servings*

Vinaigrette Dressing

Beware the fools or charlatans who tell you there's only one way—one recipe—to make anything. How many pompous headwaiters and captains have I suffered through their insistence: "There's only one way to make a vinaigrette and it's 7 to 1." The classic ratio of oil to vinegar is said to be nine to one. Ah, but what vinegar, whose oil? Use light, pure oil, and the vinegar needed decreases. Use mellow balsamic vinegar and the vinegar can be increased easily to 30 percent or 3:1. Use rich, unfiltered extra virgin oil *and* balsamic vinegar, and 50:50 is not out of the question when dressing freshly picked full-flavored greens such as escarole.

½ teaspoon Dijon mustard
¼ cup red wine vinegar
¼ teaspoon sugar
½ teaspoon dried chervil
½ teaspoon chopped fresh parsley
   Salt and freshly ground pepper to taste
1 clove garlic, bled (scored)
   Dash of cayenne
7 ounces olive oil, pure or extra virgin

1. Whisk the mustard with the vinegar until the mustard dissolves. Whisk in the seasonings.
2. Whisk in the oil in a thin stream and let marinate for at least 30 minutes before using. Whisk again before serving.

Variation

•

Place all ingredients in a small jar and shake vigorously until smooth. Let sit for at least 30 minutes and shake again before serving.

YIELD: *1 cup*

Al Limone

LEMON AND OIL DRESSING

This is especially good over Bibb lettuce garnished with finely sliced white onions.

6 tablespoons fresh lemon juice
   Pinch of cayenne
1 tablespoon Dijon mustard
1 teaspoon dried chervil
½ cup plus 2 tablespoons extra virgin olive oil
   Salt and freshly ground white pepper to taste

1. Place lemon juice, cayenne, mustard, and chervil in a small, high-sided bowl and whisk to combine.
2. Begin adding the oil, drop by drop, while whisking constantly to form an emulsion. Continue adding the oil while whisking constantly until all is added. Season with salt and pepper and serve within a few minutes.

YIELD: *1 cup*

PASTA

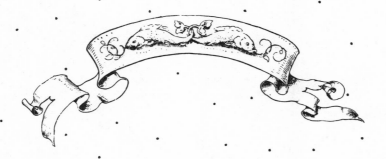

Pasta

PASTA

PASTA ALL'UOVO PASTA FRESCA

From *agnolotti* to *tufoli*—in broth *(in brodo)*, with sauces (hundreds), baked in the oven *(al forno)*— Latin *nodellus* (little knots) or German *nudeln, Kartofflekoesse* (potato dumplings) or *gnocchi,* Chinese rice noodles, *spätzle, nouilles,* or American spaghetti and meatballs—from as far away as Japan, and as close as the nearest stove, "pasta" is being celebrated continuously.

And so well it might. The simplicity and fulfilling nature of pasta in all its variety is unequalled by any other basic food. As we mentioned earlier, the true cooking of Italy is the mother cuisine of western civilization and certainly not limited to pasta. But *pasta secca* (dried commercial pasta) and *pasta fresca* (homemade egg noodles), with their unlimited potential, can well be Italy's greatest contribution to gastronomy.

The origin of pasta has been disputed for centuries. A little research indicates that the story that Marco Polo brought pasta to Italy from his travels in the Far East actually originated in an unsigned article appearing in the October 1929 edition of the *Macaroni Journal,* an American trade

journal of the pasta industry. But nowhere in the writings of Marco Polo does he relate anything more than the fact that he ate something similar to lasagne in Sumatra that was made from the flour of the breadfruit tree.

Whether Marco Polo was given some rice noodles to take home, or some ingenious woman in Bologna first combined eggs and flour to make tagliatelle is not as important as knowing a few of the more than 230 ways of making pasta.

In the whole history of cooking there have been very few genuine inventions. Most everything is extremely derivative. What most likely happened was that pasta and pasta cooking arose spontaneously—like roasted birds or broiled meat, vegetable soup, or flat bread—from the populace; from all those ladies cooking every day and exchanging recipes while they gossiped. The simplest and probably most ancient form of pasta was most likely lasagne, or *lagana*—sheets of flour bound with water or eggs—which date back to the third century A.D. according to certain references found in the writings of Cicero.

However, if one had to select one pasta of all the varied types of *pasta fresca* and *pasta secca* that could be said to be the most typical of Italy, it would be *tagliatelle.* These long, ribbonlike noodles are found almost everywhere in Italy where they have eggs and flour, and appear daily on the dinner table with the also ubiquitous *ragù* or *sugo*. It is generally recognized that they have been raised to perfection as "golden threads" in Emilia Romagna. Interestingly enough, while all of Italy reveres the quality of Emilian tagliatelle, they don't follow the recipes prevailing there, which omit oil and salt.

There are enough distinctions and preferences concerning ingredients and methods for making pasta for us to spend a few moments of analysis of the basic components before eliciting our own particular recipes and comments on "how to" and "how not to" make pasta.

The Flour

From the number of questions I have heard over the years concerning the relative merits of "durum," "hard wheat," and "semolina," it appears important to draw the distinction between these and soft wheat flours at the outset.

Wheat flour (as opposed to rye or corn, etc.) is the only one that forms gluten. Gluten is the result of the mixing of two proteins by hydration (the addition of a liquid). The higher the protein, or gluten, content, the greater the pasta's ability to expand. Therefore "durum" or "hard wheat" flour has the greatest expansion potential since it has a greater protein content than soft wheat.

Many students have asked, "But I thought semolina makes the best pasta." Well, it does, but only for *pasta secca,* because the dough requires a flour richer in protein in order to stand up to the heavy compression it is exposed to as it passes through the dies of the extrusion machine. Semolina is the inner core, or endosperm, of hard winter wheat and its very high protein content produces a more resilient dough that can withstand the stronger treatment of commercial machines.

But for *pasta fresca all'uovo,* by hand or machine, finely milled, medium strong, soft wheat flour is preferred. This produces a malleable, all-purpose dough that is easier to knead and roll out than one made of semolina, since it is softer, with less protein, less gluten, and more starch.

The traditional Italian choice for *pasta fresca* is "00" flour, the closest American equivalent being unbleached all-purpose flour. Unbleached all-purpose flour, however, is slightly more gluten-rich and hence stronger, and therefore does not lend itself as well as Italian soft wheat flour to the extensive extension technique of Emilia Romagna, where they prefer to make pasta by hand stretching.

Be that as it may, there are other factors, such as the quality and freshness of the eggs and the love, care, and knowledge of the pasta maker, that render the distinction between Italian "00" and American unbleached all-purpose flour relatively unimportant. You can make great pasta with American flour; it's just a little harder to roll out.

It is important to note that while a major percentage of *pasta secca* is made with semolina flour and *pasta uova* with "00," there are, nonetheless, many other flours used in pasta making as well. Whole wheat is used for *bigoli,* for example, and buckwheat for *pizzocheria,* pastas found extensively in the far north of the Valtellina and the Friuli-Venezia Giulia districts. They are usually combined, however, with a bit of regular flour to avoid too dense a product.

The Liquid

Although the type of liquid used is variable, it always has a very definite effect.

The 70-gram, wonderfully fresh and deeply colored Italian eggs are an ideal medium. The firm, fresh whites provide albumen to assist in binding, and the yolks supply the color, rich flavor, and silky feel of their oils. Being 73 percent water, eggs provide a rich liquid for making attractive and delicious pasta.

The equivalent in American stores to the 70-gram Italian egg would be Grade A jumbo; although unless you find a store with *farm* fresh eggs they are never quite as good as their Italian counterpart.

Certain handmade, or machine-made, but not extruded, pastas, such as *stringozzi* or *lombrichelli* and *pinci* from Umbria, or *trenette* from Genoa, use water as the liquid and when prepared correctly are unusually delicious and different from a boxed-extruded linguine, for example. Many recipes for these types of pasta require the addition of egg whites, which produce a "bouncier" noodle, pale in color, and also very much lower in calories.

By contrast, many recipes call for an extra egg yolk, or in some cases two or three egg yolks, which will add proportionately more color, flavor, and a cakier texture.

The normal formula or ratio of eggs to flour for one portion is ¾ cup flour to 1 egg, and as a standard operating recipe it is pretty foolproof, bearing in mind that these ratios vary as the type of flour and size of the eggs vary. The further question of the addition, or omission, of oil and salt can be decided according to your own preference, once you understand that the oil reduces the gluten's strength and makes a softer dough, whereas salt does just the opposite, working chemically to toughen it.

Whether by hand or by machine (but not extruded), the omission of oil (all taste considerations apart) as a textural matter for *pasta al forno* (an oven-baked pasta dish) makes "technical" sense, since a stiffer dough will probably stand up better to double cooking, first in water and then in the oven. However, I should immediately admit that for some thirty odd years I have preferred the taste of oil and salt in my pasta to such an extent that it is not omitted even for the oven pastas. I have never found the product to suffer and to this day I will reach for salt, oil, 2 eggs and 1½ cups of flour to make most pastas except the fabulous Emilia Romagnan *tagliatelle,* where I think their recipe without salt is unbeatable.

Equipment

- A wooden surface—pasta board—work table—chopping block, etc. Marble should be avoided since it's cold and makes the dough less elastic. Most teachers say a 3- to 4-foot square or rectangular work surface is ideal. That certainly is true, especially if you're making a 6- to 20-egg pasta, where such a large space is essential. However, if one were to make a 2-egg pasta at home for a dinner for two, a 16- by 32-inch chopping block would be fine.

- Rolling pin. A rolling pin is, after all, just a wooden cylinder and therefore one might say that any old pin will do. Not so. A proper rolling pin for pasta is essential when it comes to stretching pasta in the Emilian manner. It should be 1½ to 2 inches in diameter and 30 to 36 inches long, depending on your reach and the quantities you think you'll most often be working with. While such pins are readily available in stores in Italy, there might still be some difficulty in locating them in America, depending on the size and sophistication of your particular city, in which case, the nearest lumber yard is an excellent source. Soft wood is cheaper than hard but certainly not as good since it is more porous.

However, I must at the same time point out that I've made excellent pasta in a kitchen where the work space was 16 inches and a vodka bottle was used to roll out the dough (full, incidentally). My reason for telling you this is not to confuse, nor to denigrate well-defined principles for making perfect pasta. As a professional chef, I am naturally inclined by training to use the best work space and tools for a particular job. But I also have cooked for friends under extremely strained circumstances and found it possible to produce a very satisfactory meal. That has taught me to temper my professional requirements with an insight into, and a recognition of, the problems of home cooking.

But getting back to the rolling, or pasta, pin, like all wood products it will have a slight taste when new and therefore should be washed well several times and seasoned with a bit of good extra virgin olive oil before using. It is preferable to store it hanging in the open air, instead of in a closed drawer, and, like all cook's tools, it should be cleaned regularly and reseasoned once in a while. It's also best to rub the pin with flour prior to each use.

- A clean sharp knife to cut the pasta.
- A large sharp metal scraper, known as a dough blade or scraper, to clean the board and keep it free from excess dough bits and flour as you're working.
- A medium-size (or large, depending on the quantity you usually make) drum sieve or flour sifter to clean the remaining flour from bits of dough, and also to provide a fine "flouring" of the board when rolling or stretching.
- A large metal or wooden spoon for mixing.
- A large fluffy pastry brush to remove excess flour.

- A pastry bag for piping in fillings, though a teaspoon will do just fine.
- Various ravioli and other molds.
- Various cutters, crimpers, and sealers, including one especially useful gadget, the krimp-kut-sealer, that does all three jobs in one pass.
- A spindle rack of any sort for hanging pasta.

The Methods

Keeping these basic principles of ingredients in mind, one is then confronted with the further question of technique. Or as I've heard asked so often . . . by hand or by machine? . . . which is better?

The Romagnans insist that the delicate and persistent stretching of the dough by hand is what makes their *tagliatelle* memorable. I tend to agree and go a step further to prefer hand-rolled pasta for stuffed and baked pastas such as manicotti, ravioli, and lasagne.

Technically, there's an obvious difference. Kneading and rolling by machine forces the dough by compression into a more uniform, elastic product. But such pasta can never be as soft and have the same taste as hand-stretched pasta.

Incidentally, the machine we are referring to here is a hand-cranked or electric roller, not the extruder used for making *pasta secca,* which forces the dough through dies by heavy compression.

There is an electric machine which is quite expensive ($350–$450) that has plastic rollers with bumps on them which enable you to avoid the finished "manufactured" texture of regular machine-made pasta. But nonetheless, even this addition does not make pasta the quality of that which has been hand-stretched or hand rolled.

Texture is not only controlled by the methods of handling, but also by the length of time spent in the kneading and stretching, or rolling, of the dough. The longer and more forcefully a dough is kneaded, the firmer the gluten strands become and the tougher the dough. That's why it is so important to stretch rather than press down, or compress, when you're rolling out pasta by hand.

It is also important to note that this entire question of stretching, rolling, etc. cannot in truth be said to have any absolutes. It is a question of texture and flavor, which are, after all, highly subjective matters. Once you know how to make pasta by various methods it is up to you to decide which is suitable for a particular dish. As long as you understand the principles involved and know how to execute them to get a desired effect, it is my opinion that your taste and opinion should be the deciding factors, not those of die-hard authorities who will try to insist that their way is the only way to make pasta.

How to Cook Pasta

Whether the pasta is an egg pasta, or one of the dried *(pasta secca)* pastas, there are a few simple rules for cooking it:

- There must be sufficient water (6 quarts to 1 pound pasta).
- The water should be salted at, or near, the end of the cooking time.
- The water should be on a slow, rolling boil, not a fast, hard boil, which will tear the outside edges of macaroni and leave the center uncooked.
- The pasta can be well-drained before saucing—or tossed with a bit of the pasta water. I prefer my pasta well-drained.
- Toss it with a bit of butter or oil before saucing—or not.
- Use hot plates. Absolutely essential.
- Serve immediately. Also essential.

The common practice of rinsing the pasta after cooking is a "no! no!" The salted pasta water has good flavor and should not be washed off. Also, the Italians cook their pasta in a broth made from the main ingredient of the sauce or dish it is to be served with. For example, if you were making pasta with broccoli, the water used to prepoach

the broccoli would be used, or added to more water if necessary, adding more flavor to the pasta itself.

Some Last Tips Before We Begin

- Always use the same flour for dusting the board and equipment as was used in the dough. Use semolina or fine corn flour to dust the finished noodles or squares.
- Always lift a sheet or strip of dough by gingerly draping it over one arm, or a rolling pin, to move or turn it. Avoid picking up or grasping with the fingertips as the dough will become misshaped or tear.
- Nest noodles carefully as they are cut. In this way you will avoid piling or overhandling. The dents and wrinkles incurred by handling will not straighten out during cooking.
- Use your best judgment as to when to cut pasta dough. If cut too "fresh," the noodles can easily stick and get misshaped in subsequent handling. If too dry, they may crack and break. A dry-to-the touch, yet supple pasta is perfect.
- Pasta made with spinach or other flavoring ingredients quickly gets sticky even if it feels well floured. Keep it well dusted, check regularly, and avoid overlapping or stacking.

Pasta all'uovo

BASIC EGG PASTA

The addition of oil and salt in this dough precludes its use for the classic Emilian method, as already discussed in the introduction. It is suitable, however, for all the other handling methods, including by machine. It is especially suited for making all types of *pasta ripiena* (stuffed pasta), as the oil helps to lubricate the dough so no additional moisture is needed to seal the edges, and keeps it supple longer, allowing time to form *tortellini,* for example, without the last few cracking.

Another departure that makes everything easier is to start the dough in a 12-inch bowl and form it into a ball before putting it on the work surface. This is an excellent way to make pasta and bread. The idea of a volcano crater, with its walls and floor, is all very mysterious sounding and looks impressive, but actually for the novice who doesn't want all that mess, a bowl is much more practical.

1¾ *cups (approximately) Italian "00" or American all-purpose, unbleached flour*

2 *freshest jumbo eggs, at room temperature*

1 *teaspoon salt*

2 *teaspoons olive oil*

1 *cup flour (as above) for rolling, dusting, etc.*

¼ *cup semolina or corn flour for nesting, etc.*

YIELD: *2 servings*

MAKING THE PASTA

1. Put the flour in a large bowl and make a well in the center. Break the eggs into the well and then add the salt and olive oil. Mix these ingredients thoroughly with a wooden spoon.
2. Incorporate the flour a little at a time as needed until a pliable dough forms. At first mix the dough with the spoon and then with the knuckles of one hand, folding and kneading lightly against the bowl.

KNEADING THE DOUGH

1. Dust a large board or work surface and your hands with flour. Place the dough on the floured surface in front of you and shape it into a ball.
2. With the fingers of your left hand (if you are right-handed), lift part of the dough up and over to fold it into itself by pressing down with the heel and palm of your right hand.
3. Turn the dough a quarter turn and repeat— lifting with the left hand and pressing down and away with the palm of your right hand.
4. As you continue to turn the dough and knead, set one foot in front of the other (whichever makes you comfortable, although I prefer the left foot in front of the right) and rock forward as you press down and back as you release. Lift the dough up with the fingers of your left hand as you rock. Naturally the procedure reverses itself if you are left-handed.
5. Maintain a steady rhythm of lift-fold-press, rocking and kneading until you have a smooth elastic ball. This will take approximately 5 minutes. The dough should not need any additional flour to prevent sticking, and if it does, it is too wet. To remedy this, open the ball of dough and insert more flour directly into it. Close it and begin kneading again.
6. When the dough is smooth and elastic, wrap it in plastic wrap, set a bowl over it, and let it rest. Since there is oil in this dough, the resting period can be as short as 10 minutes or as long as several hours.

ROLLING OUT THE DOUGH

1. Unwrap the ball of dough and flatten it into a disk on the floured surface in front of you. Cut the disk into quarters (depending on size) and roll each quarter out till it is thin and slightly transparent. If you hold the dough to the light, your hand behind it should be visible.

2. This rolling can be accomplished by simply turning the disk a quarter turn and rolling it out and away from you, while pressing down lightly with the rolling pin. Continue turning the disk and rolling out and away until the dough is properly thin and transparent. For making lasagne and other specialty items, you might prefer a slightly thicker dough, but generally the transparency test is accurate.

3. Let the rolled dough rest again to dry. Place the sheets on a board or baking sheet dusted with corn flour and leave it exposed to the air for 1 to 1½ hours, depending on the temperature and humidity. Spinach and filled pastas will take longer to dry because of their moisture content. But in all cases, allow substantial drying time before trying to cut the noodles. This was the reason for all those sheeted beds of pasta I observed in so many households in my youth.

CUTTING THE DOUGH

Various shapes and sizes are possible at this point for all kinds of pasta. I refer you to the individual methods of cutting found in specific recipes. However, I will explain here how to cut what we refer to as noodles. They are *capelli d'angelo* (angel hair), *taglierini, tagliolini, tagliatelle, fettuccine, trenette, pappardelle, lasagnette* (small lasagne), and *maltagliati* (badly cut). The difference between these long noodles is one of thickness or broadness. *Capelli d'angelo* are the finest as is signified by a literal translation of "angel's hair." *Lasagnette* are the fattest, or broadest, if you will, at about 2 inches wide. *Maltagliati* means "badly cut" and refers to a sheet of pasta being cut randomly into squares, triangles, or other shapes. I sometimes use the

leftover trimmings from pasta sheets for this purpose. Those leftover pieces are also good deep fried and then sprinkled with sugar and cinnamon. When made with a sweetened pasta dough, they are called *cenci*.

The Italians sometimes take this business of the thickness and broadness of their noodles quite seriously. In Bologna there is a pasta museum in which the perfect *tagliatelle*, in gold, mind you, are displayed in a glass case. Rather than try to frighten you with such specifics, the following are the general widths of the better-known noodles.

Capelli d'angelo	¹⁄₃₂ inch
Taglierini	¹⁄₁₆ inch
Tagliolini	⅛ inch
Tagliatelle	¼ inch
Fettuccine	¼ inch (interchangeable)
Trenette	¼ inch (interchangeable but water instead of eggs)
Pappardelle	½–¾ inch
Lasagnette	1–1½–2½ inches
Maltagliati	1½ inches approximately (random slices in squares, triangles, and diamonds)

The method for cutting all these sizes of long noodles is the same.

1. Trim all four sides of the pasta disk so that you have a square or rectangle.

2. Fold the straight edges toward the center from the right and left sides in 2-inch segments. Proceed from each of two outside edges.

3. You should now have two "scrolls" of pasta.

4. Fold one on top of the other and cut the noodles with a sharp chef's knife, making a brisk clean downward thrust to get evenly sliced noodles. You can use a ruler in the beginning if you like to achieve the different sizes, but in a very

short time (after five or six tries), you should be able to cut them by eye.

5. To unroll the noodles from the scroll, slip the dull edge of the knife under the scroll at the seam and lift carefully and evenly. The noodles will unravel at once on either side of the knife.

6. Dust your free hand with flour and remove the noodles from the knife, wrapping them around your fingers to form a nest.

7. Lay the nest on a board or an inverted pan which has been dusted with cornmeal.

8. Now cover them lightly with cheesecloth or a light cotton towel; the Italians say cover *i nidi* (the nests) *con un velo di cotone* (with a veil of cotton). The reason for the lightness of covering is to allow the pasta to breathe but not dry out totally. This is not to say that you can't take leftover fettuccine and dry them totally in a covered container to use days later. It is not the same thing, however. If you refrigerate them for the next day's use, take them out and allow them to sit two hours at room temperature before using to allow the humidity from the refrigerator to dry out. Again, it's not the same, and, in my opinion, fresh pasta, *pasta all'uovo*, should be made fresh, according to the procedures outlined above, and eaten soon thereafter.

The Classic Emilian Pasta all'Uovo

With this stretching method you will need ample space to work the dough. A 37- by 26-inch (approximately) board or work surface will be needed as well as a minimum 22-inch rolling pin.

1¾ cups (approximately) Italian "OO" or American all-purpose, unbleached flour

2 fresh jumbo eggs, at room temperature

½ cup flour (as above) for rolling, dusting, etc.

¼ cup semolina or cornmeal, for nesting, etc.

YIELD: *2 servings*

Technique 1—The Classic Emilian Method
•

MAKING THE PASTA

1. Mound the flour on the work surface. Form a crater in it, leaving ample "walls" and "floor."

2. Lightly mix the eggs and pour them all at once into the crater. Begin incorporating the flour with the eggs, little by little, using your fingertips. Continue until the mass becomes thicker and you have used all, or nearly all, the flour. Then, using your whole hand and a dough scraper, work the dough until it is as firm as you can make it.

3. Set the dough aside, scrape the surface clean and gather the remaining scraps and flour into a pile at the corner of the board for later use (or not). Wash and dry your hands.

KNEADING THE DOUGH

1. Dust a board or work surface and your hands with flour.

2. Place the dough in front of you and compress it lightly with the palm of your hand into a thick disk.

3. With the edge of your right hand (if you are right-handed), lift one third of the right edge of the disk and fold it down against the center of the dough. Switch the weight to the heel of your hand and press down firmly.

4. With the edge of your left hand, rotate the disk counterclockwise a quarter turn while adjusting its distance from you as well.

5. From now on the edge of your right hand will find a knob of dough where the smooth edge was on the first knead. This knob is folded over and pressed into the center of the evolving dough as the kneading progresses.

6. Maintain a steady rhythm of lift-fold-press-turn until tiny blisters are clearly visible on the dough's surface. This will take at least a full 10 minutes. The dough should not need any additional flour to prevent sticking as long as it remains in motion. If it does stick, it is too soft and more flour should be worked in. Wrap the pasta in plastic and set it aside to rest for at least 30 minutes but for no longer than two hours.

7. Scrape the board clean and prepare to roll out the rested dough.

ROLLING OUT THE DOUGH

1. Place the rested dough in front of you and flatten it slightly into a disk.

2. Enlarge the disk gradually by lightly rolling out the center with a rolling pin, turning the dough and rolling out again. Continue until it is thin enough, using the transparency test (see page 57).

STRETCHING THE DOUGH

1. Roll the dough around the rolling pin, starting at the far edge of the circle and stopping within 3 to 4 inches of the near edge. Gently pin down the near edge with the palm of your left hand.

2. With the heel of your right hand, gently push the pasta-encased rolling pin away from you, keeping an even tension between it and the pasta in your left hand. Proceed slowly and carefully in 4 to 6 movements to stretch the pasta away from you while simultaneously allowing it to unroll.

3. Turn the dough 90 degrees counterclockwise and repeat. Turn the dough without disfiguring it by picking it up with your fingertips, rolling it back onto the pin, and then unrolling it away from you at whatever new angle is needed. Repeat this process until you've obtained the largest circle possible without tearing the dough.

FINISHING THE PASTA

1. Roll the dough toward you around the rolling pin. Using both palms in rapid massagelike motions, stretch the pasta lightly away from the center of the pin while allowing it to unroll slowly. Repeat this procedure, rolling the pasta around the pin to expose a new area, smooth the pasta, and complete its stretching.

2. Lay the pasta out on a sheet or towel to rest uncovered until you are ready to cut and the pasta is well dried but not brittle.

The cutting and nesting procedures are the same as in the basic recipe (see pages 56–58).

CUTTING THE PASTA

1. For *tagliatelle,* dust the pasta lightly with flour. Trim the tops and bottoms of the circular sheet of pasta by cutting 2 inches off those edges in a straight line.

2. Fold or roll the straight edges toward the center, like joined scrolls. Using a sharp chef's knife and a brisk clean downward thrust, slice across the scrolls at $1/4$-inch intervals.

3. To unroll the noodles, slip the dull edge of the knife lengthwise under the scrolls at the seam, as far in as a single portion, and lift carefully. The noodles will unroll on either side. For *fettuccine,* simply stretch the dough less thin and cut at intervals closer to $1/8$ inch than the $1/4$ inch *tagliatelle.* For *taglierini,* cut the "classic" sheets extremely fine, technically $1/16$ inch wide. For *pappardelle,* do not roll the dough for cutting. Instead, use a fluted pastry wheel to cut $1/2$ inch strips directly from the open sheet.

NESTING THE NOODLES

1. Rest the unfurled noodles, still on the blade, against the table and shower them thoroughly with semolina or corn flour.

2. Slide the *tagliatelle* off the blade into the palm of your other hand, simultaneously "nesting" them, or forming them into a loosely piled spiral.

3. Place the "nests" carefully on whatever lined and dusted pan you are using and shower them again.

STORING THE NOODLES
(THEY'RE BEST WHEN FRESH)

1. Let the nests dry thoroughly in a cool, dark place before slipping them into individual plastic storage bags.
2. Keep the bags away from direct sunlight, extremes of temperature, and humidity. They should last for many weeks before crumbling.

Technique 2—The Modified Emilian Method

•

We call this the "modified" method because, while it maintains most of the benefits of the stretching procedure, it's really a compromise between stretching and rolling. You'll find this a more natural technique to adopt, and far easier to work quickly. It makes consistently superb noodles.

A "pizza pin," a 12-inch version of the classic Emilian rolling pin, is needed for this technique. It's a wonderful pin to have around in any event; it's ideal for those times when a larger pin is just too unwieldy.

The steps for making and kneading the dough are identical to those of the classic Emilian method (see pages 58–60). We begin with the rolling and stretching of the dough, which are here combined into one step.

ROLLING AND STRETCHING THE DOUGH

1. Cut the rested dough into as many equal pieces as the number of eggs in the recipe. Lay one piece in front of you on a floured surface; cover and set aside the rest.
2. Flatten the dough into a strip with the palm of your hand. Gently pin down the near edge of the strip with the flat palm of your left hand (if you are right-handed).

3. With the shorter rolling pin in the other hand, use it to simultaneously roll and stretch the strip away from you. Turn the rectangle sideways, and roll and stretch it to a width of 6 to 8 inches.
4. Turn the dough again lengthwise and continue to make short, firm stretching and rolling movements, always away from you.
5. Flip the dough strip over lengthwise to expose the end that the left hand was holding and repeat the stretching and rolling, flouring the pasta as needed.
6. When the strip gets too long to handle, cut it in half and set one half aside as you work with the other to achieve the desired thinness using the transparency test.
7. Flour the finished halves well and stack them to one side as they accumulate.

CUTTING THE PASTA
(IF USING FOR *PASTA RIPIENA,* PROCEED AS
INDICATED IN INDIVIDUAL RECIPE)

1. For noodles, make stacks of two strips folding or rolling their ends toward the center—like joined, short 6- to 8-inch-wide scrolls.
2. Cut across the scrolls at the desired widths. Unfurl, nest, and store the noodles as explained in the classic Emilian method on pages 58–60.

Technique 3—The Pasta Machine Method

•

The invention of the pasta machine put homemade pasta within the reach of even the busiest person. This is wonderful, as long as it is remembered that it yields a totally different product from that made by hand. Pasta can be "homemade," but certainly not "handmade," with a machine.

In any case, here are a few special guidelines for using the machine most efficiently, after making the dough according to the instructions on page 58.

1. Watch the dough strips carefully for sticky spots. If dough gets stuck in the gears, you're in for an hour's work with toothpick and brushes. Keep the work surface dry while using the machine and dust liberally with flour.

2. Conversely, as the pasta gets smoother, avoid clumps of flour on the strips by dusting them with flour, then sweeping them off. A fluffy brush is excellent for this. Keep the strips smooth to avoid gummy noodles.

3. Use your judgment as to how many times (six to eight) to knead the dough through the rollers. Keep in mind that the strips should be smooth enough to handle without sticking, but that during rolling they will pass through the rollers many more times. The pasta will eventually toughen if passed through the rollers too many times. Adjust by decreasing or increasing the folding and adding or eliminating a notch in the rolling.

4. Never get the machine wet. Use a dry toothbrush if bits of dough get in the cracks.

5. Work on the biggest surface you can. Have plenty of space to lay the increasingly larger strips.

6. Although not critical, avoid stopping the rollers with a strip in them. This increases the risk of dough getting stuck in the gears and sometimes the strip will split in half. As a rule, once you start cranking, don't stop until all the pasta is through the rollers.

KNEADING THE DOUGH

1. Take the coarse wad of dough from the bowl, cut it in half if more than two eggs were used in the recipe, in quarters if more than four were used, etc. Flour the work surface in front of the machine lavishly and lay one piece of dough on it; cover and set aside the rest.

2. Form a strip of dough half as wide as the rollers with the palm of your hand, turning and flouring as needed.

3. With the rollers set at their widest, pass the well-floured strip through once, guiding it away from the rollers as it emerges.

4. Fold the strip in half, flour thoroughly, and pass it through again on the same setting. Avoid letting the emerging strip pile up. Alternatively, you can sandwich the dough into itself in thirds, and using the tips of your fingers, seal the dough into itself, making it easier to pass through the rollers.

5. Decrease the width of the rollers two notches, flour the strip, and pass it through. You may have to cut it in half. Fold it in half, flour it, and pass it through again. (The previous sticky mass should now begin to resemble pasta. If still too coarse and sticky, repeat the procedure at this setting.)

6. Set the first strip aside and flour it well. Repeat steps 1 to 5 with the remaining pieces of dough.

ROLLING OUT THE DOUGH

1. Bring out the first strip of resting dough, dust it with flour (though more lightly now), and pass it through the rollers set one notch narrower than the last time.

2. The emerging strip will be at least twice as long now, so cut it in half, setting one piece aside.

3. Fold the half in half and dust lightly, checking for sticky spots and sweeping off the excess flour with the hand or a brush. Pass it through again and set aside.

4. Repeat with remaining strips, dusting lightly and setting aside.

5. Adjust the width of the rollers to the final thickness of pasta you prefer. Pass the strips through, cutting them in half as required, and setting them aside, dusted and stacked. Allow to dry slightly before cutting.

CUTTING THE PASTA

The strips of pasta can now be cut by hand, if you prefer, into whatever shape is required. If using the automatic cutters of the pasta machine, proceed as below:

1. Dust each strip and cut it to the length you prefer the finished noodles to be.
2. Insert the crank into the cutter side of the machine. Gently guide one end of a strip into the cutters and begin turning the crank.
3. As the noodles emerge, let the remainder of the strip rest on the machine, freeing your hand to collect the noodles.
4. Nest the noodles as indicated in the basic technique or our classic Emilian method (see pages 56–60).

Pasta Matta

CRAZY PASTA

Pasta matta—crazy pasta, the joker, the wildcard in the deck—is made by hand with soft wheat flour and water and no eggs, although an egg white might be added to make these rustic noodles bouncier. Although they are made in many parts of Italy, they are really a specialty of Umbria and have different names in different parts of that region. In and around Perugia they are called *lombrichelle* (worms) because of their uneven fat shape resembling worms. Further south near Terni they are called *stringozzi* (laces) because they are made a bit more evenly and look like shoelaces, while in the north of Umbria around Città di Castello they refer to *pasta matta* as *pinci,* supposedly because they pinch the dough out into little cylinders before rolling it with the palms and fingers, as is done in making *gnocchi. Cirioli* are rather thick and are distinguished by using half semolina and half regular wheat flour. The use of

egg whites is optional but a method that is much preferred by the ladies here at the school. They also insist on very warm water (just under boiling) to mix the pasta with. The result is a very chewy and quite delicious pasta of its own type.

Basic techniques for rolling out, cutting, and nesting are relatively the same for *pasta matta.* The recipes are as follows.

> 2 cups (approximately) Italian or American all-purpose, unbleached flour
> 1 jumbo egg white
> ½ cup simmering water
> 1 teaspoon salt

YIELD: *2 servings*

STRINGOZZI

Make the dough following the instructions for Basic Egg Pasta (on pages 56–58) or Classic Emilian Pasta (on pages 58–60). Proceed as directed here when you reach the instructions for rolling and cutting the dough.

Roll out the dough rather quickly, about ⅛-inch thick. Roll up and cut across evenly at ⅛- to ¼-inch intervals, which will produce a nearly square circumference. Shake them freely, dust with semolina and nest them.

LOMBRICHELLE

After proceeding with techniques 1, 2, 3, or 4, continue as follows:

1. Mix the ingredients together and knead for 2 to 3 minutes till elastic.
2. Flour the work surface and cut the dough in half.
3. Form a long cylinder, as in making *gnocchi,* with the palms of your hands by rocking it back and forth against the surface.
4. Work the cylinder finer and finer until it is the general thickness of an earthworm.

5. You can also pick up the cylinder and by rubbing one end back and forth between the palms of your hands and letting the remainder hang and bounce up and down in a pendulum motion. The cylinder will stretch and lengthen. Return it to the table and finish rolling with the palms of your hands.

6. Repeat using all the remaining *pasta matta* and form all into spirals; dust with semolina on a well-floured plate and nest them.

TRENETTE

There seems to be some confusion concerning eggs (whole, with yolk) or not, with *trenette*. Some authorities treat *trenette* as another *pasta all'uovo,* and since they are cut approximately ¼-inch thick, similar to *tagliatelle,* there would be no real distinction. But our research in Genoa, where *trenette* originates, indicates it is a water and flour pasta with the white of an egg optional, but never made with whole eggs or egg yolks.

The method is the same as for *stringozzi,* but it is rolled out thinner, as when making *tagliatelle,* and then cut in ¼-inch widths.

NOTE: The addition of egg white in this flour and water dough helps bind the dough and makes a bouncier noodle. There is a further variation possible, by eliminating the water and adding a cup of egg whites (three jumbo) to approximately 2 cups of flour.

These noodles are cooked very little (3 or 4 minutes), not only because people in Umbria and Genoa prefer them very firm (al dente) but also because they will crumble in the water if cooked longer.

A typical saucing for *trenette* is a type of *filetto di pomodori* (tomato filets) spiced with *peperoncini.* They work equally well to soak up the savory juices of hearty roasts and braises . . . like a cross between a German spätzle and a potato *gnocchi.* Of course, the traditional treatment for *trenette* in Genoa is with pesto, and all of these noodles find a perfect marriage with this famous basil sauce.

FLAVORED PASTAS

Spinach pasta, beet pasta, herb pasta, mushroom pasta, pesto pasta, saffron pasta, tomato pasta, carrot pasta, red pepper pasta, onion pasta, garlic pasta . . . even chocolate pasta can be made by adding an ingredient. I'll provide you with a master recipe for spinach pasta and then a number of variations. Once understood, it is easy to incorporate whatever flavoring you'd like. The three I use most frequently are: spinach, *peperoncini,* and saffron pasta. Spinach pasta can be used almost interchangeably with regular egg pasta, while *peperoncini* (red hot pepper) pasta is a bit more restricted in use, in my opinion (I find an onion sauce—made from long-sweated white, red, and yellow onions—to be the best accompaniment). Saffron pasta is wonderful with light cream sauces and fish sauces that are not too "tomatoey." One of my favorite uses of saffron pasta is with leftover sauce and bits of meat from an osso buco.

On to the recipes.

Pasta all'uovo Verde agli Spinaci

EGG PASTA WITH SPINACH

8 ounces frozen chopped spinach or 1
  pound fresh spinach, cleaned
½ teaspoon salt
  Pinch of freshly ground black pepper
  Pinch of freshly grated nutmeg
2 teaspoons unsalted butter
3½ cups (approximately) Italian or
  American all-purpose, unbleached flour
2 jumbo eggs, at room temperature
½ cup flour (as above), for rolling,
  dusting, etc.
¼ cup semolina or cornmeal, for nesting,
  etc.

1. Steam spinach in its own water with salt, pepper, nutmeg, and butter until just tender. Frozen spinach should be thawed first but not squeezed dry; fresh spinach should be washed and the water still clinging to it used to steam it. Fresh will take a little longer than frozen.
2. Drain, and when cool enough to the touch, squeeze as dry as you can. Chop spinach very finely. Do not puree. Proceed as in either basic pasta method (see page 56 and page 58), adding the spinach with the eggs.

Variation

•

Spinach Pappardelle: Use 2 ounces frozen spinach, 1 egg, and about 2 cups flour. Proceed as above. Roll finished dough into thick sheets, and cut into noodles 1½ inches wide and 3 to 4 inches long.

Other Egg Pasta Variations

•

Peperoncini Pasta: Use 2½ to 3 cups flour, 2 eggs, 1 tablespoon cracked red pepper finely ground, and 1 tablespoon red pepper flakes. *Saffron Pasta:* Use 2½ to 3 cups flour, 1 egg, and 1 tablespoon saffron threads soaked in ½ cup warm water or 2 tablespoons ground saffron dissolved in ¾ cup warm water. *Tomato Paste Pasta:* Use 2½ cups flour, 2 eggs, and one 6-ounce can tomato paste. *Carrot and Tomato Paste Pasta:* Use 2¾ cups flour, 2 eggs, 1 cup cooked, drained, and pureed carrots, and 1 teaspoon tomato paste. *Beet Pasta:* Use 2½ cups flour, 2 eggs, and ¼ cup thoroughly cooked, peeled, and grated beets. *Egg Yolk Pasta:* Use 1¾ cups flour and 8 egg yolks. *Pesto Pasta:* Use 1¾ cups flour, 2 eggs, and 3 tablespoons finely ground pesto.

YIELD: *2 servings*

Gnocchi

Ah, *gnocchi!* The divine pillows of a childhood feted with dumplings. To me there was always something medicinal about them, in the better sense of the word—like the alleged medicinal properties of chicken soup. Good for what ails you. And a plate of *gnocchi* always has, and still does, make me feel extra good. Somehow there's nothing sinful about this indulgence.

    The most popular form of *gnocchi* is made with potatoes and all-purpose flour, but they are also made with semolina flour and/or cornmeal instead of, or in combination with, regular flour. There are also many forms of flavored *gnocchi*—

alla zucca (pumpkin), *alla gorgonzola* (with gorgonzola cheese), with ricotta, parmigiano, zucchini, basil, mushrooms, pesto, or tomatoes. The only problem with flavored *gnocchi* is that you have to add more flour than I like because of the moisture content of the additive. This goes against the basic principle of making *gnocchi*, which is to have them as soft and light as possible without their melting into the water they are cooked in. By adding more flour *gnocchi* will keep better and are easier to handle, and there's no danger of their melting in the water. But my God, how awful they are! So, if you're intent on mastering *gnocchi*, you must have the nerve to hold back on the flour and suffer a few "meltdowns" till you get the balance right. As with most supposedly difficult things in cooking, persistence and repetition (four or five times, not hundreds) are necessary, but the payoff is double when you sauce them with pesto or a ragù Bolognese, or simply butter and cheese. A special favorite of mine is called *ravioli nudi alla gratinata*. The name comes from the fact that the spinach and ricotta that these dumplings are made of is the filling for most ravioli served throughout Italy. In this gratin version the gnocchi are first poached till they rise to the surface, then drained and coated with an enriched *balsamella* to be finished browned under the broiler. A very delicate and savory dish.

I provide a basic potato *gnocchi* to get you started on making *gnocchi*. Once having mastered these basic recipes, you shouldn't have any trouble expanding into the flavored ones.

  2 *large potatoes*
  1 *extra large egg, beaten*
      Pinch of salt
      Pinch of freshly ground white or black pepper
  1 *tablespoon freshly grated parmigiano*
      Freshly grated nutmeg to taste
 ½ *cup all-purpose flour (or less if possible)*

1. Peel and dice the potatoes. Boil them gently in lightly salted water to cover until tender. Drain well and, while still warm, put them through a food mill or potato ricer into a bowl.
2. Beat the egg with the salt, pepper, cheese, and nutmeg. Add to the potato.
3. Gradually add the flour and mix well. Shape into a loose ball in the bowl. Divide the ball into three parts.
4. Dust a board or work surface with flour and roll each ball into long, ¾-inch rolls, keeping them floured to avoid sticking. Use the palms of your hands to roll these into long snakes. Handle lightly.
5. The long snakes will be very soft and hard to handle at first—if they don't already have too much flour. Move your palms over them, rolling them back and forth until they are shaped. The flour on the work surface will be gently worked into them this way.
6. Cut the rolls in ½-inch pieces and toss and roll them in the flour, shaping as you do. By pressing gently as you shape the pieces into ovals, you will incorporate a bit more flour. It is only through trial and error, however, that you'll be able to determine the proper texture: soft, but firm enough to cook without falling apart.
7. Lay the tiny ovals on a floured tray covered with plastic in a dry cool place till needed. Do not refrigerate or they will become gummy.
8. To cook, carefully remove the *gnocchi* from the tray with a floured spoon and ease them into gently boiling water. Cook for 3 to 5 minutes and remove with a slotted spoon as soon as they pop to the surface. Drain and serve with whatever sauce you choose. My favorites are butter and cheese, pesto (see pages 125–26), or *ragù bolongese* (see pages 108–9).

Some variations are spinach *gnocchi*, carrot *gnocchi*, and pumpkin *gnocchi*.

YIELD: *about 24 pieces or 2 servings*

It's one thing to make noodles, or open a box of *pasta secca* and cook it, and another to reach for the stars, so to speak, and make perfect little *tortellini, tortelli, agnolotti,* ravioli, *manicotti, cappellacci,* or the incredible *pasticcios, pasticiattas,* and lasagne of Italy.

Savory stuffings can be as simple or as complex as you like and as economical or expensive as you can afford. Leftovers make some of the best fillings and give you a chance to use up odd bits of meat and vegetables that would otherwise be wasted, though, to my mind, nothing can replace fresh calves' brains, chicken livers, pistachios, and truffles, which are the bases of my own filling for tortellini. *Pasta ripiena* also provides an opportunity to combine sauces, fillings, and pastas with cheeses and seasonings in as creative a manner as you like.

Fortunately for us, all of the strange-sounding names, shapes and fillings can be reduced to a less intimidating concept quite easily. After all, we're only talking about a piece of dough wrapped around a filling or layered in a pan.

For example, *manicotti,* which means hand-rolled, or handcooked, is a square of *pasta all'uovo* rolled around a filling of ricotta, eggs, prosciutto, and Parmigiano, sauced and baked. It comes from the name in Italian for a woman's hand muff —*mani cotto.* You might be more familiar with it as *cannelloni,* since the long, cylindrical tubes made from pasta squares are the same; it's the filling and the region that determine the name. If you change the filling from ricotta to chicken livers and ragù, it becomes *cannelloni* in some parts of Italy. In fact, if you add spinach to the ricotta filling, it becomes *cannelloni di ricotta e spinaci.* The term *manicotti* is rarely used north of Naples.

Tortellini (little stuffed rings), *tortelli* (larger *tortellini*), *cappellacci* (little hats), ravioli (little squares), and *agnolotti* (larger ravioli) are usually stuffed with ricotta and spinach although, like *tortellini,* they can also be the subject of wonderful savory meat fillings. These are all basically envelopes, which are sealed after stuffing.

The secret of presenting these and other types of *pasta ripiena* lies in the particular recipes that have been developed over the years to provide the best combinations of pasta, stuffings, and sauces.

Pasta all'uova alla Pasta Ripiena for Stuffed Pasta

EGG PASTA

The pasta sheets for *manicotti* or lasagne can be made from any of the egg pasta recipes in this chapter. We, however, prefer this special recipe that we developed which contains a bit of the ricotta filling for the *manicotti.*

3 to 4 cups (approximately) Italian "OO" or American all-purpose, unbleached flour

4 jumbo eggs, at room temperature

1 tablespoon Ricotta Filling (see page 70)

1 teaspoon salt

1 tablespoon olive oil

½ cup flour (as above), for rolling, dusting, etc.

¼ cup semolina or corn flour, for nesting, etc.

The method is the same as our easy one for making Pasta Uovo (see pages 56–58).

YIELD: *4 to 6 servings*

Manicotti al Sugo

PASTA ROLLS WITH CHEESE

1 cup Ricotta Filling (see page 70)
Two *5-by-7-inch pieces homemade Egg
    Pasta for Stuffed Pasta, cooked briefly
    in salted water (see page 66)*
Two *¼-inch slices mozzarella*
½ *cup Sugo di Carne (see page 106)*
2 *tablespoons freshly grated parmigiano*

1. Put ½ cup ricotta filling on each piece of pasta. Add a mozzarella slice and roll into a cylinder. Press the edges together to seal.
2. Line a casserole with *sugo,* lay the *manicotti* on top, and cover with the remaining sauce. Bake at 350°F for 30 to 40 minutes.
3. Remove from the oven, place on a warm plate, and serve garnished with parmigiano.

YIELD: *1 serving, 2 pieces*

There is a maxim we use in training cooks for professional kitchens that is useful to the amateur as well: "The simpler the dish, the more vivid the consequence of any variation in its preparation." This is never truer than in pasta recipes. The seemingly picayune differences between a square ravioli, round *cappellacci,* and crescent-shaped *agnolotti* render totally different flavors and textures. Even the differences between several square ravioli, all stuffed with, say, ricotta, one thicker, one finer, one with straight instead of fluted edges, one smaller, or one larger, provide a huge variety of possible sensations. The best part is, they're the easiest of the small *paste ripiene* to assemble, and the quickest to adapt to a personal style of presentation.

They're all made generally in the same manner: A bottom sheet of pasta is dotted with filling, a top sheet is applied, and the pasta is sealed and cut around the mounds in squares, circles or crescents. Any of our basic recipes and techniques for making *pasta all'uovo* can be used for *pasta ripiena.* In particular, the all-purpose basic pasta (see pages 56–58) is recommended as its oil content helps keep the pasta moist longer for sealing edges. For larger dumplings like *tortelloni,* the egg pasta for *manicotti* made with ricotta (see page 66) makes a special textural treat, but is too soft for shaping tiny *tortellini.*

Two methods for making ravioli are presented here, to account for variables in equipment, space, and type of pasta.

Basic Ravioli

*½ recipe Egg Pasta for Stuffed Pasta (see
pages 66–67), or other as desired*

*2 cups filling of your choice (see pages
70–72)*

METHOD NO. 1—TO MAKE BY HAND

1. If using hand-rolled pasta, trim the sides of a
sheet of pasta to form a rectangle. Dust the work
surface and center the pasta on it.
2. If pasta seems a bit dry, brush half lightly with
an eggwash (an egg beaten with a little water).
Lay on the filling, using a pastry bag or spoon, in
mounds on half of the sheet (the wet half if using
the egg wash). These should be at least one
mound-length apart.
3. Fold the other half of the sheet carefully over
the first, repositioning the mounds if they're too
close to any edge. Press down around the mounds
with your fingers to seal, starting at the closed
side and working across to expel air.
4. Cut between the rows of filling and across to
shape the ravioli, or stamp them out with round
cutter or glass. Scoop them up with a spatula and
place them on a lightly floured pan, tray, or plate.

ALTERNATIVES TO METHOD NO. 1

Instead of using a single sheet or strip of pasta
and folding, twice as many can be made at once
by using two sheets or strips, though you need a
larger work space.

To make the crescent-shaped *cappellacci,* use a
wide-mouthed glass or jar that fits over two
mounds at once, then a cutter to form half-
moons. Or, use the traditional round cutter, then
fold by hand, as in the beginning of *tortellini.*

YIELD: *36 to 40 cappellacci*

METHOD NO. 2—
TO MAKE WITH A RAVIOLI FORM

If you want perfectly square, uniform ravioli, this
is the method. Strips of dough from pasta machine rollers just happen to fit perfectly over the
form but, as you know, we're not crazy about the
machine. In any case, hand-stretched or rolled
dough only needs to be trimmed to fit.

Whether using either type, the form calls for
a slightly thicker pasta, another factor that determines the uniformity of the ravioli from it.

1. Trim the sheets or strips of dough to fit the
form by placing the form directly on the pasta
and cutting around it. Leave a 1-inch border or
overhang. You'll need two such pieces of pasta.
2. Thoroughly dust 1 piece of pasta and place it,
floured side down, on the form. Press down
gently into the holes with the top part of the
ravioli forms to form the pockets for the filling.
Remove the top.
3. Fill the pockets, using about 1 slightly rounded
tablespoon of filling.
4. Place a second, unfloured piece of pasta over
the form. Press down gently to flatten the fillings,
evening out the surface. Roll a pin over the form
lengthwise, back and forth, until the jagged cutters of the form come through the dough. Tilt the
form directly over a pan, releasing the ravioli.
Gently nudge out any that are reluctant.
5. Cut the individual pieces apart with a cutter or
a knife. Place pieces separately on a floured plate
or tray and store in a dry, cool place if serving
within a half hour. Failing that, cover with plastic
wrap and store in refrigerator. Make sure they
come to room temperature before using to avoid
gumminess.

• PASTA RIPIENA •
BASIC TORTELLINI/CAPPELLETTI

The only difference between these two ring-
shaped dumplings is that *tortellini* start as circles
and *cappelletti* as squares. Making either takes only

a quickly acquired knack. First, some useful hints:

- Work with small amounts of pasta at one time, while it is still moist. This is the secret to avoiding the frustrating sticking and tearing that inevitably occur when water is used in sealing dry edges.
- Keep the sheets or strips of pasta not in use covered with a damp towel or plastic wrap to maintain moisture.
- Make the dumplings huge the first few times and then progressively smaller as your technique develops; larger ones are much easier to handle. Call the giant ones *tortelloni.*
- Make more pasta than you really need the first few times to cover experiments, and practice with squares or rounds of paper before trying pasta.
- Use any filling you wish, as long as it's ground finely. Jagged chunks will tear the pasta. It's amazing how little filling actually fits in these dumplings . . . ¼ teaspoon usually suffices or sometimes even less.
- Set the finished *tortellini* on floured plates or towels as they are made, and keep them spaced apart so they don't stick.
- The leftover scraps of dough may be rerolled and shaped, but the dough becomes considerably tougher. Better to gauge carefully and cut closely to minimize waste.
- The freshly made *tortellini* begin to suffer perceptibly after the first hour or so; make them in the late afternoon before dinner. If you must hold them, refrigerate them loosely covered, well floured, and spaced apart. They'll take up lots of room, though, as they can't be stacked, and the amount of flour needed to keep them dry tends to make their surfaces gummy when cooked.
- Alternatively, they hold well in the freezer. Freeze them, well spaced, on cookie trays, then transfer to Zip-loc bags for storage up to 6 to 8 weeks. Cook them frozen; do not thaw.

A Note on Store-Bought Tortellini

With all the precise, careful handling requirements in recipes for homemade *tortellini,* you may be wondering how manufacturers manage to package them for storage on supermarket shelves next to the spaghetti or in the refrigerator cases. All jumbled together without so much as a single grain of *semola* to keep them apart.

The differences in texture and taste between these and homemade dumplings are clues to the answers.

First of all, the fillings are made extremely dry, and ground very finely. Store-bought *tortellini* generally do contain the classic ingredients—mortadella, prosciutto, and parmigiano—but the mortadella is made especially low-fat and not studded with nuts, the parmigiano may be Grana (a cheaper variation), and the prosciutto from other than Parma, all specified with an eye toward consistency, the needs of the machine, and a long shelf life.

Second, the pasta, which admirably must, by Italian laws at least, contain durum semolina and eggs and little else, is nonetheless worked through giant pressure rollers into glossy, hard sheets that the machine can deal with. And don't think that the scraps, of which the machines give off plenty, go to waste—back into the rollers!

Third, the actual *tortellini* are stamped out (very cleverly, and in an interesting, syncopated rhythm) by machines.

Finally, and more important for shelf life, they're *pasteurized,* steamed quickly but thoroughly until fully cooked, and then passed on to blowers to dry them.

This is the general procedure for *tortellini* that require refrigeration. The *really* dried ones are made similarly but, as you can imagine, much more extremely. In any event, it is not easy to find handmade *tortellini* in restaurants, even in Italy. All the more reason to make your own—a very special treat.

Tortellini

½ recipe Egg Pasta for Stuffed Pasta (see pages 66–67), or other as desired

2 cups filling of your choice (see below)

1. Cut 2-inch squares or circles from freshly rolled sheets or strips of pasta. Work with twelve at a time.
2. Line the squares or circles in front of you on a floured work surface and place ¼ to ½ teaspoon (for 2-inch pieces of pasta) or less stuffing in the center of each. If squares, fold them to make triangles. If circles, fold them to form half moons. In either case, seal the edges together by pressing down against the work surface.
3. Pick one up between the thumb and index finger of the left hand (if you are right-handed). Pull the two ends together around your index finger to form a ring. With the left thumb, bend back the "brim" or flared edge of the *cappelletti*, or pointed "peak" of the *tortellini*. Press the ends together firmly to close, and let the pasta rest until you are ready to cook and serve it.

YIELD: *48 to 60 pieces*
(about 20 pieces to a portion)

Ricotta Filling

4½ cups whole milk ricotta

1 jumbo egg

4 ounces prosciutto, thinly sliced and coarsely chopped

½ cup chopped fresh parsley

½ cup diced or shredded whole milk mozzarella

1 teaspoon freshly ground black pepper

1 teaspoon freshly grated nutmeg

1 tablespoon sugar

½ teaspoon salt

1. Mix all ingredients thoroughly in the order given.
2. Use as a filling for *manicotti, lasagne, tortellini,* and other pastas.

YIELD: *6 cups*

Spinach and Ricotta Filling

½ pound fresh spinach, cleaned and washed, or 5 ounces frozen chopped spinach

Salt and freshly ground black pepper to taste

Freshly grated nutmeg to taste

1 tablespoon unsalted butter

1 cup ricotta cheese

1 large egg

1. Steam whichever type of spinach you are using with salt, pepper, nutmeg, and butter. Drain well and cool.
2. Squeeze the spinach against a strainer until very dry. Chop finely. Do not puree in a blender.

3. Mix together the ricotta and egg. Season to taste with salt, pepper, and nutmeg. Add the drained spinach and mix lightly. It should look like a ricotta and spinach filling, not a totally green mixture.

YIELD: *1½ cups*

Swiss Chard and Ricotta Filling

4 ounces Swiss chard, cleaned
1 tablespoon unsalted butter
   Freshly grated nutmeg to taste
   Salt and pepper to taste
1 cup ricotta cheese
1 large egg
2 teaspoons freshly grated parmigiano

1. Steam the Swiss chard with butter, nutmeg, salt, and pepper. Squeeze the chard as dry as possible and chop fine. Do not puree.
2. Mix the ricotta with egg and parmigiano. Add the Swiss chard and adjust the seasonings.

NOTE: A heartier alternative to the regular spinach or Swiss chard and ricotta stuffing is to use the filling to stuff larger ravioli or agnolotti. The pungency of a caper or fresh sage butter sauce makes the perfect counterpoint.

YIELD: *1½ cups*

Savory Filling

2 tablespoons unsalted butter
8 ounces calves' brains
2 ounces chicken livers
2 teaspoons finely diced shallot or white onion
   Salt and pepper to taste
2 tablespoons dry white wine
½ cup plus 2 tablespoons Mornaia (see page 116)
¼ cup unsalted, shelled pistachios, roughly chopped
1½ cups Ragù Bolognese (see pages 108–9)

1. Heat the butter in a large skillet or sauté pan and sauté brains and livers with the shallots, letting them set on one side.
2. Turn the meat over in the pan and season to taste with salt and pepper. Deglaze the pan with the wine. Stir well, breaking up the brains and livers.
3. Add the *mornaia* and pistachios, and mix well. Add the *ragù bolognese* and simmer gently, stirring, for 5 minutes.

Variation for agnolotti

•

Add ½ pound of chopped, cooked spinach, squeezed dry. Mix thoroughly and moisten with a little extra *mornaia* or cream, if necessary.

YIELD: *4 cups*

Pumpkin Filling

1 *cup unsweetened pumpkin pulp, fresh or*
canned
1 *large egg*
½ *cup freshly grated parmigiano*
  Freshly grated nutmeg to taste
  Salt and freshly ground pepper to taste
½ *cup crushed amaretti cookies*
1 *teaspoon lemon juice*

1. If using a whole sugar pumpkin, bake for about
1 hour at 400°F. Quarter, seed the pumpkin, and
then scrape the pulp from the rind and mash with
a fork. Freeze extra pulp if you have too much.
2. Place the pulp in a bowl and mix in the other
ingredients. Beat well with a wooden spoon to
make the filling smooth.

YIELD: *2 cups*

• LASAGNE AND PASTA AL FORNO • BAKED PASTA

Lasagne refers to pasta squares cooked with a
sauce of any description, tossed, and usually
topped with grated cheese.

Lasagne al forno (from the oven) is similar in the
use of sauces and varietal ingredients, but is
usually further enhanced by the addition of
cheeses—grated parmigiano, shredded or whole
mozzarella slices, or fontina. Both as fillings and
toppings these cheeses add a lustrous quality to
an already impressive dish.

Pasticcio and *pasticciata* refer to tossed or baked
lasagne that combines several sauces and/or ingredients. An example of this type of dish is
lasagne imbottita, a mixture of meat sauce, ricotta,
hardboiled eggs, sausage, butter, and parmigiano,
baked in the oven.

To get a fuller understanding of these baked
pastas, let's take a culinary tour of the country.
We'll start in the far north of Valle d'Aosta, with
its particularly alpine type of cooking. Fontina is
the cheese here, and the forests of Alba due south
in the Piedmont region provide rare white truffles
to this rich cuisine. A beautiful vegetarian lasagne
comes from this region, called *lasagne di cavolfiore
Valle d'Aosta.* This calls for a coating of *balsamella*
over cauliflower buds with sliced white truffles as
an addition and fontina in layers with yellow egg
pasta.

One of the most unusual and, at first preju-
diced blush, perhaps the most unattractive
sounding lasagne comes from the northern
reaches of the Piedmont area. It's called *lasagne al
sangue* and is made with sweetbreads, sausage,
onions, and pig's blood cooked in milk; reduced,
the blood is thick enough to make a proper sauce.
It's a tossed lasagne and is finished with liberal
toppings of parmigiano.

Right below Piedmont and directly on the *Mar
Ligure* is Liguria, with its famous seaport city of
Genoa, from which we have the classic pesto
sauce. Our recipe in this case, known as *lasagne al
pesto* or *lasagne al basilico,* calls for lasagne squares
tossed with sweet butter and pesto. When ricotta
is added, it becomes *piccage al pesto—piccage* meaning handkerchiefs, another name for the squares
of lasagna when they are folded loosely.

Although Lombardy and its leading city,
Milan, are famous for risotto and *cotoletta di vitello*
(veal cutlet), the Milanese are not without their
own version—alternate layers of pasta, *balsamella,*
and prosciutto, baked in a slow oven until golden
brown. Or *lasagne mascolata,* as prepared currently
by chef Luciano Parolari, at the world-famous
Villa d'Este at Lago di Como. This is a simple
mixture of meat sauce and *balsamella* tossed with
lasagne squares and baked with a parmigiano
topping over a final coating of *balsamella.*

In the region of Trentino–Alto Adige, just south of the Austrian Alps, it's not surprising to find sauerkraut, smoked pork, and *knoedel* instead of *gnocchi* (potato dumplings). But that doesn't prevent our northernmost Italians from making a lasagne of *sugo* made of pork and tomatoes with slices of the meat layered with pasta, mozzarella, and parmigiano. It's called the *lasagne ei maiale* (pork) and is one of the sweetest of the meat lasagnes.

Luganega sausage is the trademark of Friuli-Venezia-Giulia in the northeastern corner of Italy and provides another sweet and zesty filling.

And from the home of Romeo and Juliet in Verona, in the Veneto, comes an ambrosial lasagne of prosciutto, meat ragù, balsamella, mozzarella, and parmigiano that should have stopped even these two ardent lovers—time out for a snack at least.

One of the oldest recipes for lasagne from this region, according to that wonderfully erudite Italophile, Waverley Root, is *lasagne da fornel,* which is a favorite first course on Christmas Eve. The layers of pasta are buttered, covered with crushed walnuts, poppy seeds, raisins, grated apple, bits of fig, and sugar—a sweet combination that predates the tomato in Italy (sixteenth century) and harks back to early Renaissance usage of honey, cinnamon, clove, nutmeg, and sugar in a variety of dishes.

Now down to Emilia Romagna, where the richest and most famous lasagne in the world dominates, named *lasagne verdi,* or *pasticcio di lasagne verdi alla bolognese.* The complete recipe for this dish will be given in detail at the end of this section. But it is important to note that as rich as the basic three sauce, two cheese, and enriched spinach noodle lasagne is, the Bolognese cooks found ways of making it even richer by the addition of truffles and alternate layers of spinach and yellow egg noodles with ricotta; and by truffling and using their finest white wines in the balsamella.

Gilding the lily? Not a bit! When done correctly, it is the quintessential pasta-cream-meat-cheese concoction, giving no quarter to the dozen or so other magnificent creations that abound in Italy. Its world fame is well-deserved and a tribute to *Bologna la grassa*—Bologna the fat.

But not all is so rich in the land of Emilia Romagna. A rather simple and different treatment is to be found in the use of wild mushrooms indigenous to the area called Spugnole. The lasagne is called *La spugnole,* and provides a departure from the usual procedures. It is made of 6 or 7 layers of pasta with balsamella and, after baking, it is cut into squares and topped with a sauce made of the wild mushrooms and tomatoes.

The contrast in cooking styles between Emilia Romagna and Tuscany is remarkable. The land of the fat gives way to one of the most austere cuisines in Italy. The food in Tuscany is plain and simple and famous for its charcoal-broiled steak *alla fiorentina.* A bit of oil, a bit of lemon, and a Chianina steak charbroiled rare; simplicity at its best, with a tossed salad, Tuscan bread, and a *fiasco di vino Chianti Classico,* for which this area is justly famous.

Nevertheless, the Tuscans are not without their own special lasagne, and from the province of Arezzo comes to us a most unusual duck lasagne, *lasagne all'anatra all'aretina.* In this unusual treatment, the duck is used only to make the sauce with a little pancetta (bacon), broth, and tomatoes. This sauce is used as the filling between squares of egg pasta and the topping is a thick coating of balsamella with grated parmigiano. A simple enough dish if you don't get extravagant and throw the duck away.

Umbria is one of four regions in Italy without a sea coast. It's completely landlocked but favored by one of the largest lakes in Italy, Lake Trasimeno, and truffles.

This is the home of black Italian truffles, those culinary jewels that defy description—mysterious tuberous growths that grow under certain trees at random and up till now could only be found by trained pigs or dogs and defied cultivation. When you have it this good, why not just a little balsamella on lasagne squares tossed with butter, nutmeg, Parmigiano and shaved truffles?

Why not indeed!

Right next door to Umbria, with a similar "peasant style" cuisine, and a smashing coastline, is the region of Marche. *Brodetto* (fish stew or soup) and polenta are the favorites here and perhaps their *Vincisgrassi* is the only lasagne made of polenta—a ragù of beef, ham, sweetbreads, white wine, tomatoes, and nutmeg is layered on sheets of semolina lasagne with a bit of mozzarella and Parmigiano and baked with a butter topping.

Rome seems to be the melting-pot that has absorbed all the regional permutations, and yet survived with a cuisine of its own. Talk about elegant simplicity—how about *lasagnette di mascarpone*? *Lasagnette* are simply thin lasagne strips, which are then layered with egg yolks and mascarpone, that creamy, rich cheese with its exquisitely delicate flavor. There is also *lasagnette agli spinaci,* with chopped, creamed spinach on top of the noodles and baked briefly (10 to 15 minutes) in the oven.

Abruzzi in southern Italy is mainly a farming community and has, as many rural communities do, retained a certain old-fashioned, restrained approach to cookery. Basically food to feed its people so they can go back to work with vigor. It has, therefore, had little effect on the interregional scene in Italy, except for Amatriciana, far less on the international one. All this notwithstanding, *lasagne all'abruzzese* is a very interesting dish. Eggs and parmigiano are added to a veal *sugo* made with white wine and tomatoes. The pieces of veal are then layered with hard-cooked eggs, mozzarella, and parmigiano in between yellow egg pasta.

Finally, Calabria has the misfortune to suffer the scorn of the north because it's at the "toe of the boot," and the insults of Sicily because it's on the mainland. Fortunately, all this prejudice hasn't affected their ability to make lasagne. *Lasagne imbottita alla calabrese* has been a favorite of

mine for many years since, as a young man, my first wife's mother and grandmother stood over my second helpings, smiling and urging in Italian: *"Mangia! Che bravo ragazzo! Un altro . . . mangia!"* (Eat! Good boy! Have another . . . eat!)

It consists of tiny meat balls *(polpettine)* made from ground pork, eggs, marjoram, and pecorino and *caciocavallo* cheeses and fried in hot oil, and a sugo of carrots, celery, onions, and pieces of pork and beef. The lasagne strips are coated with the sauce and layered with slices of beef and pork, as well as the meat balls, hard-cooked eggs, mozzarella, and pecorino.

Talk about alchemy! It was baked in a hot oven (450°F) for about 30 minutes and then a very low oven (245°F) for another 45 minutes to an hour. The resultant dish is a masterpiece of brown and bubbly flavors.

In addition to the foregoing descriptions we will also now provide you with some detailed recipes. As you learn to make one or two of these you will find the previously mentioned descriptions easy to convert into acceptable dishes. *Buon appetito!*

Pasticcio di Lasagne Verdi Alla Bolognese

SPINACH LASAGNA WITH BOLOGNESE SAUCE

This is one of the richest and most interesting specialities of Bologna, the so-called land of butter and cream. The combination of spinach noodles, a Bolognese sauce, and a truffled mornay sauce in layers is an enrichment that would have brought cries from the cardinal who exhorted his parishioners, "It is not enough to boil your pasta and drench it with butter. No. You have to add cream and mushrooms and then top it off with a fistful of your best parmigiano. For shame."

Poor fellow. Must have had his hands full. So do we, for this recipe requires a bit of work with its three sauces and the spinach noodles. So, let's get cooking.

3 cups Sugo di Carne (see pages 106–7)
1 recipe Egg Pasta with Spinach (see page 64)
4 pounds Ragù Bolognese (see pages 108–9)
4 cups Mornaia (see page 116)
1 pound parmigiano, freshly grated
Freshly grated nutmeg to taste
Salt and freshly ground black pepper to taste
2 pounds mozzarella, sliced ⅛ inch thick

1. Coat the bottom of a 12- by 16- by 2½-inch baking pan with some *sugo,* then line with a layer of spinach noodles.
2. Spread some bolognese sauce evenly over the noodles. Top this loosely with *mornaia* and sprinkle with parmigiano and a light dash of nutmeg and pepper.
3. Cover this layer roughly with mozzarella and then another layer of spinach noodles.
4. Repeat this entire procedure twice more, omitting the nutmeg and pepper in the middle layer.
5. After topping with the last spinach noodles, coat the top of the lasagne with another application of *sugo* (reserve some to top each serving).
6. Bake the *lasagne* in a 350°F oven for 20 to 30 minutes and then set aside to rest for 5 minutes before cutting and serving. Cut into squares of desired size and place on warm plates, topping with hot *sugo* and grated parmigiano.

YIELD: *14 to 16 servings*

Lasagne ai Funghi

MUSHROOM LASAGNA

This is a very rich filling. Omit the ricotta and hard-cooked eggs to make it simpler. Mushrooms alone, or mushrooms and mozzarella, will make a different but completely satisfying dish. You could also omit the *sugo di funghi* and just use *balsamella.*

2 pounds mushrooms, thickly sliced
4 tablespoons (½ stick) unsalted butter
4 cups Sugo di Funghi (see pages 107–8)
1 recipe Egg Pasta for Stuffed Pasta (see pages 66–67), cut into lasagne noodles
2 cups Balsamella (see page 116)
1 pound Ricotta Filling (see page 70)
2 to 3 cups freshly grated parmigiano
1 pound whole milk mozzarella, sliced ⅛ inch thick
Freshly grated nutmeg to taste
Freshly grated black pepper to taste
3 hard-cooked eggs, finely diced

1. Heat the butter in a skillet and lightly sauté the mushrooms over medium heat for about 5 minutes. Set aside.
2. Coat the bottom of a 12- by 7½- by 2-inch baking pan with *sugo di funghi.* Line with a layer of egg noodles.
3. Spread *balsamella* over the noodles. Add one third of the ricotta filling, spreading it over the sauce. Sprinkle with a third of the parmigiano and lay on slices of mozzarella. Dust with nutmeg

and pepper and then evenly distribute a third of the mushrooms and 1 chopped egg over the top. Lace the layers with a few tablespoons of *sugo*.

4. Repeat the layering procedure twice more, omitting the pepper and nutmeg in the middle layer. Coat the top, layer liberally with *sugo* and sprinkle parmigiano on top.

5. Bake in a 425°F oven for 20 to 30 minutes and remove and let the *lasagne* sit for 2 to 3 hours, or preferably overnight, refrigerated. To serve, heat in a 350°F oven for 45 minutes and set aside to rest for 5 to 10 minutes before cutting into it. Place each portion on a white or creamy white warmed plate. Add hot *sugo* and garnish with parmigiano.

YIELD: *14 to 16 servings*

MUSHROOMS FOR LAYERING:

2 tablespoons unsalted butter
1 tablespoon olive oil
2 pounds mushrooms, including stems, sliced about 1/8 inch thick
1 shallot or small white onion, finely diced
1/8 teaspoon each dried thyme, basil, and chervil
2 tablespoons chopped fresh parsley
    Salt, pepper, and cayenne to taste
1 slice lemon

1. Put butter and oil in a sauté pan on a brisk flame. When bubbling, add the mushrooms and stir, until they take on a good color. Add the shallots and cook for another minute or so.

2. Add the thyme, basil, chervil, and parsley and toss. Season with salt, pepper, and cayenne, and stir gently. Squeeze the lemon slice over the mixture, stir, toss and cook for another minute or so. Remove from heat and reserve.

YIELD: *14 to 16 servings*

Perciatelli ai Quattro Formaggi

BAKED PASTA WITH FOUR CHEESES

1½ cups diced bread cubes, for croutons
1/3 pound (1½ sticks) unsalted butter
1 pound **perciatelli** or other long-stranded pasta
1 cup shredded mozzarella
1 cup diced Gruyère
1 cup roughly chopped gorgonzola
2 cups freshly grated parmigiano
½ teaspoon freshly grated nutmeg
    Salt and pepper to taste

1. To make croutons, sauté the bread cubes in a skillet over medium heat in 2 tablespoons of butter till golden brown. Crush half a cup and reserve this for topping. Melt ½ stick of butter and keep warm.

2. Cook the *perciatelli* very al dente, drain, and immediately toss in a warm bowl with the melted butter. Add the mozzarella, Gruyère, gorgonzola, and 1 cup of parmigiano. Add the croutons and nutmeg, salt, and pepper and toss again.

3. Liberally butter 4 individual ceramic casseroles (or 1 large, if you prefer) and place the *perciatelli* mixture in each. Liberally dot the tops of each with butter and cover with the crushed croutons and remaining parmigiano.

4. Bake, uncovered, in a 375°F oven for approximately 20 minutes. Remove and finish under a hot broiler, browning them as much as you'd like.

YIELD: *4 servings*

Rigatoni al Forno
con Salsa Aurora

BAKED RIGATONI WITH CREAM AND TOMATO SAUCE

This is a different, but equally brown-bubbly delight. The sauce is a (50–50) combination of *balsamella* (or *mornaia*) and *salsa di pomodoro*. Its creamy, pink consistency is perfect for baking all forms of pasta.

> 1 **pound rigatoni or rigati (with lines preferred)**
>
> 1 to 1½ **pounds mozzarella, half shredded and half sliced**
>
> 2 **cups freshly grated parmigiano**
>
> 2 **tablespoons unsalted butter**
>
> 2 **cups Balsamella or Mornaia (see page 116)**
>
> 2 **cups Salsa di Pomodoro (see page 103)**
>
> **Salt and pepper to taste**

1. Cook the pasta al dente and drain. While steaming hot, toss it in a warm bowl with half the shredded mozzarella, 1 cup of parmigiano, and the butter. Mix the sauces together, add half to the pasta, and toss again.

2. Line four individual casseroles with enough sauce to coat the bottoms. Place some *rigatoni* mixture in each and top with the remaining sauce. Lay mozzarella slices over the tops and sprinkle with the remaining parmigiano.

3. Bake, uncovered, in a 375°F oven for approximately 20 minutes. Remove and finish under a hot broiler, browning them as much as you'd like.

YIELD: *4 servings*

LE SALSE
ITALIANE

Italian Sauces

ITALIAN SAUCES

AS I have already pointed out, I was lucky enough to grow up in an Italian American household where Sunday wouldn't be Sunday if there wasn't a big black cast-iron pot of sauce simmering on the back of the stove.

The ladies (mother, grandmother, and sometimes an aunt or two) were first to rise, and we'd awaken to the irresistible smell of garlic and meat searing together before being flooded with dark, rich, juicy Italian plum tomatoes.

What a way to wake up! The salivary glands were working before my feet even hit the floor. As a matter of fact, these wonderful aromas were not always confined to Sunday mornings. Preceding holidays, birthdays, or when my mother was preparing for a special party—which was never less than two or three times a month—I'd go to bed with these same ambrosial smells and fall into a sleep full of gastronomic dreams. To this day I can't go to sleep without thinking of what I've eaten, what I'm going to eat, or, more interesting, what I can create in the coming week in the way of menus and new dishes, or some subtle refinement of a dish that I've made a thousand times before.

The purpose of this little treatise on sauces is to share with you what I've learned as a professional and thereby save you the time and trouble of experimentation, research, and rejection that is essential to developing professional techniques of sauce making.

To get back to that big cast-iron black pot with sauce simmering on the back of the stove . . . what would a plate of pasta be without a sauce? If only with a little butter and cheese, pasta has got to be sauced! And how about roasted meats, game, or poultry? Fresh fish can be enhanced delightfully by an aromatic white wine sauce, or cooked to perfection by poaching it in a court bouillon or fish stock, which are, after all, the foundations of fish sauces.

Whether dealt with on a professional level, or confined to *cucina casalinga* or *casareccio* (home cooking), stocks and sauces are one of the most important aspects of any cuisine; and certainly of *la vera cucina italiana*—the true cooking of Italy.

In spite of its very basic nature, however, the entire subject seems to be misunderstood on both levels of cooking, professional and home cooking. How many times have we heard from close friends, relatives, and various acquaintances, "My grandmother makes the best tomato sauce in the world, bar none—not even my mother's sauce can touch it."

We've often wondered what secret alchemistic tricks this wizard of the kitchen must possess to get her progeny to wax that enthusiastically . . . only to be totally disappointed by a barely edible, over-reduced bit of tomato paste that was thinned out with water, then reduced again, and laced with the unmistakable taste of garlic powder and dried oregano, when we finally accepted an invitation to dinner.

Since living in Italy, I have eaten hundreds of pasta dishes with an equal number of sauces from many grandmothers, mothers, sisters, aunts, cousins, cooks, chefs, and cooking teachers; and while there have been some enthusiastic comments and strong recommendations, nonetheless we've found the Italian attitude toward sauces more reasonable than the American "grandma" stories. Perhaps it's because *everybody* here makes sauce (at least two or three kinds) and they seem to take a certain standard of quality for granted. Whatever the reason, there seems to be an intelligent restraint in the use of adjectives. At most you might hear *eccezionale* (exceptional), and generally you will find an Italian who invites you to his mother's home for dinner (a serious sign of acceptance since the Italians do not generally extend themselves in this way) restricting his comments to a banal *"Si mangia bene, la salsa è buona"* (You can eat well, the sauce is good).

On a professional level, it's taken for granted in every restaurant in Italy—and there are literally thousands—that the chef makes the best *ragù*, *sugo*, or *salsa di pomodoro* in the world. No need to talk about it. It's just a fact.

This conceit is probably at the root of the sincere disdain most French chefs have for their Italian colleagues as professionals, and more particularly, for Italian sauces. The unknowledgeable French chef (of which, thank God, there are not too many, the younger breed being less chauvinistic and more sophisticated) will maintain that the majority of Italian sauces are not sauces at all since they are by and large one-step procedures that are not based on "classic" stocks and reductions.

The truth of the matter is that sauce, as defined by Webster, is, "A fluid, semi-fluid, or sometimes semi-solid accompaniment of solid food." Or, as stated in *Larousse Gastronomique,* the bible of French cuisine, "any liquid seasoning for food." This is hardly French or difficult, and it is immediately apparent that the "gravy" in mom's "grits and gravy" would certainly qualify.

Sauces are at the heart of all cuisines and are the one area, aside from native ingredients, that best distinguishes one cuisine from another. Italy is no exception. Sauces are an essential aspect of Italian cooking, and if one thinks they have been without consideration here, it's worth repeating the description by Luigi Carnacina, dean of Italian chefs and author of *Great Italian Cooking,* among other works.

"A sauce is to a dish as a piano accompaniment is to a singer; it isn't the same as the voice part, but it enriches the main theme, underlines its beauty and fills in the rest with a flavor of its own . . ."

Seems to us this is neither reticent nor conceited and lays a proper foundation for pursuing further one of the most essential aspects of all cuisines.

As an Italian chef, I am delighted to see the surge of popularity in America of *alta cucina italiana.* It seems every town has its *pastificio* (fresh made pasta store) and books on general, *casalinga,* regional, or *alta cucina* Italian cooking line the shelves of bookstores. However, aside from recipes given for particular sauces as part of an overall work, it appears to us that there is a gap or lack, if you will, of a specific instructional treatise that provides a coherent presentation of Italian sauces such as Louis Diat, and Escoffier before him, did for French sauces.

The intention of this chapter, therefore, will be to lay the foundation for such a work. In the meantime, my goal is quite modest . . . to provide you with a clear understanding of Italian sauce making and eliminate some of the misconceptions that proliferate. In other words, I'd like to help you to make Italian sauces with an awareness of the "whys," "hows," and "wherefores." Mastering the basics is not hard if you understand the principles involved. Most Italian sauces are easy, direct, and expandable. With understanding and a little practice you will suddenly see hundreds of ways to sauce your pasta, as well as countless other foods, and feel confident that what you're presenting is delicious and Italian.

STOCKS AND BROTHS

Both stocks and broths are enriched liquids; the distinction between them being that a broth is the by-product of cooking a main dish, such as boiled beef, whereas a stock is the end product in itself and the result of skimming and reducing. Since the most important aspect of making a good sauce lies in the initial liquid, broth, or stock used, perhaps it would be advantageous for us to describe what goes into one before providing you with the recipes.

INGREDIENTS

There is no getting around using beef in a beef stock or veal in a veal stock. But even when one is willing to pay for it, the modern product doesn't make it. I often hear home cooks complain that they can't get any flavor into a chicken soup. "It just doesn't taste like it used to when I was a kid . . ."

The reason is that the most basic principle of making broth is to use heavy old animals with tough solid muscle since they have much higher flavor content. Of course they're not readily available today and younger animals just don't provide the same flavor.

Well, it's not nostalgia—it's the chicken.

So the problem is not whether to use meat in the stock, but how to boost the flavor of modern meat. This is where prepared bases come in. They are so commonly used as a substitute for a stock with such terrible results, that their tremendous usefulness as a *seasoning* for organic stock is overlooked.

We're talking minute quantities here; add too much, or too late in the cooking, and that unmistakable taste comes through. But, added judiciously at the beginning of the cooking, and used in conjunction with other seasonings, they make the difference between bone water and rich, full-flavored stock.

The choice of base, both by type and brand, is one of the keys to avoiding any artificial tastes. I find a combination of natural, fat-suspended extract with liquid, natural consommé concentrate to be the most effective. Avoid the powders; they are the furthest removed from their organic source, and taste like it. Likewise, many canned broths and bouillon cubes are derived from powdered bases. So, read the ingredients label when buying. Organically derived bouillon cubes are on a middle ground, as long as the main ingredient is fat, rather than MSG (monosodium glutamate). For brands, I like Minor's, and especially Liebig for meat extracts, and Campbell's and Swanson's for liquid broth or consommé. Therein lies an interesting comparison. Just open the two, and look, smell and taste.

The choice of bones is best understood by their functions of adding gelatin and flavor to the stock. Gelatin is the product of water-soluble proteins being extracted, giving the stock "body," the feeling in the mouth of something silkier, richer, and denser than just broth. It is what makes stocks congeal when chilled and is the base for aspics.

The proteins that form it as they are dissolved are concentrated mostly in the connective tissues of muscle and bone, especially cartilage. All the joints, and especially feet, shanks, and vertebrae, are rich sources. Other bones to "stock" up on and freeze as you come across them are the neck, breast (of veal, particularly), short ribs, knuckle bones, and oxtail.

Younger animals yield more gelatin quicker because less of their cartilaginous tissue has formed into hard bone.

As I mentioned, for meat cuts, the general rule is the tougher, the better. The more use a muscle gets, the tastier it is. The shoulder, rump, and particularly the shank and neck are rich in both flavor and cartilage and are all well suited to make stock with. Look for any cut that combines a good gelatin source with a good meat source and comes ready-cut, such as oxtail. Buy when available and freeze until you've accumulated enough to make a good, strong stock.

Also, take advantage of the broth if you're making boiled chicken or beef. By simply adding a few good gelatin bones and meat scraps, you can increase the yield so it includes the soup for supper and stock besides.

Avoid pork and lamb as main ingredients for stock as they give off a very unique taste that would be incompatible with other ingredients . . . not to say, though, you can't make a lamb broth.

Use only fresh, unclouded, cold water. This will readily expel the loose fats and proteins to the surface, aiding in the process of skimming.

The other important ingredients are the aromatics and seasonings. Common herbs such as bay, thyme, and parsley augment the ubiquitous carrot, celery, and onion. Other vegetables include leeks, tomatoes, and an occasional turnip or parsnip. Cut them large or small depending on the cooking time of the stock. Try to time it to fully extract the vegetables before they are mushy and cloud the stock. Salt is a no-no; do not even use in minute quantities, because when reduced, the stock may become too intense. It's easier and safer to add salt later.

Brodo

BROTH

2 *pounds beef bones*

2 *pounds veal bones*

1 *pound beef scraps*

1 *pound veal scraps*

1 *pound turkey wings or other turkey parts*

2 *pounds chicken pieces (feet, backs, necks, head)*

2 *medium-large yellow onions*

2 *large ribs celery with tops*

1 *large carrot*

4 or 5 *parsley stems with leaves*

1 *fresh tomato*

1 *small leek*

2 *bay leaves*

1 *tablespoon whole black peppercorns*

Water

1. Carefully wash the veal and beef bones (any blood left on them will cloud the broth) and trim the meat and poultry pieces of fat.

2. Place all the ingredients in a large stock pot and fill the pot with cold water till it comes to about 4 inches above the ingredients.

3. Place over medium heat and cook till the scum begins to rise; skim the impurities continuously until they cease to appear. Then turn the heat down to low and let the broth simmer for 1 to 1½ hours.

4. Strain the broth, let it cool to room temperature, then refrigerate. Before reheating it, skim off the congealed fat.

YIELD: *4 quarts*

Fondo Bruno

BROWN STOCK

3 *ribs celery with leaves*

2 *large carrots, unpeeled and split lengthwise*

2 *large white or yellow onions with skin, split in half*

2 *large leeks, split in half and cleaned*

2 *whole heads garlic, split in half*

3 *pounds beef shank, neck, or tail, split into 2- to 4-inch pieces*

3 *pounds veal joint bones, split into 2- to 4-inch pieces*

2 *pounds fowl backs and wings, split into 2- to 4-inch pieces*

½ *cup vegetable oil*

1 *tablespoon natural beef extract or base*

8 to 10 *sprigs fresh parsley*

2 *bay leaves, cracked in half*

1 *tablespoon dried thyme*

12 *whole black peppercorns*

¾ *cup dry red wine*

One *10- or 12-ounce can concentrated beef broth or consommé*

Water to cover by 2 inches

ROASTING THE MEATS

1. Preheat the oven to 450°F. Arrange the celery, carrots, onions, leeks, and garlic in a roasting pan big enough to hold all the meat and poultry in no more than two layers. Make sure the onions and garlic are face down against the bottom so they brown well.

2. Rub the bones with the oil and extract, then place the meats on this bed, with the fattiest portions most exposed, on top. Scatter the seasonings throughout, tucking them in to prevent scorching, then pour the wine and broth evenly over the top.

3. Place the pan on the floor of the oven; after about 15 minutes, or when you hear the pan sizzling, check the meats for progress in browning, repositioning them if necessary,

After 30 minutes, or when the top layer of meats is well crusted, reposition the ingredients to expose the remaining meaty parts. Check the bottom of the pan for excessive burning, and to see that the onions are browning well. If the bottom is too dry, add a little wine or water, but not too much; there should be very little liquid left by the end of cooking.

4. Remove the pan from the oven when most of the meats are well browned, the vegetables are soft, the onions brown, and a good, dark juice remains in the bottom. Then transfer the meats, bones, and vegetables to a large stock pot, leaving the juices in the pan.

5. Set the roasting pan over medium-high heat and bring the juices to a boil. Reduce the liquid while stirring to dissolve the browned crust stuck to the pan and concentrate the whole. Add a few tablespoons of wine or water if the pan is too dry. When the bottom deposits are dissolved, add this deglaze to the stockpot. Fill the pot with cold water till it comes to about 2 inches above the contents.

SKIM THE STOCK

1. Set the stockpot over a brisk flame, and set a crock or pot with a ladle and a large spoon to its side for skimming. As the stock comes to a simmer, adjust the heat to prevent boiling. Do not stir the pot's contents. Allow 5 to 10 minutes from the time it simmers for the frothy impurities to coagulate on the stock's surface.

2. Remove the scum with the ladle, pouring it

into the crock. Try to avoid carrying off too much water with the scum. Adjust the heat, lowering it to prevent the rapid boil that will occur as the scum is removed and the surface exposed to the air.

Once you have cleaned the surface, reach into the bottom of the pot with the long spoon and reposition the ingredients to aid in releasing more impurities. Do this gently, and by no means stir the stock or it may cloud up.

3. Allow another layer of scum to accumulate on the stock, about 10 minutes, and remove it as before. Repeat this cycle of skimming, adjusting the heat and meats, waiting, and skimming until the impurities that accumulate become minimal, 3 to 4 times, about 40 minutes total.

COOKING THE STOCK

1. Once the stock is cleared, raise the heat to a low boil and adjust the pot to one side of the burner so only half of the liquid boils. This will concentrate the remaining impurities to the opposite side, where they can be easily skimmed off.

2. Continue cooking at this temperature, skimming occasionally as needed, for a further 3 to 3½ hours, or until the desired character is obtained.

STRAINING, COOLING, AND STORING

1. Remove the pot from the stove. Set a large wire strainer or colander over a large bowl or pot that will hold all the stock. Ladle off as much stock as possible from the pot, pouring it through the strainer. Tilt the pot as needed.

2. Remove the solids from the pot with a large spoon into a separate bowl and set aside to cool before discarding them. Pour the remaining stock through the strainer. Do not press down on any semisolids left in the strainer to extract their juice. Instead, shake the strainer gently and allow it to rest over the bowl to drain.

3. Set the stock to cool surrounded by cold water or near a cool, drafty window. Do not refrigerate prior to cooling.

4. Finally, skim off the fat that rises to the surface, and strain through moistened cheesecloth into smaller containers for storage in the refrigerator or freezer.

YIELD: *4 quarts*

Fondo Bianco

WHITE STOCK

White stock is the base for a whole range of sauces that do not want the depth of flavor and color of beef stock nor the particular poultry flavor of chicken stock. Seen mostly in braises, stews, and fricassées.

4 ounces veal fat

3 pounds veal joint bones, split into 2- to 4-inch pieces

3 pounds veal breast or neck or meaty shank, etc., in 2- to 4-inch pieces

2 pounds fowl backs and wings in 2- to 4-inch pieces

1 cup white wine

1 tablespoon natural chicken extract or base

One 10- or 12-ounce can or ¾ cup fresh, concentrated chicken broth

About 5 quarts cold water

2 medium-size carrots, unpeeled

3 ribs celery with leaves

2 medium-size leeks, split and washed
2 whole cloves
2 large white onions with skin, split in half
2 whole heads garlic, split in half
6 to 8 sprigs fresh parsley
2 bay leaves, cracked in half
2 teaspoons dried thyme
12 whole black peppercorns

DEGLAZING THE MEATS

1. Place the veal fat in a heavy-bottomed 12- to 16-quart stockpot over medium heat; allow the fat to partially melt without browning.
2. Add the meats and turn them in the hot fat for 2 to 3 minutes to warm them. Do not brown.
3. Pour in the wine, then dissolve the extract in the chicken broth and add to the meats. Turn the meats as the liquid evaporates to glaze them evenly. Before the liquid evaporates completely, add all the water.

SKIMMING THE STOCK

Follow the exact same procedure for skimming outlined on pages 85–86 for *fondo bruno*.

COOKING THE STOCK

1. Once the stock has cleared, add all the remaining ingredients. Place the carrots, celery, and leeks vertically between the meats as best you can. Insert a clove into the root end of each of two of the onion halves, and place them face down in the stock.
2. Raise the heat to a low boil and adjust the pot to one side of the flame so only half of the surface is active. This will concentrate the modest scum from the vegetables and any remaining impurities from the meats to the opposite side of the surface, where they can be skimmed off easily.
3. Continue cooking at this temperature, skim-

ming occasionally as needed, for a further 2 to 2½ hours, or until the desired character is obtained.

STRAINING, COOLING, AND STORING

Follow the exact same procedure as outlined on pages 85–86 for *fondo bruno*.

YIELD: *About 4 quarts*

Brodo di Verdure

VEGETABLE STOCK

Good vegetable stock can make all the difference in making vegetable risottos or soups and is worth the effort. It's quite simple to make and any combination of vegetables on hand will do. Always try to add the aromatic *battuto* of carrot, celery, onion, leek, and parsley, if possible, and bay leaves, a clove-stuck onion, and peppercorns, to help make a richer broth. If you want a single accent, by all means just use asparagus to make an asparagus broth or zucchini to make a zucchini broth, but bear in mind that the broths might be even richer if they were made with a vegetable stock instead of water. Straining and reducing by a third will give you a stronger and clearer product.

2 tablespoons extra virgin olive oil

1 large carrot, roughly cut

1 large rib celery, roughly cut

1 large onion, roughly cut

1 clove garlic, cut in half

1 large leek, roughly cut

1 medium-size white onion,
stuck with 2 whole cloves

1 zucchini, roughly chopped

2 medium-size ripe tomatoes, roughly
cut

2 to 3 cups roughly chopped mixed
vegetables

6 sprigs fresh parsley

2 tablespoons finely chopped
fresh parsley

1/8 teaspoon dried thyme

1/8 teaspoon dried basil

1/8 teaspoon dried chervil

2 bay leaves

Salt and freshly ground black
pepper to taste

1 1/2 quarts water

1. Heat the oil in a deep saucepan over medium-high heat and sweat the carrot, celery, chopped onion, and garlic a few minutes, not letting the onion brown. Add the leek, whole onion, zucchini, tomatoes, parsley sprigs, mixed vegetables, and chopped parsley and sauté a few minutes longer. Season with the herbs, salt, and pepper.
2. Add the water and bring to a boil, skimming all the while. When there is no more foam, turn the heat down and simmer over low heat for 20 to 30 minutes.
3. Remove from the heat and strain the stock through cheesecloth set in a china cap. Return to the stove and reduce by a third over high heat.

Will keep in the refrigerator for up to a week. Reboiling will not preserve it. Stock can be frozen.

YIELD: 1 quart

Consommé

Brown stock is equally as important to the making of soup, or consommé, as it is to sauces.

The methods for thus converting a stock into consommé are rather straightforward. However, particular attention should be given to the clarification, not just for the clear look of it, but also because the flavor of properly clarified soup or consommé is cleaner and richer.

8 ounces finely ground beef

1 cup combined and finely diced carrot,
celery, and onion

1 medium-size fresh tomato, split in half
Whites and crushed shells from 2 large
eggs

5 cups strong Fondo Bruno, cold or room
temperature (see page 85)

1. Make sure all ingredients are cool. Combine all ingredients, except stock, in the bottom of a heavy pot. Add stock in a stream, stirring thoroughly.
2. Set the pot over medium heat and bring to the simmer while stirring almost continuously, to avoid scorching the egg whites. The solids will rise to the surface and coagulate there with the egg whites, forming a "raft." As this happens, stir

less frequently to avoid impeding this process. Once the raft is formed, turn the heat down to low and allow the stock to simmer undisturbed for about 40 minutes. Do not stir.

3. Take the pot off the heat and remove about a third of the raft with a skimmer or spoon and discard. Gently ladle out the clear consommé, passing it through a double thickness of cheesecloth. Cool and store.

YIELD: *1 quart*

Brodo di Pollo

CHICKEN OR POULTRY STOCK

This recipe was developed using only the backs, necks, and gizzards for those who would like to save the breasts, legs, and thighs for other uses. If you don't have this extra meal in mind, then one large stewing hen instead of two will do the job. In either case, to obtain maximum gelatin from these birds, follow the procedures for dismembering, since the more open cuts you make into the bone, the more gelatin will be released. In fact, it is good procedure to hack into all the bones indiscriminately, to help this process as much as possible, particularly all the knuckle joints. Extra gizzards, as called for here, are wonderful flavor boosters. As in all stock making, careful scumming and skimming go a long way to giving you a better finished product.

1 *lemon, cut in half*

Two *5-pound stewing hens or large chickens*

2 *pounds chicken gizzards and hearts (in addition to those from the stewing hens)*

2 *pounds chicken backs and necks*

1 *pound turkey meat*

1 *tablespoon natural chicken extract or base*

One *10- or 12-ounce can or ¾ cup fresh concentrated chicken broth*

About 5 quarts fresh cold water

2 *carrots, unpeeled and thinly sliced*

2 *ribs celery with leaves, coarsely chopped*

1 *leek, split, cleaned, and coarsely chopped*

2 *whole cloves*

2 *white onions with skin, split in half*

6 to 8 *sprigs fresh parsley*

2 *bay leaves, cracked in half*

2 *teaspoons dried thyme or marjoram*

6 to 8 *whole black peppercorns*

PREPARING THE POULTRY

1. Rub the work surface with one of the lemon halves. Remove the sacks from inside the birds and empty. Remove the neck fat and reserve. Reserve the liver for another use. Combine the remaining contents with the bought gizzards. Rub the birds all over with the lemon halves.

2. Cut the birds open down the back, running the knife from the wing end, along one side of the back bone, through the thigh joints. Lay the birds skin side down and flatten them out. With a heavy knife, cut the birds in half, angling carefully between the breasts.

Remove the backs, then remove the wings at their joints. Clip off the last segment, or tip, and reserve with the backs and gizzards. Set aside the wings for another use.

Remove the breasts from their bones, and reserve with the wings for another use. Also set aside the thighs and legs from one bird. Separate the remaining legs and thighs and set aside with the backs and gizzards.

3. With a cleaver or heavy, sharp knife, split open the necks vertically to expose the gelatinous vertebrae. Discard half the fatty skin. Repeat with the backs, thighs, legs, and wing tips, always splitting any joints to expose gelatins.

DEGLAZING

Follow the exact same procedure as outlined on page 87 for *fondo bianco,* except substituting the reserved neck fat for the veal fat and omitting the white wine.

SKIMMING

Follow the same procedure as outlined on pages 85–86 for *fondo bruno.*

COOKING

Follow the same procedure as outlined on page 87 for *fondo bianco,* only reducing the final cooking time to 1 to 1½ hours.

STRAINING, COOLING, AND STORING

Follow the exact same procedure as outlined on page 86 for *fondo bruno.*

NOTE: You can also follow the simple *brodo* method for making stock on page 84.

YIELD: *4 quarts*

Brodo di Pesce

FISH STOCK

Making fish stock is the same as making brown, white, or poultry stock, except that the cooking time is less and the aromatics are lighter. The addition of lemon and juniper berry is interesting and provides another dimension to the seasoning of stocks. You will also encounter these seasonings in making game stocks. In both cases, the seasoning is used to tone down some of the higher flavors that are found in fish and game.

> 1 **tablespoon unsalted butter or vegetable oil**
> 2 **teaspoons finely chopped carrot**
> 2 **teaspoons finely chopped celery**
> 1 **tablespoon finely chopped onion**
> 2 **pounds fish heads, bones, and trimmings, split and washed**
> 1 **cup dry white wine**
> 1 **lemon, cut up and juice reserved**
> 2 **sprigs fresh parsley**
> 1 **bay leaf, cracked in half**
> 1 **teaspoon juniper berries (about 4 berries)**
> 3 to 4 **whole white peppercorns**
> **Pinch of salt**
> 1 **quart cold fresh water**

DEGLAZING

1. Melt the butter in a 4- to 6-quart narrow pot over medium heat, add the chopped carrots, celery, and onion, and sauté for 1 minute or so.
2. Add the fish head, bones, and trimmings and sauté briefly to set their flesh and warm them.

3. Add the wine and shake the pot to moisten the ingredients. Immediately add the remaining ingredients.

SKIMMING

Follow the exact same procedure as outlined on pages 85–86 for *fondo bruno.* Take note, however, that the fish stock will require only 15 minutes or so of skimming, as compared to 40 minutes for the brown stock.

COOKING

Follow the exact same procedure as outlined on page 86 for *fondo bruno,* only reducing the final cooking time to 30 to 40 minutes.

STRAINING, COOLING, AND STORING

Follow the same procedures as outlined on page 87 for *fondo bruno.*

NOTE: As with chicken stock, you can also follow the simpler *brodo* method of making stock on page 84.

YIELD: *1 quart*

6 to 8 *parsley stems with leaves*
1 *bay leaf, cracked in half*
2 *sprigs fresh thyme*
2 *cups cold water*
1½ *cups dry white wine*
½ *large lemon*
4 to 6 *whole black peppercorns*

1. Melt the butter in a medium-size saucepan over medium-low heat. Add the vegetables, parsley stems, bay leaf, and thyme, and let cook several minutes with the top on, making sure not to let them brown.
2. Raise heat to medium, cover with two cups of cold water, stir, and bring to a simmer, skimming for 5 to 10 minutes.
3. Add the remaining ingredients and simmer gently over low heat for another 20 minutes, Strain and cool before storing, covered, in the refrigerator.

YIELD: *3 cups*

SOUPS

Court Bouillon (for Poaching Fish)

2 *tablespoons unsalted butter*
½ *cup thinly sliced onion*
¼ *cup thinly sliced carrot*
½ *cup thinly sliced celery*
¼ *cup thinly sliced leek*

Minestrone alla Genovese

VEGETABLE SOUP FROM GENOA

Vegetable soups are made in every region of Italy. Some start with ham or bacon fat, oil, garlic, herbs, and/or beans of various kinds—*cannellini, ceci, borlotti*—and some include pasta, whereas others do not. As with *Pasta e fagiolo* (beans and pasta), there are various way of thickening them. Some recipes pass the entire soup, vegetables and all, through a food mill (passatutto), while others just pass the base with the beans and then add the vegetables, and others won't puree anything.

This recipe was brought into my family by my uncle from Genoa and typifies the Ligurian style of cooking by the use of potatoes and pesto.

1 cup 1-inch mixed green and yellow string bean pieces

1 cup halved and thinly sliced zucchini

3 to 4 cups Brodo di Verdure (see pages 87–88)

1 cup fresh or frozen peas (if frozen, let thaw)

4 cloves garlic, bled (scored)

2 tablespoons extra virgin olive oil

3 tablespoons finely diced carrots

3 tablespoons finely diced celery

3 tablespoons finely diced onion

2 tablespoons finely diced prosciutto

2 tablespoons finely diced pancetta or bacon

½ teaspoon dried thyme

½ teaspoon dried basil

½ teaspoon dried chervil

½ teaspoon dried marjoram

Crushed red pepper to taste

½ cup white wine, preferably Gewürztraminer

Salt and freshly ground black pepper to taste

1½ cups cannellini beans with their liquid

1 medium-size ripe tomato, diced into large cubes

1 cup cubed potatoes, cooked

2 tablespoons finely chopped fresh parsley

6 to 8 fresh basil leaves, torn

3 tablespoons freshly grated parmigiano

1½ cups pasta shells, cooked al dente and tossed with a little olive oil

4 teaspoons Pesto (see pages 125–26)

1. Blanch the string beans and zucchini in the vegetable stock over medium-heat, remove, and set aside. If using fresh peas, cook in the stock until tender, then remove and set aside. If using frozen, just allow to thaw out before adding to the soup.

2. Over medium-high, heat the garlic cloves in the oil, then add the carrots, celery, onion, prosciutto, and pancetta, and sweat until the vegetables are tender. Add the herbs and crushed red pepper and cook about 1 minute.

3. Deglaze the pan with the white wine and allow everything to evaporate partially. Season with salt and pepper, then add the cannellini beans with their juice. Add the tomatoes and cook over medium heat for 1 minute. Add the vegetable stock, potatoes, and half of the parsley. Stir and allow to cook gently for 3 or 4 minutes.

4. Add the string beans, zucchini, and peas and cook again for 3 or 4 minutes. Add the basil leaves. Add 1 tablespoon of the parmigiano and cook another 3 or 4 minutes, stirring occasionally. Add the pasta, then pour the soup into warm bowls. Top each with the remaining parmigiano and parsley, and finally the pesto. Serve immediately.

YIELD: *4 servings*

Carabaccia

RENAISSANCE ONION SOUP

This onion soup is so surprisingly sweet and elegant that it can be used at the most formal dinner parties. The onions are cooked till soft and then passed (pureed) before adding lemon juice, cinnamon, sugar, and sliced almonds. It is cooked again a few minutes to amalgamate and is garnished again without stirring so that when eaten there are textural and sweet and sour sensations. that are brightly up front. The soup is very unusual and delicious.

> 3 quarts *Fondo Bianco* or *Brodo di Pollo*
> (*see pages 86–87 or 89–90*)
> 3 large red onions, peeled
> ¼ cup extra virgin olive oil
> 3 large white onions, peeled
> 2 large yellow onions, peeled
> Salt and freshly ground black pepper to taste
> 1½ cups fresh lemon juice
> 12 ounces sliced blanched almonds
> ¼ cup freshly grated parmigiano
> 5 teaspoons ground cinnamon
> ¼ cup sugar

1. In a large pot bring the stock to a slow simmer over medium heat. Skim as necessary. Meanwhile, chop all the onions coarsely, keeping the colors separate.
2. Cook the onions in three stages: Sweat the yellow onions first in the olive oil in a large sauce-pan over medium heat till softened, about 5 minutes. Brown only slightly. Add the red onions and sweat likewise. Finally, add the white onions, and season with salt and pepper. Immediately add 1 quart of the stock to the pan, increase the heat to medium-high, and stir to reduce slightly.
3. Transfer all the contents of the pan to the remaining stock. Simmer until the white onions are soft, about 15 minutes. Skim as necessary.
4. Meanwhile, in a small saucepan, heat the lemon juice over medium-low and add three quarters of the almonds. Allow to simmer very gently for 5 minutes.
5. Strain the stock to remove the onions. Purée them in a food mill or processor, with half the warmed almonds and lemon juice, and the parmigiano, and return them to the pot with the stock. Return to medium heat, stirring and simmering. Taste for salt and pepper. Add 1 teaspoon of the cinnamon. Add the remaining warmed lemon juice and almonds and simmer over medium-low 4 to 5 minutes.
6. In a small saucepan, over medium heat, toast the remaining almonds.
7. To serve, ladle the soup into heated bowls, mix the sugar with the remaining cinnamon and sprinkle 1 teaspoon of the mixture over each bowl. Garnish with the toasted almonds.

YIELD: *8 generous servings*

GLAZES

Glazes, whether of beef, veal, fish, or other flavor, are all simply super-concentrated versions of the original stock or mother sauce. In all cases, the stock or sauce is reduced to a quarter of its original volume, or until it has the consistency of a thick syrup. A glaze should be as translucent as possible, have the intense and agreeable flavor of the main ingredient, and be gelatin-rich enough that it solidifies completely when chilled.

In home kitchens, glazes are great friends. A drop of the appropriate glaze added to any sauté intensifies the flavor, while the concentrated gelatin gives a most desirable natural body to the sauce.

I'll present here recipes for glazes produced from stocks, sauces, and convenience products. The last give satisfactory results if their saltiness and other drawbacks are adjusted for. They are, of course, the easiest and quickest to make.

Other suitable sources for making glazes are commonly found in the home. For example, whenever you have a good broth as a byproduct of a dish such as chicken soup, boiled beef, or poached fish, set aside two cups or so for reducing to a glaze. This will yield approximately a half cup of concentrated glaze that will last for weeks or months by simply recooking it every week. Just be sure to cover the glaze completely with plastic for airtight protection. Freezing breaks down the concentrated gelatin and is not recommended.

Equipment

The time required to make a glaze can be cut considerably by using a wide pan rather than a pot. However, such a pan should only be used if the stock or sauce is extremely clear, as the larger surface area, which allows for quicker evaporation, also causes whatever scum there is to be dispersed, making it more difficult to skim.

Whether using a narrow pot or sauté pan, you may need to transfer the glaze to a smaller vessel as it reduces, to prevent scorching. As a matter of fact, if you were reducing a gallon of stock to three cups of glaze, you would probably use four pots of progressively decreasing sizes.

Thickening

Arrowroot can be used to give the glaze its characteristic syrupy consistency when:

1. A stock or broth is used that is too low in gelatin to yield the consistency desired. The rich body a good, gelatin-rich glaze contributes to any sauce will be missing, however, since the arrowroot will not reproduce it. Keep in mind that if the glaze is to be added to a sauce or dish that is being thickened by other means, the addition of arrowroot is unnecessary.

2. A mother sauce such as a demi-glaze is used, but its thickener has broken down from prolonged heating or freezing. Again, such an addition is necessary only if the glaze is intended to help thicken as well as flavor the dish it's going to be added to.

3. The glaze is being made from convenience products that don't contain thickeners or sufficient gelatin.

4. A lighter intensity of flavor is desired, or the desired intensity is achieved before the glaze gets syrupy.

One teaspoon arrowroot or cornstarch will thicken one cup of liquid to a medium sauce consistency. If the arrowroot is stale, a little more may be needed. Always dissolve the starch in an equal quantity of *cold* liquid before stirring it in. Its thickening power is usually activated only by boiling, although arrowroot may begin to work at a somewhat lower temperature occasionally.

Glazes from Stock

GLACÉ

2 cups clear stock of any flavor, or better yet, consommé
Iced water as needed

1. Pour the stock in a small, narrow pot that will comfortably hold it. Set a small bowl of iced water and a tablespoon nearby.

2. Bring the stock to a gentle boil over medium heat. Adjust the pot to one side of the flame, so only half of the surface is active.

3. Skim the stock as necessary. Add the iced water, a teaspoonful at a time, if needed, to help bring the scum to the surface. Maintain a gentle boil while the stock reduces to about a quarter of its original volume, or until a consistency of maple syrup is reached. This should take approximately 5 to 10 minutes.

4. Strain the finished glaze through moistened cheesecloth or a fine cloth and allow it to cool before refrigerating. It will not freeze well. If left in the refrigerator, reboil every 3 or 4 days for 2 or 3 minutes, adding a bit of water or stock, and then return to the refrigerator.

Variation

•

If you don't have consommé or stock on hand, you can make a glaze while making a stock. As soon as the stock has cleared, borrow from it two or three of the meatiest bones or pieces of meat and put them in a narrow pot. Add enough of the liquid from the stockpot to cover them. Season this second potful with a teaspoon or so of an appropriate base, extract, or broth and bring it to a rapid boil over medium heat. Skim quickly and carefully around the meats as the liquid reduces. When it reduces by half, refill it with the main stock, reduce it again by half as before, then remove from the heat. Remove the meats and return them to the main pot. Pass the liquid through a cheesecloth and put it in a sauté pan. Bring to a rapid boil, skim carefully, and taste for intensity. Add stock from the main pot in successive stages as the newly formed glaze reduces, reducing each addition by three fourths until the desired intensity and thickness is reached.

YIELD: *about ½ cup*

Glaze from Sauces

Leftover sauces can also be made into glazes. Even the juices of a hearty beef stew, or the liquid portions of a vegetable soup, may be concentrated down to a form of glaze that is quite useful. Keep in mind the clarity of the sauce or juices you intend to use during the reduction. In the case of a thick sauce from a stew, for example, extra stock or water should be added to it before the boiling begins to thin it, allowing the scum to rise to the surface. Also, remember that the reduction is less because the sauce has already been reduced.

About 2 cups of any sauce, such as a chicken, velouté, or brown sauce

1. The same procedure is used as outlined in Glaze from Stock (see recipe at left), except the sauce should be reduced by half till almost syrupy.

YIELD: *About 1 cup*

Quick Demi-Glaze

Assuming you don't have stock or consommé on hand, there is a way to boost a canned product by the addition of meat scraps, extract, vegetables, and wine, which is then cooked, skimmed, and reduced. This is called a quick demi-glaze. To make a glaze out of it, simply reduce it further till you reach the desired syrupy consistency.

1 tablespoon vegetable oil

½ pound beef shank or other meaty cut, or scraps

¼ cup coarsely chopped carrots

¼ cup coarsely chopped celery with leaves

½ cup coarsely chopped onion

1 small tomato, roughly cut

2 bay leaves, cracked in half

1 tablespoon meat extract or beef base

1 cup Marsala, Madeira, tawny port, or red wine

1 quart canned beef stock or consommé diluted as per directions (or a combination)

1 tablespoon arrowroot, dissolved in 2 tablespoons water or stock

Salt and pepper to taste

1. In a heavy-bottomed, narrow pot large enough to hold all the ingredients, sauté the meat in the vegetable oil over high heat until browned thoroughly. Add the chopped vegetables and bay leaf and sauté them till soft.

2. Dissolve the extract in the wine and add it to the pan, stirring the contents to glaze them evenly as the liquid evaporates. When the wine has reduced by half, add 1 cup of the stock, or consommé, stirring constantly while it reduces by half. Add the remaining stock or consommé and skim thoroughly (see pages 85–86 for guidelines), maintaining an even, gentle boil.

3. Once the sauce has cleared, add the arrowroot, dissolved in a little cold water or stock, and stir well with a whisk to incorporate it.

4. Allow the sauce to cook, skimming occasionally, until the desired intensity is attained. Season to taste with salt and pepper.

5. Strain through a cheesecloth or fine cloth, let cool, and refrigerate. *Do not freeze.*

YIELD: *About 4 cups*

Espagnole

CANDY GLAZE

2 cups brown stock or canned consommé or 1 cup demi-glaze (previous recipe)

1 cup sweet Marsala

½ cup sweet vermouth

1 teaspoon arrowroot, dissolved in 1 teaspoon water

1. Combine all the ingredients except the dissolved arrowroot and proceed as for Glazes from Stock on page 94, reducing by ½ to ¾. Add the arrowroot at the end and let thicken before straining.

YIELD: *½ cup*

ITALIAN SAUCES

The following recipes are all classic Italian sauces, beginning with *aglio e olio* through *paglia e fieno*. The use of stocks, glazes, and wine throughout is optional. Most often I've opted to provide recipes without these enhancers. This is not done to imply there is anything negative, or even unauthentic, in their use, but rather to let you see how they work without them and because, in many cases, that's my personal preference.

I might also mention that the use of aromatics is also highly personal and where you will hardly ever encounter oregano in my recipes, that does not imply that there's anything wrong in using it. I just don't like it—with rare exceptions, such as clams arregenata or artichokes arregenata.

The methods presented are intended to provide maximum Italian flavor and therefore it might be worthwhile to try to adhere to them in the beginning till you develop the confidence of technique to execute things in your own personal manner.

Aglio e Olio

GARLIC AND OIL

Most all Italian sauces begin with a bit of oil and garlic (except for cream sauces naturally), just as the French begin with butter and shallots. However, *aglio e olio* sauces have garlic and oil as their main quantitative ingredients. They begin with a sauté of garlic and oil and whatever seasonings are desired. Quick and simple. From this, the character or taste can be changed in innumerable ways by the addition of meat, fish, vegetables, and herbs, such as *con peperoncini* (red pepper).

As simple as this primary sauce sounds, and is, it nevertheless is at the heart of Italian cooking and needs careful attention, since the true flavor that separates Italian from French and other cuisines begins here.

There are several components necessary for making a "foolproof" *aglio e olio*. First, use the best virgin olive oil available. If possible, keep a bottle in reserve with some garlic cloves for use especially in this dish. Failing that, or in addition to it, to guarantee good garlic flavor, before beginning the recipe, sauté several bled (scored) garlic cloves in the oil over low heat for 5 minutes so the oil is well permeated with its flavor. Then brown the garlic to darken the flavor. Lastly, have the pasta ready before finishing the sauce. Toss the pasta with half of the sauce and then after plating, finish with the sauce and some more fresh chopped parsley.

- 1 to 1½ cups garlic-infused Italian extra virgin olive oil
- 4 large cloves garlic, bled (scored)
- 2 cloves garlic, chopped
- 1 cup chopped fresh parsley
  Salt and freshly ground black pepper to taste
  Crushed red pepper to taste

1. Heat the oil and garlic in a large, heavy saucepan over low heat until the garlic begins to take on color.
2. Remove the pan from the stove and add half the parsley; if oil is very hot, wait 30 seconds before doing so. Return the pan to the stove and cook, stirring, approximately 1 minute.

Add the salt and pepper and crushed red pepper if desired. Turn up the heat for a brief ½ minute to make the sauce properly hot. Be careful not to burn the parsley.
3. Pour half the sauce over well-drained al dente pasta in a warm bowl and toss thoroughly until the pasta is coated evenly. Reseason with salt and pepper to taste. Plate into 4 warm dishes and top it with the remaining sauce. Garnish with the remaining chopped parsley.

Variations

•

The addition of thyme, basil, chervil, oregano, marjoram, sage, coriander, cumin, curry, mace, lemon rind, orange rind, saffron, raisins, pine nuts, walnuts, pistachios, crushed red pepper, and/or white wine are optional and will change the basic sauce dramatically. These additions should be made at the time the first half of the parsley is added.

One half cup white wine can be added at the beginning after the oil is heated and before the garlic is browned. Be sure to heat the wine before adding it to the oil to avoid explosions.

If substantial additions are made to this sauce in the way of fish or vegetables, the amount of oil can be reduced by half since it is no longer just a garlic and oil sauce.

YIELD: *4 servings*

Salsa alla Liguria

GARLIC AND OIL SAUCE IN THE LIGURIAN MANNER

My uncle Frank the baker from Liguria taught me this delicious extension of *aglio e olio* many years ago. It's particularly wonderful on linguini as a light, late evening snack, as we used to say in Queens Country thirty-five-odd years ago. Now I'd probably serve it as an entrée with a salad, a crusty loaf of homemade bread, and a bottle of Chianti. Times change, and so do appetites.

> 1 to 1½ *cups garlic-infused extra virgin oil*
> 4 *large cloves garlic, bled (scored)*
> 2 *cloves garlic, chopped*
> ½ *cup raisins*
> ½ *cup pine nuts*
> ⅛ *teaspoon each dried thyme, basil, and chervil*
> *Crushed red pepper to taste*
> *Salt and pepper to taste*

> 1 *cup freshly grated parmigiano*
> 1 *cup chopped fresh parsley*
> 1 *cup small toasted croutons*
> 1 *pound stranded pasta, any kind (linguine preferred), cooked al dente*

1. Heat the oil with the garlic over low heat till the garlic cloves begin to color.
2. Remove from the stove, allow to settle, and add all the remaining ingredients, except for the parmigiano, half the parsley, half the croutons and the pasta.
3. Return the pan to moderate heat and cook until the garlic just begins to brown. Don't let anything burn.
4. Place well-drained steaming hot pasta in a warm bowl and pour half the sauce over it with one half the remaining parmigiano. Toss until well coated. Place in warm bowls and garnish each with the remaining sauce, parmigiano, croutons, and parsley. Serve immediately.

YIELD: *4 servings*

Salsa alle Vongole in Bianco

WHITE CLAM SAUCE

I suppose white and red clam sauces on linguine and spaghetti are almost as popular now in America as Mom's apple pie. And why not? There's a universal appreciation of garlic, oil, and clams that defies description. It seems to be the ultimate seafood dish without being fishy. And then, of course, who doesn't like spaghetti?

2 dozen littleneck clams

½ to 1 cup garlic-infused extra virgin olive oil

4 cloves garlic, bled (scored)

2 large garlic cloves, chopped

1 cup finely chopped fresh parsley

⅛ teaspoon each dried thyme, basil, and chervil

Crushed red pepper to taste

Salt and pepper to taste

½ cup best available white aromatic wine

1 pound stranded pasta, any kind (linguine preferred)

1. Heat the oil in a large, heavy skillet over low heat, add the garlic, and sauté until browned slightly.

Turn the heat up to medium, add the clams, and cover them till they steam open (approximately 2 to 3 minutes). Those that don't open, force open with a knife and smell. It's not necessarily true that they're bad because they don't open, nor is it true that they're bad if they're open ahead of time; the smell test will tell you for sure.

2. Remove the cover, stir, and add the herbs and seasonings, reserving half the parsley for a garnish. Deglaze immediately with the wine and turn the heat up to high to reduce the liquid slightly, stirring all the while. If you want a thicker sauce, remove the clams and reduce further.

3. In any event, remove the clams and take the meat out of 1 dozen of them, discarding the shells. Return the clam meat to the sauce. With the other dozen, release the clam from its muscle and put it back in the shell. These are to be used as garnish.

4. Place well-drained, steaming pasta in a warm bowl and add half the sauce, tossing till coated evenly. Plate in warm bowls and garnish with the remaining sauce and parsley. Place 3 clams in their shells on top in each bowl, and then serve immediately.

YIELD: *4 servings*

Stringozzi ai Tartufi

SHOELACE PASTA WITH TRUFFLES

While we're on the subject of garlic and oil, why not with truffles? Why not, indeed? This dish is an Umbrian specialty; the center of the truffle industry is at Norcia. Naturally there are several ways to make this pasta. The simplest, but unfortunately most expensive, presentation is pasta tossed with some butter along with a few diced truffles, and then a shave of giant truffle on top. Absolutely fabulous, especially if it's a fresh winter truffle. However, the recipe that's used in most restaurants doesn't require that expenditure and is still very delicious. Here, then, is the cheaper version.

2 anchovy fillets, minced

1 large clove garlic, minced

¼ cup extra virgin olive oil

Two 1-ounce fresh black Norcia truffles, cleaned but unpeeled

½ pound Stringozzi (see page 62)

1. Mash the anchovies and garlic together in a small bowl with the back of a fork, adding enough oil, drop by drop, to form a thick paste.

2. Heat the remaining oil in a small heavy skillet over very low heat, then "sweat" the minced truffle in the oil, over very low heat, without

sizzling, to perfume the oil thoroughly, no more than 2 minutes.

3. Mix the paste into the truffle oil, raise the heat slightly, and warm through, no more than a few minutes.

4. Place well-drained, steaming, al dente *stringozzi* in a warm bowl and toss with the hot sauce. Place into hot bowls and top with the remaining truffle, thinly sliced.

NOTE: Stringozzi are eaten nearly raw in Umbria, where they originate. Though you may certainly cook them more, or to taste, the extremely firm center is essential texturally to the success of the dish. Also, waiters in Umbria will actually try their best to refuse any request for parmigiano to accompany *Stringozzi ai Tartufi*—but it's an extremely rich addition.

YIELD: *2 servings*

Marinara

This is also known as *filetto di pomodoro* if the sauté is quicker, leaving the tomatoes practically whole. Fresh plum tomatoes also make an interesting sauce but not as dark red as the best canned Italian plum tomatoes, recommended here, can provide. It is one of the few cases where a canned product is preferable for a certain effect.

Bear in mind that there are many degrees of oiliness and spiciness to be found from region to region with this sauce. The recipe I present here is a mild non-oily version.

Also, my technique in the original sauté is quite different. Everything is done on very high heat. I brown the garlic almost to burning and sear the tomatoes by flaming them as you might do in a flambé.

⅓ *cup olive oil (enough to coat the pan liberally but not be present in the final sauce)*

4 *large cloves garlic, bled (scored)*

6 *cups canned Italian plum tomatoes, with juices*

Optional herbs, spices, and wine as desired

Salt and freshly ground black pepper to taste

1 *cup chopped fresh parsley*

6 to 8 *fresh basil leaves, torn in half*

2 to 3 *large cloves garlic, minced*

1 *pound linguine or other pasta*

1. Heat the oil over medium-high heat. Add the garlic and sauté until well browned.

2. Turn up the heat further and add the tomatoes. Do not be afraid if it flames up. The idea is to scorch the tomatoes. However, it must be done quickly and with a pot cover to shield the rest of the stove. Stir with one hand and hold the cover above the pot with the other.

3. Turn the heat down to medium, add the seasonings, wine, half the chopped parsley, the basil, and diced garlic. Stir well and cook for 3 to 5 minutes.

4. Place well-drained, steaming pasta in a warm bowl and toss with half the sauce. Plate in warm bowls and garnish with the remaining sauce and chopped parsley. Serve immediately.

YIELD: *4 servings*

Variations

A further enrichment of these marinaras is made by pureeing some of the additional ingredients and/or poaching some and using the liquor to accent the dish. Anchovy paste, clam juice, shrimp or vegetable fumets would be prime examples of this technique. The pastes would be added to the oil before the addition of tomatoes and the juices or fumets are added after the tomatoes and before the seasonings.

Pizzaiola is a special version of these marinaras. In this case, meat (steak, veal, or chicken livers) is browned in the oil before the tomatoes and seasonings are added, along with sliced or rough cut green peppers.

Make a light (rather than stewed) *chicken alla cacciatora* in a similar way. Or, make a mélange of vegetables (broccoli, zucchini, or string beans) and you have a *primavera,* although to my taste, the best *primavera* is made from a rosé, or better yet, a simple butter sauce.

Of course, *diavolo* is one of the most unique and exciting forms of marinara. The addition of a diced red pepper as well as cayenne and Tabasco gives it its rightful name. A classic *diavolo,* however, is made with a fumet (lobster, shrimp, or other fish) or glaze, a *battuto,* and white wine, and is stewed for a considerable time before being pureed. In the *ristoranti* I have owned, we reduce by half *salsa di pomodoro* and marinara together in equal parts with an infusion of fish stock. After this, we devil it according to the customer's preference—mild, hot, or *diavolo.*

All these sauces can be taken a step further by starting with a *battuto,* 1/8 cup more oil, and then adding red wine or Marsala.

Cooking or stewing these sauces for a longer time (30 to 40 minutes) also reduces them, making them *stretto* rather than liquidy.

By using ham (or classically, pork jowl), onions and red pepper, we create *sauce all'amatriciana.*

Combining black and green olives, anchovies, and capers with our basic marinara, you can create a *sauce alla meretrice,* otherwise known as harlot sauce. Supposedly it was created by the prostitutes of Naples because it could be prepared quickly between assignments.

YIELD: *4 servings*

Salsa Rossa alle Vongole

RED CLAM SAUCE

This is probably the most abused dish in the world aside from scrambled eggs. It seems that everybody in America has the secret recipe for clams "red sauce" in spite of the fact that the components are too simple to require much elaboration.

In Italy, we use a very tiny clam called *verace,* which is quite different from littleneck or cherrystone clams, more commonly encountered in America. The *verace* are about 1/8 the size. Our recipe is for use in the States, however.

In any case what we're really talking about is a dish of clams enhanced by tomatoes and aromatics and tossed with pasta. Not much of a secret if you think about it. So let us proceed to a simple basic recipe and let those in the "know" adulterate it as they will.

1 *dozen small cherrystone clams*
1 *dozen small littleneck clams*
1/4 *cup best available olive oil*
4 *cloves garlic, bled (scored)*
    Salt and pepper to taste
1 *teaspoon each dried basil and thyme*
1/8 *teaspoon crushed red pepper*
2 *tablespoons best available dry, aromatic white wine*
1/4 *cup finely chopped fresh parsley*
6 *to 8 fresh basil leaves, torn*
1 *teaspoon minced garlic*
6 *cups canned Italian plum tomatoes, with juice*
1/2 *pound pasta, cooked al dente (optional)*

1. Scrub and rinse the clams several times with cold water. Smell those that are already opened and discard any that have an "off odor."

2. Place oil in a large, heavy-bottomed skillet and heat with the whole garlic cloves over medium heat. When the cloves begin to take on color, add the clams and continue to cook over medium-high heat, covered, stirring occasionally, until they are more or less opened, about 2 minutes.

3. Remove the cover and season with salt, pepper, thyme, dried basil, and red pepper, and mix well. Deglaze with the wine. Add half the chopped parsley, the fresh basil, and minced garlic. Stir in the tomatoes and cook over medium-high heat for 3 or 4 minutes until they amalgamate with their natural juices, the wine, and aromatics. Turn off the heat.

4. Remove the clam meat from 1 dozen shells; cut off the beard or "lip" and cut them in half if large; otherwise, leave them whole. Place the clam meat in the sauce and stir.

5. Place well-drained, steaming pasta in a warm bowl and toss with half the sauce. Lace the 12 clams in their shells in the pasta in a random fashion. Plate into warm bowls and add the remaining sauce. Garnish with the rest of the chopped parsley. Serve immediately.

YIELD: *4 servings*

Rosé

LIGHT, FRESH TOMATO SAUCE

By reducing the amount of oil used by ½ cup and adding 2 medium size fresh tomatoes, roughly cut up, you create an interesting sauce that lies be-

tween an *aglio e olio* and a marinara. I call it *rosé.* It's best with *tagliolini* and *angeli di capelli.*

- 1 cup best available olive oil
- 2 cloves garlic, bled (scored)
- 2 medium-size fresh tomatoes, roughly cut
  Salt and freshly ground black pepper to taste
- 1 cup finely chopped fresh parsley
- 2 leaves fresh basil, torn
- 1 clove garlic, minced
  Optional herbs, spices, and wine added as you wish
- ½ pound pasta

1. Heat the oil and half the garlic in a large, heavy-bottomed saucepan over low heat until the garlic is golden.

2. Add the tomatoes and cook over high heat for 2 or 3 minutes, pressing the juice out of the tomatoes. Do not overcook the tomatoes or it will turn into an oily marinara.

3. Season with salt and pepper. Add half the parsley, the basil, the remaining minced garlic, and any optional ingredients, and stir to incorporate.

4. Pour the sauce over well-drained, steaming pasta in a warm bowl and toss until the pasta is coated thoroughly. Plate into warm dishes and garnish with the remaining parsley. Serve immediately.

YIELD: *2 servings*

Salsa Cruda

RAW, FRESH TOMATO SAUCE

Here is the perfect summer sauce made with fresh red-ripe tomatoes, garlic, oil, and fresh basil leaves and buds. The crushed red pepper and pecorino Romano are optional but in my opinion give the sauce an added piquancy that is very refreshing. I've often carried this piquancy thought further by adding some balsamic vinegar. Of course the surprise aspect of this dish is the combination of the cold, or room temperature, sauce with hot pasta. It's a big favorite in summer here in Umbria and makes a very pleasant luncheon pasta when the heat of the day cries out for something different. It's traditionally served with penne or spaghetti.

    2 fresh ripe tomatoes
   10 fresh basil leaves with buds, torn
   ¼ cup extra virgin olive oil
    2 cloves garlic, minced
      Salt and freshly ground black pepper to
      taste
      Crushed red pepper to taste (optional)
      Freshly grated pecorino Romano to taste
      (optional)

1. Cut the tomatoes in half and shake out excess water and seeds. Remove the cores and chop them coarsely.
2. Combine all the ingredients in a large bowl and toss. Cover and refrigerate for at least a half hour.
3. When the pasta is ready, divide the chilled salsa between 2 hot, oversized pasta bowls.
4. Drain the pasta well and add it to the bowls. Toss vigorously and quickly, adding grated

cheese to taste. Serve immediately while the sauce is still cool on the hot pasta. Drizzle a little extra olive oil on top if desired.

YIELD: *2 servings*

·SALSA DI POMODORO· TOMATO SAUCE

You wouldn't believe there could be so much discussion about a simple tomato sauce. Yet one authority after another will insist:

- there are no vegetables, oil, garlic, onion, herbs used, just tomatoes cooked in their own juice till thick and pulpy.
- the tomatoes have to be fresh, not canned.
- if using a *battuto* (diced carrot, celery, and onion), it should be added raw not sautéed.
- if using a *battuto,* it should be sautéed before adding.
- the *battuto* should be sautéed and added after the tomatoes are three-quarters cooked.
- the *battuto* should be sautéed and the tomatoes added to the sauté.
- garlic and onions are a no-no.
- garlic and onions are essential.
- the only herb possible is basil and it must be fresh. God forbid a sprig of thyme should sneak in.
- the tomatoes should be passed through a food mill before cooking.
- the tomatoes should be puréed after cooking.
- the tomatoes should be long stewed (1½ to 2 hours).
- the tomatoes should be cooked only till they thicken (20 minutes).
- sugar is a no-no.
- sugar helps to moderate the acidity.

Upon due consideration it seems to me that they're all right. It's just a question of what you're after. Certainly the purity of the tomatoes is best maintained if they're not even cooked in oil. But the question remains as to the taste you want—pure or not. Each one of these "rules" will produce its own variation of a basic tomato sauce. Certainly the result will be different if the *battuto* is sautéed or not; if fresh or canned tomatoes are used; if garlic is added or not. But my advice is, let the battle rage on, and in the meantime, enjoy it all. For different moods and different times of the year, any and all of these theories will produce a fine-tasting sauce. My own three preferred versions follow:

Salsa di Pomodoro I

PASSED TOMATO SAUCE I

This next one is my own favorite, if I had to choose only one of all the possible ways to make *salsa di pomodoro*. For me it accomplishes the light freshness that is characteristic of these sauces and at the same time is enriched by the *battuto* and the butter.

> 2 tablespoons finely chopped peeled carrot (about 1 small carrot)
>
> 2 tablespoons finely chopped celery (about 1/2 rib)
>
> 1/4 cup finely chopped white onion (1 small onion)
>
> 1 tablespoon chopped fresh parsley
>
> 2 cloves garlic, bled (scored)

> 2 tablespoons extra virgin olive oil
>
> 6 cups canned Italian plum tomatoes, with juice
>
> Salt and freshly ground pepper to taste
>
> 4 to 6 fresh basil leaves, torn
>
> 1 clove garlic, minced
>
> 1 teaspoon sugar
>
> 2 tablespoons unsalted butter

1. Sauté the carrots, celery, onion, parsley, and whole garlic in the oil in a medium-sized saucepan over medium-low heat until softened and translucent; do not brown.
2. Add the canned tomatoes. Simmer, stirring occasionally until the tomatoes begin to break apart, about 5 minutes.
3. Season with the salt and pepper, add the basil, minced garlic, and sugar, and simmer for another 15 to 20 minutes.
4. Pass the sauce through a food mill and return to low heat to reduce as desired. Finish with the butter before serving by swirling it into the sauce. The procedure is called "mounting."

YIELD: *4 servings, about 2 cups*

Salsa di Pomodoro II

PASSED TOMATO SAUCE II

When I first came to Italy four years ago, the mother of a friend I was staying with in Todi had won a poetry contest, sponsored by a national newspaper, and the presentation awards ceremony was to take place on a Sunday in the town of Pompei, south of Naples. We all got spiffed up in our Sunday best and glided down the *autostrada* on a beautiful sunny afternoon in May. The town hall had been flowered and polished for the occasion and as I took my seat among the well-dressed crowd, made doubly festive by the pleasant smell of intermingled expensive perfumes, I was handed a program for this event and proceeded to read it as I listened to the murmuring crowd, keening at each other in Italian stage whispers.

"*Grazie a Dio! I fiori nel giardino sono bellissimi quest'anno.*" (Thank God! The flowers are beautiful this year.)

"*Ha visto la sorella della contessa ieri sera? Che faccia brutta! Sembra una putta, no?*" (Did you see the Countess's sister last night? She looks like a whore, no?)

Then suddenly there it was in the program, "*Azienda agricoltura Soviero.*" An ad for a company that made farm machinery. And then another, "*Azienda vinicoltura Soviero*" . . . So they made wine, too!

As I continued through the ads I encountered seven that bore my family name. Very impressive, I thought, and I knew I had to introduce myself to my *parenti* (relations). I'm afraid it would take far too long to relate those nostalgic encounters as much as I'd like to. Suffice it to say that they all make *salsa di pomodoro* and naturally have pet theories as to which version is the best. After tasting and enjoying several, I was completely bowled over one night by a particular rendition that was different from all I had tasted previously. It was more dense and oilier at the same time, and seemed richer than all the rest. Naturally I had to get the recipe. So here it is. By the way, this is wonderful on *rigatoni rigati*.

> 4 large cloves garlic, bled (scored)
> ½ to ¾ cup extra virgin olive oil

> 6 cups canned San Marzano plum tomatoes (very special, vacuum packed by cousin Francesco Soviero), if available, or any high-quality Italian plum tomatoes, with juice
> 1 teaspoon sugar
> Salt and pepper to taste
> ⅛ teaspoon crushed red pepper

1. Sauté the garlic in the oil over medium-high heat till very lightly browned.
2. Add the tomatoes and sugar and season with the salt and black pepper. Reduce the heat to very low and cook for at least 1½ hours or until the sauce reaches the desired consistency. Pass through a food mill and serve.

YIELD: *4 servings, about 2 cups*

Salsa di Pomodoro Fresco

FRESH TOMATO SAUCE

Since I make this only in the summer, when my own vine-ripened plum tomatoes are at their red ripest, I suppose it could be called a summer sauce. And since I prefer to use onion and garlic, I suppose it could also be called a *pommarola*, although according to certain authorities the fact that these aromatics are sautéed first would possibly disqualify it . . . whatever.

1 clove garlic, diced

1 small white onion, diced

2 tablespoons extra virgin olive oil

1½ to 2 pounds fresh, ripe plum tomatoes, diced

Salt and pepper to taste

1 teaspoon sugar

6 to 8 fresh basil leaves, torn

1. Sweat the garlic and onion in the oil in a casserole. Add the diced tomatoes and season with salt, pepper, and sugar. Stir well.
2. Cook on very low heat for 30 to 40 minutes without stirring.
3. Pass through a food mill.
4. Return the sauce to the stove and add the basil leaves. Cook for another 10 minutes on very low heat. Adjust the seasonings and serve on whatever pasta you like, although homemade egg pastas seem to marry this delicate sauce better than *pasta secca*.

YIELD: *4 servings, about 2 cups*

SUGO

This is a stewed and usually pureed tomato sauce that has as many variant recipes as there are Italian pastas. *Sugo* means juice of, and the meat is usually removed after lengthy cooking, leaving the "juice" or *sugo* good flavor.

Some start with oil and garlic, carrots, ham, thyme, and bay leaf. Others use bacon, celery, onion, garlic, and oil. The sauces are then enriched with pieces of beef, veal, pork, or a combination thereof, or game such as rabbit, duck, pheasant, or goose, and the addition of wine.

Basically sauté the meat or game in a bit of oil until brown, preferably in a good old cast-iron or other casserole. Add the garlic and herbs for a further sauté. Use wines (burgundy, claret, Italian wines, spirits or fortified wines such as Marsala, port, sherry, or Cognac) either to deglaze or flambé. Then puree the tomatoes through a food mill, discarding the seeds (they tend to make the sauce bitter), and add to cover the meat. Season with salt, pepper, and a bit of sugar (to temper the acidity), bring to a low boil for 5 minutes, and then simmer on the lowest possible heat for an hour or so. In many Italian kitchens, this sauce is left on the back of the stove (away from direct heat) to thicken naturally.

This *sugo* recipe is made with a piece of top, or bottom, round of beef and lamb shank. The pureed tomatoes with some onion and a bit of sugar are added to the browned meat. This is my own recipe and a personal favorite. Its sweet simplicity is what appeals most and it is the best sauce I know for all kinds of pasta. As a basic puree of tomato it can be used in a hundred other ways as well. *Sugo* is really one of the most important staples in Italian cooking. Big pasta such as *tufoli*, rigatoni, *mostaccioli, lumache,* and *maruzzelle* (seashells) are ideal with this sauce. My all-time favorite is *maruzzelle,* preferably from De Cecco or Barilla.

Sugo di Carne

MEAT SAUCE

2 tablespoons extra virgin olive oil

4 cloves garlic, bled (scored)

1 pound beef in 1 piece, top or bottom round

1 medium-size lamb shank

⅛ teaspoon each dried thyme, basil, and chervil

⅛ teaspoon crushed red pepper

⅛ teaspoon freshly grated nutmeg

1 teaspoon salt

1 teaspoon freshly ground black pepper

½ cup Marsala

6 cups canned Italian plum tomatoes, pureed in a food mill, blender, or food processor

1 tablespoon sugar

1 medium-size white onion, peeled

1 teaspoon minced garlic

1. Heat the oil in a large saucepan over medium-high heat and sauté the whole garlic until lightly browned; remove and reserve.

2. Add the meat to the pan and brown well over medium-high heat. Once browned, season with the red pepper, nutmeg, and a touch of the salt and pepper, and return the garlic cloves to the pan.

3. Deglaze with the Marsala, scraping the bottom to loosen any brownings. Let the Marsala reduce slightly to caramelize the meat. Then add the tomatoes, sugar, the rest of the salt and pepper, and the onion. Turn the heat up and bring the tomatoes to a soft boil for approximately 5 minutes.

4. Add minced garlic, then turn the heat down as low as possible and simmer for an hour or so until the sauce reaches its desired thickness.

5. Remove the meat, slice, and serve separately with some of the sauce.

YIELD: *1 quart*

Sugo di Funghi

MUSHROOM SAUCE

This one is for our vegetarian friends. If you brown the mushrooms nicely and deglaze properly, you will get a rich, dark sauce that no one will ever find lacking. A porcino mushroom or two (fresh or dried) in the sauté will also give the sauce a deeper dimension.

½ cup extra virgin olive oil

4 large cloves garlic, bled (scored)

¼ pound medium-size mushrooms with stems, sliced

⅛ teaspoon each dried thyme, basil, chervil, and marjoram

⅛ teaspoon crushed red pepper

⅛ teaspoon freshly grated nutmeg

Salt, java pepper, and freshly ground black pepper to taste

⅛ cup sweet Marsala

1 cup canned Italian plum tomatoes, drained and passed through a food mill

1 teaspoon minced garlic

1 teaspoon sugar

1 medium-size white onion, bled (scored)

1. Place three of the whole (bled) garlic cloves in oil in a medium-size copper sauté pan or cast-iron pot and cook slowly over low heat until they take on color.

2. Sauté the mushrooms, tossing and turning, until they begin to take on color. Then add the thyme, basil, chervil, and marjoram. Stir, then add the crushed red pepper and nutmeg. Stir,

then add the salt and two peppers to taste. Stir and toss.

3. Pour in the Marsala, add the tomatoes, then reseason with salt and pepper. Stir and add the minced garlic and sugar. Stir, then add the onion. Cook over medium-high heat, for 5 minutes, till the sauce gently boils.

4. Reduce the heat to a very low simmer and cook slowly for an hour or so until the sauce reaches the desired consistency.

YIELD: *4 servings, about 2 cups*

Ragù Bolognese

BOLOGNESE SAUCE

In America ragù is what people relate to as a meat sauce. Ground meat, usually hamburger, is what is expected. In Italy a ragù can be made of almost anything, and you'll encounter chicken liver, sausage, calves' brains, sweetbreads, and fish of various kinds in different ragù. The most famous is ragù bolognese, which was probably the inspiration for the Italian-American meat sauce. When made as they do in Bologna, it's the richest version I've seen anywhere, with its heavy cream finish. Unfortunately, it's used in making lasagne throughout Italy ad nauseam. By itself, on a plate of homemade *tagliatelle,* it can be the quintessential meat sauce, particularly when made only with ground veal.

The recipe below is made with veal and beef and can be said to lie on the middle ground between the rich and lighter versions. Once you understand this one, however, it will be easy to move on to others that use stock and go up and down the scale from richness to lightness. Three ingredients that you'll seem to find in all the recipes for meat ragù are: diced carrots, veal (in some ratio to other meats, or alone), and heavy cream. Stock and wine are optional but generally garlic, oil, and bacon (or other fat) are used in varying ratios.

- ¼ *cup extra virgin olive oil*
- ¼ *pound bacon, coarsely chopped*
- ½ *cup medium-diced carrots*
- ¼ *cup medium-diced celery*
- ¼ *cup medium-diced onion*
- 3 *pounds ground veal*
- 2 *pounds ground beef*
- ¾ *cup good white wine (Gewürztraminer recommended)*
- Two *6-ounce cans tomato paste*
- 1 *teaspoon salt (or to taste)*
- 1 *teaspoon freshly ground black pepper (or to taste)*
- 1 *teaspoon freshly grated nutmeg (or to taste)*
- 2 *cloves garlic, finely diced*
- 1 *cup heavy cream*

1. Heat the oil and bacon together in a large saucepan over medium heat until the bacon is very light brown, stirring constantly.

2. Add the carrots and celery and stir while they cook, until they take on color. Add the onions, stir, and cook briefly.

3. Add the veal and beef and cook for approximately 3 to 5 minutes, stirring constantly. When the veal and beef have taken on color, add the wine and cook, stirring all the while, until it partially evaporates, about 3 minutes.

4. Add the tomato paste and stir thoroughly, mixing it in well. Add the salt, pepper, nutmeg, and garlic. Combine and cook for 45 minutes on the lowest possible heat. Finish with the cream, cooking a few minutes longer to amalgamate and heat thoroughly.

5. Place well-drained, steaming pasta on warm plates and heap a mound of the Bolognese sauce in the center of it; drizzle some olive oil around the sauce. Serve with a fork and large spoon so that each guest can mix the sauce with the pasta.

YIELD: *2 quarts*

Tagliatelle ai Funghi

TAGLIATELLE WITH MUSHROOMS

2 tablespoons extra virgin olive oil

2 tablespoons unsalted butter

1 pound champignon mushrooms, sliced

2 pieces dried porcini mushrooms, soaked in 1 tablespoon water until soft, drained, and minced

½ cup finely diced shallot or onion

⅛ teaspoon each dried thyme, basil, and chervil

   Crushed red pepper to taste

½ cup finely chopped fresh parsley

   Salt and pepper to taste

   Fresh lemon juice to taste

1 pound tagliatelle

1. Heat the oil and butter over low heat in a skillet. Add the mushrooms and shallots and sauté until they begin to take on color. Add the seasonings and lemon juice and combine thoroughly. Toss well-drained, hot pasta with half the sauce, then plate up in warm bowls and top with the remaining sauce, if desired.

YIELD: *4 servings*

Vermicelli alla Siracusana

VERMICELLI WITH EGGPLANT AND OLIVES

An extension of a basic *aglio e olio,* this Sicilian dish is a rich combination of oil and garlic, tomatoes, wine, capers, anchovies, and black olives.

¾ cup garlic-infused extra virgin oil

4 large cloves garlic, bled (scored)

2 medium-size green bell peppers, cut into 2-inch pieces

1 cup canned Italian plum tomatoes

1½ cups diced fresh tomato (about 2 tomatoes)

2 large cloves garlic, minced

2 tablespoons jumbo capers

2 tablespoons mashed anchovies

1 cup marinated pitted black olives

⅛ teaspoon each dried thyme, basil, and chervil (optional)

½ cup finely chopped fresh parsley

⅛ teaspoon crushed red pepper

½ cup best available dry white wine

   Salt and pepper to taste

1 pound vermicelli or other stranded pasta

   Freshly grated pecorino Romano to taste

1. Heat the olive oil in a skillet and lightly sauté the garlic cloves over medium-low heat. Add the green peppers and brown slightly.

2. Turn the heat up to high and add the canned tomatoes, searing them.

3. Turn the heat back down to medium and add the fresh diced tomatoes, minced garlic, capers, anchovies, olives, thyme, basil, chervil, half the parsley, and the red pepper flakes, and mix well. Add the white wine, season with salt and pepper to taste, and cook on moderate heat for 3 to 5 minutes.

4. Remove half the sauce to a warm bowl for topping, and toss well-drained, steaming hot pasta in the saucepan with the remaining sauce, coating well. Plate in warm bowls and top with the remaining sauce and parsley, and grated pecorino Romano (or other sharp) cheese. Serve immediately.

Variation
•

To make a *pasta al forno* (baked pasta) dish out of this you must first undercook the pasta since it will be cooked again in baking. Then:

1. Toss very *al dente* pasta with half the sauce, then with a mixture of 1 cup diced mozzarella, 1 cup shredded Gruyère or Swiss cheese, and 1 cup grated parmigiano.

2. Place some of the more liquid part of the sauce on the bottom of a casserole dish, then nest in the pasta. Top the dish with the remaining sauce, parsley, and the pecorino Romano as before.

3. Bake in a preheated 400°F oven for 15 to 20 minutes, then remove and brown under a broiler for a minute or two before serving if the oven baking hasn't already browned it.

4. Let the casserole rest for 2 to 3 minutes before serving and pass some more pecorino for individual topping.

YIELD: *4 servings*

Fusilli Lunghi al Tonno

FUSILLI WITH TUNA SAUCE

The *fusilli lunghi* in this recipe are a long (spaghetti length) corkscrew type of pasta.

1	cup garlic-infused extra virgin olive oil
4	large cloves garlic, bled (scored)
1½ to 2	cups canned tuna fish, in oil
2	tablespoons jumbo capers
½	cup green, brown, and black pitted marinated olives
2 to 3	sprigs fresh thyme or 1 teaspoon dried thyme
2	cloves garlic, finely diced
¼	teaspoon crushed red pepper (optional)
1	cup finely chopped fresh parsley
½	cup best available white wine
½	cup Brodo di Pesce (optional—pages 90–91)
	Salt and pepper to taste
1	pound fusilli lunghi
1	cup freshly grated pecorino Romano

1. Heat the oil in a saucepan and lightly sauté the garlic over medium-low heat. Add the tuna fish, capers, olives, thyme, minced garlic, red pepper, and half the parsley.

2. Cook over medium heat for 3 to 5 minutes, reducing the liquids slightly, then season to taste with salt and pepper.

3. Reserve half the sauce in a warm bowl, then

toss well-drained, hot fusilli in the saucepan with the remaining sauce, coating thoroughly. Toss with half the pecorino Romano. Plate in warm bowls and top with the remaining cheese and parsley. Serve immediately.

YIELD: *4 servings*

Rigatoni alla Pizzaiola

I've encountered several versions of this *aglio e olio* enhanced by tomatoes. In the *campagna* (country-side) outside Naples it refers to a simple marinara with oregano, while in Naples and elsewhere it can be a marinara that is then passed through a food mill and simmered for 20 to 30 minutes—also with oregano. There is also a steak *pizzaiola* recipe that works itself into a sauce recipe for pasta when the meat is cut into small pieces—*pez-zetti.*

¾ *cup garlic-infused extra virgin olive oil*

4 *large cloves garlic, bled (scored)*

10 *ounces steak (good tender beef needed), in 1-inch cubes*

Salt and pepper to taste

⅛ *to ¼ teaspoon crushed red pepper*

1 *teaspoon dried oregano*

1 *cup chopped fresh parsley*

½ *cup Florio sweet Marsala*

½ *cup best available dry red wine*

2 *cups canned Italian plum tomatoes, with juice*

2 *cloves garlic, minced*

1 *pound rigatoni*

Freshly grated pecorino Romano or parmigiano to taste

1. Heat the oil in a saucepan and lightly sauté the garlic over medium-low heat. Add the meat, turn the heat up and sauté till the meat is browned but still rare. If the garlic starts to burn, remove and return to the pan later.

2. After it's browned, season the meat with salt and pepper, half the red pepper, half the oregano, and ¼ cup of the chopped parsley.

3. Immediately pour in the Marsala, cooking it till it evaporates slightly and caramelizes the meat lightly. Then, add the red wine, stir, and add the tomatoes and stir.

4. Season the tomatoes with the minced garlic, the remaining red pepper and oregano, and another ¼ cup of the parsley. Adjust seasonings and cook over medium-low heat for 3 to 5 minutes.

5. Remove and reserve half the sauce in a warm bowl. Toss well-drained, steaming hot *rigatoni* in the saucepan with the remaining sauce, then plate in warm bowls and top with the remaining sauce and the remaining parsley. Top with grated pecorino Romano, or parmigiano, or both and serve immediately.

Variation

•

The sauce can be deepened with a few table-spoons of tomato concentrate, which would be put in right after the red wine and before the tomatoes, and then passed through a food mill at its completion. I prefer the rougher texture of the pieces of tomato as presented in the recipe above, however.

YIELD: *4 servings*

Manfrigoli alla Fattoressa

MANFRIGOLI WITH EGGPLANT
AND ONIONS

Manfrigoli are the same flour and water pasta made with hot water and an egg white as *stringozzi* (see pages 99–100 for the recipe), except that they are more even and slightly thicker than the other two.

2 large cloves garlic, bled (scored)
½ cup extra virgin olive oil
1 red bell pepper, cut into 2-inch pieces
1 cup cubed eggplant (about 1-inch cubes)
1 medium-size ripe tomato, diced
  Salt and pepper to taste
⅛ teaspoon crushed red pepper
1 pound manfrigoli
  Freshly grated pecorino Romano or other sharp cheese to taste

1. In a small saucepan, sauté the garlic in the oil over medium heat and immediately add the red bell pepper and eggplant. Cook over medium to low heat for 8 to 10 minutes, then add the tomatoes. Season with the salt, pepper, and red pepper flakes.
2. Remove and reserve half the sauce in a warm bowl. Toss the well-drained *manfrigoli* in half the sauce in the saucepan, then plate up in warm bowls and top with the other half of the sauce. Garnish with pecorino Romano or another grated sharp cheese.

YIELD: *4 servings*

Fusilli Delicati

FUSILLI WITH SPRING VEGETABLES

These are the short *fusilli* (corkscrews) called *fusilli corti* and are sauced with what some might call a *primavera* (spring vegetable) sauce. For better presentation and taste all the vegetables are cut the same length as the fusilli.

½ cup zucchini sticks (¼ to ½ inch thick), blanched
½ cup carrot sticks
½ cup asparagus tips (cut to same length as fusilli)
½ cup thinly sliced scallions
1 cup peas (if frozen, thawed)
2 tablespoons unsalted butter
1 tablespoon extra virgin olive oil
1 teaspoon dried chervil
1 cup finely chopped fresh parsley
1 cup Brodo di Verdure (see pages 87–88)
1 tablespoon arrowroot slurry (dissolve 1 tablespoon arrowroot in 2 tablespoons water)
1 pound fusilli corti

1. Blanch all vegetables in gently boiling water or a vegetable stock for 1 to 3 minutes, drain, and set aside.
2. Place the butter and oil in a saucepan over low to medium heat. When the butter foams, add the vegetables and stir in the chervil and half the parsley. Add the vegetable stock and simmer for a few minutes, slightly reducing the stock and cooking the vegetables. Do not overcook the vegetables.

3. Add the arrowroot and water mixture by the teaspoonful and bring the sauce to a boil (remember root starches do not thicken until the liquid they are in boils). Be careful to add only a little at a time. The goal here is an almost imperceptible thickening of the watery broth into a sauce.

4. When you achieve the right consistency, remove half the sauce to a warm bowl. Toss well-drained, steaming hot *fusilli* with the sauce in the saucepan and coat well, then plate in warm bowls and top with the remaining sauce and parsley. Serve immediately.

NOTE: The freshness of the sauce is better left without a grating of cheese, but if you want cheese, parmigiano is the one to use.

YIELD: *4 servings*

Sverzini al Limone

SVERZINI WITH LEMON SAUCE

Lemon-sauced pasta seems to be so popular today that I feel compelled to include my own recipe for it. I've found that a very thin spaghetti-type pasta, called *sverzini*, with very slight ridges in it works very well for the delicacy of this dish. If you can't find it, *vermicelli* will also do very nicely.

> 3 to 4 *lemons for thinly julienned lemon rind*
>
> 3 to 4 *lemons for finely diced rind and freshly strained juice*

> 1 *cup water*
>
> 2 *tablespoons unsalted butter*
>
> 1 *tablespoon extra virgin olive oil*
>
> 1 *tablespoon chopped fresh dill*
>
> 1 *tablespoon chopped fresh mint*
>
> ½ *teaspoon dried dillweed*
>   *Salt and pepper to taste*
>
> 1 *tablespoon arrowroot slurry (dissolve 1 tablespoon arrowroot in 2 tablespoons water)*
>
> 1 *pound sverzini*

1. Blanch the julienne lemon strips in a cup of water, reserving the water for the sauce and half the strips and half the diced rind for a final garnish.

2. Heat the butter and oil in a large saucepan over medium-low heat. When the butter foams, add half the blanched lemon rind, the lemon juice, fresh dill, mint, dried dill, salt, and pepper.

3. Reduce the liquid slightly by turning up the heat and bringing the sauce to a gentle boil. Then add the arrowroot and water mixture a teaspoon at a time, being careful not to make the sauce too thick.

4. Remove and reserve half the sauce in a warm bowl. Toss well-drained, steaming hot pasta with the sauce in the saucepan, then place in warm bowls and top with the remaining sauce and the julienne of lemon and the diced rind. Serve immediately.

YIELD: *4 servings*

Mezze Maniche al Cavolfiore

MEZZE MANICHE WITH CAULIFLOWER SAUCE

Here's a gilded lily recipe if ever there was one.

> 1 medium-size head cauliflower, in small florets
> 2 tablespoons unsalted butter
> 1 medium-size red bell pepper, in short julienne strips
> ½ cup olive oil
> Salt and pepper to taste
> 3 cups heavy cream
> 6 to 8 fresh basil leaves, torn
> 1 tablespoon chopped fresh tarragon
> 1 tablespoon diced lemon rind
> 1 jumbo egg, hard-cooked and diced
> 1 cup croutons (tiny cubes, not crumbs) sautéed in 1 tablespoon unsalted butter
> 2 medium-size ripe tomatoes, diced
> 2 large cloves garlic, bled (scored)
> ½ cup chopped toasted hazelnuts
> ⅛ to ¼ teaspoon crushed red pepper
> 1 pound mezze maniche
> ½ to 1 cup freshly grated parmigiano

1. Cook the cauliflower in enough salted water to cover over medium heat for 3 to 5 minutes; it should be somewhat tender, but not cooked through. Drain and toss with 1 tablespoon of the butter. Set aside.

2. Sauté the julienne strips of red bell pepper in a third of the oil in a small saucepan over medium heat for 3 to 5 minutes. Season with salt and pepper and set aside in a small bowl.

3. Pour the cream in a large, heavy skillet and reduce by a third over medium heat. Add the basil, tarragon, and lemon rind, stir and then set aside in a medium-sized bowl.

4. Sauté the croutons in the remaining 1 tablespoon butter in a medium-sized saucepan over medium heat until light brown. Set aside in a small bowl.

5. Sauté the tomatoes in another ⅓ of the oil with one of the garlic cloves in a medium-sized saucepan over medium heat and combine with the cream mixture.

6. Sauté the cauliflower in the remaining oil with the other garlic clove in a large saucepan over medium heat for about 3 to 5 minutes. Add the croutons, hazelnuts, red pepper julienne, red pepper flakes, and stir. Then add half the cream, basil, tarragon, and tomato mix, and let heat through.

7. In a warm bowl, toss well-drained, hot pasta with half the sauce and half the parmigiano. Place the pasta in warm bowls and top with the remaining sauce, cream and tomato mixture, and parmigiano. Serve immediately.

Variation
•

A simpler version of this is to just toss the croutons and the blanched cauliflower with some diced anchovies in a sauté of butter.

YIELD: *4 servings*

·SALSE BIANCHE·
WHITE SAUCES

❦

Making a basic white sauce might not be as easy as rolling off a log, but it's close to it. A little butter and flour to make a roux and some milk cooked over low heat, and you have it. In Italian it's called *balsamella,* in French béchamel. If you add cheese and wine, and traditionally start with a bit of diced veal and onion or shallot in the butter, you have a *mornaia,* or mornay sauce. A *vellutata,* or in French and international cooking language velouté, simply has chicken stock, veal stock, or fish stock added to the basic roux instead of milk.

Aside from these academic distinctions there are very practical uses for these sauces. Quite frequently in Italy, they are enriched with wine and truffles to serve as bases for a host of dishes that work particularly well in the oven. For example, a lasagne that requires long cooking at moderately high heat needs the stability of a white sauce rather than cream, since cream would tend to soak into the noodles and make them mushy. But it is not only stability that makes these sauces valuable to any cuisine. They provide the rich, creamy contrasts that can be used in hundreds of dishes to make more interesting menus and provide a certain delicacy that is otherwise unobtainable. In this regard, *sogliole alla parmigiana,* a favorite treatment of sole, immediately comes to mind. Hot fish stock is poured over fish fillets to poach them for under a minute. Then, the fillets are placed in a casserole with a light fish stock based mornay sauce under and over (lightly, mind you) them. It is topped with a parmigiano whipped cream and parmigiano, then browned under a broiler. Brown, bubbly, and yet lusciously delicate, this dish always brings out those soul-satisfying comments that are so pleasant to hear.

The following recipes provide the basics. There is nothing, however, to prevent you from adding different wines, cheeses, and aromatics to expand these sauces. For that matter, you can also combine them with other sauces to make interesting combinations. But whatever you do with these sauces, think light and make sure you cook out the flour in the roux without browning it. Add the milk, wine, chicken, veal, or fish stock warm or cool, but not hot-hot, or ice cold, to avoid lumpiness or excess fat solids. The ratio of butter (or other fat) to flour in the making of a roux is 50/50 and it takes a quarter of a pound of roux to a quart of milk to make a quart of white sauce. The ratio goes up or down depending on whether you want a thicker or thinner sauce.

Arrowroot and cornstarch can also be used as thickeners in making white sauces. They require much less to thicken equally; generally you need half as much arrowroot or cornstarch as you would flour. White sauces made with these starches, however, are not as stable as those made with a flour-based roux and, because they break down from prolonged cooking, will not serve you well in lasagne or other long-cooked oven dishes. Remember that you also control the thinness or thickness of a sauce by reduction, so it is not necessary to rely solely on the roux to achieve a desired texture.

To change these sauces, finish them in various ways. Swirl cream and/or butter in at the end and/or pass them through a cheesecloth set in a china cap for a further satinizing finish. In the beginning, however, exercise restraint till you see the result. You can always add more cream, butter, or cheese after you observe what has happened from your first addition. As usual, remember:

"Start with the finest natural ingredients, cook with love, knowledge and devotion . . ."

Balsamella

WHITE SAUCE

1 tablespoon diced white onion or shallot
8 tablespoons (1 stick) unsalted butter
  Salt to taste
  Freshly ground white pepper to taste
½ teaspoon freshly grated nutmeg
  Pinch of cayenne
1 cup all-purpose flour
1 quart whole (not skimmed) milk, scalded
1 small bay leaf

1. In a large saucepan, sauté the onion in the butter over medium heat till translucent, not brown.
2. Season lightly with some of the salt, pepper, nutmeg, and cayenne. Mix and turn the heat as low as it will go.
3. Add the flour in thirds, whisking the while. When fully amalgamated, set on low heat with diffusers to cook evenly and slowly without browning (3 to 5 minutes). In other words, cook out the cereal taste of the flour.
4. Add the hot scalded milk in thirds, whisking all the while, then the rest of the seasonings. When fully amalgamated, let cook for another 10 to 15 minutes.
5. If making for *lasagne,* use directly. If needed for something finer, strain through a cheesecloth set in a china cap. If you want a finer sauce still, strain it again. Brush the top of the sauce with melted butter; this will prevent a skin from forming. *Balsamella* will hold in the refrigerator for 3 or 4 days; *do not* freeze.

YIELD: *1 quart*

Mornaia

MORNAY SAUCE

1 tablespoon diced white onion or shallot
3 ounces best available white veal, diced
8 tablespoons (1 stick) unsalted butter
  Salt to taste
  Freshly ground white pepper to taste
½ teaspoon freshly grated nutmeg
  Pinch of cayenne
1 cup all-purpose flour
1 quart whole milk, scalded and hot
½ cup best available dry white wine
1 small bay leaf
1 cup freshly grated parmigiano

1. In a large saucepan, sauté the onion and veal in the butter over medium heat till the onion is translucent and the veal has lost its pinkness; *do not* allow either to brown.
2. Season lightly with some of the salt, pepper, nutmeg, and cayenne. Mix and turn the heat down as low as it will go.
3. Add the flour in thirds, whisking all the while till smooth. Let cook, without browning, for 3 to 5 minutes.
4. Add the hot scalded milk in thirds, whisking all the while, and then add the wine and the rest of the seasonings. When fully amalgamated, stir in the parmigiano till fully incorporated. Let cook for another 10 to 15 minutes.
5. If making for use in *lasagne,* use the sauce just as it is. If it is needed for something finer, strain through cheesecloth set in a china cap (conical strainer). If you want a still finer sauce, strain it again.

YIELD: *1 quart*

Vellutata

VELOUTÉ

Once again, this is basically the same as *balsamella* except we use chicken, veal, or fish stock instead of milk. If you later finish the sauce with cream, or milk, and cheese it becomes a mornay based on a chicken, veal, or fish *vellutata*.

1 tablespoon diced white onion

3 ounces veal, chicken, or fish, diced

8 tablespoons (1 stick) unsalted butter
  Salt to taste
  White pepper to taste

¼ teaspoon freshly grated nutmeg
  Pinch of cayenne

1 cup all-purpose flour

1 quart Fondo Bianco, Brodo di Pollo, or
  Brodo di Pesce (see pages 89–91)

1 small bay leaf

¼ cup best available dry white wine

1. In a large saucepan, sauté the onion and veal in the butter over medium heat till the onion is translucent and the veal has lost its pinkness; *do not* allow either to brown.
2. Season lightly with some of the salt, pepper, nutmeg, and cayenne, just a little part of the whole. Mix and turn the heat down as low as it will go.
3. Add the flour in thirds, whisking all the while till smooth. Let cook, without browning, for 3 to 5 minutes.
4. Add the stock in thirds, whisking all the while, then add the wine and the rest of the seasonings. Let cook for another 10 to 15 minutes.

5. If making for use in *lasagne,* use the sauce just as it is. If it is needed for something finer, strain through cheesecloth set in a china cap (conical strainer). If you want it still finer, strain it again.

YIELD: *1 quart*

·BURRO FUSO·
BUTTER SAUCES

Ravioli di ricotta e spinaci—burro fuso con parmigiano . . . There aren't many menus in Italy that don't have this dish, particularly in the north. And what they mean by *burro fuso* is a liaison of melted butter with cheese. It's that simple and that good! It extends itself to all kinds of pasta with all kinds of aromatics. The king of the *burro fuso* dishes, of course, is Fettucine Alfredo.

Whether the butter is simply melted or browned with capers, anchovies, pine nuts, walnuts, or other ingredients and/or whether aromatics are used, there is usually a fusion with parmigiano.

The amazing thing about these sauces is that in spite of their extreme simplicity they are never boring. I don't believe a week goes by in my life without some pasta *burro fuso*. I'll provide you with a favorite recipe of mine as an example which should set you off in indulging in your own imaginative creations.

YIELD: *4 servings*

FETTUCCINE ALFREDO

There is a story in connection with this dish that I think is worth repeating. When I first arrived in Italy to live, some friends and I decided to eat at the famous "original" Alfredo's of Rome. We were all living in Siena and planned a day trip to Rome. We forgot to bring the guidebook that warned us there were now three "original" Alfredo's in Rome and only one of them, which was not the original, was any good. It seems the original owner had died and relatives, a former head waiter, and a stranger were running the three different establishments, all claiming to be the original "original." Unfortunately, when we arrived in Rome we couldn't remember which was which and after explaining the predicament to a taxi driver were whisked to:

"Senz'altro questo è l'originale, lo so, lo so." Without doubt the original, I know! I know!

We entered somewhat reassured and it wasn't long before the head waiter settled the question quite emphatically.

"You will of course want our famous Fettuccine Alfredo," he intoned imperiously.

Out came a bowl of noodles which he immediately dumped into a cold unattractive stainless steel bowl—the kind of restaurant supply house equipment that is reserved for utilitarian purposes in the back of the house. When asked about the gold spoon, he sneeringly snapped, "A myth. We don't need a gold spoon. This pasta is gold."

Whereupon he practically flung some cut-up pieces of very suspicious (yellow—like margarine) looking butter in the bowl with the noodles and began to beat them vigorously with two steel kitchen spoons. Supposed parmigiano was also flung into the bowl to be accompanied by the same angry beating as before. The plates were then flung in front of us and, "Now you are privileged to eat the original Fettuccine Alfredo."

One of the ladies in our party was born in Modena and brought up in Bologna, where proper *tagliatelle* making is still taught to little girls before they even enter grade school. After one bite, she began to shake her head vigorously.

"No! No! It's terrible. They're overcooked and salty. The butter has salt in it," she lamented incredulously.

The head waiter, who had not moved away from serving, stepped forward as if to hit the lady. And by God, I'm not sure that he wouldn't have had not my friend and I risen in righteous indignation and forcefully escorted him away from the table. Mad, absolutely mad! Screaming, in English, "What you tourists know. You never eatta so good inna yu life."

Needless to say, we left.

When you have a dish as simple as this one, the quality of the ingredients stands out dramatically. You must have properly made and cooked egg noodles, the freshest and richest sweet butter possible, and freshly grated parmigiano reggiano—the king of all cheeses. That's all there is to the dish—noodles, butter, and cheese, which can be embellished by nutmeg and black pepper. But even if the ingredients are the best, the dish must be made carefully with love and devotion. Some of the butter has to be melted so the noodles can be tossed gently, the bowl must be hot, the rest of the butter near melting, and these ingredients, as well as the cheese, must be added in three applications so that the fettuccine are well coated. It's all done very rapidly and lightly and served in hot plates. As simple as this dish is, I never tire of it and will probably have fettuccine or another pasta "Alfredo" once a week for the rest of my life.

Fettuccine Alfredo (not the original)

12 tablespoons (1½ sticks) best available unsalted butter

1 pound freshly made fettuccine or tagliatelle

1½ cups freshly grated parmigiano reggiano

*Freshly grated nutmeg to taste
(optional)*
Black pepper to taste (optional)

1. While heating a bowl large enough for tossing the pasta in, an oversized fork and spoon, and the serving plates, melt half the butter and cook and drain the *fettuccine* or *tagliatelle* pasta.
2. Place the pasta gently in the warm bowl, pour a third of the warm butter over it, and toss lightly. Add a third of the parmigiano and continue to toss lightly.
3. Repeat the procedure with another third of the butter and parmigiano.
4. Add the nutmeg and black pepper and repeat the procedure with the remaining butter and parmigiano.
5. Top with grated parmigiano and serve immediately in warm bowls.

Variation

•

Try adding shaved truffles or toasted pine nuts.

Yield: *4 servings*

Burro Fuso con Acciughe e Pane Grattugiato

FUSED BUTTER WITH ANCHOVY AND BREAD CRUMBS

½ cup bread crumbs
1½ to 2 cups freshly grated parmigiano
Salt and pepper to taste

*¼ to ⅓ pound (1 to 1⅔ sticks) unsalted
butter*
Juice of ½ lemon
6 to 8 anchovy fillets, chopped
2 tablespoons capers
⅛ teaspoon crushed red pepper
1 cup finely chopped fresh parsley
*1 pound shell macaroni or other
similar pasta*
1 cup toasted croutons

1. Toss the bread crumbs with 1 cup of the parmigiano, and season with salt and pepper.
2. Melt the butter in a medium-sized saucepan and brown slightly over medium heat. Stir in the lemon juice. Add the anchovies and capers, season with the black and red pepper, and then add one half the parsley.
3. In a warm bowl, toss well-drained, steaming pasta with half the butter sauce. Add the seasoned bread crumbs and half the croutons, tossing all the while.
4. Plate in warm bowls and top with the remaining butter sauce, parmigiano, and parsley.
5. Serve immediately.

Yield: *4 servings*

•SALSE ALLA PANNA•
CREAM SAUCES

Alla panna (with cream) in its purest state would simply be warm cream; or, taking it a step further, an infusion of parmigiano into a reduction of cream.

Naturally, the use of cream sauces is not limited to pasta dishes, but since heavy cream evaporates readily, they're not very practical for dishes requiring long cooking where the stability of a balsamella or vellutata is more suitable. Pasta is a natural for cream sauces since only a slight reduction is necessary. The three most famous *alla panna* dishes in Italy are *tortellini alla panna, paglia e fieno,* and *rigatoni alla norcina.*

Once you understand these three, it should be no problem for you to give reign to your own creative imaginings.

Tortellini alla Panna

TORTELLINI IN CREAM SAUCE

Throughout the centuries there are writers who proclaimed, "It wouldn't be Italy without *tortellini alla panna.*" Tortellini are those wonderful ring-shaped pasta filled with delicious forcemeats and so often served with a reduction of heavy cream infused with parmigiano.

> 4 tablespoons (½ stick) unsalted butter
> 2 cups freshly grated parmigiano (reggiano preferred)
>   Salt to taste
> ⅛ teaspoon freshly ground pepper, or to taste
> ⅛ teaspoon freshly grated nutmeg, or to taste
>   Pinch of cayenne (optional)
> 2 cups heavy cream
> 1 to 2 pounds tortellini, preferably homemade

1. In a large saucepan, melt the butter over medium heat and stir in 1 tablespoon of the par-migiano and a touch of the salt, pepper, nutmeg, and cayenne.

2. Add the heavy cream in thirds, whisking all the while, and then add 1 cup of the parmigiano, stirring till fully incorporated. Add the remaining seasonings. Reduce by one third, stirring all the while.

3. Remove half the sauce to another saucepan set on very low heat. Toss well-drained, steaming hot tortellini in the saucepan with half the remaining parmigiano. Plate in warm bowls and top with the remaining sauce and parmigiano. Serve immediately.

YIELD: *4 servings*

Paglia e Fieno

STRAW AND HAY

For all its sophistication and prettiness, *paglia e fieno* is basically a rustic dish inspired by the incredible quality of the produce, hams, and cheese of the regions of Emilia Romagna and the mountains to the north. Its literal translation, "straw and hay," refers to the plain egg noodles (the straw) and the spinach noodles (signifying the green hay fresh from the fields). So this dish comes to us "fresh from the fields" with the wonderful smoky flavor of air-cured prosciutto contrasted with sweet green peas set in rich farm-fresh cream and laced with parmigiano. Oh, and don't forget the butter, because it's really a *burro fuso* with prosciutto, peas, and cream. Sounds rather rich? Not a bit! That's the genius of the combination of these wonderful natural ingredients.

Traditionally, this dish is made with *tagliolini* and not *fettuccine* or *tagliatelle* as is seen so often in the United States. *Tagliolini* are very thin noodles, just a step or two above *capelli d'angeli* (angels' hair), and require quick, careful, gentle handling to prevent them from sticking together or gumming up. Use plenty of boiling salted water and stir with a long fork frequently to separate them. When tossing with cream and cheese, use a many-pronged spaghetti fork or similar utensil to avoid mishandling.

    4 *tablespoons (½ stick) unsalted butter*
    2 *cups freshly grated parmigiano (reggiano preferred)*
   ⅛ *teaspoon freshly grated nutmeg*
      Freshly ground black pepper to taste
4 to 6 *ounces short julienned prosciutto (⅔ to 1 cup)*
    2 *cups heavy cream*
      Salt to taste
6 to 8 *ounces fresh or frozen peas*
   ½ *pound tagliolini (½ pound green noodles), preferably homemade*

1. In a large saucepan, melt the butter over a moderate heat and stir in a bit of the parmigiano, nutmeg, and pepper. Add the prosciutto and cook lightly for 1 to 2 minutes, without browning the ham or the butter.

2. Add the cream, 1 cup of the parmigiano, and the remaining seasonings and turn the heat up to medium-high. Reduce the sauce by one third, whisking all the while.

3. If the peas are frozen, they need only to be blanched in salted water for 1 or 2 minutes. If fresh, they will have to be cooked in water till tender. Once cooked or blanched, drain thoroughly and add to the sauce.

4. Remove half the sauce to another saucepan over low heat. Add the well-drained, hot *tagliolini* to the saucepan with a bit of the remaining cheese and toss carefully and gently. Adjust the season-

ings if necessary. Plate in warm bowls and top with the remaining sauce and parmigiano. Serve immediately.

YIELD: *4 servings*

Rigatoni alla Norcia

RIGATONI WITH CREAM AND SAUSAGE, NORCIA STYLE

When I first had this Umbrian cream sauce speciality, I was pleasantly surprised by the pieces of crumbled sausage, flecks of red pepper, and diced lemon rind that combined with a very *stretto* or *concentrato* (concentrated) cream sauce to make the most unusual rigatoni presentation I had seen. Of course, if you add some diced truffles as well, so much the better and certainly in keeping with the character of Norcia, the center of the black truffle industry in Italy.

    4 *tablespoons (½ stick) unsalted butter*
    2 *cups freshly grated parmigiano*
      Pinch freshly grated nutmeg
      Ground black pepper to taste
 Two *4- to 5-ounce sausages, crumbled*
 1½ *cups heavy cream*
    1 *scant tablespoon grated lemon rind*
      Salt to taste
   ¼ *teaspoon crushed red pepper*
    1 *pound rigatoni or other large macaroni with lines*

1. In a large saucepan, over a moderate heat, melt the butter and stir in a bit of parmigiano, nutmeg, and pepper.

2. Add the crumbled sausage meat and cook until any pinkness is gone; be careful not to brown the butter or sausage.

3. Add the cream, 1 cup of the parmigiano, the lemon rind, and the rest of the seasonings.

4. Remove half the sauce to another saucepan over low heat. Add the well-drained, hot *rigatoni* to the saucepan with a bit of the remaining cheese and toss gently and carefully. Adjust the seasonings; reseason if necessary. Plate in warm bowls, and top with the remaining sauce and parmigiano. Serve immediately.

YIELD: *4 servings*

·BURRI COMPOSTI·
COMPOUND BUTTERS

Compound butters are important to those who wish to produce a full range of taste sensations when they cook. A bit of anchovy butter made with anchovies, lemon juice, white pepper, and cayenne makes a wonderful additive to many otherwise plain presentations, as will the rest of these creamed butters.

A general rule of thumb for quantities of additives is 2 tablespoons of fine diced or pureed herbs, green vegetables, tuna, capers, anchovies, mustard, garlic, or sundried tomato, to ¼ pound (1 stick) of unsalted butter. (Mustard butter seems to work best when equal parts of dry and Dijon mustard are used.) The lemon juice, cayenne, salt (or not), and white pepper are in "to taste" quantities.

The best method for making compound butters is to warm the butter to room temperature first so that it is easily creamed. *Do not heat it.* Mix thoroughly to work the ingredients in. Place the

mixture on a piece of parchment, wax paper, or aluminum foil, and roll it into a 2-inch thick log. Seal both edges tightly and keep refrigerated. Slice off as much as is needed for use without opening the paper, since it is easily removed from the individual slices. Compound butters will keep in the refrigerator for a week; *do not freeze.*

YIELD: *½ cup*

Burro di Acciughe

ANCHOVY BUTTER

2   tablespoons minced anchovy fillets (about 12 fillets or 1 can)

1   tablespoon oil from anchovy can
    White pepper to taste
    Pinch of cayenne

⅛ teaspoon fresh lemon juice

8   tablespoons (1 stick) unsalted butter, softened to room temperature

1. Combine all the ingredients in a medium-sized bowl and cream with a wooden spoon or in a food processor.

YIELD: *½ cup*

Caper Butter

¼ cup large capers, finely minced
⅛ teaspoon fresh lemon juice
⅛ teaspoon cayenne
   Salt and pepper to taste
4 tablespoons (½ stick) unsalted butter, softened to room temperature

1. Combine all the ingredients in a medium-sized bowl and cream with a wooden spoon or in a food processor.

YIELD: ½ cup

Maionese della Casa

MAYONNAISE OF THE HOUSE

Mayonnaise is basically an emulsification of oil into egg yolks. The addition of lemon juice, vinegar, salt, pepper, cayenne, and sugar are optional, as is the type of oil used. As usual, the choice depends on what you're after. There are those who prefer the lighter vegetable oils to make a milder product, while others will reach for the greenest, richest tasting, extra virgin, cold-pressed olive oils to produce a heavier dressing that is practically green in color. In between lie a dozen degrees of intensity of flavor.

Choose the lightness or intensity of the oil depending on what the mayonnaise is to be used for. The vegetable oils make a nice light all-pur-pose dressing, flavored differently depending on type, with safflower being the lightest (and most expensive).

The range of olive oils is even broader. From the light yellow-gold Tuscan oils to the opaque green Calabrian extra virgin oils, your choice will depend on the accompanying dish. A lighter, golden, extra virgin is right as a dip for cold steamed vegetables eaten al fresco. A heartier oil is perhaps better suited as a sauce to accompany cold lamb or hot grilled scampi.

While purists will decry the addition of pepper and cayenne, and shout "criminal!" to those who add sugar, there is complete agreement that the fresher and richer the egg yolks, the better the mayonnaise. While we see no damning objection to the use of sugar if you want a sweeter product for certain types of salads or vegetables, nonetheless our own preferred recipe is without sugar. The hue and cry, incidentally, about commercial mayonnaise is that it contains too much sugar.

2 egg yolks, as fresh as possible
2 cups extra virgin olive oil (lighter yellow preferred)
   Salt to taste
1 tablespoon fresh lemon juice or white wine vinegar
   Cayenne to taste
   White pepper to taste

1. All the ingredients and equipment (the whisk and a bowl) should be at room temperature unless you are working in above 90°F summer heat, in which case, refrigerate everything slightly before using. Warm ingredients will not thicken whereas cold ingredients will not emulsify.
2. Beat the egg yolks thoroughly with a fork and then add the oil in miniscule drops, whisking all the while to incorporate. Do not add more oil until the first addition is completely emulsified. Continue to add oil in this manner until you

reach the desired consistency. Do not rush or increase the flow of oil.

3. Dissolve the salt in the lemon juice and add cayenne and white pepper, if desired. Drop by drop whisk the lemon juice into the emulsification, being careful again to incorporate each addition totally before adding more. Refrigerate the mayonnaise until needed; it will keep in the refrigerator about 10 days.

NOTE: If the weather is warm and the mayonnaise is slightly thin, it will thicken in the refrigerator. If the sauce breaks, not to worry. Simply beat another egg yolk and add the broken or curdled sauce to the egg yolk and it should restabilize. If it doesn't, we're afraid you'll have to start all over again.

The variations on mayonnaise are as rich as your imagination, and include every known herb, pickle, spice, fumet, or whatever.

For example, add a bit of curry and you have *salsa all'indiana,* or some whipped cream folded in and it's called *chantilly,* or if you add diced gherkins, anchovy paste, mustard, capers, parsley, thyme, basil, chervil, and tarragon, and sometimes a few drops of a fumet made from the main ingredient such as mussels, the result is *salsa remolata.*

YIELD: *2 cups*

Aïoli

GARLIC MAYONNAISE

Use this for tuna tartar, salmon, and *carpaccio.*

¼ *cup plus 3 tablespoons virgin olive oil*

¼ *cup plus 3 tablespoons Maionese della Casa (see above) or store-bought mayonnaise*

2 *tablespoons fresh lemon juice*

4 *cloves garlic, diced and squeezed through a garlic press*

1 *tablespoon dry mustard*

½ *teaspoon ground cumin*

1 *teaspoon ground coriander*

1 *teaspoon ground cardamom*

Pinch of cayenne

2 *tablespoons chopped fresh parsley*

Salt and freshly ground black pepper to taste

1. Whisk the oil into the mayonnaise in a large mixing bowl.

2. Add all ingredients in the order listed, and mix well.

3. Let marinate, refrigerated, for at least 4 hours before using.

YIELD: *1 cup*

Pesto

Salse verdi (green sauces)—sauces made of herbs and lemon juice or vinegar—were found in ancient Rome and then again in the Renaissance.

They were, and are still, used to accompany one-dimensional dishes such as grilled meat or fish, or a *bollito misto* (mixed boiled meats), to provide a balance between a savory and tart accent for these otherwise plain entrees.

The addition of nuts and cheese, and other ingredients, was also quite pervasive and led to the development of the now world-famous *pesto alla genovese,* a sauce that is recognized everywhere and appears on hundreds of menus of restaurants in America. Unfortunately, it's not always (or perhaps hardly ever would be more apt) a *pesto alla genovese* made in the classic style, with a mortar and pestle, using only the youngest and most tender tiny leaves of a special basil plant that I've not encountered in America.

This is not to say that any sauce of pounded, chopped, ground, or torn basil leaves of any plant, of any age, won't serve to make a delicious sauce. The distinctions are subtle and refined . . . but worth it if you can grow the real thing.

There are also such subsidiary questions as the addition of spinach leaves and parsley to stabilize the green color. There is nothing discreditable in this, since it is common practice today in Genoa, where pesto originated. From personal experience, we've found these ingredients help to preserve the pretty green color that otherwise will blacken if the basil is unassisted. The important thing is to use them sparingly so that they don't weaken or change the flavor of the fresh basil.

Everyone agrees on the necessity for the best virgin oils and the use of parmigiano and pecorino cheeses, although the ratio may change from recipe to recipe, as will the amount of garlic needed. Pine nuts are also agreed upon, while the addition of walnuts seems to be disputed by the less knowledgeable. I say less knowledgeable because walnuts are definitely used in Genoa, and always have been.

The use of butter, while encountered in so-called reliable cookbooks, seems to us way off the mark, and upon due enquiry, found to be a modern addition, having nothing to do with the original Genoese pesto.

The omission of acid (lemon or vinegar) in this sauce opens a broad spectrum of uses that were not previously possible. But from there begins a multitude of applications in soups, lasagne, breads, pizzas, eggs, potatoes, *gnocchi,* and wherever else one could desire . . . although I don't think it could ever become my favorite flavor for ice cream.

The truly wonderful thing about pesto is that it will store easily in or out of the refrigerator and will keep for a month if you put a covering of oil on the top of the jar and keep it out of the sun.

There's a hard way and an easy way to make pesto. If you have the time and elbow grease, a hand-ground pesto made in a mortar and with a pestle is the ultimate method for this dish. The bruising of the leaves and gradual breakdown into a sauce in this manner imparts more aromatic flavor than any other technique. But you do need a half hour of continual pounding to achieve it. Two or three pulses of a Cuisinart or other good kitchen machine will, however, produce a satisfactory product which, according to your taste, can be very smooth or somewhat rough, as we personally prefer it. A combination of both rough and smooth (half and half) releases all of the juice of the basil and yet leaves you with an interesting textural sauce rather than a puree.

40 to 60 *fresh basil leaves (depending on size)*

2 *tablespoons pine nuts*

1 *tablespoon pistachios*

1 *tablespoon walnuts*

½ *cup freshly grated parmigiano*

¼ *cup freshly grated pecorino Romano*

2 *ounces chopped, drained spinach*

½ *cup extra virgin olive oil*

Salt and fresh ground pepper to taste

1. Mix all ingredients together in a large bowl in the order listed, then place in a blender one third at a time. Puree to the desired consistency, periodically scraping down the sides of the blender with a spatula. This can be kept in the refrigerator in a tightly covered jar with a bit of oil on top.

2. When serving heat the pesto gently with a little butter until softened, then place approximately 1 tablespoon in the center of a plate of hot, well-buttered noodles.

Each person should toss his or her own pesto with a fork and spoon. Serve with freshly grated parmigiano and freshly ground black pepper.

YIELD: *2 cups*

RISI E POLENTA

Rice and Polenta

RICE AND POLENTA

RISO · RICE

Rice, unlike many ingredients in Italy that have pre-Christian origins, is a relative newcomer to Italian cuisine. Although the Romans knew about rice through the traders and expeditionary forces that had made contact with India centuries before, rice wasn't cultivated in Roman times. It is reputed to have been brought by the Arabs through Spain to Sicily in the ninth or tenth century A.D., but didn't appear in recipes with any frequency in Italy until the Renaissance in the 1400s, when the vast rice production of the Po Valley began. Today, Italy is the largest producer of rice in Europe at about a million tons a year.

Italian rice evidently presents a confusing picture to many authorities, so disparate are their views. I won't name names to spare embarrassment, but here is a sampling from some famous cooking authors.

"The best rice for risotto is Italian Arborio, a long grained rice . . ."

"Medium grain rice is particularly suitable for risotto since it is slightly starchier than long grain. Arborio is the best for this purpose."

"Italian short grain rice (arborio) is the best choice for risotto if it is available."

"Superfino, a long grain rice (⅕ inch), is ideal for risotto. The best varieties of superfino are Arborio, Roma, and Canaroli."

I suppose the confusion comes from the fact that Italian "fino" and "superfino" rices are fatter and bigger looking than other rice and therefore appear to be long grained and/or short grained depending on what you're normally accustomed to seeing. They're definitely "bigger" than other rices. The truth of the matter is that the rice Italians prefer for making risotto is a species of medium grained rice with larger than normal dimensions in width.

There are many varieties of fino and superfino that are better rices for risotto. The best are:

Fino—Europa and RB

Superfino—Arborio, Canaroli, Roma

If I had to make a choice for the best risotto possible it would be Arborio of the superfino class. But any of these rices will make good risotto because these thicker, fatter, medium grain rices have more starch and will withstand the longer, slower cooking necessary to properly infuse risotto with the particular flavor you're after—beef, veal, chicken, fish, mushrooms, truffles, or vegetables—without gumming up.

To make puddings and other desserts *originario* works very well since it absorbs liquids more readily and clings together better, which is desirable in those cases. Semifino is the preferred rice in Italy for soups and salads because of its middle ground nature as to separation of kernels and absorption of liquids. But risotto is the King of rice dishes in Italy and one of the superfinos is the rice of choice.

There is also this much misunderstood theory of stirring. Misbeguided amateurs will tell you that it is absolutely essential to stir the risotto continually as you might do for polenta or in making ice cream. Nonsense! A thorough stir at the addition of each liquid application is more than enough. I've been making risotto for thirty-five years and never paid more than minimal attention to stirring. And in all my years as a chef and a consultant I've never seen a professional chef hovering over a pot of risotto and stirring constantly as he might when skimming a stock. No, my dears, somebody got it all wrong and they have been perpetuating this mistake ever since—in book after book, article after article, ad nauseam.

Risotto should, however, be served immediately upon completion, or else the grains will continue to cook.

The key ingredient in making any kind of risotto is the liquid. It's worth the effort to have the best homemade beef, chicken, veal, fish, game, or vegetable stock available. In fact, as in making a good *velutatta*, you are even better served by using specific accents rather than generic, such as shrimp stock for shrimp risotto (not fish stock); veal stock for a risotto with veal sweetbreads; and a vegetable stock with extra zucchini to make a risotto with zucchini and zucchini flowers instead of just regular vegetable stock.

To carry this idea of maximizing flavor further, it is also good to introduce a bit of the main accent into the initial sauté of diced onions as we

do also with *velutattas,* for instance a few shrimp diced up; a few pieces of diced sweetbreads; or a few zucchini flowers and pieces of zucchini.

Once the principles outlined above are understood it is very simple to make any kind of risotto you desire.

Risotto alla Milanese

MILANESE STYLE RISOTTO

The term "risotto" (from the Italian word for rice —*riso*) implies not just a series of recipes for rice, but a technique for cooking a specific type of rice that is unique in the world. Arborio rice is particularly suited to the sauté and braise of this technique as it is medium, very wide grained and untreated. The key to the success of this dish lies in having the rice still *al dente,* before the grains burst totally, while it remains in a creamy, saucy state. The starches in the rice thicken the broth as it reduces and is absorbed, making the timing somewhat crucial.

Some add a beaten egg, as we do here, in the final "mounting" with butter and cheese for an increased creaminess. Saffron is also added in the next to last cooking as well.

- 2 *tablespoons extra virgin olive oil*
- 2 *cups Arborio rice*
- 2 *tablespoons finely diced white onion*
- 1 *cup marrow from veal shanks*
- ½ *cup dry white wine*

6 cups *Fondo Bianco or Brodo di
Pollo, heated (see page 86 or 89)*

1½ to 2 teaspoons *saffron, pulverized with
a mortar and pestle and soaked in
1 tablespoon hot stock*

1 tablespoon *unsalted butter*

1 large *egg, beaten*

2 tablespoons *freshly grated
parmigiano*

*Salt and freshly ground pepper to
taste*

*Freshly grated parmigiano to
garnish*

1. Heat the oil over medium heat in a large sauté
pan; add and sauté the rice, tossing and stirring to
coat it with the oil.
2. Add the onion and cook till it becomes clear,
then add the marrow, tossing and stirring.
3. Deglaze with the wine, stirring thoroughly as
it sizzles, until absorbed.
4. Add 2 cups of the stock, still stirring to prevent
sticking and browning, and cook quickly until
almost all the liquid is absorbed. When the simmering liquid changes to a sizzle, or slightly
before, add another cup of stock and stir, still
over medium heat, until it's absorbed.
5. Repeat with as much of the remaining stock as
is needed, 1 cup at a time. After the third or
fourth cup, taste frequently to catch the rice just
as it becomes al dente, is still rather saucy, and
before the grains burst totally. This whole procedure will take about 20–30 minutes.
6. Add the saffron before the next to last cup of
broth is used. Incorporate it thoroughly.
7. The moment it is done, remove the pan from
the heat and stir in the butter, beaten egg, and
parmigiano. Season with salt and pepper.
8. Serve immediately with an abundance of additional grated parmigiano.

YIELD: *4 to 6 servings*

Risotto ai Gamberi

SHRIMP RISOTTO

Of all the risottos there are to make (hundreds),
if I were asked which is my favorite it would be
shrimp risotto. I think the delicacy of shrimp and
the stock made from them is the perfect ingredient to expand the natural flavor of rice without
overpowering it. Purists might decry the use of
parmigiano at the end—and I'm one of them—
but I must admit that it's not as "out of place" as
it would be on a linguine with clam sauce. No, the
delicacy of parmigiano (not pecorino) almost
matches the delicacy of the shrimp and is generally unobtrusive. To some it adds the proper finish to the dish.

The recipe I'm about to provide can easily be
applied to cooking all sorts of fish and shellfish.
To gain the proper accent make a fish stock and
then poach whatever you're using—crab, mussels, clams, bass, bluefish, trout—in it. Or you can
make stock from the main ingredient.

1 pound *shrimp, unpeeled*

5 to 6 cups *Brodo di Pesce (see page 90) or
fish and shrimp stock, heated*

2 tablespoons *olive oil*

2 cups *Arborio rice*

2 tablespoons *finely diced celery*

2 tablespoons *finely diced onion*

1 cup *aromatic white wine
Salt and pepper to taste*

1 tablespoon *unsalted butter*

1 egg, *beaten*

1 tablespoon *freshly grated parmigiano
(optional)*

1. Poach the shrimp in the simmering fish stock or a court bouillon (see page 90) for 2 to 3 minutes only.

2. Remove the shrimp from the stock, peel and dice, and set the shrimp aside for later use. Return the shrimp shells to the stock and cook for 10 to 15 minutes. Strain, clarify, and reserve.

3. Heat the oil in a sauté pan and sauté the rice, tossing and stirring to coat it with the oil. Add the celery and onion and cook briefly till the onion is translucent. Add a few diced shrimp also.

4. Deglaze with the white wine, stirring thoroughly as it sizzles and allow to be absorbed. Add 2 cups of the shrimp stock, covering the rice liberally, and still stirring to prevent sticking and browning. Cook over medium heat so that the liquid bubbles gently till it's almost absorbed.

5. Add another cup of stock, stir well, and allow to almost be absorbed again. Repeat twice more, adding 1 cup at a time. Taste the rice for doneness. (You will have added 5 cups of stock at this point.)

6. Add the shrimp and mix well before the last cup of stock.

7. Season with salt and pepper.

8. When the rice is still creamy and liquidy, remove the pan from the stove and add the butter and the beaten egg, again mixing well. Add the parmigiano if you chose it. Serve immediately in warm bowls.

YIELD: *4 to 6 servings*

Risotto con Tartufi alla Piemontese

RISOTTO WITH TRUFFLES IN THE MANNER OF PIEDMONT

The interesting thing about this risotto, aside from the use of white truffles, is that it's made with a beef and pork broth and the rice is cooked directly in the broth and then removed and tossed with butter, truffles, and parmigiano instead of the usual method of gradually adding in the stock until it's absorbed. The advantage to making the rice this way is that you don't need Arborio rice; semifino (a shorter grained rice) and others will do just as well. The white truffles are even the essence of this dish but are nonetheless replaceable with black truffles or even mushrooms should white truffles be beyond reach. The grated lemon rind and julienne strips of lemon are nice tart accents to the sweet, almost greasy taste of the broth.

BROTH

1 *pound ground beef*

4 *ounces prosciutto*

4 *ounces salt pork*

2 *cloves garlic, bled (scored)*

1 *tablespoon olive oil*

Salt and pepper to taste

1 *small carrot, peeled and coarsely chopped*

2 *ribs celery with leaves, coarsely chopped*

1 *onion*

2 *whole cloves*

8 *cups water*

1 *bay leaf*

1 *tablespoon roughly chopped*
   fresh parsley
3 *egg whites*
2 *cups rice*
1 *large white or black truffle*
   (1 ounce), with three quarters
   peeled and sliced (reserving peelings)
   and a quarter left whole and
   unpeeled
1 *teaspoon finely diced lemon rind*
½ *cup julienne strips of lemon zest*
1 *tablespoon unsalted butter*
2 *tablespoons freshly grated parmigiano*
1 *egg, beaten*
   Salt and pepper to taste

1. Sauté the meats and garlic in the oil in a large casserole. Season with salt and pepper and add the carrot, celery, and onion stuck with the 2 cloves. Cook briefly.
2. Add the water and bring to a light boil, skimming any foam as it rises to the top.
3. Cook on low heat for 1 hour, covered. Uncover and cook on low heat for another hour, reducing it by 2 cups.
4. Strain through a cheesecloth set in a china cap. Set aside to let the grease rise. When cool, blot the surface with a paper towel to remove the grease. (If you can, after degreasing refrigerate overnight and then remove the solidified fat.)
5. Set the pot over medium high heat with the egg whites. Bring to a light boil and clarify the stock (see pages 85–86 for instructions). When clarified, strain again through a cheesecloth.
6. Bring the broth to a boil and add the rice, truffle peelings, and diced lemon zest. Cook for 15 to 20 minutes, depending on the type of rice, until al dente. During the last 2 or 3 minutes of cooking add the julienned strips or rind.
7. Strain the rice and lemon from the broth and immediately toss with butter, sliced truffles, par-

migiano, and the beaten egg. Season to taste with salt and pepper. Shave more truffles on top and serve in warm bowls.

Yield: *4 to 6 portions*

Risi e Bisi

RICE AND PEAS

Bisi is a shortened Venetian dialect word for *piselli* (peas) and *risi e bisi*—not surprisingly—is a specialty of the Veneto. If you listen to Mazzotti, a fifteenth century Venetian writer, there's no *risi e bisi* outside of Venice:

A real Risi Bisi can only be found in Venice in its season. To make it well, you must follow all the rules, especially this one. The peas must be fresh (from Veneto), shelled at the last minute (purists even add that the peas must come from the vegetable farms between Chioggia and Burano, which means those which border the lagoon of Venice itself).

You prepare a soffritto of oil, butter, and chopped celery (garlic, onions, and parsley seem optional as long as the taste of celery dominates). When it is lightly browned put in the rice. You boil the pea pods separately to give flavor to the water. Moisten the rice with this water and a few tablespoons of beef and chicken consomme. After 7 or 8 minutes of cooking add the peas, stirring them until the rice has finished cooking. Two minutes before the end add grated parmigiano and serve with solicitude.

And butter, I might add.

The use of beef and chicken stock can also be improved upon by using a vegetable stock to which the pea pods have been added. I also prefer a bit of pea pods and peas in the initial sauté with the onion to maximize flavor.

I am also quite skeptical about the need for peas from Chioggia. American fresh peas will do fine and, as much as it may sound sacrilegious, I've made the dish with frozen peas and pea pods with good results. I don't attribute that opinion to a non-discerning palate and actually feel very strongly that the broth used to make this risotto will have more to do with the flavor than the peas—assuming of course that the peas are decent.

>   2 *pounds unshelled peas*
> 4 to 6 *cups Brodo di Verdure (see page 87), heated*
>   2 *tablespoons extra virgin olive oil*
>   2 *tablespoons unsalted butter*
>   2 *cups Arborio rice*
>   1 *medium-size rib celery, finely diced*
>   ½ *cup best available dry aromatic white wine*
>   *Salt and pepper to taste*
>   2 *tablespoons freshly grated parmigiano*
>   1 *large egg, beaten*

1. Shell the peas, reserving the pods, and soak them in salted water for 30 to 40 minutes.
2. Poach the peas and the pea pods in simmering vegetable stock for 30 to 40 minutes till soft and tender. Discard the pea pods except for 3 or 4, which you will dice fine. Strain and reserve. Mash or cut up 6 peas.
3. Heat the oil and 1 tablespoon of butter in a pan and add the rice, cooking over medium heat and stirring. When the rice is well coated, add the celery and cook briefly. Add the diced pea pods and the mashed peas.
4. Deglaze with the white wine, stirring thoroughly as it sizzles until absorbed.

5. Add enough stock to cover and stir thoroughly. Cook till almost all the liquid is absorbed. Add about 1 more cup of stock and cook again. Season with salt and pepper.
6. Add the peas and more liquid and stir again. Taste the rice for doneness. When the liquid is absorbed the risotto should be done. Take it off the burner and add the remaining butter, the parmigiano and the beaten egg. Correct the seasoning for salt and pepper and serve immediately in warm bowls.

NOTE: This recipe is useful for all kinds of vegetable risottos. For example, to make risotto with zucchini and zucchini flowers, simply substitute them wherever the peas and pea pods come into play in the foregoing recipe. The same would apply to leafy vegetables such as *bietola* (Swiss chard) or spinach, only they would be cooked less because of their more delicate nature.

YIELD: *4 to 6 servings*

Arancini di Sicilia

DEEP FRIED RICE BALLS

Arancini means little oranges and is used to describe risotto shaped into a ball, breaded, and deep fried. The filling at the center can be most anything and in the case of the similar *suppli al telefono* of Rome it is composed of prosciutto and mozzarella bound with egg. The *al telefono* indicates the long strands (telephone wires) of mozzarella that are visible after it is deep fried and broken open.

This version has chicken livers, veal, and peas at the center and is tinted with a bit of *profumato* (perfumed) saffron. When deep fried golden brown they make an interesting antipasto, a side dish with some soup, or a creamy entree. You can also make them the size of walnuts and pass them as finger food with a cold aperitif.

2 tablespoons olive oil

2 to 4 cloves garlic, bled (scored)

¼ pound chicken giblets or livers, finely chopped

¼ pound best available ground veal

2 tablespoons finely diced onion

2 tablespoons finely diced celery

½ teaspoon minced garlic

1 cup aromatic white wine
  Salt and pepper to taste

1 cup Salsa di Pomodoro (see page 103) or canned Italian plum tomatoes, drained

1 cup Brodo di Pollo or consommé (see pages 88–90)

1 cup peas, precooked

2 hard-cooked eggs, finely chopped

2 cups Risotto alla Milanese (see pages 130–31)

FOR THE ANGLAISE:

2 cups flour, seasoned with salt and pepper

3 jumbo eggs, beaten and seasoned with salt and pepper and a bit of parmigiano

2 cups white bread crumbs

2 quarts vegetable oil
  Lemon wedges or Marinara (see page 100) for garnish

1. Heat the oil and whole garlic over medium heat in a pan and add the chicken giblets and veal. Cook on a moderate heat. Add the onion, celery, and minced garlic and cook till the onion is translucent. Do not brown.

2. Deglaze with the white wine, allowing it to evaporate by half. Season with salt and pepper. Add the *salsa di pomodoro* and cook all for 3 to 5 minutes over a moderate heat.

3. Add the chicken stock and cook over medium-high for 3 to 5 minutes. Turn the heat to low and cook very gently for another 15 to 25 minutes, or till the sauce thickens.

4. Five minutes before the sauce is finished add the peas, mixing them in thoroughly and cooking them for the last 5 minutes. Add the hard-cooked eggs and set aside to cool.

5. Form the rice into balls the size of small oranges; make an indentation in the center of each and fill with the sauce. Close the rice ball up, adding a little more rice to seal the place where the indentation was, and set aside.

6. Lay out the flour, egg, and bread crumbs for an anglaise (see page 5), putting each in a shallow bowl, and pass the rice balls from flour to egg to bread crumbs, coating them thoroughly.

7. Fill a deep-fat fryer with vegetable oil and heat the oil to 350°F. Deep fry the rice balls rather slowly so the center cooks before the outside turns golden brown.

8. Drain on paper towels, season with salt and pepper, and serve with lemon wedges or a tomato sauce such as marinara.

NOTE: To make *suppli al telefono* instead, simply omit the sauce with ground veal and chicken giblets and, for the filling, substitute 4 ounces of small diced prosciutto, 8 ounces diced mozzarella, and 3 tablespoons of parmigiano mixed together and bound with a beaten egg.

Yɪᴇʟᴅ: *4 servings*

Timballo di Risotto alla Montefalchese

RICE MOLD IN THE MANNER OF MONTEFALCO

Here in Umbria Sagrantino, from Montefalco, is the Amarone of the hill towns—Assisi, Spoleto, Norcia, Gubbio, Spello, Trevi, Todi, Città di Castello, Città della Pieve, and Montefalco. Although this big red wine is little known beyond the province of Perugia, its fame within is well deserved. This robust red is deep purple in color and is perfect with game or roasts of any kind. Its use here, in the risotto, as well as in the accompanying sauce, is properly reflective of Umbrian cooking at its best. If you can't find Sagrantino in America, any dark, rich, red wine will suffice. Corvo from Casa Vinicola Duca di Salaparuta comes to mind as a good inexpensive substitute. I've also made this dish with an *abboccato* (sweet) Sagrantino that is now made in the old manner from *passito* grapes (dried like raisins). The wine develops 15 to 16 percent alcohol content because of the sugar content. I found the result to be exquisite.

Timbale is defined in *Webster's Third New International Dictionary* as a kettledrum, but also "a creamy mixture (as of chicken, lobster, cheese, or fish) cooked in a drum-shaped mold or in various individual molds or cups."

This *timballo* is a further variation in that a ring mold is used and the center is filled with chicken livers and pieces of chicken in a rich sauce.

FOR THE FILLING OF THE RING MOLD:

- ¼ pound mushrooms, thinly sliced
- 1 tablespoon unsalted butter
- Salt and pepper to taste
- 3 tablespoons extra virgin olive oil
- 4 cloves garlic, bled (scored)
- ¼ cup finely diced prosciutto
- 2 cups cubed chicken meat, reserved from the stock, cut into 1½-inch pieces
- 1 cup chicken livers and hearts (approximately 4 livers and 2 hearts)
- 2 tablespoons finely diced onion
- ⅛ teaspoon freshly grated nutmeg
- Pinch of cayenne
- ½ cup Marsala (Florio sweet preferred)
- 1 cup dry red wine
- 2 tablespoons tomato paste
- 4 to 5 fresh sage leaves or 1 teaspoon dried sage
- 1 bay leaf
- 2 cups Brodo di Pollo (see page 89)

FOR THE RISOTTO:

- 2 tablespoons extra virgin olive oil
- 2 cups Arborio rice
- 1 medium-size rib celery, finely diced, about ½ cup
- 2 tablespoons finely diced white onion
- ½ cup Marsala (Florio sweet preferred)
- 1 cup Sagrantino (passito preferred)
- 5 to 6 cups Brodo di Pollo (see page 89), heated
- Salt and pepper to taste
- 1 tablespoon unsalted butter
- 2 tablespoons freshly grated parmigiano
- 1 jumbo egg, beaten

1. To make the sauce filling, sauté the mushrooms in the butter over medium-high heat, season with salt and pepper, and set aside.

2. Heat the oil and garlic cloves in a sauté pan and add the prosciutto, cubed chicken, chicken livers, and hearts. Stir and cook over high heat until lightly browned.

3. Add the onion and cook till translucent. Add the mushrooms.

4. Season with salt and pepper, nutmeg, and cayenne. Deglaze with Marsala, allowing the liquid to evaporate slightly and partially caramelize the meat.

5. Add the red wine and reduce it by a quarter. Add the tomato paste and stir. Add the sage, bay leaf, and the chicken stock and cook over low, diffused heat covered for 30 to 40 minutes. Check and stir occasionally to see that it's cooking gently and the liquid has not evaporated. It should be a saucy mixture.

6. To make the risotto, heat the oil over medium heat in a pan and add the rice, tossing and stirring to coat it with the oil. Add the celery and the onion and cook all till the onion is translucent but not brown.

7. Deglaze with the Marsala. Add the red wine and let it cook over a medium-high heat till it is nearly absorbed. Add 2 cups of chicken stock, covering the rice totally, and stir well. Cook over high heat so that the liquids bubble and are nearly absorbed again.

8. Repeat the procedure three more times, adding only one cup of chicken stock each time. Before the last application, season with salt and pepper and stir well. Do not let the last cup of stock evaporate too much. The rice should be slightly soupy. Remove the pan from the stove and add the butter, parmigiano, and the beaten egg.

9. Mix well and spoon the risotto into a 5-cup, 9-by-2¼-inch ring mold that has been thoroughly but lightly buttered. (You may use another size ring mold as long as it's approximately the same size. You may have to adjust the cooking time slightly.)

10. Place the ring mold in a pan with hot water three quarters up its sides and bake in a 375°F. oven for 20 to 30 minutes.

11. To unmold, remove the mold from the water and invert a large oval plate (11- to 12-inch minimum) on top of it. Turn the plate and mold over so that the bottom of the ring mold (open side) is on the plate. Wait 1 or 2 minutes for the rice to settle and then tap and shake the ring mold till it breaks free from the rice. Lift the ring mold off; the rice will be perfectly situated on the plate.

12. Spoon the meat pieces from the sauce into the center of the ring. Some will fall over the top. Spoon the sauce over the meat and the rice and serve immediately on warm plates.

YIELD: *4 servings*

Riso Nero da Sicilia

BLACK RICE FROM SICILY

Riso nero usually is made with squid ink, which is quite black. Hence the *nero*. But this rice dish from Sicily is really a dessert rice made black with chocolate and sweetened with sugar and cinnamon. It is an unusual, simple dessert that can be elaborated on with raisins, and candied orange slices, or whatever you'd like.

2 cups water (approximately)
Salt to taste
2 cups rice (originario, not Arborio)
1 teaspoon ground cinnamon
1 teaspoon finely diced orange rind
1 tablespoon sugar
2 to 3 ounces grated semisweet or
    bittersweet chocolate, about ¼ cup
4 cinnamon sticks

1. Bring the water to a boil and add salt to taste. Add the rice and cook over medium-low heat for 10 to 15 minutes, or until done.
2. It helps to combine the cinnamon, zest, sugar, and chocolate. Drain the rice well and, while still hot, add the combined ingredients and mix well.
3. Cool or serve chilled with a cinnamon stick in each dish.

YIELD: *4 servings*

POLENTA

"Eat your oatmeal!" "Eat your spinach!" "Think of the poor starving children in Europe."

Does that sound familiar? Not to me! *Grazie a Dio!*

How blessed I was to have always loved both, although I must admit to some confusion as to why I love grains and cereals so much, and especially *granoturco* (Turkish grain), as polenta is called. Is it because I know it's good for me, healthy and digestible, or is it because it is so intrinsically delicious?

But love it I do, steaming bowls of farina or oatmeal, in spite of their bland reputation, really turn me on. And then when it comes to the won-derful cornmeal mush called polenta—pure ambrosia; for here you can dress it with all sorts of wonderful *sugi* and *ragùs* from meat, liver, sausages, game birds, and fish. Or you can chill it, slice it, and then fry it and serve it with butter and parmigiano. Or layer slices of it with a *balsamella*, fontina, and truffles and bake it in the oven. Or pile it steaming hot on warm plates and top it with spit roasted quails and their juices. Or make large round disks out of it and bake it with nutmeg, butter, and parmigiano *alla romana*.

The history of polenta is deceivingly recent. While puls—*pulmentum* in Latin—was the grain mush that, it might rightly be said, the Roman Empire was built upon, puls was the forerunner of bread and was the daily ration of the famous Roman legions. This early porridge was made of faro and spelt and not corn, which was introduced from Mexico in the 1800s. Polenta as we know it today developed in the Northern regions of Piedmont, Lombardy, and the Veneto in the late 1800s and has remained a Northern specialty since then. Unlike dried pasta which became ubiquitous throughout Italy, the polenta line seems to stop at Rome, although every region seems to have at least one or two specialties.

How do you make the best polenta? To begin with, there are three basic types of cornmeal: coarse grain, fine grain, and that which has been pulverized into a flour—*farina di mais,* in Italian.

While it's a matter of personal preference as to how coarse or how fine you want your polenta, after considerable experimentation I've come to prefer a composition of 50 percent coarse and 50 percent fine ground cornmeal in my recipes. The ratio of water to cornmeal is also important and I've found 3 cups of water to one of cornmeal to be just about right. However, always have a little extra scalding water standing by just in case to get the thickness or looseness you prefer. As to the use of a *paiolo*—an unlined round copper pan shaped like an upside down hat—there is nothing better. If you can find one at Williams Sonoma or one of the other gourmet cookware shops, by all means get it. However, don't let its lack or expense stop you from making polenta. Any decent stainless steel pot will do a fine job. I've made polenta repeatedly in such vessels with exactly the same results as in a *paiolo*. As is the case with the mythical need for cutting it with a string. A knife and stainless spoon will do as well. Whether to pour it out directly onto a board, a marble slab, or a wet towel on a board is equally a matter of personal preference. Taking it off the stove and shaking it to free it from the sides and the bottom of the pan is a very good procedure since it is liable to stick otherwise. But other than these little tricks, bear in mind, you're only making a bowl of porridge, a simple procedure that's been done since the beginning of cooking.

In spite of these comments of practical necessity to demythologize the mistaken "essentials" in certain recipes, I want to be quick to point out that I am a strong believer in the alchemical aspects of cooking. A favorite pot, particular knife, and "essential" spoon are part of my own personal rites of cooking. And if a piece of string and an unlined copper pot will bring you closer to the love that is the *sine qua non* of all good cooking, then by all means so ritualize. But understand what you're doing; and if you find yourself a guest with a group who are dying for polenta, don't refuse to make it because they haven't got an unlined copper pot or a piece of string. You might make the polenta of your life without the so-called "proper utensils" if the group desire inspires you to infuse the dish with enough love. "Finest natural ingredients; cook with love, knowledge, and devotion . . . "

Other considerations:

- Pouring the cornmeal in a steady stream into the boiling water while you stir continually with a long wooden or stainless steel spoon is essential; otherwise the polenta will be lumpy.
- Adding butter and/or parmigiano at the end, while looked down upon by purists, is fine if you like it.

- If you're going to slice it and fry it—which is perfectly delicious—or make it into a lasagna type baked dish, is better, I've found, with leftover 1-day old polenta. It can be done with fresh polenta also; just let it chill to stiffen before using.
- Cooking times are fairly standard in spite of the fact that some authors say 20 minutes and others insist on an hour and a half. It seems to me that between 30 and 45 minutes lies a proper doneness. Perhaps a little less if you're going to bake it again later.

Polenta

6 *cups water*
1 *cup fine cornmeal*
1 *cup coarse cornmeal*
2 *tablespoons unsalted butter (optional)*

1. Bring the water to a boil in a large pot, preferably unlined copper but stainless steel is fine, and add the salt. Meanwhile, mix the cornmeals together in a small bowl.
2. With one hand, or an assistant, dribble the cornmeal onto the water in a steady stream while stirring vigorously all the while with a long wooden paddle or stainless steel spoon. Stop the stream of cornmeal occasionally but continue stirring.
3. Continue adding and stirring the cornmeal until it's totally absorbed in the water and without lumps. If there are a few, you can get rid of them by pressing them against the side of the pot.
4. Adjust the heat to low so that the polenta is just bubbling occasionally and softly. Stir steadily but much less vigorously and much slower. If you have an electric *paiolo* equipped with a pad-

dle, so much the better. Cook in this manner for 30 to 40 minutes until the polenta is thick and smooth.

5. Remove from the stove and slap the bottom of the pot smartly on a stiff surface, freeing the polenta from the bottom and sides of the pot.

6. Return the pot to the stove and mix in the butter. When the butter is thoroughly amalgamated the polenta is done.

7. Put a wet towel on a countertop or table. Immediately turn the polenta out onto the towel by turning the pot upside down. You will have a good egg-shaped pile of polenta. Cut (with a string, knife, spoon) and serve as you wish in hot bowls. From here on you can treat it like cooked pasta and sauce it as you wish. Grated cheese, butter, and truffles can be exquisite, as can a sauce made with sausage or other meats.

Variation

•

POLENTA FRITTA FRIED POLENTA

1. Allow the polenta to cool, shaping it into a square or rectangular loaf. Chill in the refrigerator.

2. Slice the polenta into 3- to-4-inch slices, ½-inch thick, and fry in oil with 2 bled garlic cloves on a medium heat for 3 or 4 minutes till golden brown.

3. Serve without dressing on the same plate with tossed green salad or serve with any one of a hundred sauces just as you would pasta—butter and cheese, *salsa di pomodoro*, *ragù*, clam sauce, mussel sauce (white or red) or whatever.

YIELD: *4 to 6 servings*

Pasticcio di Polenta e Mascarpone

POLENTA AND MASCARPONE LASAGNA

These *pasticcios* and *pasticciatas* can be made with most anything and signify a mixture of ingredients usually layered in a dish and baked. In this case, we make polenta and layer it with a meat *ragù* and mascarpone and parmigiano cheeses before baking it.

If you have another sauce on hand it is certainly not necessary to make this ragù. While not just any sauce will do, a well made tomato sauce with or without meat will suffice. Just don't switch to one of the canned or jarred products and hope to get the same results.

      1   tablespoon unsalted butter
      1   tablespoon extra virgin olive oil
3 to 4   cups thinly sliced mushrooms
      1   tablespoon finely diced white onion
      1   cup Salsa di Pomodoro (see page 103)
    *1½   pounds polenta, chilled and cut into
          ½-inch slices (see page 139)*
 1 to 1½   cups mascarpone
 *1 to 1½   cups Ragù Bolognese (see page
          108)*
          Salt and pepper to taste
      3   tablespoons shredded Gruyère
*4 to 6   tablespoons freshly grated
          parmigiano*
          *Freshly grated nutmeg to taste
          (optional)*

1. Heat the butter and oil in a sauté pan over medium heat. When the butter melts, add the mushrooms and cook for 1 to 2 minutes. Add the diced onion and cook for 2 to 3 minutes more, stirring.

2. Line a 7-by-10-inch baking pan with the *salsa di pomodoro* and lay in a third of the chilled polenta.

3. Spread the polenta with half of the mascarpone, half of the mushrooms, and top with half of the *ragù*. Season with salt and pepper and sprinkle with Gruyère and parmigiano. Add nutmeg if you wish.

4. Repeat the procedure with the polenta, sauces, mushrooms, and cheeses and then close up the *pasticcio* with another layer of polenta. Top with the remaining *ragù*, sprinkle with grated parmigiano, and bake in a 375°F oven for approximately 1 hour. Serve immediately in warm bowls.

YIELD: *4 servings*

Gnocchi di Polenta alla Romana

POLENTA DUMPLINGS IN THE ROMAN STYLE

This variation on regular polenta calls for milk instead of water. It also has eggs, butter, and nutmeg worked in at the end as well as parmigiano to give you a richer, more finished type of polenta *gnocchi*. The polenta is then spread onto a cookie sheet with 1 to 2 inch sides, chilled, and cut with an approximately 2-inch round disk cutter. The gnocchi disks are laid in a baking dish, somewhat overlapping, with butter and cheese, baked in a moderately hot oven (375°F) for 20 minutes or so, and finished under a broiler till golden brown. Deliciously simple and simply delicious. In Umbria I've seen the same dish done with sage leaves added. And so we will do it here.

¾ *cup fine cornmeal*

¾ *cup coarse cornmeal*

4 *cups whole milk*

Water as needed

2 *jumbo eggs, beaten*

1 *tablespoon unsalted butter, for the polenta*

¼ *cup freshly grated parmigiano, for the polenta*

Salt and pepper to taste

Freshly grated nutmeg to taste

2 to 3 *tablespoons unsalted butter for baking*

20–24 *sage leaves (4–6 per serving)*

1¼ *cups freshly grated parmigiano, for baking and topping*

1. Combine the cornmeals in a small bowl. Bring the milk to a gentle boil and add the cornmeals, dribbling in a steady stream, stirring all the while with a long wooden paddle or large spoon.

2. Cook for roughly 30 to 40 minutes, stirring steadily, until thick. Add a little water during cooking if it's too thick. Remove the pot from the stove and slap it on a hard surface, freeing the polenta from the sides.

3. Mix in the beaten eggs, butter, ¼ cup parmigiano, salt, pepper, and nutmeg and spread the hot polenta on a cookie sheet.

4. Cool and chill in the refrigerator for at least 1 hour. When chilled, cut the polenta into 2-by-

½-inch-thick disks. You should get 24 ½-inch disks.

5. Melt the remaining butter and coat the bottom of a baking dish with half of it. Set the disks in the butter so that they overlap slightly. Dribble more butter on top, season with salt, pepper, and grated cheese, and bake in a 375°F oven for 20 minutes or so. Place under a hot broiler until golden brown. Serve in warm bowls with another topping of parmigiano.

YIELD: *4 servings*

Verdure

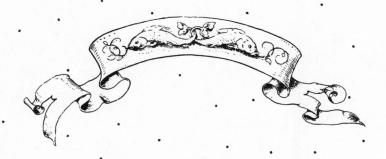

Vegetables

VEGETABLES

It's hard to say which Italians love most—fish, game, pasta, or vegetables. Historically, grains and vegetables were the staple diet for the larger part of the population in Italy; only the rulers and aristocracy were well off enough to have meat and fish regularly. From early Roman times through the Renaissance to modern Italy, vegetables (including salads and herbs) were not only an important part of the everyday diet but also held an honored place on the tables of all Italians as courses in their own right. The modern practice of serving vegetables as accompaniments to entrees has never been a standard part of Italian eating habits; the development of *sformati* (puddings) and *timballini* (small timbals of souffléd or pudding vegetables) as separate courses was considered a high art in Renaissance cooking, as it is today.

It wouldn't be an exaggeration to say that Italy is the garden country of the world. Gardens and gardeners have always proliferated, and there aren't many vegetables that the Italians haven't raised and made love to through their cooking. Fortunately, produce is grown seasonally and in very small quantities, thus avoiding the necessity to breed and raise special vegetables and fruits that will withstand long-distance shipping and are so obviously lacking in flavor. The old "small farm" system still exists here, providing the markets with fresh, flavorful produce that can rarely be found in America.

Here at the school we raise enough vegetables, lettuces, and herbs for our own needs and then some. Many's the summer day I'll be traveling in a loaded station wagon and stopping at the homes of various friends and partners to leave a flat of fresh produce from our *orto* (garden). When I "pick and eat" from our own garden the produce can't be matched even by the local markets, and I find myself eating a succession of vegetables as they mature without ever being bored. By God they're good. Vine-ripened tomatoes, fresh spinach, peas, corn, Swiss chard, mustard greens, broccoli, cauliflower, eggplant, carrots, zucchini, peppers, scallions, radishes, celery, and all the lettuces, except "iceberg," are just a few of the garden delights available; and when added to sorrel, thyme, basil, chervil, tarragon, sage, rosemary, borage, parsley, leeks, onions, and garlic, they provide us with a kitchen garden that is, for me, the dream of a lifetime.

In spite of the fact that the Italians make all kinds of vegetable preparations, they are most partial to the simplest, like lightly boiled or steamed, called *lessati* or *in vapore,* vegetables dressed in the best extra virgin olive oil. There isn't a vegetable or salad that can't be treated in this manner. The trick is to make sure the vegetables are not overcooked. The more you cook a vegetable the more the nutrients leach out and the wonderful freshness disappears into a tired, mushy, tasteless mess. That's why the Italian system for simply boiling or steaming lightly and dressing with oil is such a foolproof winner.

But that's not the end of the story by any means, as you will see from the recipes that follow. While it is beyond the scope of this book to be the definitive study of vegetables, nonetheless I hope to provide you with enough "method" information and particular recipes to enable you to present and serve Italian vegetables, salads, and herbs with confidence.

Here is a listing of the most generally used produce and their cooking times in gently boiling, salted water.

Vegetables (Legumi—Verdure—Ortaggi)	Cooking Time	Vegetables (Legumi—Verdure—Ortaggi)	Cooking Time
Asparagi (asparagus)	12–15 minutes	*Fagiolini gialli* (yellow string beans)	5–10 minutes
Barbabietole (beets)	30–40 minutes	*Fave* (broad beans)	10–15 minutes
Broccoli (broccoli)	15–20 minutes	*Finocchi* (fennel)	15–20 minutes
Broccoletti di rape or *cima di rape* (turnip) greens)	6–8 minutes	*Patate* (potatoes)	10–15 minutes, depending on type
Carciofi (artichokes)	15–20 minutes	*Piselli* (peas)	10–15 minutes, depending on type
Cardi (cardoons)	40–60 minutes	*Pomodori* (tomatoes)	10–15 minutes
Carote (carrots)	15–20 minutes	*Porri* (leeks)	15–20 minutes
Cavolfiore (cauliflower)	10–15 minutes	*Rape* (turnips)	20–30 minutes
Cavoli (cabbages of all types)	10–15 minutes, depending on type	*Scalogne* (shallots)	5–10 minutes
Cavolini di Bruxelles (Brussels sprouts)	10–15 minutes	*Scorzanera* (black thistle root)	15–20 minutes
Cipolle (onions of all types)	15–20 minutes	*Sedano* (celery)	15–20 minutes
		Spinaci (spinach)	5–8 minutes
Fagioli (green lima beans)	15–20 minutes	*Topinambur* (Jerusalem artichokes)	20–30 minutes
		Zucca (pumpkin)	15–20 minutes
Fagiolini (green string beans)	5–10 minutes	*Zucchini* (zucchini)	5–10 minutes

The above cooking times are obviously quite general. Actually, however, this is my least favorite method for preparing vegetables. Most do much better with very little water, a bit of butter, salt, and pepper, and cooked gently in a covered pot for a few minutes, or until tender. The variables of size and toughness of type are so great as to render most charts meaningless.

The trick here is not to rely on charts and to test the particular vegetable frequently for doneness. The alternative to this is to cook them covered with a bit of water so that the steam descends as they are braised (in effect) below. Of course, most tubers—carrots, potatoes, turnips, parsnips—would require boiling first to tenderize them before using this semi-braise technique; but they are certainly improved by being finished in this manner.

The next method is called *strascinato* (meaning "dragged through the pan") in Italian and refers to a quick sauté. In most cases (absolutely with roots and tubers) this technique works better if the vegetables are blanched, or prepoached till almost tender, so that the sauté can be done quickly. However, as you've no doubt seen with stir-fry cooking, or sauté, precooking the vegetables is hardly essential. Starting with raw produce just requires a lower heat to give a chance for the sauté to tenderize the vegetable before browning.

Another area where precooking (blanching, poaching, boiling) is normally necessary is deep frying. Most vegetables work better if they are almost tender before being batter-dipped, or bread crumb–coated, and deep fried. The golden-brown color of the outer covering then determines doneness and not the vegetable inside, whose tenderness has already been assured by precooking.

Some of the more structured vegetables, such as stems of celery, Belgian endive, and cardoons, as well as the tubers, lend themselves very nicely to braising, stewing, and fricassee; not to imply, however, that you can't braise almost anything

(including leafy vegetables). The procedure is quite simple. Put the vegetable in a covered pot with a bit of liquid—water, stock, wine (or combinations thereof)—a bit of butter or oil, and a herb or two of your choice. Then, cook in the oven on moderate (370°F) heat or on top of the stove. It is much easier in the oven, since you don't have to worry about the heat from the stove burning the bottom of the vegetable. Check every 3 to 5 minutes to make sure the cooking is proceeding properly and that there is enough liquid.

Vellutata, particularly when made with chicken or veal, works well in these braises which then become stews or a *fricassea* of vegetables. *Balsamella* and *mornaia* also are used very frequently as sauces for vegetables as well as binders and thickeners in the making of *sformati* and soufflés. You might have broccoli baked in mornay sauce or a soufflé of green peppers, made with a puree of roasted peppers in combination with a bit of *mornaia*. In most cases for all these baked dishes, puddings, and soufflés, the vegetables are cooked previously.

In any event, the key to good vegetable cooking can be summed up in the Italian expression *al dente* (to the bite). Overcooking is the no! no! here and is to be avoided at all times. If a dish has to be finish-baked, make sure the vegetable is only half cooked to allow for further cooking during the baking. And if you want a nice brown topping, don't overbake the vegetable to achieve it. Spread a bit of whipped cream with parmigiano on top and put the dish under a broiler. In one minute you'll have a bubbly brown, gratiné top without having overcooked the vegetables.

We don't have the time and the space to do a systematic presentation of all the vegetables and all the ways to cook them. However, we do have quite a few favorite recipes we'd like to share with you and hope you'll continue to explore this wonderful aspect of cooking on your own. For our vegetarian friends we'd like to point out that

Italian presentations will add another dimension to vegetable cookery. I think it is the easiest country in the world in which to be a vegetarian . . . as long as there's pasta. With vegetables and pasta I've created many a dinner where diehard meat eaters never felt the lack. In Italy there's enough variety of vegetable dishes in each season with an endless variety of taste sensations to keep you from being bored year round.

CARCIOFI • ARTICHOKES

What wonderful hidden treasures lie ensconced inside the thorny artichoke thistle. I'm always amazed at man's ingeniousness in making edible the unapproachable. Whether it's ugly dogfish, catfish, great skate, pig, boar, honey from busy bees, or even "ugly fruit" and thistles, we seem to have a knack for making it all digestible. There must have been some rude surprises along the gastronomic way that involved throwing caution to the wind as man continued to experiment—to see, to look, to feel, to taste, to enjoy all the world's offerings. It seems most of the real work was done thousands of years ago. The historical record shows that appreciation of the ugly and difficult to deal with as foodstuffs goes back to ancient Egyptian civilization and was well established in Rome at the time of Christ. In spite of this enjoyment of "offputting" items by the Romans there were, and are, always the naysayers. Pliny wailed at what some then called the lowly artichoke as "monstrous productions of the earth."

But he was an aberration. The Romans loved and developed wonderful recipes for all kinds of artichokes that are still popular today. In fact, all kinds of artichoke dishes are featured on Roman menus, and *carciofi alla romana, carciofi fritti alla romana,* and *carciofi alla giudea* have become part of the national cuisine just as pizza, tagliatelle, and *costolette alla milanese* are found throughout Italy.

Of course, to be able to appreciate artichokes, someone has to be involved in a somewhat complex cleaning/preparation process. The seeming waste of discarding leaves and cutting down the cone to reach the tenderest morsels must be borne stoically, for the treat of the bittersweet yet sharp, indescribable flavor that awaits is well worth the effort.

The guidelines we're about to set out will apply to all recipes for artichokes throughout the book, to avoid repetition. If a different preparation is required it will be noted in the particular recipes.

Cleaning and Preparing Artichokes

1. Wash the artichoke in cold water.
2. Snap off the stem.
3. Cut the remaining stem off at the base with a stainless steel knife.
4. Rub the cut bottom with a cut lemon.
5. Pull off the outer bottom leaves and discard.
6. Cut off the top third of the artichoke, placing it on its side and slicing down with the knife.
7. Cut the sharp points off the remaining leaves with a pair of scissors.
8. If you have to set the artichoke aside for even a few minutes, put it in water with the juice of one or two lemons, depending on quantity; otherwise it will discolor quickly.

You now have an artichoke that is ready to cook in various ways:

- Simply steam it and serve with drawn butter or hollandaise.
- "Lard" it by putting thin slices of garlic in between the leaves with some mint leaves interspersed. Season with salt and pepper, then steam-braise it in a covered pot with some aromatic white wine, oil, and water.
- If you want the bottoms and the hearts made into a *fricassea,* simply trim the bottoms, discard (reserve) all the leaves, and remove the choke with a sharp knife. Steam the bottoms

and hearts, then sauté them in oil and garlic, adding broth and tomatoes, and let "stew" for 30 to 40 minutes.

- Thin-slice leftover leaves into julienne and sauté with garlic in oil—again, the leaves are better if presteamed. Use in a *carbonara* with spaghetti. Toss the leaves with the spaghetti, a beaten egg, and grated cheese and you have a delicious *carbonara ai carciofi*.

Carciofi alla Romana

ARTICHOKES ROMAN STYLE

4 *large artichokes*
60 to 80 *slivers garlic*
2 *cups extra virgin olive oil*
1 *cup white wine, preferably Gewürztraminer*
Salt and freshly ground black pepper to taste

1. Clean and prepare the artichokes as described on page 148.
2. Open the leaves and place the garlic slivers randomly throughout. Place them in a casserole and pour the oil, then the wine, over each artichoke. Season with salt and pepper. Cook covered for 30 to 40 minutes, on a low diffused heat, or till they're as done as you like them
3. Serve on hot plates with extra salt for dipping on the side.

YIELD: *4 servings*

Carciofi Fritti

FRIED ARTICHOKES

Artichokes *fritti alla romana* and *alla toscana* are very similar in that they are both deep fried in oil after being dipped in batter, the only difference being that in the Roman style they mix flour and egg together with oil and salt and pepper for the batter, whereas the Tuscans dredge the artichokes in flour and then dip the pieces in beaten eggs with salt and pepper. If you wish to avoid precooking, in either case it is best to use the miniscule baby artichokes—and even then cut into small pieces—rather than normal-size or *mamme* artichokes, which are better for steaming and stuffing. Frying in olive oil gives them a special heavier taste, so if you prefer a lighter finish by all means use vegetable oil. Also make the batter lighter by adding a stiffly beaten egg white just before frying. Our own favorite batter is closer to that for a tempura.

Artichokes, cleaned, prepared, and precooked
1 *cup all-purpose flour*
½ *teaspoon baking powder*
1 *teaspoon sugar*
Pinch of salt
1 *jumbo egg*
6 to 9 *ounces best available beer, at room temperature and slightly flat*
1 *egg white (optional)*
Vegetable oil, for deep frying

1. Clean and trim the artichokes as described on page 148.
2. Sift together all dry ingredients.

3. Break the egg into a large bowl and add the flour mixture, whisking with a wire whisk. While whisking, begin adding the beer little by little to avoid lumps. Add more or less depending on the absorbency of the flour.

4. Let the batter rest, covered, at room temperature for at least 1 hour before using.

5. Dip bite-size pieces of artichokes in the batter and deep fry in 2 to 3 inches of vegetable oil at 350° to 360°F for approximately 5 minutes, or until golden brown. Serve with a lemon wedge, and possibly a garlic mayonnaise sauce, *aïoli*, for dipping (see page 124).

YIELD: *1½ cups*

Crocchette o Fritti di Carciofi

FRIED ARTICHOKE CROQUETTES

Crocchette or *fritti* of artichokes are wonderful finger food with champagne or apéritifs. They can be made in advance up to the point of deep frying and are therefore convenient for large parties.

This recipe is slightly different from the one discussed earlier and merely presents another version. The difference between *crocchette* and *fritti* is simply one of size; the *crocchette* is four times as big and should be served as an accompaniment to an entree.

    4 *medium-size artichokes*
1 to 2 *lemons*
    1 *medium-size white onion, coarsely sliced*
    2 *cloves garlic, bled (scored)*

   ¼ *cup olive oil*
   ⅓ *cup best aromatic white wine available*
     Salt and pepper to taste
   2 *jumbo eggs*
   1 *tablespoon milk*
   1 *cup (approximately) plain bread crumbs*
   ¼ *cup (approximately) flour*
   2 *tablespoons freshly grated parmigiano*
   1 *tablespoon finely chopped fresh parsley*
   ½ *cup (approximately) thick Balsamella (see page 116), warm*
   8 *cups vegetable oil*
   1 *lemon, cut into 6 to 8 pieces*

1. Clean the artichokes by peeling away the outer, toughest leaves, trimming away the stem, and cutting off the top half of the leaves. Rub them with cut lemons. Keep the trimmed artichokes in ice water with cut fresh lemons.

2. Slice the artichokes in half through the heart. Remove the chokes with a small knife and thinly slice the artichokes lengthwise. Sauté the sliced artichokes with the onion and garlic in the olive oil over medium heat until they just begin to take on color.

3. Deglaze the pan with white wine, let it reduce by half, and then add 1 cup cold water, or enough to cover the artichokes by about 1 inch.

4. Season with salt and pepper and simmer, uncovered, until the artichokes are tender but not mushy and all the liquid has evaporated. Taste them during cooking and add more water as necessary. Set them aside to cool.

5. Beat 1 egg with a little milk in a deep bowl. Set the bowl in a row with the flour and bread crumbs, all in bowls.

6. Finely chop the cooled artichoke mixture and combine with the other egg, the cheese, and the parsley.

7. Add the warm *balsamella* and mix well. Adjust

the stiffness of the mixture with some bread crumbs if necessary. Chill the mixture thoroughly (it will stiffen considerably).

8. Shape the chilled mixture by spoonfuls into one *crocchetta* or *fritto* at a time and coat with the flour, dip into the egg, and coat with the bread crumbs. Adjust the shape, checking for overcoating, and place on a bed of bread crumbs spread on a plate. You may chill the *fritti* at this point for later frying. If you do, make sure they are brought to room temperature before frying.

9. Heat the vegetable oil in a heavy, deep pan to 375°F and fry the *fritti,* 2 or 3 at a time, until well crusted and heated through. Remove to a nest of paper towels and toss lightly to drain. Serve hot with lemon wedges.

YIELD: *24 fritti or 6 croquettes*

Carciofi alla Giudea (or Giudia)

ARTICHOKES JEWISH STYLE

Carciofi alla Giudea, however, is another story altogether. Edda Servi Machlin, in her very fine book *The Classic Cuisine of the Italian Jews,* states a surprising fact if true. She says that the Jews represent only 0.1 percent of the Italian population. And yet they have made a number of important contributions to Italian cuisine. *Carciofi alla Giudea* (or *Giudia)* is so well respected it has become part of the Italian national cuisine. Since she learned the recipe from her mother, a Roman Jew, and cites its authenticity, we are pleased to pay tribute to its influence on our own recipe to follow:

4 *large (mamme) artichokes*
Salt and pepper to taste
2 *cups extra virgin olive oil*
4 to 8 *large lemon wedges*

1. Clean and prepare the artichokes as described on page 148, leaving an inch or two of stem. Open up the leaves on each by prying them apart with your fingers and then pressing down on your work board. They won't open completely without breaking, but this treatment will prepare them for a later flower-like opening.

2. Drain them well on paper towels, shaking vigorously so that you free them from as much of the acidulated water as possible. In this case they are not precooked.

3. Sprinkle them thoroughly, inside each leaf and out, with salt and pepper.

4. Heat the oil in a sauté pan large enough to hold all 4 artichokes when their leaves are open.

5. Cook them in the hot oil on all sides for 15 to 20 minutes, or until tender and golden brown. The trick to "sizzling" them without burning your hand is to spray them with water from a plastic sprayer, or failing that, to dip your closed fist in water and then shake the water into the pan by opening your fingers and shaking your hand. This creates a steam sizzle that fries the artichokes in a special way and is not as dangerous as it sounds. The spray sizzles, but does not explode, as it would had you left too much water in the artichokes when cleaning them.

6. Remove the artichokes from the pan and place them right side up on a plate, leaving the oil that remains in them. Pick them up one by one with a fork in the stem end and return them one at a time to the hot oil, pressing down and opening the leaves by applying pressure against the bottom of the pan. Remove; drain on paper towels.

7. Serve right away with salt and pepper and a lemon wedge or two.

YIELD: *4 servings*

Carciofi Origanata

ARTICHOKES WITH OREGANO

3 to 4 *tablespoons of dried oregano*
1½ *cups bread crumbs*
1 *clove garlic, chopped*
3 to 4 *tablespoons extra virgin olive oil*
½ *teaspoon crushed red pepper*
2 *tablespoons freshly grated parmigiano*
2 *tablespoons freshly grated pecorino Romano*
   Salt and pepper to taste
4 *large, cleaned, cooked Carciofi alla Romana (see page 149)*
1 *cup coarsely crumbled toasted bread crumbs, for topping*

1. Mix all the ingredients together, except artichokes and coarsely crumbled bread crumbs, reserving some cheese and a bit of the oil to drizzle on top of each artichoke.
2. Stuff the prepared artichokes with the bread crumb mixture by prying the leaves open. Arrange the artichokes so that they stand upright in a shallow baking pan.
3. Top with the coarsely crumbled bread crumbs and reserved cheeses. Drizzle some oil over them. Bake in a 375°F oven for 20 to 30 minutes or until nicely browned. Serve hot or cold. They're wonderful cold the next day.

Variation

•

Carciofi alla siciliana (Artichokes Sicilian Style): An interesting variation of the foregoing Neapolitan artichoke *originata* is found in Sicily, where they eliminate the oregano but add capers and anchovies to a bread crumb mixture. The quantities are not important since the capers and anchovies are "to taste." As much or little as you'd like is fine, as is the addition of anchovy oil and/or caper juice. I prefer squeezing a whole lemon into this breading, however, to acidify the fish taste of the anchovies. All other ingredients and procedures are the same as found in *Carciofi Origanata*.

YIELD: *4 servings*

Sformato di Carciofi

ARTICHOKE PUDDING

This, like all vegetable *sformati* (puddings) in the Italian repertoire, can be made denser or lighter by the omission or addition of egg whites. The most dense version uses just egg yolks. Use whole eggs for a lighter version. Separate the yolks and the whites, then fold soft peaked whites into a *balsamella*, egg yolk, and artichoke mixture for a soufflé that's even lighter. The Italians generally prefer the densest version, which is given here.

4 *large, cleaned, cooked Carciofi alla Romana (see page 149)*
4 *tablespoons (½ stick) unsalted butter*
   Salt and freshly ground pepper to taste

Freshly grated nutmeg to taste

4 *egg yolks*

2 *cups Balsamella (see page 116), cooled*

3 *tablespoons freshly grated parmigiano*

3 *tablespoons freshly made bread crumbs*

1. Remove the leaves from the prepared artichokes and reserve. Discard the choke and trim the bottoms and the hearts. Coarsely chop all the artichoke pieces.

2. Heat the butter in a sauté pan and gently cook the chopped artichokes till very tender. Season with salt, pepper, and nutmeg.

3. Pulse half the artichokes in a food processor and then pass through a food mill to puree. Set all aside to cool.

4. Thoroughly mix the egg yolks into the *balsamella.* Mix in the parmigiano and season to taste. Add the artichoke pieces and the puree to the bowl and mix gently but thoroughly.

5. Butter a 9-by-5-by-3-inch loaf pan and coat it with bread crumbs. Gently lay in the artichoke mixture.

6. Place the loaf pan in a hot water bath and bake in a preheated 400°F oven for 30 to 40 minutes, or until the top is nicely browned and the center tests clean. Allow to cool and settle somewhat before turning out onto a serving platter, top down. Serve warm.

YIELD: *6 to 8 servings*

ASPARAGI · ASPARAGUS

Both cultivated and wild asparagus are found extensively in Italy and referred to as *del giardino* (of the garden) and *selvatici* (wild). Robust ladies in rubber boots, carrying sticks to ward off vipers, can be seen constantly patrolling the highways and back roads here in Umbria from March through June in a perennial search for wild asparagus *(asparagi selvatici)* that grow along the roadways, so fond are the Umbrians of *spaghetti alla boscaiola* and *tagliatelle con salsa di asparagi.* This type of asparagus is long and thin and has a special bittersweet tang that is not present in the garden-grown varieties.

But it's not just the Umbrians who are wild about asparagus. Ancient and present-day Romans were and are dedicated devotees, as is the rest of Italy for that matter.

Asparagus can be steamed or boiled, in bundles or singly, but the Italians prefer, as I do, a combination of both methods. Wash the asparagus and prepare the stems by trimming off the ends—¼- to ½-inch will do—and then slitting up the stems with a sharp knife (make several incisions in each stalk). Then, using a vegetable peeler, lightly skin the bottom half of the remaining stems. From here on in there are three methods of preparation:

1. Place the asparagus, tips up, on a rack placed in a large, flat, covered pan filled with a few inches of water so that one end of the rack is propped up on the edge of the pan. This way the tips are steamed while the tougher stems are boiled. If you have trouble fitting a cover over the pan, use tinfoil instead.

2. Use an asparagus steamer. This has a few inches of water on the bottom with a perforated rack that allows the asparagus to steam standing up. Once again, the bottoms cook while the tips steam gently.

3. Or use a double boiler and invert the top part to use as a cover, boiling the bottom stems of the standing asparagus spears in a few inches of water while the tips simultaneously steam.

To bundle or not to bundle is a matter of preference. The reason for bundling is that the delicate tips may break by rubbing or bumping against one another. This will hold true if you like the tips cooked very much. I don't and therefore never find it necessary to bundle them.

Whatever recipe or method you prefer when cooking asparagus, as with most vegetables, freshness is the key to the best flavor. Asparagus is best bought or picked and used immediately, if you can.

In all of the following recipes we will assume that you have read our previous comments on washing, stemming, peeling, scoring, and steam-boiling so that we may avoid repetition.

Asparagi Olandese

ASPARAGUS WITH HOLLANDAISE

This is the classic dish—hot steam-boiled asparagus with *salsa olandese* (hollandaise). Aside from drawn butter, this is my own preferred accompaniment for cultivated asparagus; the wild ones are too strong for this simple butter and egg yolk emulsion.

> 3 *fresh jumbo egg yolks*
> ⅓ *pound (1⅔ sticks) unsalted butter*
> 1 to 2 *teaspoons fresh lemon juice*
> *Cayenne to taste*
> *Salt and white pepper to taste*
> 1½ *pounds fresh large asparagus*

1. Place the egg yolks in the top half of a double boiler set over water that has been heated so that it is boiling gently without touching the bottom of the top half. Whisk briskly. Add a third of the

butter and whisk constantly as it melts. When amalgamated add the next third and continue whisking till it melts and is incorporated. After amalgamating the last third by continued whisking, add the lemon juice and cayenne and whisk in.

2. Season with salt and pepper and continue to whisk and cook until you have a desired thickness, about 2 to 3 minutes. Do not scramble the eggs by cooking too much.

3. If the sauce breaks, to correct it:

a) add 1 tablespoon of scalding water and whisk;

b) if still no good, add 1 tablespoon of cold water and whisk;

c) if still broken, add 2 egg yolks, 1 at a time, and whisk the while;

d) if that doesn't do it, throw it away and start all over again.

4. Steam the asparagus until fork tender. Drain and place on a warm plate. Top with the sauce. The hollandaise will keep when removed from the stove by being stored in a covered bowl away from the heat at room temperature. To reheat, simply place the bowl in a hot water bath till warm enough to serve. *Buon appetito!*

YIELD: *4 servings*

Asparagi con Salsa Vinaigrette

ASPARAGUS WITH VINAIGRETTE

This is a favorite cold presentation of mine that dresses steam-boiled asparagus with a vinaigrette enriched with diced gherkins and finely diced hard-cooked eggs. It's quite easy to make.

2 hard-cooked eggs, finely diced
¼ cup chopped gherkins (sweet pickles)
1½ cups Vinaigrette Dressing (see page 47)
2 tablespoons finely chopped fresh parsley
1½ pounds fresh asparagus

1. Combine the hard-cooked eggs and the chopped gherkins with the vinaigrette. Stir in 1 tablespoon of parsley.
2. Steam the asparagus until fork tender. Drain and chill. Arrange the asparagus on a chilled plate and top liberally with the dressing and the remaining parsley.

YIELD: *4 servings*

Asparagi alla Florentina

ASPARAGUS IN THE FLORENTINE MANNER

1 pound fresh asparagus
Salt to taste
4 to 6 tablespoons unsalted butter
1 cup freshly grated parmigiano
4 large eggs
Pepper and cayenne to taste

1. Clean the asparagus and snap half the stems off. Make 1-inch incisions in the bottoms of the stalks and slight incisions along the sides.
2. Place a rack in a pan of water large enough to hold the asparagus and rest one end of the rack on the top edge of the pan so that when racked

the bottoms of the asparagus are submerged in water but the tips remain suspended above the water. Salt the water, cover tightly with aluminum foil and cook on medium heat for 10 to 12 minutes, or until tender.
3. Heat the butter in a large sauté pan. Drain the asparagus and carefully toss them in the butter.
4. Remove the asparagus to warm plates and sprinkle with the parmigiano.
5. Fry the eggs sunnyside up in the asparagus butter and season with salt, pepper, and cayenne. Place the eggs on top of the cheesed asparagus and top with more parmigiano and salt and pepper.

YIELD: *4 servings*

Asparagi allo Zabaione

ASPARAGUS WITH ZABAGLIONE SAUCE

1 pound fresh asparagus
3 jumbo egg yolks
1 jumbo egg
1 cup best available aromatic white wine
2 tablespoons unsalted butter, softened
½ cup heavy cream, warmed
Salt, white pepper, and cayenne to taste

1. Clean, prepare and steam the asparagus as directed in recipe for *alla florentina* (see above).
2. In a double boiler on medium heat, combine the egg yolks, whole egg, and white wine by whisking vigorously until the mixture foams and thickens. Scrape the corners with a spoon to make sure all is amalgamated.
3. Remove the egg mixture from the heat and fold

in the softened butter, whisking lightly. Whisk in the warmed heavy cream and season with salt, pepper, and cayenne.

4. Drain and plate the asparagus on warm plates and pour the sauce over them.

YIELD: *4 servings*

Salsa di Asparagi

ASPARAGUS SAUCE

½ *pound fresh asparagus*

2 *cups Marinara (see page 100)*

2 *anchovy fillets in oil, pounded in a mortar*

1 *tablespoon diced lemon rind*

1 *cup dry white wine*

1 *cup fresh bread crumbs tossed with 2 tablespoons parmigiano*

Salt, pepper, and cayenne to taste

1. Clean and prepare the asparagus as described in the recipe on page 153 but do not steam.

2. Slice the asparagus in half lengthwise and again in half horizontally so that you have 2- to 3-inch batons.

3. Place the asparagus and the marinara sauce in a saucepan over medium heat. Add the anchovy paste, lemon rind and white wine and cook on medium heat for 20 to 35 minutes, covered, until the asparagus are well integrated into the sauce.

4. Remove the cover and add the bread crumbs. Correct the seasoning and use as a sauce for pasta, eggs, vegetables, or fish.

YIELD: *2 cups*

Sliced, buttered beets with tarragon have always been a favorite of mine in spite of the fact that, like a lot of roots and tubers, they are held in low esteem by many people. They're also surprisingly delicious when batter-fried and add an interesting color note to a *fritto misto* (mixed fry) of vegetables. But my favorite use is as a pickled contrast to many dishes. *Vitello tonnato* (cold poached veal slices with a tuna fish, heavy cream, and caper sauce), for example, cries out for the sweet and tart contrast of diced pickled beets; as does *bollito misto* (boiled mixed meats), or cold salmon trout in a light fish jelly; or a warm duck salad with Bibb lettuce and walnuts; fried chicken; and dozens of other specialities.

Barbabietole in Aceto

PICKLED BEETS

2 *cups small dried beets*

1 *tablespoon fresh lemon juice*

½ *lemon*

2 *teaspoons sugar*

Salt to taste

1 *tablespoon finely diced white onion*

1 *tablespoon best available white wine vinegar*

1 *tablespoon aromatic Gewürztraminer white wine*

Freshly ground black pepper to taste

1 *tablespoon chopped fresh mint*

1 *tablespoon finely chopped fresh parsley*

1. Wash the beets and cook them in gently boiling, salted water with the juice of half a lemon—leave the rind in the water—½ teaspoon of sugar, and a pinch of salt until fork tender. When cool enough to handle, peel and dice the beets into small cubes.

2. Place them in a bowl and add all the other ingredients, reserving ½ tablespoon of parsley for garniture. Let the mixture marinate, covered, in the refrigerator for at least 2 hours.

3. Garnish with the remaining parsley before serving.

YIELD: *4 servings*

CARDI · CARDOONS

Cardoons or *cardi* look like celery with their long stalks and leafy tops and taste like artichokes. They are members of the thistle (artichoke) family and, like artichokes, need a bit of lemon juice or acidulated water to prevent them from turning brown. They have a special bittersweet flavor that makes them a great accompaniment to roasts and braises. There are many ways to prepare them once you trim the ends, and cook them in lemon water to tenderize for 20 to 30 minutes. In Emilia Romagna cardoons are served *alla parmigiana,* the tenderized pieces layered with parmigiano and butter and baked. In Milan they do the same thing but add hazelnut butter as a topping for the final browning. In Puglia they use pecorino and capers and in Tuscany they have a rather involved recipe called *cardi trippati alla toscana,* in which the cardoons are boiled, fried, and then baked in the oven with parmigiano and cinnamon.

Cardi all'umbro

CARDOONS UMBRIAN STYLE

1 *pound cardoons, cleaned, trimmed, and cut into 4-inch strips*

1 *lemon*

1 *teaspoon sugar*

Flour

¼ *cup extra virgin olive oil*

4 *cloves garlic, bled (scored)*

1 *tablespoon chopped fresh garlic*

¼ *cup best available aromatic white wine*

1½ *cups canned Italian plum tomatoes*

2 *tablespoons chopped fresh* **mentuccia** *(wild, mild mint—see note below)*

Salt and pepper to taste

¼ *cup freshly grated parmigiano*

1. Cut off the ends and trim the cardoons as you would celery. Cut the stalks into 4-inch pieces and rub them with lemon. Squeeze the juice of the lemon into a pot of water with a bit of salt, sugar, and flour.

2. Cook the cardoons in the water until tender, approximately 30 minutes. Remove, pat dry, and sauté in the oil with the whole garlic cloves for 2 to 3 minutes over medium heat. Deglaze with white wine till it evaporates by half.

3. Add the tomatoes, break them up, and cook briefly. Add the *mentuccia,* salt, and pepper to taste and cook on a very low heat, covered, for 20 to 30 minutes. Stir occasionally.

4. Add 2 tablespoons of parmigiano without stirring, recover, and cook for another 15 minutes on the same low heat. Place on warm plates and top with a sprinkle of parmigiano on each.

NOTE: *Mentuccia* is a very mild variety of mint that grows wild and is much more delicate than regular mint. If you can't find it, use regular mint but cut the quantity in half unless you're really fond of mint.

YIELD: *4 servings*

Cardi alla Perugina or Parmigiana di Gobbi

CARDOONS PERUGIAN STYLE

1½ to 2 *pounds large cardoons, cleaned, trimmed, cut into 4 pieces*
2 *jumbo eggs, lightly beaten*
1 *cup (approximately) flour*
1 *cup (approximately) plain bread crumbs*
¼ *cup olive oil*
1½ *pounds lean ground beef*
¼ *cup diced onion*
1 *tablespoon dried porcini mushrooms, soaked and minced*
3 *cups canned Italian plum tomatoes*
3 *tablespoons fresh lemon juice*
   Salt and pepper to taste
1 *pound mozzarella, thinly sliced*
1 *cup freshly grated parmigiano*

1. Blanch the cardoons in boiling, salted water till they begin to soften. Drain and cool slightly. Bread the cardoons by first dipping the pieces in the egg, and then the flour and bread crumbs.
2. Heat the vegetable oil in a deep, heavy saucepan and deep fry the cardoons.
3. Heat the olive oil in a skillet and brown the beef. Add the onions, porcini, tomatoes, and lemon juice and simmer over medium-high heat till thick, 30 to 40 minutes.
4. Layer the cardoons in a casserole, similar to lasagna. Cover with half the sauce, slices of mozzarella, and a sprinkling of parmigiano. Repeat the process, ending with meat sauce, mozzarella, and parmigiano. Bake in a 375°F oven and remove when brown and bubbly, roughly 20 to 30 minutes.

YIELD: *6 servings*

CAROTE • CARROTS

In addition to the obvious carotene (Vitamin A) benefit of carrots, they also happen to be a natural aromatic sweetener in cooking. The list of preparations that use carrots as a base (in a *soffritto* or *batutto*) or as an aromatic in stocks and soups is endless; not to mention the ubiquitous presence of carrots in stews and braises of all kinds. Like the onion, it is the handyman of the kitchen.

It is also quite delicious as a separate vegetable course, or as a contrast to *bollito misto* (mixed boiled meats). In Sicily, they glaze them with Marsala, to which I add a bit of mint and honey. Another interesting use is in purée *(in purea)* with cardamom and coriander, which is excellent served with roasts of all kinds.

Carote in Purea

CARROT PUREE

1 pound young, fresh, tender carrots
2 tablespoons sugar
1 tablespoon unsalted butter
½ teaspoon ground coriander
½ teaspoon ground cardamom
   Salt and pepper to taste

1. Wash, peel, and slice-dice the carrots. Cook them in boiling, salted water with the sugar till very tender.
2. Drain, mix with the butter, and pass through a food mill while hot.
3. Add the seasonings, mixing well, and serve hot.

YIELD: *4 servings*

Salsa di Carote

CARROT SAUCE

This sweet and sour wine tomato compound of shredded carrots is wonderful with vegetables, but it also works as a very unusual pasta sauce.

3 medium-size young carrots, shredded
1 tablespoon extra virgin olive oil
1 tablespoon unsalted butter

¼ cup finely diced onion
2 tablespoons dry white wine
   Salt and freshly ground black pepper to taste
2 teaspoons sugar
¼ cup beef glaze (see page 93)
2 tablespoons red wine vinegar
½ teaspoon balsamic vinegar (optional)
3 tablespoons tomato paste
1 tablespoon fresh lemon juice

1. Sauté the shredded carrots in oil and butter over medium-high heat. Add the onion and continue to cook till the onion softens. Deglaze with the white wine and season with salt and pepper and sugar.
2. Add the vinegars, tomato paste, and lemon juice. Stir well and cook for 5 to 10 minutes on low heat.
3. Add water if necessary, but cook until the mixture forms a thick sauce. Serve hot or cold with vegetables or pasta.

MELANZANE · EGGPLANT

It's strange to think that prior to the eighteenth century eggplant was considered dangerous, leading to madness. It took the braveness of the Sicilians to cast aside all doubts and create their wonderful caponatas. Today it's a very popular vegetable throughout Italy but still more appreciated in Sicily, Naples, and the south. The two most well known treatments are caponata and *melanzane alla parmigiana,* both of which are now made in practically all the regions in one form or another. For this reason I'll provide a few different recipes of each, and then two extra special eggplant recipes of my own.

Caponata or Caponatina

There are as many ways to make caponata as there are regions in Italy . . . and then some. Practically every household, trattoria, and ristorante has its particular versions, with added variations from a multitude of *salumerias* (delicatessens). Although its origin and fame are purely Sicilian, it is basically a mélange of eggplant and vegetables that has echoes of Indian chutneys.

Falzone, the great Italian food writer, as quoted by Waverley Root in *The Food of Italy*, waxes poetic about it:

He who has not eaten caponatina of eggplant has never reached the antechamber of the terrestrial paradise . . .

A mixture of vegetables, greenery, and essence of the sea, which figures as the base eggplant cut into cubes and fried, with an addition in a fantastic sauce of tomatoes, sweet and sour, celery, capers, olives, tuna roe, crayfish tails, or lobster claws, a composite flavor comparable to no other, but which recalls nostalgically exotic lands and seas, whose mingled aromas evoke the chief characteristic of Sicilian cuisine, the field on which all the other cuisines give battle to each other.

It seems that there is no distinction between *caponata* and *caponatina*, the latter diminutive merely being a sign of affection and feminine grace. Root attributes motherhood to Catania, to the capital of Palermo, and claims it has no comparison on the mainland. And we must be ever vigilant, on the lookout, for the dead give-away of an ersatz product called *caponata alla marinara*, which is usually just stale bread rubbed with garlic and oil, tomato, anchovies, and perhaps a few olives.

I found Root's description of the method used worth repeating in that it captures the importance of techniques to this dish. To wit:

It consisted simply in cooking each of its chief ingredients—eggplant, pepper, tomatoes, onions, and celery—separately. Thus each could be sautéed in the soffritto most appropriate to it, with the dosage of cooking fats (chiefly olive oil) which it could most advantageously absorb. Each could be seasoned by its own selection of herbs and spices. The different components of my Catania caponatina had been started on their way at different times, so that all of them reached simultaneously the perfect state for being combined to finish their cooking in an iron skillet with vinegar, capers, olives, a little tomato sauce, and a hint of anchovy juice; it was served still sizzling in the skillet.

My own improvisation allows the delight of "skillet sizzle" and the advantage of deep enough cooking to serve it chilled as an antipasto; it will last for several weeks if refrigerated tightly covered. I also add the crunch of pine nuts and the soft richness of plump raisins to accentuate the *agro dolce* (sweet and sour) aspect of this dish. A northern trait, I suppose.

With that in mind, let's make some.

Eggplant
Salt
1 cup olive oil
4 large cloves garlic, bled (scored)
    Java pepper and freshly ground
    black pepper to taste
1 cup finely chopped fresh parsley
1 large carrot, cut semi-thin on bias
2 medium-size ribs celery, cut semi-thin
    on bias
1 medium-size red or green pepper, seeded,
    cut into 6 strips, then halved
6 large mushrooms, quartered and stems
    halved
1 medium-size white onion, sliced into
    ¼-inch slices

1 tablespoon dried thyme (if herbs
  are fresh use only half)

1 tablespoon dried basil

1 tablespoon dried chervil

1 tablespoon dried marjoram

1 cup best available dry white wine

One 16-ounce can whole Italian
  plum tomatoes (not pureed or
  crushed)

1 cup black olives, sliced into large
  pieces

1 cup green olives, sliced into large
  pieces

1 clove garlic, finely chopped

1 teaspoon crushed red pepper

1 cup fresh, soft raisins (can be plumped
  in hot water)

1 cup pine nuts

½ cup jumbo capers

2 tablespoons sugar

1 cup homemade red wine vinegar, or
  add good red wine to red wine
  vinegar (½ cup of each)

½ tin anchovies with some oil (optional,
  4–6 pieces)

1. Slice the eggplant and sprinkle on both sides
with salt. Let it drain in a colander or large
pan for 20 minutes. Then dry well and cut into
cubes.
2. In a large skillet, heat ½ cup oil with 2 whole
cloves garlic. Add the eggplant cubes and sauté
over high heat, gently stirring and turning occasionally till golden brown. Add more oil to the
pan if needed. Season with salt, peppers (the java
and black), and ¼ cup parsley.
3. Heat the remaining oil and garlic cloves in another skillet and gently sauté the carrot, celery,
pepper, mushrooms, and onion in a descending
order so that all finish at the same time and are

lightly golden—or as they say, taking on color is
the goal. Add the thyme, basil, chervil, marjoram,
¼ cup parsley, salt, java, and black pepper.
4. Combine all the vegetables in the large skillet,
giving a good shake and a stir for equal disper-
sion. Keep heat on high and add the white wine
at once, scraping bottom and sides to complete a
deglaze. Add the tomatoes, breaking them up
with a spoon. Add the olives, reduce the heat to
a vigorous simmer and cook till half the liquid
evaporates, about 5 minutes. Stir in the remaining
parsley.
5. Add the diced garlic and crushed red pepper,
sprinkling them evenly over the mixture.

Melanzane alla Parmigiana

EGGPLANT PARMESAN

1½ to 2 medium-size eggplants, washed
         and sliced ¼ inch thick

2 to 3   cups milk

4   large eggs, lightly beaten

1½ to 2 cups all-purpose flour

4   cups bread crumbs
         Freshly grated nutmeg to taste
         Salt and black pepper to taste

1 to 1½ cups freshly grated parmigiano

1   pound mozzarella, sliced ¼ inch
         thick

2   cups vegetable oil for frying

1½ to 2 cups Salsa di Pomodoro (see page
         103)

1. Lay the eggplant in a shallow pan and cover with milk. Soak for 30 minutes, turning them over once or twice.

2. In the meantime set up a breading (anglaise) with the beaten eggs in one bowl, flour in another, and bread crumbs seasoned with salt, pepper, nutmeg, and parmigiano in a third. Season the egg and flour with a little salt and pepper.

3. Dust the eggplant slices with seasoned flour. Dip them in the egg wash, using a spoon or fork (in one hand to keep it dry) and the fingers of your other hand. Make a well in the center of the seasoned bread crumbs and bury the slice of eggplant in it. Shake off the excess bread crumbs and set aside.

4. Heat the oil to 375°F and deep fry the breaded eggplant slices until golden brown. Drain well on paper towels.

5. Spread the bottom of a casserole with *salsa di pomodoro*. Make a layer of the eggplant slices and season with salt, pepper, and nutmeg. Layer some mozzarella slices over the eggplant and dust with parmigiano. Repeat the layering twice more, ending with eggplant slices on top. Coat the top layer with *salsa di pomodoro*.

6. Bake in a 375°F oven for 30 to 40 minutes, or until done as you like. Let rest for 2 to 3 minutes before serving with a bit more sauce on the side. Garnish with more parmigiano if you'd like.

YIELD: *4 to 6 servings*

Melanzane con Ricotta

EGGPLANT WITH RICOTTA

The use of a ricotta pudding on top makes this a very light presentation of what used to be in America a very heavy dish as I remember it— tough breaded eggplant slices swimming in an acidy tomato concentrate sauce—yuucchh! a goppy goopy mess. Try this lighter version!

2 to 3	*medium-size eggplants, uniformly sliced ¼ inch thick*
2	*cups milk, to soak eggplant slices*
	Ricotta
	Milk for ricotta mixture
4	*jumbo eggs*
4	*cups bread crumbs*
	Salt and pepper to taste
	Freshly grated nutmeg to taste
1 to 1½	*cups freshly grated parmigiano*
1½ to 2	*cups all-purpose flour*
8	*cups vegetable oil for frying*
1½ to 2	*cups Salsa di Pomodoro (see page 103)*
1	*pound mozzarella, cut into ½-inch slices*
2	*cloves garlic, bled (scored)*

1. Soak the eggplant slices in milk for 30 minutes.

2. Drain the slices and sauté in hot oil with the garlic until all are nicely browned. Drain on paper towels.

3. Season both sides liberally with salt and pepper and set aside.

4. Line a casserole with *salsa di pomodoro* and top with a thick layer of eggplant slices.

5. Layer the mozzarella slices on top and sprinkle with parmigiano.

6. Add another layer of the eggplant slices and parmigiano—no mozzarella.

7. Coat with *salsa di pomodoro* and top with basil slices.

8. Mix the ricotta with the eggs, parmigiano, milk, parsley, and nutmeg, and season with salt and pepper. Add the ricotta mix to the casserole as a thick topping.

9. Sprinkle with grated parmigiano and bake at 400°F for 30 to 40 minutes, until nicely browned.

YIELD: *4 large servings*

Crocchette o Fritti di Melanzane

FRIED EGGPLANT CROQUETTES

These eggplant balls, puffs, *crocchette,* or *fritti* are wonderful to pass with cold champagne, cheese fritters, and fried artichokes. A platter of this combination of golden fried delicate morsels is a wonderful opening to any festive occasion.

> 1 *large eggplant*
> 1 *cup milk*
>   *Salt*
>   *Pepper*
> 2 *tablespoons olive oil*
> 1 *tablespoon pine nuts*

> 2 *jumbo eggs*
> 3 *tablespoons freshly grated parmigiano*
> 1 *cup plain bread crumbs*
> ¼ *cup all-purpose flour*
> 4 *cups vegetable oil for deep frying*
> 6 to 8 *lemon wedges*

1. Peel the eggplant, cut into small cubes, and soak in a bowl with 1 cup milk and salt for about 30 minutes.

2. Remove the eggplant and squeeze dry. Heat the 2 tablespoons oil in a sauté pan and cook the eggplant gently until soft, about 10 minutes. Sprinkle in the pine nuts, remove to a cutting board, and chop finely, in batches. Place the chopped eggplant in a large bowl.

3. Lightly beat 1 egg and mix it into the eggplant. Add the cheese and season with salt and pepper. Mix thoroughly.

4. Stiffen the mixture with some of the bread crumbs, adding it in parts until the mixture is dry enough to handle but still moist. You will not need all the bread crumbs. Place in the refrigerator and allow to chill thoroughly (it will stiffen with the chilling). It can be held as long as overnight.

5. Beat the other egg with a little milk in a deep bowl. Set the flour, egg mix, and remaining bread crumbs in separate bowls in a row on the table *(anglaise).*

6. Shape the chilled mixture by spoonfuls into one *crocchetta* or *fritto* at a time, immediately passing it through the flour, then egg, and finally the bread crumbs. Adjust the shape, checking it for an even coating, and place on a plate that's been coated with bread crumbs. The *crocchette* or *fritti* can be held in a cool place for several hours before frying.

7. Heat the oil to 375°F and fry the *fritto* or *crocchetta* until it is well crusted and heated through. Remove to a nest of paper toweling and toss lightly to drain. Season with salt and pepper to taste.

8. Squeeze lemon wedges over them freely and serve immediately.

YIELD: *24 fritti or croquettes*

Melanzane Orientali

EGGPLANT ORIENTAL

I've been making this recipe for so many years now that I can't remember where it came from, except that I dimly remember first tasting it at the home of some relatives in Brooklyn when I was very young. It's obviously an extension of the sweet and sour (raisins, pine nuts, sugar, vinegar) aspect of caponata, only the filling is used as a stuffing between two slices of eggplant that make it a sandwich of sorts which is baked with tomato sauce over and under and then served cold with lemon wedges. It's an unusual and delicious presentation.

3 *large eggplants*

2 *cups milk*

½ *cup extra virgin olive oil*

2 *cloves garlic, bled (scored)*

  Salt and pepper to taste

½ *cup finely diced onion*

1 *tablespoon finely chopped fresh garlic*

¼ *cup raisins (can be plumped in hot water)*

¼ *cup pine nuts*

⅛ *teaspoon each dried thyme, basil, and chervil*

⅛ *teaspoon each dried marjoram and oregano*

⅛ *teaspoon crushed red pepper*

¼ *teaspoon ground fennel seed*

¼ *teaspoon ground coriander*

⅛ *teaspoon freshly grated nutmeg*

⅛ *teaspoon ground mace*

1 *cup best aromatic white wine*

½ *cup white wine vinegar*

¼ *cup red wine vinegar*

2 *tablespoons sugar*

  Rind of ½ lemon

4 *fresh basil leaves, torn*

6 *fresh mint leaves, torn*

½ *cup freshly grated parmigiano*

1½ *cups tomatoes, either canned or fresh, or Salsa di Pomodoro or Marinara (see pages 103 and 100)*

½ *cup finely chopped fresh parsley*

½ *cup bread crumbs, seasoned with salt, pepper, and freshly grated parmigiano*

24 *thin lemon slices, cut in half, for garnish*

8 to 12 *sprigs fresh parsley for garnish*

1. Slice 2 eggplants into eight ½-inch slices. Cut the remaining eggplant into ½-inch cubes.

2. Soak all of the eggplant in milk for ½ hour.

3. Drain the slices well on paper towels and fry them in hot vegetable oil till golden brown on both sides. Drain well again on paper towels and set aside.

4. Sauté the cubes of eggplant in the oil over medium-high heat with 2 garlic cloves, till lightly browned, then add all the ingredients in the order

listed above except add only half the parsley, and do not add the lemon slice and parsley sprigs. Stir to amalgamate thoroughly after several additions. Add the salt and pepper when sautéing, to correct the seasoning.

5. Remove half the tomato sauce for baking.

6. Spread some of the filling between 2 slices of eggplant. Repeat 3 times so that you have sandwiches.

7. Coat the bottom of a sheet pan with tomato sauce and place the four sandwiches in it.

8. Coat the sandwiches with sauce and bake in a 350°F oven for 20 to 30 minutes.

9. Remove from the oven, cool (or even refrigerate), and serve garnished with lemon slices—3 to a side, tucked slightly under, and 2 or 3 parsley sprigs. Sprinkle chopped parsley on top of each as a further garnish.

10. Serve as an appetizer or vegetable course. The sandwiches can also be cut into bite-size pieces as *antipasti* (hors d'oeuvres).

YIELD: *4 sandwiches*

FINOCCHIO · FENNEL

This aromatic licorice-scented bulb grows wild and is heavily cultivated in Italy. Its most popular use is sliced plain as one might cut celery hearts or in salads. Thin juliennes add a wonderful taste and textural addition to mixed green salads. Or, thin slices with a lemon and oil dressing make a refreshing salad by themselves with sugar, salt, white pepper, chervil, and cayenne added to the dressing; and the tart sweet contrast of the dressing to the super fresh crunchy taste of the fennel will provide you with a refined salad that can be used on the most formal menu.

But aside from this natural fresh use, fennel is also very popular braised with butter and chicken stock, and many times finished in the oven or under a broiler with parmigiano. The Umbrians have a favorite recipe called *finocchio al trasimeno* (from Lake Trasimeno) where they sauté the fennel pieces after steaming them and then stew the fennel with garlic, oil, and tomatoes laced with *mentuccia* (wild mint).

Our own favorite of favorites is *crostata di finocchio.* These individual fennel and cheese pies have many possible uses: first as an appetizer, second as a separate vegetable course, and last as a proper accompaniment to game birds and roasts of all kinds.

Crostata di Finocchio

FENNEL TARTLETS

DOUGH:

    1 *cup all-purpose flour*
       Pinch of salt
2½ *tablespoons unsalted butter, cut into 1-inch pieces*
    1 *teaspoon cold aromatic white wine*

FILLING:

1½ *pounds fennel bulb*
  ½ *lemon*
    1 *tablespoon unsalted butter*
      Salt and pepper to taste
    1 *teaspoon chopped fresh dill*
    1 *teaspoon chopped fresh mint*
1¼ *cups shredded Gruyère*
5 to 6 *tablespoons freshly grated parmigiano*

1. For the dough, sift the flour and salt into a bowl. Cut the butter into the flour with a knife. Keep cutting with a knife and fork until the consistency is mealy.

2. Add enough wine to bring the dough together and knead very lightly. Form into a ball. Wrap the ball of pastry dough in plastic and let rest for 1 hour or more.

3. For the filling, cook the fennel until fork tender in boiling salted water with the half lemon and its juice, approximately 5 minutes.

4. Cool and cut the fennel in half and then into 2- to 3-inch strips. These strips will be used as a decorative fan on the tart with the cheeses underneath.

5. Sauté the fennel strips in butter on high heat till they take on color and are lightly browned. Season with salt, pepper, and herbs, and set aside.

6. Roll out the pastry to about ⅛-inch thickness. Cut out 4 circles about ½-inch larger than the tops of the tartlet pans. Place the dough in the tartlet pans and press down the bottom and the edges.

7. Sprinkle the dough with the Gruyère and parmigiano, reserving some of both for topping. Season with salt and pepper.

8. Arrange the fennel slices on top in a decorative fan shape and dust the tops with the remaining cheeses.

9. Bake in a 375°F oven for 15 to 20 minutes, or until done, and serve directly, garnished with sprigs of fennel leaves.

YIELD: *4 tartlets*

FUNGHI • MUSHROOMS

Not being an aficionado of wild porcini mushrooms, or goat cheese for that matter, I seem to have become isolated from contemporary and Italian tastes in this regard. Here in Italy, when it's time to gather wild mushrooms, there is a positive frenzy among the entire populace, and every menu in all the restaurants is taken over by porcini—the king of the wild mushrooms. Strangely enough, the rich, dark, woodsy flavor that most people find delectable is too strong for my tastes. I do, though, love a few slices of dried porcini, along with the water-juice that comes from recapturing them, mixed in regular mushroom dishes for added flavor, and I use it extensively to enrich stocks, soups, and sauces. But a plate of *tagliatelle* overflowing with freshly picked porcini is something I can't get beyond a few bites of, in spite of the ecstasies I behold on the faces of my dinner companions.

All this is not to say I don't like mushrooms. It's just the wild ones that turn me off. In fact, one of my favorite *lasagne* recipes is *lasagne ai funghi* (see page 75), in which some porcini are infused with the rest of the mushrooms. I'm also very fond of baked mushroom caps, as my uncle, the baker from Liguria, used to make them—stuffed with anchovies, mushroom stems, onions, bread crumbs, and marjoram. Mushroom caps are also the perfect garniture, or side dish, with *costolette milanese* (breaded veal cutlet, bone in), where the mushrooms are sautéed simply in butter, or grilled, till golden brown. These are perfect with grilled fish and meats of all kinds. And of course, if you really want to get fancy, there's nothing more elegant than a turned mushroom cap as a garniture for a multitude of dishes.

The use of mushrooms in salads is also very refreshing. The Italians prefer to slice them thin and toss them in extra virgin oil—*au naturel,* so to speak. My own recipe is a bit more complex and makes a very elegant salad, particularly when plated properly on Bibb lettuce and garnished with parsley and diced scallions.

Funghi Ripieni alla Liguria

STUFFED MUSHROOMS IN THE MANNER OF LIGURIA

There are dozens of wonderful stuffings that are interchangeable with mushroom caps, zucchini boats, eggplant shells, tomatoes, and artichokes. This one is a Ligurian speciality in which you achieve a surprisingly different taste by combining anchovies and mushrooms.

8 *extra large mushroom caps*

3 *tablespoons unsalted butter*

2 *tablespoons extra virgin olive oil*

2 *tablespoons finely diced white onion*

3 *tablespoons chopped anchovy fillets*

1 *teaspoon dried marjoram*
Pinch of crushed red pepper

1 *tablespoon finely chopped fresh parsley*
Salt and pepper to taste

2 *tablespoons best available aromatic white wine*

3 *tablespoons bread crumbs*

1 *cup tiny cubed croutons sautéed in oil*
Freshly grated parmigiano

1. Remove the stems from 6 of the mushrooms. Dice the stems and remaining 2 mushrooms.
2. Heat 2 tablespoons of butter and 1 of oil in a sauté pan. Add the onion, anchovy, marjoram, crushed red pepper, and parsley, salt, and pepper and gently sauté until the onions begin to soften.
3. Deglaze with white wine and add the bread crumbs and half the cheese and cook briefly. If too dry add a bit of oil.
4. Sauté the mushroom caps in very little oil and butter so that they turn golden brown quickly without really cooking them. Turn them over and sauté the underpart for just 30 seconds.
5. Now toss the croutons into the mixture and fill the caps—nicely mounding and filling each one. Sprinkle parmigiano on top and bake in a 375°F oven for 10 to 15 minutes. Finish under a broiler to brown. Serve directly or chill and then serve later at room temperature as part of an antipasto.

YIELD: *6 mushroom caps*

Funghi Crudi al Limone

RAW MUSHROOM SALAD WITH LEMON

8 *ounces medium-size and tightly closed Champignon mushrooms, washed, dried, and thinly and uniformly sliced*

¼ *cup scallions or white onion tops, cleaned, peeled, and sliced thinly on the bias*

1 *tablespoon dried chervil*

2 *tablespoons finely chopped fresh parsley*
Salt and freshly ground black pepper to taste

¼ *cup fresh lemon juice*

½ *cup extra virgin olive oil*

1 *teaspoon Dijon mustard*
Lemon wedges

1. Toss the sliced mushrooms with the scallions, chervil, 1 tablespoon of the parsley and season well with salt and pepper. Add half the lemon juice and half the oil and let the mushrooms marinate for at least one hour, but not more than 3.

2. Drain the mushrooms by lifting them with a slotted spoon. Mound them on plates lined, if you wish, with lettuce leaves.

3. Make a dressing by whisking together the mustard and remaining oil and lemon juice. Spoon the dressing over the mushrooms and garnish with chopped parsley, sliced scallion, and lemon wedges.

NOTES: Using "turned" mushroom caps would be an additional garnishing touch. Buy perfect, large mushrooms for this.

Use fresh chervil sprigs in the marinade if you have them instead of the dried chervil by increasing the quantity to 3 tablespoons of chopped leaves.

Large mushrooms should be split before slicing to provide uniform size for marinating and handling. In any case, the caps should be tightly closed, and the stems trimmed to within 1 inch of the caps.

This salad is a lovely addition to a traditional antipasto when mounded on a platter, as well as making an unusual first course for a luncheon or light supper.

YIELD: *2 cups*

CIPOLLE • ONIONS

More essential to cooking than even carrots and celery, onions are the staple aromatic vegetable of the kitchen. I imagine it would be virtually impossible to list all the culinary uses of onions—so many are they—since I doubt there's a cuisine to be found without them. Their popularity stretches all the way back to ancient Egypt and continues unabated to this day throughout the world.

Within the onion family there is a delicious variety of types that range from the strongest yellow onions that are perfect for stocks and soups, to the sweetest white of white onions from Vidalia, Georgia, and Maui Maui in Hawaii, which you can almost eat like an apple. Sweet white onions are the centerpiece of *battuto,* marrying the celery and carrot to parsley and prosciutto to make an aromatic base for roasts, braises, stews, and sauces of all kinds. Red (or Spanish) onions, whose bright, sharp flavor contrasts so well with green peppers and tomatoes for a special salad on a hot summer day, have become so popular in America today that they have begun to replace white onions in the basic *battuto* in many instances. And then, of course, where would we be without scallions, chives, leeks, and shallots? When was the last time you had a plate of brandied shallots in cream? Never, you say? Well, try them instead of creamed onions on one of the holidays. Delicious!

The use of all kinds of onions, including shallots, is as extensive in Italy as anywhere in the world, and perhaps more so. Stuffed onions and *cipolle all'agrodolce* (sweet and sour) are prevalent everywhere and part of the ubiquitous antipasti of Italy when not served as a separate vegetable course. Onion sauces for pasta, sliced and served as a salad, and sweet and juicy on *pizza bianca* are just a few of the thousands of dishes you're bound to find an onion hiding in. In fact, onions are so popular that, like chestnuts, they're sold by street vendors in Italy, roasted in their skins to be taken home, peeled and seasoned, and eaten directly.

Whatever your preference, just remember to bite on a piece of bread before and during the peeling and you won't have to cry over them. Works for me—and about 90 percent of the apprentices who work here at the school, except for the diehards who think soaking them in cold water works. Funny to see when we're preparing for Renaissance onion soup *(Carabaccia), pizza bianca,* and our own special onion pizza, all in the same day, and four apprentices are peeling onions with slices of bread in their mouths.

Cipolle all'agrodolce

SWEET AND SOUR ONIONS

1½ to 2 *pounds small onions*

2 to 3 *tablespoons extra virgin olive oil*

½ *cup best aromatic white wine*

1 *tablespoon tomato paste*

2 *cups water*

2 *bay leaves, torn*

2 *whole cloves*

1 *teaspoon juniper berries*

   Salt and pepper to taste

½ *cup white wine vinegar*

1 *teaspoon fresh lemon juice*

2 *tablespoons sugar*

1. Peel the onions without removing the bottom stem so that they stay together. Sauté them lightly in olive oil, adding the white wine and tomato paste.

2. Add the water and season with the bay leaves, cloves, juniper berries, salt, and pepper. Cook gently for 30 minutes, uncovered.

3. Add the white wine vinegar, lemon juice, and sugar, and cook for 45 minutes to an hour, stirring occasionally and adding more liquid if necessary. This should be done on a very low diffused heat. The onion will turn golden brown. Serve hot, at room temperature, or chilled. All equally good.

YIELD: *4 servings or 12 antipasti*

Cipolle Farcite

STUFFED ONIONS

These stuffed onions are wonderful as an appetizer, side dish, or separate vegetable course.

FOR THE ONION SHELLS:

5 *extra large onions*

8 *cups water*

1 *bay leaf, torn*

1 *teaspoon sugar*

FOR THE SAUTÉ:

1 *onion, cut in half and thinly sliced*

½ *teaspoon olive oil*

   White wine to taste

   Freshly grated nutmeg to taste

   Salt and pepper to taste

½ *cup bread crumbs*

2 *tablespoons freshly grated parmigiano*

FOR THE FILLING:

1 *tablespoon diced gorgonzola*

1 *tablespoon diced Gruyère*

1 *tablespoon diced taleggio (or Camembert or any soft cheese)*

½ *cup tiny cubed croutons, sautéed in oil*

2 *tablespoons freshly grated parmigiano*

1. To prepare the onion shells, put the peeled onions in gently boiling water with the seasonings and cook for 5 to 7 minutes, or until tender.

2. Drain them and carefully remove the insides of

4 of them, leaving a thick ¼-inch wall intact. Set the onion shells aside.

3. Chop up the insides along with the extra onion and reserve for the sauté.

4. Sweat the reserved chopped onions and the sliced onion in oil and wine for 10 to 15 minutes on low heat, depending on toughness. They should be very soft.

5. Turn the heat up and brown the onions with nutmeg, salt, and pepper. Add water if liquid is necessary to keep the onions from sticking. Add the bread crumbs and parmigiano and mix briefly in the pan. Remove and set aside.

6. Lightly mix the gorgonzola, Gruyère, and faleggio with the sautéed sliced onions. Add the croutons and toss gently.

7. Fill the onion shells with the onion mixture, rounding or mounding the tops. Garnish with parmigiano.

8. Bake in a 375°F oven for 20 to 30 minutes. If not brown on top, finish under a broiler. Serve immediately.

YIELD: *4 servings*

PISELLI • PEAS

These are perhaps the only vegetables I know of that can be equally as good bought frozen as fresh. Unless you have your own garden to raise the right variety you can be unpleasantly surprised by the toughness and lack of flavor you might encounter in fresh peas. I've had to cook some store-bought peas for over an hour, and they still weren't any good. The better frozen product companies give you consistently sweet and tender peas, and while they certainly aren't as good as the right fresh garden pea, nonetheless the quality and flavor can be depended upon.

The Italians have been very fond of peas since ancient Roman times as can be seen by the nu-merous recipes Apicius provides. And today, although peas are popular throughout Italy, the Romans are as well known for their dishes with peas as the Tuscans are for their beans.

Aside from particular dishes of peas, they are also used as part of a very fine pasta dish, *paglia e fieno.* The first is shell macaroni tossed with butter, peas, and parmigiano, and the second is straw and hay (regular and spinach egg noodles) with a butter sauce enriched by prosciutto, peas, heavy cream, and parmigiano (see page 120). Yet another interesting pasta combination is with peas, mushrooms, onions, and a mayonnaise dressing in a cold pasta salad. But whatever pea recipe you might choose, be sure to cook them till they're properly done and add a bit of sugar to accent their sweetness. If using frozen, they need not be cooked at all. Simply steaming them over hot water (pasta water will do) till they're hot is all that's needed.

Piselli alla Marinara

PEAS WITH MARINARA SAUCE

1 pound baby sweet peas (frozen acceptable)
1 teaspoon sugar
   Salt and pepper to taste
1 cup Marinara (see page 100)
2 tablespoons finely chopped fresh parsley

1. Steam the peas in a bit of water with the sugar until tender (1 minute if frozen). Season with salt to taste.

2. Drain the peas and add the cup of marinara to

them in a saucepan set over medium heat and cook for 5 minutes. Correct the seasoning and toss all lightly together. Serve in warm bowls and garnish with the parsley.

YIELD: *4 servings*

Piselli al Prosciutto alla Romana

PEAS WITH HAM ROMAN STYLE

This recipe was given to me by a Roman chef in New York many years ago, and upon returning to Rome I've found it to be authentic all right, except perhaps for the use of a chiffonnade of lettuce included, which doesn't seem to be part of the present-day standard recipe. This is also wonderful as a tossed pasta dish.

10 to 12 *ounces fresh or frozen peas*
       Salt
  1 *teaspoon sugar*
  1 *tablespoon unsalted butter*
  1 *tablespoon olive oil*
  2 *tablespoons thinly sliced prosciutto*
½ *cup finely diced white onion*
½ *cup Brodo di Pollo (see page 89)*
½ *cup chiffonnade (thin shreds) of romaine lettuce*
      Salt and pepper to taste
⅛ *teaspoon each dried thyme, basil, and chervil*

1. Cook the peas in boiling salted water over medium-high heat with a pinch of salt and the sugar (or steam if frozen and add sugar later) until tender. Drain.
2. Heat the butter and oil in a sauté pan. Cook the drained peas briefly, adding the prosciutto. Add the onion and cook 1 to 2 minutes. Add the chicken stock and amalgamate all, cooking for another 2 to 3 minutes.
3. Add the lettuce, cook for 30 seconds or so, season with salt, pepper, and herbs. Add a little more sugar and serve in warm dishes.

YIELD: *4 servings*

Pisellini e Funghi alla Menta

BABY PEAS AND MUSHROOMS WITH MINT

  1 *pound baby sweet peas (frozen acceptable)*
  4 *tablespoons (½ stick) unsalted butter*
½ *pound mushrooms, thinly sliced*
  2 *tablespoons finely diced white onion*
      Salt, pepper, and cayenne to taste
  1 *teaspoon sugar*
  2 *teaspoons dried mint or 4 teaspoons diced fresh mint*

1. Steam the peas in a bit of water until tender (1 minute if frozen).
2. Melt 2 tablespoons of butter in a sauté pan on medium heat and, when foaming, add the sliced

mushrooms. Cook, turning frequently until lightly browned, 3 to 5 minutes, and then add the diced onion. Season with salt, pepper, and cayenne, and add the peas. Sprinkle all with the sugar.

3. Separately pound the remaining butter with 1 teaspoon of the mint in a mortar to make a composite mint butter. Add the mint butter to the peas, mushrooms, and onions and stir all thoroughly. Serve in warm bowls and top with the remaining teaspoon of mint.

YIELD: *4 servings*

PEPERONI • PEPPERS

I suppose if I were limited to a choice of two vegetables for the rest of my life they would be spinach and peppers. And yet for a variety of menu uses it would have to be peppers first. Whether roasted and served hot or cold, sliced in a salad, sautéed with onions, pickled, pureed, braised alone or in combination with chicken, veal, steak, fish, or game, or as part of a wonderful eggplant caponata, peppers will lend their special flavors without overpowering, at the same time adding great eye appeal with their bright green, red, or yellow accents. I've been having great fun lately creating various types of pepper lasagne:

- red pepper *lasagne,* which consists of egg noodle sheets layered with a sauce of red pepper puree, tomatoes, and mozzarella.
- green pepper *lasagne,* made of egg noodle sheets layered with a sauce of green pepper puree and mozzarella.
- yellow pepper *lasagne,* made from green spinach noodle sheets layered with a yellow pepper puree and mozzarella.
- green and yellow pepper *lasagne;* alternate egg noodle sheets with green pepper puree and spinach noodle sheets with yellow pepper puree.

Somehow I couldn't bring myself to create the Italian flag (red, white and green), although I suppose it too could be delicious.

You'll find many pepper uses spread through a variety of recipes in this book, but I'll now provide three of my favorites.

Peperoni Arrosti

ROASTED PEPPERS

2 **large bell peppers (green are preferred)**
1 **tablespoon extra virgin olive oil**
2 **large cloves garlic, bled (scored)**
 Salt and freshly ground pepper to taste
4 to 6 **anchovy fillets in oil or 2 tablespoons of anchovies and/or capers**
½ **cup Vinaigrette Dressing (see page 47)**
1 **tablespoon chopped fresh parsley**

1. Holding a pepper on the end of a long fork, blister each one evenly over an open flame to char about half of the surface.
2. Place the peppers in a gratin dish or other small casserole. Rub with the oil and garlic and season with salt and pepper. Roast in a 375°F oven for about 12 minutes, leaving still quite firm. They will continue cooking after being removed. Allow to cool in the casserole to room temperature

before serving, or refrigerate if you prefer them cold.

3. To serve, lay anchovy fillets across them (or capers), sauce with vinaigrette, and garnish with the parsley.

YIELD: *2 to 4 portions*

Soufflé di Peperoni

PEPPER SOUFFLÉ

Easy enough if you're into making soufflés. The trick is to drain the pepper puree before adding it to the *balsamella.* Otherwise there is too much liquid and it won't dry out without overcooking the rest of the soufflé. I also add some thin juliennes of peppers cooked lightly in white wine and butter for added flavor and textural contrast.

    2 *large green bell peppers*
4 to 5 *tablespoons extra virgin olive oil*
      Salt and pepper to taste
    6 *cloves garlic, bled (scored)*
    1 *tablespoon julienned green bell pepper*
      White wine to taste
    1 *tablespoon extra virgin olive oil*
    1 *cup Mornaia Sauce (see page 116)*
    4 *jumbo eggs, separated*
    1 *tablespoon unsalted butter, softened*
    2 *tablespoons fine, white bread crumbs*
    1 *large red bell pepper*
    2 *tablespoons best available aromatic white wine*

1. Holding a pepper on the end of a long fork, blister it lightly and evenly over an open flame (using the top of a stove will do).

2. Place the peppers in a baking pan, coat them with about 3 tablespoons of oil and season with salt and pepper.

3. Add 4 garlic cloves and bake in a 375°F oven for 20 to 30 minutes until they begin to collapse.

4. Remove from the oven and peel the peppers. Pass through a food mill and set the pulp in a strainer over a bowl to allow the liquid to drain off. Set aside the puree.

5. Sauté the julienne of peppers in wine and oil, season with salt and pepper, drain, and set aside.

6. If the *mornaia* has just been made, let it cool. Add the egg yolks, 1 at a time, whisking all the while. Season to taste. Fold in the pepper puree and julienne of peppers.

7. Beat the whites to soft peaks and mix a bit into the *mornaia* base. Fold the rest of the egg whites into the soufflé base.

8. Butter and crumb individual soufflé ramekins (or 1 large soufflé dish). Place extra dab of butter on the bottom of each dish. Spoon the soufflé mixture into the ramekins and place them in a pan with water three quarters up the sides. Bake in a 375°F oven for 15 to 20 minutes until puffed and golden. Test for doneness with a sharp knife or a toothpick; it should come out clean. Unmold with a sharp knife onto a warm plate with red pepper puree underneath.

9. Oil pepper thoroughly, using 1 to 2 tablespoons of olive oil, and season with salt and pepper.

10. Roast it in a baking pan with 2 garlic cloves at 375°F for 15 to 20 minutes, or until it starts to collapse. Remove from the oven and puree (without peeling) the pepper through a food mill. Do not drain it since you need the liquid for the sauce.

11. Heat the puree in a bit of oil and reseason with salt and pepper. Serve hot on a warm plate under the unmolded soufflés.

YIELD: *4 to 6 servings, 6 small 2½-inch soufflés*

Purea di Peperoni

PEPPER PUREE

This can be made with less *salsa di pomodoro* or none for that matter. It can be used for soufflés, as a liner for *anitpasti*, a sauce for pasta, or as a base for sauces and salad dressings.

> 10 to 12 *ounces red bell peppers*
> 1 *tablespoon olive oil*
> 2 *cloves garlic, bled (scored)*
> *Salt and pepper to taste*
> 1 *cup (approximately) Salsa di Pomodoro (see page 103)*

1. Split and seed the red peppers and chop them coarsely. Stew them in the oil over low heat with the garlic till soft, Season lightly with salt and pepper
2. Puree in a processor or food mill and return to the pan. Cook briefly over low heat to lighten.
3. Add the *salsa di pomodoro* to the pan and continue to cook lightly to amalgamate. Serve with pasta, roast potatoes. . . .

YIELD: *2 cups*

PATATE · POTATOES

Potatoes were not always popular in Italy. They were mainly used in the north since *pasta secca* was the favored starch throughout the rest of Italy. In the last hundred years or so, however, they have come into their own and now there aren't many menus in Italy without potatoes in one form or another. Fried, stewed, made into pies with onions, *crocchette,* or braised in wine with parmigiano, the so-called lowly potato—is that because they're cheap or because they're grown underground?—is now a staple in the Italian diet and considered one of the finer vegetables. Of course their contribution to the world of pasta has given us those wonderful soft pillows of delight called *gnocchi.* For the recipe for gnocchi see page 64.

Here are three other marvelous uses of our friend the potato.

Crocchette di Patate

POTATO CROQUETTES

I was first brought up on potato croquettes as a child and later was exposed to them as the proper accompaniment to many game and poultry dishes from the classic French (haute cuisine) and *alto livello* Italian presentations, where they are the perfect foil to sop up juices, gravies, and sauces. To this day potato croquettes are my own preferred addition to *anitra all'arancia* (duck à l'orange), *fagiano in salmis* (roast pheasant), *coniglio* (rabbit), *lepre* (hare) or quail in red wine *alla Perugina*. They are also delicious when formed into little balls and served as part of a *fritto misto.*

The trick in making these croquettes is just as in making *gnocchi*—you want to eliminate flour as a binder altogether (or at least keep it to a minimum), so that they remain soft inside as a proper contrast to the crunchy fried bread crumb outside.

3 pounds potatoes, peeled
2 tablespoons unsalted butter
2 jumbo eggs
¼ cup freshly grated parmigiano
1 teaspoon freshly grated nutmeg
1 cup combined finely diced
   mozzarella and prosciutto
   (optional)
   Salt and pepper to taste
1½ to 2 cups flour, seasoned with salt and
   pepper
4 eggs, lightly beaten for eggwash
4 cups bread crumbs for breading
   Vegetable oil for frying

1. Cook the potatoes in boiling salted water until tender.
2. Drain and, while still hot, pass through a food mill with the butter
3. Beat in the 2 eggs. Add the parmigiano, ½ teaspoon of nutmeg, mozzarella, and prosciutto, if you so decide. Since the water starch content of potatoes differs, you will have to adjust the parmigiano accordingly. If the batter is still too wet, add a little flour. Season with salt and pepper and mix well. Chill the potato mixture for at least 30 minutes before shaping it.
4. Arrange 3 bowls on the counter, one holding seasoned flour, another the eggs for the eggwash, and a third the bread crumbs seasoned with salt, pepper, and the remaining ½ teaspoon of nutmeg.
5. Shape the chilled potato mixture into small logs using a spoon and the palms of your hands. Pass the logs through the flour, eggwash and bread crumbs, place on a crumbed plate and chill.
6. When ready to serve, heat the vegetable oil in a deep pot to 350°F. Fry the logs, a few at a time, till golden brown. Drain on paper towels and serve directly.

YIELD: *10 to 12 pieces*

Patate alla Parmigiana

POTATOES PARMIGIANO

2 large potatoes, peeled
6 to 8 tablespoons unsalted butter
   Salt and pepper to taste
1 cup Fondo Bruno or consommé (see
   page 85 or 88)
¼ cup best available dry red wine
1 cup freshly grated parmigiano
   Freshly grated nutmeg to taste

1. Thinly slice the potatoes and place in an ice water bath.
2. Blanch the potatoes in salted, boiling water for just 2 minutes, drain, and shock with cold water until cooled.
3. Thickly butter a 6-cup, shallow casserole and arrange an overlapping layer of potato slices in it. Season with salt and pepper, dot with a third of the remaining butter, moisten the layer with a third of the stock and wine, sprinkle on a third of the parmigiano, dust lightly with nutmeg, and repeat the procedure for 2 more layers, ending with the parmigiano. Bake in a 425°F oven until well browned and tender, about 30 to 40 minutes.

YIELD: *6 servings*

Tiella di Patate

POTATO CASSEROLE

Tiella in Pugliese dialect means casserole and the use of tomato sauce in this potato-and-anchovy casserole makes it unusual.

2 pounds medium-size potatoes, 10, peeled
    and sliced ¼ inch thick
    Salt
1 cup Salsa di Pomodoro (see page 103)
    Freshly ground black pepper to taste
½ cup shredded Gruyère
½ cup freshly grated parmigiano, plus some
    for topping
2 tablespoons grated pecorino Romano
    Two 2-ounce cans anchovy fillets in oil

1. Parboil the potatoes in salted water till just tender.
2. Coat the bottom of a 9-inch casserole dish with half of the *salsa di pomodoro* and lay in a third of the potato slices. Season with salt and pepper and sprinkle with ½ of the Gruyère, parmigiano, and pecorino. Top with half of the anchovy fillets.
3. Repeat the process and then cover with a third layer of potatoes. Season that with salt, pepper, and some parmigiano, and top with the remaining *salsa di pomodoro*.
4. Bake in a preheated 375°F oven for approximately 1 hour, until crisp and golden brown. Serve directly on warm plates as a vegetable course or a side dish.

YIELD: *4 to 6 servings*

Patate "Rissole"

RISSOLE POTATOES

18 to 20 small potatoes, 3 to 4 ounces each,
    peeled
2 to 3 tablespoons unsalted butter
2 to 3 tablespoons olive oil
    Salt and pepper to taste

1. In a heavy-bottomed pan or casserole, cook the potatoes over very low heat in the butter and oil for about 40 minutes. Turn frequently as they cook so that they crust evenly on all sides. The potatoes should be well crusted outside and tender inside.
2. Season at the end of cooking.

NOTE: These potatoes can also be cooked in beef or veal drippings while a roast is cooking.

YIELD: *6 servings*

• SPINACI E GLI ALTRI •
SPINACH AND OTHER LEAFY GREENS

Aside from the lettuce family there are a number of leafy green vegetables, or greens from the tops of tubers, such as turnips and beets, that exude good health as well as flavor. Spinach, sorrel, Swiss chard, kale, mustard greens, and even grapevine leaves all have a multiplicity of uses—from the most simple steaming or sauté, through packets filled with forcemeats, to creaming, braising, or raw in salads. Leafy greens not only look good and taste good, but they also make you feel good. For me it's the best of all possible worlds when my taste buds are sated with something that I know is also healthy and nutritious. My favorite of favorites in this area is spinach. Whether steamed, sautéed, creamed, or in salads, spinach to me has the quintessential bittersweet dark green flavor that makes it consistently the most satisfying vegetable. Not to denigrate mustard greens, sorrel, and others, but as delicious as they are my liking for them is only occasional, whereas spinach remains available as often as I'd like, with never a fear of disappointment.

As far as cooking methods go, they are all interchangeable except that a recipe calling for spinach might take 10 to 15 minutes longer to cook if it were for mustard or beet greens. But other than that you can use the same recipes for all of them.

Spinaci Rosolati o Strascinati

SPINACH SAUTÉ

¼ cup extra virgin olive oil
2 cloves garlic, bled (scored)
2 pounds fresh leaf spinach
Pinch of salt
½ teaspoon freshly ground black pepper
½ teaspoon crushed red pepper (optional)

1. Heat the oil over medium-high heat and lightly brown the garlic.
2. Add the spinach and sauté for 1 or 2 minutes. Add the salt and pepper, toss, and serve. The crushed red pepper is a *sine qua non* in some Italian homes and is added at the end of the toss.

Crema di Spinaci

CREAMED SPINACH

Vegetables of all kinds, and particularly greens, are an essential part of Italian cooking. In fact, the Italians will sneak spinach in everywhere they can: in soups, pasta, frittatas, and ravioli fillings. In Bologna they learned early how to chop and cream spinach into a truly luscious vegetable dish. As with all greens, of course, a bit of oil, a clove or two of garlic, and freshly ground pepper are the most natural, and the Italians will invariably sauté greens on a brisk heat in this manner. But for a richer, gentler presentation you can't beat creaming these wonderful vegetables.

1 garlic clove, bled (scored)
4 tablespoons (½ stick) unsalted butter
2 to 3 tablespoons all-purpose flour
Salt and pepper to taste
1 teaspoon finely grated nutmeg
2 cups milk, scalded and hot
2 pounds fresh or 10 ounces frozen spinach (cooked with 2 tablespoons butter, pinch nutmeg, salt, and pepper, drained and squeezed of excess liquid, then finely chopped)
½ cup heavy cream

1. Brown the garlic in 3 tablespoons of butter over medium-low heat. Add the flour and cook, whisking all the while, till the mixture browns. This is a brown roux. Season the roux with salt, pepper, and ½ teaspoon of nutmeg and whisk thoroughly.
2. Add the scalding milk in thirds and whisk

again. Add the spinach and mix well. Add the remaining spices and mix again.

3. Cook for approximately 25 minutes over low, diffused heat, stirring occasionally, and then add the heavy cream and the remaining teaspoon of butter to finish. Serve immediately.

YIELD: *4 servings*

FAGIOLINI • **STRING BEANS**

Wonderful when simply steamed and buttered and perhaps tossed with almonds and/or hazelnuts, string beans are especially good if you use the thin, round, green beans that always seem to have better flavor and texture. You can also use yellow in this recipe, although being more delicate I'm partial to yellow beans with hazelnuts and butter.

Fagiolini alla Pizzaiola

STRING BEANS WITH TOMATO AND OREGANO

12 ounces young green string beans

1 cup canned Italian plum tomatoes, with juice

3 cloves garlic, bled (scored)

1 tablespoon extra virgin olive oil

1 tablespoon dried oregano

1 tablespoon large capers

1 tablespoon unsalted butter

Salt and pepper to taste

½ teaspoon crushed red pepper

Fresh lemon juice to taste

2 tablespoons chopped fresh parsley

1. Cook the beans in salted water until tender but still *al dente.*

2. Pass the tomatoes through a food mill or puree quickly in a food processor so that they are still course.

3. Sauté the beans in the garlic and oil over medium heat and add the pureed tomatoes, oregano, and capers.

4. Add the butter and stir over low heat so that it melts slowly. Add the salt, pepper, and crushed red pepper. Stir in the lemon juice.

5. Turn the heat to medium-low and cook for 5 to 10 minutes until the tomatoes thicken.

6. Serve hot, garnished with parsley.

YIELD: *4 servings*

ZUCCHINI • **ZUCCHINI**

In America when one thinks of Italian vegetables it's zucchini and eggplant that immediately come to mind. Throughout Italy these small green squashes are almost the national vegetable. There are different types of zucchini. The smaller tastier kind, called *cocuzze* in Puglia and Bari, are superb when simply steamed with good oil and a bit of onion. In Liguria they prefer to sauté zucchini slices with garlic, oil, and tomato, which is probably the forerunner of zucchini provençale. My personal favorites are the two that follow.

Zucchini in Vapore

STEAMED ZUCCHINI

2 large or 4 small zucchini (1 pound)
2 medium-size onions, sliced
2 tablespoons unsalted butter
½ teaspoon dried chervil
   Pinch of cayenne
1 teaspoon sugar
   Salt and pepper to taste
1 tablespoon finely chopped fresh parsley

1. Wash the zucchini, trim the ends, and slice into ⅛-inch pieces.
2. Place in a pot to cook with a few tablespoons of water and the remaining ingredients, reserving half the parsley. Cook, covered, over medium heat for 3 to 5 minutes until tender and serve in the juice, garnishing each dish with the remaining parsley.

YIELD: *4 servings*

Zucchini Ripieni con Uva Secca

STUFFED ZUCCHINI WITH RAISINS

3 medium-size zucchini, about 1 pound
2 tablespoons olive oil
1 clove garlic, bled (scored)
1 tablespoon raisins, plumped in water, drained
1 tablespoon toasted pine nuts
1 tablespoon chopped fresh mint
   Pinch of crushed red pepper
   Salt and pepper to taste
2 tablespoons dry white wine
¼ cup bread crumbs
¼ cup freshly grated parmigiano
1 cup tiny cubed croutons

1. Wash the zucchini, trim the ends, and cut 2 zucchini in half lengthwise. Scoop out inside pulp, leaving a ¼-inch-thick shell. Roughly chop the pulp and the other zucchini.
2. Heat the oil in a sauté pan over moderate heat with the garlic clove. Add the chopped zucchini and cook for 1 to 2 minutes. Add the onion and continue to cook for 1 minute. Add the raisins, pine nuts, mint, crushed red pepper, salt, and pepper. Deglaze with white wine.
3. Stir in the bread crumbs and half the parmigiano. Mix well, add the croutons, and mix again. Garnish with the remaining parmigiano.
4. Remove from stove and stuff the zucchini shells, mounding each.
5. Oil a pan, place the zucchini in the pan, and bake in a 375°F oven for 30 to 40 minutes. Finish under a broiler if not brown. Serve immediately.

YIELD: *4 servings*

PESCE

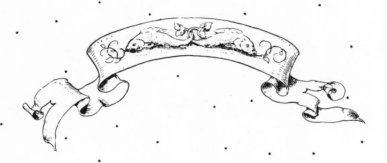

Fish

FISH

PESCE · FISH

Nine-tenths of Italy is surrounded by the sea. Those few areas that are landlocked abound with rivers, lakes and streams that always have been, and still are, regularly fished by the Italians. Here in Umbria, in the center of Italy, and two hours from either coast, the *trota salmonata* (salmon trout) from the many rivers and streams are prized throughout Italy as are the eels from nearby Lake Bolsena. Since no point in Italy is far from the water, fish is an important staple in the Italian diet.

The Romans were inordinately fond of fish of all kinds, particularly oysters and caviar from their own privately cultivated sturgeon which, when combined together, make one of the most exquisite antipasti possible. The original cultivation of oysters in beds is attributed to Sergius Orata in the fifth century B.C. In the "heydays" of the Roman Empire (100–200 A.D.), enormous sums were spent on the upkeep of these beds and for special ponds to raise *morene* (lamprey or sea eels). No banquet in those days was considered complete without oysters and those long undulating sea snakes. According to Waverley Root

in *The Food of Italy*, lamprey were cultivated so extensively that Caesar is said to have served 6,000 of them at a banquet to celebrate a victory.

Although the Italians were not loathe to create tasty dishes out of what some might consider the strangest inhabitants of the sea (dogfish, sea urchin, cuttlefish, octopus, frogfish, sea strawberry, sea cat, squid, and skate or ray), they were, and are, equally adept at utilizing all the more normal types of fish and have given us a broad fish cuisine that is classically simple and yet wonderfully inventive.

What could be simpler and yet more delicious than to steam clams or mussels in their shells and combine their juice with a bit of wine, herbs, and aromatics? Or to add soft- and hard-fleshed fish and perhaps saffron to create the delicate richness of a Venetian *Zuppa di pesce*?

The list of fish used throughout Italy is endless and the variety of presentations inexhaustible. I'll provide a list of the major saltwater and freshwater fish in suitable categories of lean and fat fish both in English and Italian, as well as the major mollusks, crustaceans, and other seafoods for your information at the end of this chapter.

In the meantime, let's discuss some of the more important aspects of buying, handling, preparing, and cooking fish in general.

BUYING FISH

Freshness is the well-known key to the purchase of all seafood. Ideally, one should go fishing or clamming, and have a lobster pot and a kitchen right at the source. If any of you have been that fortunate and privileged to eat fresh catch, you will agree, I'm sure, that there is no better way to eat seafood. I remember reading somewhere that the Russians in the old days were so fond of their "fresh" fish that fishmongers maintained boats on the rivers and the seas where customers could shop and pick out live fish from large tanks hanging on the sides of the boats. Failing this, there were horsedrawn carts, and later trucks, that went through the larger cities selling live fish from tanks. The Italians don't go quite that far but it is refreshing to see that all the better fish restaurants have lobster and trout tanks on display to assure the freshness of at least those products.

This attention to freshness and the benefit of improved flavor is particularly important for clams, oysters, and mussels, where eating direct from the sea can't be beat. But with fish generally, the flavor of a fresh catch will be improved if you let the fish rest (chilled) for three or four hours after catching it, strange as that may seem.

Unfortunately, these considerations are hardly the problem when you purchase fish from your local fish market. Here you have to look carefully and feel, see, and touch to determine freshness.

What do you look for?

General appearance. Fresh fish are shiny and bright, healthy looking, and not slimy.

Texture The flesh is firm, springy and elastic to the touch with a taut, moist skin. The abdomen is not soft or flaccid. Nothing is wrinkled or dry.

Eyes. The eyes of a fish are a dead giveaway as to freshness. When fresh, they are bright and shiny, not in the least bit cloudy or filmed over— and definitely not opaque. The pupils are a brilliant shiny black and the cornea is transparent and clear. A fish eye that's fresh looks exaggeratedly open.

Gills. The inside of the gills should be moist and a dark burgundy color with a transparent mucous. After a few days the dark wine color fades into a brownish red color and the inside filaments are separate and become unhealthy looking.

Odor. A fresh fish smells of fresh (unpolluted) seawater with its pleasant briny odor. If it's a freshwater fish, the smell is like seaweed and still unmistakably fresh smelling. The smell deteriorates rapidly and becomes putrid and sickly sweet as the fish deteriorates. The nose test is particularly useful for shellfish and mollusks, where the other tests of eyes and gills don't apply; although general appearance and texture are important tests for those types of seafood also. Lobster, crabs, and other shellfish should be alive when purchased and if they look too sleepy and refuse to wake up on prodding, you can bet they'll be dead by the time you get them home. Clams and mussels should close up tightly when tapped, if alive. If they refuse to close, smell them and you'll be able to tell if it's stubbornness or death.

It is also important to note that freshwater fish deteriorate more rapidly than saltwater fish and should really be consumed the same day, whereas a fresh catch of bluefish, for example, if properly lemoned and iced will be usable for two or three days . . . assuming one had to wait for some reason. When you buy any kind of fish in the normal market, however, consumption the same day is the best policy since they are probably two or three days old already.

All fish should be gutted immediately upon catching since the innards deteriorate the fastest. Assuming you have a gutted fish, however, which is what is normally available in the markets, the first thing to do is to wash it in clear cold running water immediately. Then, pat it dry with toweling of some sort and wash it with lemons. A lemon is to a fish as butter is to bread—a marriage of significant natural consequence. The acid not only cleanses the fish but also kills bacteria and thereby slows down spoilage. The next trick is to chill the fish thoroughly without freezing it. The best technique for achieving this is to refrigerate it on a bed of crushed ice, with cut-up lemons in a perforated drip pan to catch the water that runs off as the ice melts. The fish should not sit in water. If you don't have a drip pan, you can make one out of plastic containers set inside one another. Puncture the inset plastic container with an icepick or skewer and set it on a rack in the second container so that the water can run off when the ice melts—unless you're fortunate to find a plastic container that will suspend itself over the other container. Then set the crushed ice in the inset with the lemons used for washing the fish, lay the fish on top, cover with a wet (damp) towel, and refrigerate.

As good as lemons are for the average fish, they are deadly for shellfish. The acid will kill clams, mussels, lobsters, and crabs, as will cold fresh water. It is best to leave the clams and mussels in the packs they're purchased in and refrigerate with damp toweling. After cleaning, use the shellfish as quickly as possible. Lobsters and crabs are best stored in seaweed in a very cool place but not refrigerated. I've held them alive in this manner for as long as three days. Wood shavings also work if you can't get the seaweed.

As for freezing—well, if you must—do it while the fish is fresh. Lean fish will be okay for six months and fat fish about three months. Lobster and crab freeze decently, but the rest of the shellfish are so far off the mark that I'd recommend a change in menu before using them.

Although you can tell your fishmonger to prepare a whole fish for you, I think it will be helpful to explain exactly what has to be done to get fish into usable portions.

The butchering technique is somewhat different for round fish and flat fish when it comes to sectioning, but remains the same for scaling and gutting except for a technique of gutting large round fish through the gills which is done to preserve the whole fish intact for baking, roasting, or grilling.

Whether round, flat, fat, or lean, in order to prepare a fish correctly and easily without undue mess it is necessary to set yourself up properly. First of all you need very sharp knives, preferably long thin fillet knives, a strong sharp pair of scissors, and a scraper for scaling. Then lemon a board and set it on a damp towel so it won't shift around. Set it near a sink so that you can rinse the fish with cold running water easily. Finally organize a waste can and a garbage can so that you can dispose of all extraneous matter directly.

Now you're ready.

Scaling. Use a fish scaler or a knife and proceed to stroke the skin from tail to head, removing the scales by scraping.

Finning. Remove the dorsal, anal, and pectoral fins with a sharp knife or scissors by slicing each side of the fin and freeing the connecting bones or cutting them off with scissors.

Gutting. Cut down the length of the fish's belly from the root of the tail to the gills. This can be done either with scissors or a sharp knife. Now run a knife down the backbone on the inside to release the blood pockets and innards, and pull them all out. Clean the fish with cold running water, pat dry, and lemon the insides.

Gutting a large round fish. This is done to preserve the whole fish. Open wide a gill with your fingers, forcing them all the way in; reach down and pull out all the innards. Rinse well with running cold water by washing out the inside through the gill.

Skinning a flat fish. Place the fish on the lemoned board, dark side down, and hold the tail firmly with your other hand. Cut the skin across the bottom where it joins the tail. Now pick up a flap of the skin with your other hand and pull or peel the skin up all the way to the head. Turn the fish over and do the other side. Again lemon the fish.

Skinning a round fish. Make an incision with a sharp knife from the gills to the tail. Now work the point of the knife under the skin and slice clear across to the other side. Hold the freed skin taut with your other hand and slice back and forth down to the tail without removing any of the flesh. Discard the skin. Lemon the fish.

Filleting a flat fish. After skinning the fish, remove the fillets by scoring the flesh at the juncture with the bone, by running down the center with the sharp pointed end of a knife. Once you have loosened this bit of flesh, it is easy to continue to work gently outward, thus loosening the whole fillet from the bones. Once freed, remove the outer fatty rim from each fillet. The same procedure applies whether the fish is skinned or not. If there are small bones remaining, pull them out with tweezers or your fingers. Lemon the fish again.

Filleting a round fish. Skinned or unskinned, but in either case cleaned and gutted, lay the fish on its side with the tail nearest you and proceed to make an incision at the backbone nearest the head, using the sharp pointed end of a knife. Hold the fish firmly with your other hand and slice down to the tail, exposing the backbone. Sever the flesh from its juncture with the head and continue to separate the flesh from the bones, working from the top to the tail. Turn the fish over and fillet the other side.

If there are small bones remaining, pull them out with your fingers or a tweezer and discard. Lemon the fish again and reserve chilled and well covered.

Filleting a cooked fish. Whether flat or round, a cooked fish is easily filleted by making an incision with the sharp pointed end of a knife at the top of the backbone near the head and continuing down to the tail. Take the top half of the fish off and the bones will be exposed on the bottom half. Simply pick the whole bone out by lifting it at the tail with a knife and fork. Pick out whatever little bones remain and you're ready to serve.

Cutting fish into steaks. There are a limited number of fish that can be properly cut into steaks. The fish should be large, round, and without a mess of tiny bones. Swordfish, tuna, salmon, and cod are prime candidates because of their size, roundness, and lack of excessive bones. First, cut through the back of the head by laying the fish on its belly and slicing down just behind the gills through the backbone. Now turn the fish on its side and remove the head by slicing down again. Reserve for the stockpot. Now slice the fish into steaks by laying it on its side and slicing straight down at a distance of 1½ to 2½ inches, depending upon your own preference for thickness. To cook properly, whether by grilling, sautéing, or baking, you need at least 1 to 1½-inch thickness in the steaks from a fish that weighs 12 pounds or better. A good portion size is 6 to 8 ounces.

Cooking times. It would be nice to think that the famous Canadian system of cooking for ten minutes for every inch of thickness of a fish measured at its thickest point was infallible as some writers would suggest. But unfortunately other writers, such as Alan Davidson in his very fine book on North Atlantic seafood, point out that

. . . heat travels gradually from the outside to the inside. The further it has to go the longer it takes.

However, the time taken does not vary in simple proportion to the thickness, but in proportion to the square of the thickness . . .

If it takes two minutes to cook a piece of fish 2 cm thick, then a piece 4 cm thick will take 8 minutes, not 4 minutes.

So much for the clever fish rule called the "Perfect Fish," which relies on a simple 10 minutes per inch formula.

As I've stated elsewhere, the *sine qua non* of good cooking is to look, see, feel, touch, and smell with love and devotion and you will quickly learn when something is done or it isn't. By all means measure the thickness and multiply by ten minutes to get an approximate idea of cooking time, but then pay attention to the fish as it cooks and test for doneness by prying open the flesh several times. None of these charts, or general rules, take into consideration that lean and fat fish cook differently, as do flat and round fish.

The strangest thing is that most everyone ignores the really foolproof method of using an interior gauge thermometer. The proper range of doneness for fish is between 135° and 145°F, with 140°F being the theoretical optimum. It's quite simple to insert the thermometer into the thickest part of the fish and determine proper doneness, regardless of whether the fish is flat, round, lean, or fat.

Since fish has very little connective tissue, it cooks rapidly even at low heat and must be handled and watched carefully to avoid being overcooked. It can be considered done if the fish is just able to be separated into flakes, the flesh separates from the bone easily and the bone is no longer pink, or the flesh has turned from translucent to opaque. Remember that fish is so delicate it keeps cooking after you remove it from the stove, thus requiring you to anticipate the desired doneness.

COOKING METHODS

Lean and fat fish should be distinguished as to cooking methods. Lean fish tends to become dry and therefore should be poached, or generously basted to preserve what moisture there is, and cooked very little.

Fat fish, however, can be poached or braised and are available to broiling or frying just as lean fish are, with only one caution, cut back on the fat in cooking since the technique for cooking fat fish is to remove the greasiness, not increase it.

Some of the more popular examples of these categories are:

Fat fish—mackerel, tuna, carp, sturgeon, swordfish, bluefish, mullet, shad, pompano, sardines, herring, smelts, trout, butterfish, and salmon.
Lean fish—cod, flounder, sole, halibut, pike, perch, red snapper, haddock, bass, pollock, whiting, catfish, turbot, monkfish, grouper, and tilefish.

No matter how you prepare your fish, remember to allow further cooking time for plating up and serving; fish continues to cook on the plate. Have warm plates ready and serve your fish directly from the stove top, oven, broiler, or grill.

If any of these recipe calls for a fish that is not available, substitute another, making sure only that the type of fish is suitable to the cooking method.

Zuppa di Pesce

FISH SOUP

To make a marvelous dinner, serve this hearty but light entree with salad, cheese, and fruit. Let the guests savor the zuppa.

½ cup olive oil

4 cloves garlic, bled (scored)

12 mussels, cleaned and debearded

12 littleneck clams, washed

3 small petit lobster tails

12 shrimp, peeled and deveined

1 cup combined diced carrot, celery, and onion

1 teaspoon finely diced garlic

1 medium-size white onion, diced

Pinch each dried thyme, basil, chervil, and marjoram

1 to 2 bay leaves

2 to 4 fresh basil leaves

2 tablespoons chopped fresh parsley

Salt and freshly ground pepper to taste

1 cup aromatic white wine

1 cup Marinara (see page 100) or fresh chopped tomatoes

4 cups Brodo di Pesce (see page 90)

3 to 4 slices orange rind

1 teaspoon grated lemon rind

1 to 2 pounds each, fillets or steaks, of 3 kinds of fish (perch, bass, flounder, snapper, rockfish)

1. Heat the oil in large casserole over medium-high heat. Partially brown the garlic cloves in the oil.

2. Add the shellfish, starting with the hardest (the mussels) and ending with the shrimp.

3. Add the carrots, celery, onion, garlic, shallots, herbs, salt, and pepper. Quickly add the wine before the garlic browns.

4. Add the marinara sauce or fresh tomatoes and the fish stock. Add orange and lemon rinds.

5. Stir gently and cook, covered, for 4 to 6 minutes over medium-low heat.

6. Add the fish fillets, placing the firmest on the bottom and softest on the top. Cook for another 4 to 6 minutes or until the top fish is done.

7. Remove and set the fish aside and continue to cook any unopened shellfish, if needed. Force any that do not open with a knife. If they smell or look bad, discard. Otherwise, serve them.

8. Place the shellfish and fish in large warm bowls, dividing all and the broth as equally as practical among your guests.

9. Garnish with slices of Italian bread rubbed with garlic and oil, topped with grated parmigiano, and toasted under a broiler.

YIELD: 6 servings

Burrida o Brodetto alla Liguria

FISH SOUP LIGURIA STYLE

2 lemons

2 to 3 pounds of assorted hard and soft fish, cleaned and cut into 2-inch pieces but not boned

1 cup extra virgin olive oil preferred

4 cloves garlic, bled (scored)

2 tablespoons diced onion

1 cup dry white wine (Soave or best available)

2 cups canned Italian plum tomatoes

1 bay leaf

⅛ teaspoon crushed red pepper

Salt and pepper to taste

4 *walnuts, finely ground*

4 *slices bread toasted with parmigiano*

¼ *cup Pesto (see page 125) for garnish*

1. Squeeze the lemons over the cut-up fish and gently toss to coat.
2. Heat the oil in a large casserole over medium heat and add the garlic cloves, cooking until slightly browned. Add the diced onion and the fish and cook gently until the onion begins to color.
3. Deglaze with the white wine and allow the wine to evaporate partially.
4. Add the tomatoes, bay leaf, and crushed red pepper, and season with salt and pepper. Add the ground walnuts, cover, and cook for 5 minutes on medium-low heat. Uncover and cook for another 20 minutes, stirring occasionally.
5. Place the toasted bread slices in four warm soup bowls and pour the *burrida* (soup and fish) over them. Top each with a tablespoon of pesto and serve.

YIELD: *4 servings*

Caciucco alla Toscana

FISH SOUP TUSCAN STYLE

2 *lemons*

2 *pounds assorted hard and soft fish, cleaned, boned, and cut into 2-inch pieces*

1 *pound hake or cod fillets, cleaned, boned, and cut into 2-inch pieces*

24 to 36 *pieces assorted shellfish such as clams, mussels, crab, and shrimp*

1 *cup extra virgin olive oil*

2 *cloves garlic, bled (scored)*

2 *garlic cloves, diced*

Salt and pepper to taste

2 *cups best available aromatic white wine*

2 *cups Brodo di Pesce (see page 90) or 1 cup white wine and 1 cup water*

2 *cups canned Italian plum tomatoes, pureed*

2 *tablespoons tomato paste*

1 *bay leaf*

⅛ *teaspoon crushed red pepper*

¼ *teaspoon each dried thyme and marjoram*

¼ *cup chopped fresh parsley*

2 *cups water*

1 *ounce* **vin santo** *(optional)*

Croutons (optional)

1. Squeeze the lemons over the fish and gently toss to coat. Rinse the shellfish several times and scrub clean.
2. Heat the oil over a medium heat in a large casserole and gently cook the whole garlic cloves. Add the boned 2-inch pieces of fish and cook lightly for 2 to 3 minutes without browning. Stir in the diced garlic and season with salt and pepper.
3. Deglaze with 1 cup of the white wine and allow to evaporate slightly. Add the fish stock (or wine and water), pureed plum tomatoes, tomato paste, bay leaf, crushed red pepper, thyme, marjoram, and 1 tablespoon of the chopped parsley. Cook, partially covered, over medium-low heat for 45 minutes to 1 hour.
4. In the meantime, steam the shellfish with the

other 1 cup of wine and the water. Remove the meat from the shells when slightly undercooked.

5. When the tomato base for the *caciucco* has finished cooking, pass it through a food mill or strainer.

6. Adjust the thickness to a desired consistency by reducing it slightly over high heat, or adding wine or water if too thick for your taste.

7. Add the fillets of hake or cod and the meat from the shellfish to the tomato base in the casserole.

8. Adjust the heat to medium-low and cook, uncovered, for 10 to 15 minutes, or until the fish and shellfish are properly done. The fillets of hake or cod will break into pieces, which is desirable. In fact, you can help them along with a fork.

9. Add *vin santo* or not and plate in warm bowls with or without croutons, as you prefer. Top each bowl with the remaining chopped parsley.

YIELD: *4 servings*

Salmone della Casa

SALMON WITH HOLLANDAISE

Although salmon is technically a "fat" fish, and can be baked, it is nonetheless a thing unto itself, being so delicate as to make poaching or steaming the techniques that automatically come to mind with this very special fish. The Italians are very fond of chargrilling their salmon with a bit of oil and lemon—and very delicious it is. Nonetheless, my own preference is to steam the salmon in a racked poacher with a court bouillon underneath and knap it with a simple hollandaise tarted with lemon and cayenne. I first had this at the Villa d'Este at Lago di Como (Lake Como) some thirty odd years ago and was pleased to enjoy the same dish again just last year.

2 *cups Salsa Olandese (see page 154)*
2 *cups warm Court Bouillon, made with Brodo di Pesce and wine (see page 90)*
4 *fresh salmon steaks, 6 to 8 ounces each*
2 *tablespoons finely chopped fresh parsley*
4 *lemon wedges*
4 *sprigs fresh parsley*

1. Make the hollandaise and reserve.

2. If you don't have a fish poacher, make one by putting a rack in a baking pan. Put the court bouillon in the pan under the rack so it does not quite touch the rack. Set this on the stove and heat to barely boiling.

3. Place the salmon steaks on the rack. Cover tightly with a lid or foil and cook by steaming the fish for 10 to 15 minutes or longer, depending on thickness, until done.

4. Quickly lift the steaks from the rack with a spatula, being careful not to break them, and plate in the center of a warm plate. Spoon warm hollandaise over the top of each and sprinkle with chopped parsley. Garnish each with a lemon wedge and parsley sprig. Serve immediately.

NOTE: Doneness is easy to determine in this case since the salmon loses its deep red, wet color and blanches out. Test with a fork, observing the red wetness as it disappears. At the precise moment before it totally disappears, the fish is cooked perfectly.

YIELD: *4 servings*

Trancie di Salmone al Basilico

SALMON FILLETS WITH BASIL

  2 lemons
  4 salmon fillets, 6 to 8 ounces each, cleaned and boned
  8 tablespoons (1 stick) unsalted butter, cut into 12 pieces
30 to 40 fresh basil leaves (dried not acceptable), torn and stemmed
    Pinch of cayenne
    Salt and pepper to taste
  1 cup heavy cream
 ¼ cup roughly chopped fresh basil for topping

1. Squeeze 1 lemon over the salmon, making sure to coat both sides.
2. Melt 4 tablespoons of butter over medium heat in a sauté pan large enough to accommodate the 4 fillets. When the butter foams, add the fillets. Cook for 3 to 5 minutes on each side and reserve on a warm plate in a 175° to 200°F oven.
3. Add the remaining butter to the pan, a piece at a time, and melt until foaming. Do not brown. Add the juice from the other lemon, the basil leaves, cayenne, salt, and pepper and stir to amalgamate all. Add the heavy cream and reduce all by a third. Correct the seasonings.
4. Plate the fish on warm plates with a small pool of the sauce underneath each fillet. Top each lightly with more sauce and sprinkle with the roughly chopped basil.

YIELD: *4 servings*

Filetti di Salmone al Barolo

SALMON FILLETS IN BAROLO

  1 lemon
  4 salmon fillets, 6 to 8 ounces each, boned and cleaned
  4 tablespoons (½ stick) unsalted butter
  2 tablespoons extra virgin olive oil
  3 cups Barolo wine
  1 cup Brodo di Pesce (see page 90)
 ½ cup fish glaze (see page 93)
  2 cloves garlic, minced
 ¼ cup finely chopped fresh parsley
    Salt and pepper to taste
    Cayenne to taste

1. Wash the salmon, making sure to cover both sides.
2. Melt the butter in a skillet large enough to hold the salmon. Add the oil and heat it. Sauté the salmon fillets over medium heat for 3 to 5 minutes on each side. Deglaze with the Barolo and then add the fish stock and stir to combine.
3. Remove the fillets to a warm plate and keep warm in a 175° to 200°F oven.
4. Add the fish glaze to the pan and season with the diced garlic, 1 tablespoon of parsley, salt, pepper, and cayenne. Stir well, raise the heat, and reduce a third, whisking the while for 3 to 4 minutes.
5. Strain the sauce through cheesecloth set in a china cup and keep warm, over low heat. Plate the fillets on warm plates with a small pool of sauce underneath. As a garnish, top partially with the remaining sauce and the remaining chopped parsley.

YIELD: *4 servings*

Sogliole alla Parmigiana

SOLE WITH PARMIGIANO

Use Dover sole, lemon sole, rex sole, or flounder fillets interchangeably for this dish. The same holds true for most soft white fleshed fish that can be boned thoroughly. After all, poaching a fish and then baking briefly with mornay is a technique that lends itself to practically all fish . . . just bake it more if it's a fat fish instead of a lean fish.

> 4 fresh sole or flounder fillets, 6 to 8 ounces each
> 2 cups (approximately) Court Bouillon (see page 91)
> 24 seedless white grapes
> 3 to 4 tablespoons fruity white wine to cover grapes
> 1½ to 2 cups warm Mornaia (see page 116)
> ¼ cup of heavy cream, whipped
> 2 tablespoons freshly grated parmigiano

1. Lay the fish in a shallow pan and add enough court bouillon to cover. Gently poach the fish at a low simmer for 2 to 3 minutes until slightly underdone to allow for further finishing under a broiler.
2. Meanwhile, put the grapes in a saucepan large enough to hold them in a single layer and add enough wine to barely cover. Bring the wine to a boil, reduce the heat, and simmer for 1 to 2 minutes. Drain and set aside, or leave on the back of the stove to stay warm. Be sure to not overcook.
3. Spoon enough hot *mornaia* in a shallow ovenproof casserole to cover the bottom.
4. Lift the poached fillets carefully out of the court bouillon with a slotted spatula so that they can drain slightly and lay them in the casserole. Handle them gently so they won't break. Coat with more *mornaia* sauce.
5. Fold about 1 tablespoon of parmigiano lightly into the whipped cream. Spoon this mixture over the *mornaia*. Dust with the remaining parmigiano.
6. Finish under a hot broiler until brown and bubbly.
7. Carefully remove the fillets from the casserole with an unslotted spatula so as to keep the attractive brown spots on top. Spoon the remaining sauce around the fish. Place the warm grapes around the fish and serve.

YIELD: *4 servings*

Sogliole in Saor

SOLE IN SWEET AND SOUR SAUCE

The Venetians, as well as most of the rest of Italy, are very fond of things in *agrodolce* (sweet and sour). The beginnings of this preference can be found in the writings of Apicius in early Roman times. The recipes were then standardized in the Renaissance and continue to this day in most parts of Italy. Vinegar, lemon juice, verjuice (sour grapes), and sugar are used in hundreds of combinations with meat, fish, poultry, and vegetables. The recipe provided here is interesting in that it employs a breaded deep-fried fillet of sole that is marinated and served cold.

4 extra large eggs

1/4 cup milk

Pinch of salt

Freshly ground black pepper to taste

2 pounds small sole or flounder fillets, cut into 2-by-4-inch pieces

2 large white onions, sliced into thin rings

1/2 cup extra virgin olive oil

1/4 cup raisins, plumped in warm water and drained

2 tablespoons pine nuts

1/4 cup finely chopped fresh flatleaf parsley

10 whole black peppercorns

5 bay leaves

1/2 cup white wine, preferably Gewürtztraminer

1/2 cup white wine vinegar

1 tablespoon sugar

1/8 teaspoon each dried thyme, basil, and chervil

Crushed red pepper to taste

1 cup water

1 1/2 cups freshly made bread crumbs

1 quart vegetable oil

1. In a large bowl, mix together the eggs, milk, salt, and pepper. Add the fish and marinate until needed.
2. Over medium-high heat, sauté the onion rings in the olive oil until they begin to sweat. Add the raisins, pine nuts, parsley, peppercorns, bay leaves, wine, vinegar, and sugar, and simmer briefly. Then season with the thyme, basil, chervil, crushed red pepper, salt, and pepper. Add water and simmer this sauce for another 3 to 5 minutes, then set aside and cool. Preheat the vegetable oil to 375°F.
3. Bread the fish fillets by pulling them out of the

egg-milk mixture and dredging them in the bread crumbs.
4. Deep-fry them till golden brown, then drain on paper towels.
5. Pour half the sauce over the warm fillets and set aside to cool. Plate on cold plates and top with the remaining sauce. Serve with a lemon wedge and parsley sprig garnish.

Yield: 6 servings

Merluzzo al Forno

BAKED COD

1 lemon

4 whole cod, 8 to 10 ounces each, cleaned and boned

1/2 cup extra virgin olive oil

3 cloves garlic, bled (scored)

1 large green bell pepper, cleaned and sliced in rings

20 ounces ripe tomatoes, roughly diced (about 2 medium-size tomatoes)

1/2 medium-size red onion, thinly sliced

9 to 10 anchovies in oil

1/4 cup Brodo di Pesce (see page 90) or 2 tablespoons water mixed with 2 tablespoons white wine

1/2 cup best available aromatic white wine

Salt and pepper

1 tablespoon unsalted butter

1 tablespoon finely chopped fresh parsley

1. Squeeze the lemon over the fish, making sure to cover both sides.

2. Spread the oil in a casserole large enough for the fish and vegetables and add the garlic cloves. Layer the casserole with the green peppers, tomatoes, sliced onions, and anchovies. Pour the anchovy oil over all.

3. Reduce the fish stock and wine by half and then pour it over the vegetables. Cover the casserole and place it in a 375°F oven for approximately 20 minutes.

4. Place the fish on top of the vegetables and season with salt and pepper, dot with butter, spoon some of the juice over the top and bake, covered, for another 10 minutes, or until the fish is done.

5. Plate on warm plates in reverse order (fish on the bottom and the vegetables on top, with the green pepper rings on the very top). Garnish with parsley and serve.

YIELD: *4 servings*

Tielle di Sgombro e Patate alla Barese

CASSEROLE OF MACKEREL AND POTATOES IN THE STYLE OF BARI

1 *lemon*

4 *mackerel fillets, 8 to 10 ounces each, cleaned and boned*

1 *pound potatoes, sliced, about 3 medium-size potatoes*

2 *large white onions, sliced*

2 *cups freshly grated pecorino Romano*

1 *pound ripe tomatoes, about 3 medium-size, roughly chopped*

2 *cloves garlic, finely diced*

½ *cup extra virgin olive oil*

2 *cups water*

Salt and pepper to taste

2 *tablespoons finely chopped fresh parsley*

1. Squeeze the lemon over the mackerel fillets, making sure to coat both sides.

2. Line an oiled casserole with the potato slices, onion rings, pecorino, tomatoes, and garlic in successive layers, moistening each with a bit of oil and the water.

3. Bake in a 375°F oven for 30 to 40 minutes, or until the potatoes are tender.

4. Place the fillets on top of the vegetables, moisten with oil, and season with salt and pepper. Sprinkle with parsley and bake for 10 to 15 minutes, or until the mackerel is done.

5. Serve on warm plates with the mackerel and potatoes side by side and garnish with the remaining parsley.

YIELD: *4 servings*

Sgombro al Forno

BAKED MACKEREL

This is one of those basic recipes that can be used to bake almost any fish. If a lean instead of a fat fish were used, I'd suggest a bit more butter in the greasing of the pan, but other than that, the recipe works just as well for either kind of fish. It's easy to omit the pepper rings if you think they're too strong for the type of fish you're using.

1½ to 2 pounds fish such as mackerel
        2 teaspoons unsalted butter
           Salt and pepper to taste
        2 tablespoons finely diced mushrooms
        1 medium-size white onion, sliced into rings
      ½ small red, yellow, and green bell pepper, thinly sliced
      ¼ cup aromatic white wine
      ¼ cup Brodo di Pesce (see page 90)
      ¼ cup Marinara (see page 100)
   1 to 2 tablespoons chopped fresh parsley

1. Wash and clean the mackerel, leaving it whole with the bones in and head on.
2. Butter a large shallow casserole dish and lay the fish on top. Season with salt and pepper and sprinkle the mushrooms over all. Add the onion and pepper slices, reserving a few for garnish, season again with salt and pepper, and pour the wine and stock over all. Pour the marinara loosely over all and sprinkle with half the parsley.
3. Bake at 375°F for 20 to 30 minutes, testing for doneness a few times in the last 10 minutes. Plate on warm plates and, after spooning the juices from the pan over each plate, garnish with the reserved onion and pepper slices and the remaining chopped parsley.

YIELD: *4 servings*

Trancie di Spigola alla Mandorle con Uva Biance

FILLET OF SEA BASS WITH ALMOND SAUCE AND WHITE GRAPES

        1 lemon
        4 fillets of sea bass, 8 ounces each, cleaned and boned
      ¼ pound (1 stick) unsalted butter, cut into 12 pieces
   1¼ cups best available aromatic white wine
      ½ cup fish glaze (see page 93)
        1 teaspoon finely diced fresh mint
        1 teaspoon dried dillweed
        1 cup finely ground almonds
        1 cup heavy cream
12 to 16 almond slices for garnish
12 to 16 seedless white grapes

1. Squeeze the lemon over the fillets, making sure to coat both sides.
2. Melt 4 tablespoons (6 pieces) of butter over a medium heat in a sauté pan large enough to hold all the fish. Add the fillets and cook gently on both sides, 3 to 4 minutes to a side. Do not brown. Deglaze with 1 cup of white wine, adding the fish glaze, mint, and dill. Amalgamate all and remove the fillets to a warm plate placed in a 200° oven to keep warm.
3. Add the ground almonds and heavy cream to the sauce and reduce the whole by a third, incorporating the remaining pieces of butter with a whisk.
4. Meanwhile, put the grapes in a saucepan large enough to hold them in one layer and add the

remaining wine. Bring to a boil and immediately reduce the liquid to a slow simmer and poach for 1 to 2 minutes.

5. Plate the fish on warm plates with a lake of sauce underneath and some over it too.

6. Garnish with the almond pieces and poached grapes.

YIELD: *4 servings*

Pasta con le Sarde della Casa

PASTA WITH SARDINES OF THE HOUSE

Fresh sardines are a special treat. I remember well first becoming a devotee by eating sardines *alla plancha* in an ancient little *bodega* in the old quarter of Barcelona in Spain called "El Portolón." The grill *(plancha)* was black with age and use and worked wonders with these shiny little fish. In less than a minute they were done on one side and, when flipped over, the skin was seared and scored as if it had been cooked on a charcoal grill. When finished, that grill had produced an alchemical reaction that made those sardines so wonderful. My sons and I would make a lunch of just the sardines with lemon—we consumed six, eight, ten, or sometimes twelve apiece, and washed them down with a sharp local white wine of the region. The only other grill that I've encountered with such magical capabilities is the one at the original Nathan's at Coney Island—where tons of hot dogs are grilled each day and the grill is so old, well worn, and magical that these delectable all-beef frankfurters are browned to perfection almost on contact.

But aside from grilling, which the Italians are

inordinately fond of, there are other interesting recipes for cooking sardines, particularly from Sicily and Sardinia. *Pasta con le sarde* is a famous dish from Palermo and uses a saffron-tinted tomato sauce with anchovies, fennel, pine nuts, and raisins to cook the sardines in. When crushing all together, it dresses *perciatelli, bucatini,* or spaghetti.

A sardine pie of sorts from Sardinia and Apulia omits the saffron, the anchovies, and the fennel, but adds capers, lemon juice, and bread crumbs to bake the sardines in a casserole.

It occurred to us here at the school to combine the two approaches and thus make bread crumbs and sardines part of an overall bake with a tomato sauce infused with saffron, fennel, anchovies, capers, pine nuts, and raisins. The result is a very delicious baked pasta with sardine casserole that successfully combines both ideas.

Of course, not everyone has fish stock on hand but I think it's worth the effort to make some for this particular dish (see page 90). The extra flavorful moisture it provides permeates the macaroni along with the sardines themselves—and enriches the saffron-tinted tomato sauce. Incidentally, the pasta *(tortiglioni* in this case) turns a lovely golden yellow from the saffron.

8 *medium-size fresh sardines, approximately 1 pound*

2 *lemons*

1 *small fennel bulb*

1 *pound tortiglioni, tagliolini, or other pasta*

2 *cups Marinara (see page 100)*

3 *tablespoons dry aromatic white wine*

3 *tablespoons plus ½ teaspoon fresh lemon juice*

½ *teaspoon saffron threads, diluted in 2 tablespoons of water*

1 *bay leaf, torn into 4 pieces*

1 *cup Brodo di Pesce (see page 90)*

Salt and pepper to taste

Crushed red pepper to taste

½ cup extra virgin olive oil

 1 tablespoon finely diced white onion

 2 tablespoons chopped anchovies

 2 tablespoons chopped capers

 1 teaspoon chopped garlic

 3 tablespoons raisins, plumped in water
   and drained

 2 tablespoons pine nuts

 1 tablespoon finely chopped fresh parsley

 2 cups bread crumbs

 2 cups tiny cubed croutons, sautéed

¼ cup freshly grated pecorino
   Romano

 2 tablespoons freshly grated parmigiano,
   plus additional for garnish

1. Wash, gut, and clean the sardines.

2. Rub them with lemon and remove the bones by cutting off the heads and cutting the flesh away from the bone as you would in filleting. Cut the bone out when you reach the tail and discard.

3. Rub the insides of the sardines with lemon and set them aside, covered with the cut-up lemons in the refrigerator.

4. Halve the fennel bulb and cook it in acidulated (lemon), salted water over medium-high heat until almost tender but still firm. Slice into ¼-inch slices.

5. Cook the pasta in salted boiling water for about 5 minutes so that it is very "al dente." Drain and set aside.

6. Heat the marinara sauce and add 1 tablespoon wine, ½ teaspoon of lemon juice, saffron, bay leaf, and fish stock. Season with salt, pepper, and crushed red pepper, if needed, and set aside.

7. Heat the oil and stir in the onion, anchovies, capers and garlic. Quickly add the raisins, pine nuts, and parsley and stir. Deglaze with the re-

maining 2 tablespoons of white wine and add the remaining 3 tablespoons of lemon juice. Season with salt, pepper, and crushed red pepper.

8. Add the bread crumbs and half the croutons, half the pecorino, and half the parmigiano to make a breaded mixture. Toss lightly with the fennel slices.

9. Toss the pasta with half the marinara.

10. Cut each sardine into three or four large pieces and toss the pieces with the pasta. Toss in the breaded mixture and the remaining cheeses. Season with salt and pepper.

11. Toss all again lightly and place in a casserole lined with a bit of the remaining sauce. Pour the rest of the sauce over all and top with the remaining croutons and some more parmigiano.

12. Bake in a 375°F oven for 20 to 30 minutes and serve directly.

YIELD: *4 to 6 servings*

Seppie in Bianco

CUTTLEFISH IN WHITE WINE

My *Webster's Third New International Dictionary* from 1961 defines a cuttlefish as:

. . . *a ten-armed marine cephalopod mollusk of the family Sepidae (order Decapoda) differing from a squid in possessing a calcified internal shell; broadly—any of various other cephalopods (as the squids and octopuses).*

And an ugly little brute he is, although not as menacing looking as your average friendly octopus. But as with all the unseemly looking fish, vegetables and animals (wild boar to wit), the

Italians found the way to make them delicious.

The bodies on all these cephalopods, as Webster calls them, are cut into rings easily and batter or bread crumb fried. The tentacles are good for chopping and thereby useful in fillings when you might stuff the bodies and bake, braise, stew, or sauté them in wine as we are going to do in this recipe. *Calamari* would be a workable substitute as would baby octopus, but you'd have to contend with the ink and discard it or make it into a sauce, which is another story altogether.

In this particular dish, I also prefer to use the smallest *seppie* possible (2 to 3 inches in length) since they are more delicate and tender.

>   12 *small cuttlefish, cleaned*
> 1 to 2 *lemons*
>   4 *cloves garlic, bled (scored)*
> 8 to 10 *chopped anchovies*
>   1/4 *cup chopped capers*
>   1 *tablespoon diced white onion*
>   *Pinch each dried marjoram, thyme, and cayenne*
>   1/2 *cup chopped fresh parsley*
>   *Salt and pepper to taste*
>   1 *cup best aromatic white wine*
>   *Juice of 1/2 lemon*
>   1/2 *cup soft white bread crumbs*
>   1 *cup Brodo di Pesce (see page 90) or water*
>   1/4 *cup tiny cubed croutons, sautéed in oil*
>   2 *tablespoons freshly grated parmigiano*
>   1 *jumbo egg*
>   1 *tablespoon each finely diced carrot, celery, and onion*

1. Ask the fishmonger to clean the cuttlefish. At home, wash them with water, pat dry, and rub with lemon.

2. Place the cuttlefish on a board and remove the tentacles with a knife. Chop the tentacles for the stuffing.

3. Sauté 2 of the garlic cloves in 2 tablespoons of the oil over medium-high heat. Add the chopped tentacles, the anchovies, capers, onion, marjoram, thyme, cayenne, and 1 tablespoon of parsley.

4. Season with salt and pepper and deglaze with 1/2 cup of white wine. Allow the wine to partially evaporate and add the lemon juice.

5. Add the bread crumbs. Stir and moisten with 1 tablespoon of the fish stock or water. Add the croutons and parmigiano and mix well. You should end up with a somewhat damp bread, fish, and cheese filling.

6. Remove the stuffing from the pot, allow to cool, and then bind with a beaten egg.

7. Stuff the cuttlefish with the bread mixture and seal each one with 2 toothpicks or sew them up with needle and thread.

8. Sauté the remaining garlic cloves with the remaining oil over medium-high heat and add the stuffed cuttlefish. Brown each lightly on both sides and then add the carrot, celery, onion, and half the remaining parsley. Season with salt and pepper and continue to sauté.

9. Deglaze with remaining white wine and add the remaining fish stock. Cover and simmer gently for 20 to 30 minutes. Serve directly on warm plates with lemon wedges and chopped parsley.

YIELD: *4 servings*

Calamari con Pisselli Dolce

CALAMARI WITH SWEET PEAS

2½ to 3 pounds calamari (squid),
cleaned and cut into
pieces

½ cup extra virgin olive oil

2 cloves garlic, bled (scored)

2 cloves garlic, finely minced

½ teaspoon each thyme, basil,
and chervil

Salt and pepper to taste

¼ cup finely chopped fresh parsley

1 cup best aromatic white wine
(Gewürztraminer preferred)

6 anchovy fillets, pounded into
a paste in a mortar

2 cups canned Italian plum tomatoes

1 pound small tender sweet peas
(frozen acceptable)

1. Sauté the calamari pieces in the oil with the whole garlic cloves for 3 to 4 minutes at a medium-high heat. Add the minced garlic, thyme, basil, chervil, and 1 tablespoon finely chopped parsley. Season with salt and pepper and stir well.
2. Deglaze with the white wine and reduce slightly by increasing the heat. Add the anchovies and plum tomatoes and stir.
3. Reduce the heat, add a bit of water if necessary to cover the fish, and cook over low heat, partially covered, for 30 to 40 minutes, or until the calamari is tender.
4. Ten minutes before the fish is done add the peas and stir well. Cook, uncovered, the last 10 minutes, still on low heat. Season again with salt

and pepper and serve on warm plates with the remaining chopped parsley garnish.

YIELD: *4 servings*

Scampi alla Veneziana

SCAMPI IN THE VENETIAN MANNER

24 large shrimp, unpeeled

1 lemon

1 cup extra virgin olive oil

4 cloves garlic, bled (scored)

2 cloves garlic, finely minced

½ teaspoon crushed red pepper

⅛ teaspoon each dried thyme, basil, and
chervil

Salt and pepper to taste

1 cup dry white wine

2 tablespoons finely chopped fresh parsley

1. Clean the shrimp and rub with the lemon.
2. Heat the oil over medium heat in a sauté pan large enough to accommodate all. Add the whole bled garlic cloves and brown slightly. Add the shrimp and, turning the heat up slightly, sauté briskly for 3 to 4 minutes so that the shells become brown and crunchy.
3. Add the minced garlic, crushed red pepper, thyme, basil, chervil, salt, and pepper and stir rapidly. Deglaze with the white wine.
4. Remove the shrimp to warm plates for serving and reduce the wine slightly over a high heat,

about 1 minute. Pour the reduced wine sauce over the shrimp on each plate and garnish with the chopped parsley.

YIELD: *4 portions*

sauce, if desired. Add the sauce to the pan and stir thoroughly. Plate on warm plates and garnish with parsley.

YIELD: *4 portions*

Gamberoni alla Marinara

SHRIMP IN MARINARA SAUCE

24 to 32 *large shrimp, peeled and deveined*
1 *lemon*
½ *cup extra virgin olive oil*
2 *cloves garlic, bled (scored)*
2 *cloves garlic, finely minced*
½ *cup best aromatic white wine*
½ *cup Brodo di Pesce or fish glaze (see page 90 or 93—optional)*
2 *cups Marinara (see page 100)*
2 *tablespoons finely chopped fresh parsley*
   Salt and pepper to taste

1. Rub the shrimp with the lemon
2. Heat the oil over medium heat in a sauté pan large enough to accommodate the shrimp. Add the whole garlic cloves and the shrimp and toss lightly before adding the minced garlic. Deglaze with the wine and reduce the liquid slightly by turning up the heat.
3. Stir the fish stock or glaze into the marinara

Code di Scampi alla Spumante

SCAMPI IN CHAMPAGNE SAUCE

24 *large shrimp, unpeeled*
1 *lemon*
8 *tablespoons (1 stick) unsalted butter*
1 *tablespoon extra virgin olive oil*
½ *pound mushrooms with stems, sliced*
2 *tablespoons finely minced onion*
2 *cups best available dry Champagne*
1 *cup heavy cream*
3 *extra large egg yolks*
   Salt, pepper, and cayenne to taste

1. Rub the shrimp with the lemon
2. Heat the butter and oil in a sauté pan large enough to accommodate the shrimp over medium heat and add the shrimp and cook lightly on both sides without browning. Add the mushrooms and cook for 2 to 3 minutes, stirring occasionally. Add the onions and continue cooking for another 1 to 2 minutes. Season to taste with salt, pepper, and cayenne.
3. Deglaze with the Champagne, allowing it to

come to a boil. Reduce the heat and remove the shrimp to a warm plate. Keep the shrimp warm in a 175° to 200°F oven.

4. Increase the heat under the sauté pan and reduce the wine by half. Add ¾ cup of cream and stir, turning the heat back down to medium.

5. Beat the egg yolks with the remaining ¼ cup of cream. Add a little of the hot, reduced sauce to the yolks to temper them. Beat well and then add the yolk mixture to the sauce. Correct the seasonings.

6. Plate the shrimp on warm, ovenproof plates and pour the sauce over all. Put the plates of shrimp under a hot broiler for 1 minute to glaze the sauce slightly.

NOTE: You can strain the sauce before pouring it over the shrimp, for a finer finish.

YIELD: *4 servings*

Vongole e Cozze in Fricassea

FRICASSEE OF CLAMS AND MUSSELS

32 *littleneck clams, rinsed and cleaned several times*

32 *small mussels, rinsed and cleaned several times*

4 *cups Brodo di Pesce (see page 90) or 2 cups water and 2 cups white wine*

1 *cup finely diced white onion*

1 *teaspoon dried thyme*

2 *cups dry white wine*

⅛ *teaspoon crushed red pepper*

1 *cup finely sliced leeks (2-inch pieces)*

2 *cups heavy cream*

2 *tablespoons of saffron, soaked in warm water*

4 *large bread slices, toasted*

2 to 3 *tablespoons freshly grated parmigiano*

2 *tablespoons finely chopped fresh parsley for garnish*

1. Steam the clams and the mussels in the fish stock with the diced onion in a covered pan over medium heat.

2. When the shells open, remove the meat from them and discard the shells. Force any that do not open with a knife. If they smell or look bad discard. Put the meat back in the liquid. Add the thyme, wine, crushed red pepper, and leeks. Poach gently on low heat for 3 to 5 minutes, uncovered.

3. Remove the clam and mussel meat and reserve it in a bit of the poaching liquid to cover and keep warm.

4. Turn up the heat and reduce the remaining liquid by half. Strain it through a cheesecloth set in a china cap and return it to a thick bottomed saucepan. Add the heavy cream and reduce by a third over a medium heat.

5. Correct the seasonings and return the clams and mussels to the sauce.

6. Sprinkle the bread with parmigiano. Toast under a broiler and when the cheese melts and begins to brown, place 1 slice in a warm bowl. Spoon the clams and mussels and sauce over the toast and garnish with chopped parsley.

YIELD: *4 servings*

Vongole Tagliate
al Vermouth Secco

MINCED CLAMS IN DRY VERMOUTH

32 to 36 *littleneck clams, rinsed and cleaned*
several times

2 *cups Brodo di Pesce (see page 90),*
or 1 cup water and 1 cup dry white
wine combined

2 *tablespoons best available olive oil*

2 *cups best available vermouth*

2 *tablespoons finely diced onion*

1/8 *teaspoon each dried thyme, basil,*
and chervil

1/4 *cup finely chopped fresh parsley*

1 *cup finely diced mushrooms*

2 *cloves garlic, finely minced*
Salt, pepper, and cayenne to taste

2 *cups finely ground bread crumbs*

1 *cup freshly grated parmigiano*

8 *pieces of toast cut into triangles,*
making 16 pieces

1. Steam the clams in the fish stock and vermouth with the onion, thyme, basil, chervil, and 1 tablespoon of the finely chopped parsley in a covered pan over medium heat.

2. In a separate pan, sauté the mushrooms over medium heat, adding the minced garlic, cayenne, salt, pepper, and cayenne to taste.

3. When the clams open, remove them from the liquid and discard the shells. Force any that do not open with a knife. If they smell or look bad discard. Roughly chop the meat.

4. Reduce the poaching liquid to 1 cup or less over high heat. Combine the reduced liquid with the clams, mushrooms, bread crumbs, and 1/2 cup of the parmigiano.

5. Toss and heat, thickening with more cheese, if necessary, or thin with more liquid.

6. Toast the bread, spread each point with the clam-mushroom mixture, and top with parmigiano. Pass under a hot broiler for a few seconds until the cheese browns slightly. Serve on warm plates garnished with the remaining parsley.

YIELD: *4 servings*

Pollame
Pollo·
Cacciagione

Poultry

·

Chicken

·

Wild Fowl· Game

POULTRY

nother well known fact about Italy and Italians is that they are crazy about birds—all kinds—and particularly the game birds of squab, pigeon, partridge, quail, snipe, woodcock, pheasant, and guinea hen. They are also as fond as Americans of turkey and prepare it year round throughout the various regions in a variety of ways.

Very briefly, poultry can be divided into the following categories:

Type of Poultry	Weight	Type of Poultry	Weight
Rock Cornish Hen (3–5 weeks)	1–2 pounds	Fowl (old hens and roosters over 10 months)	over 4 pounds
Poussins (4–6 weeks)	1–2 pounds	Turkeys (over 12 months)	10–20 pounds
Broilers (2–3 months)	1½–2½ pounds	Turkeys (under 6 months)	10–12 pounds
Fryers (2–5 months)	2–2½ pounds	Duckling (7–8 weeks)	4–5 pounds
Roasters (3–5 months)	over 4 pounds	Duck (over 10 weeks)	5–8 pounds
Capons (male castrates) (7–10 months)	over 4 pounds	Goose (4–6 months)	6–14 pounds

The proper use of these different types of birds is not as universally practiced as one might expect. People normally seem to have a laissez-faire attitude that echoes Gertrude Stein's "A rose is a rose is a rose"—a chicken is a chicken is a chicken. Not so!

You'll never get a rich broth with that heavy gelatinous content that is so desired in a chicken stock no matter how many broilers or fryers you use. Old hens and roasters are what is needed here—just as it is impossible, in my opinion, to make a proper *chicken alla cacciatora* with fowl or roasters. One needs young, small broilers or fryers for this quick sauté with tomatoes. Otherwise you are relegated to a hunter's stew where an older, larger chicken, or originally a game bird, is cut up, sautéed, and then braised in tomato sauce with mushrooms and onions for considerable time.

Aside from proper size there is also the question of freshness. The ideal chicken is fresh killed. And that means exactly what it says—killed, cleaned, bled, and into the pot. Failing a supply of live chickens, which is becoming more difficult to encounter each day, you should confer with your butcher and make sure that he supplies you with birds that have been prepared within 8 to 24 hours. I recognize this difficulty as well as that of insisting on range bred and corn fed birds, but there are farms in practically every state in the U.S. that do this. You just have to search them out. But believe me, the difference is worth it. There is no comparison in flavor to a Perdue chicken, for example. We no longer even know what a real chicken tastes like, such are the practices of modern producers with their synthetic coloring agents.

GUIDELINES FOR BUYING

The best tasting birds are not only fresh killed, but are farm raised on a natural diet and have had a normal amount of exercise. Force feeding penned up birds with special feeds that produce more weight in a shorter amount of time does not give you a bird with good flavor. Look for young and tender birds with a breastbone that is flexible to the touch. The skin should be smooth with minimum fat and a creamy white to yellow color. Avoid birds that are highly colored. This is the result of being fed chemicals to produce more weight and make them look good. As always, let your nose also be your guide. Fresh meat smells sweet and healthy. Avoid birds with any kind of tired smell.

The U.S. government grades chicken and poultry in categories of A, B, and C. Always buy grade A, since B and C are really good only for processing and canning. If the birds are ungraded you can bet they're a B or C and you should expect a much lower price.

Frozen birds, of any type, are anathema, since this process sucks up and dries out the natural juices, thereby removing whatever natural flavor the bird had. If you have to use frozen birds of any kind, however, the best process is to thaw them out slowly in a moderate refrigerator. At least twenty-four hours is needed.

Chicken and other birds have ten times the amount of salmonella bacteria on their skin than pork, veal, or beef, and since water acts as an incubation tank for salmonella I avoid it completely when cleaning birds. Lemon is an acid that kills bacteria and also imparts good flavor to the chicken. Use cut up lemons, squeezing and rubbing as you clean the birds. Incidentally, this should always be done immediately upon receiving the birds and before storing. Refrigerate your chicken under plastic wrap with lemons. Of course, if the bird is very dirty it will have to be washed. But avoid it if possible. Let a lemon do the job.

Duck and goose (*anatra* and *oca*) are excessively fatty and need to be rendered on a rack before being braised, roasted, or stewed. Since there is not much meat yield from these birds, they are best bought at four to six pounds minimum. The average meat yield requires approximately one and a half pounds per person.

Squabs *(piccioncelli)* are very young pigeons that weigh in at one pound or less and can be treated in most all ways: spit roasted, sautéed, braised, stewed.

Pigeon *(palombacci* or *piccione),* being a little older, gamier, and larger, needs to be breast-larded and braised slowly.

Pheasant *(fagiano)* should be aged by hanging in a dry cooler for three or four days with full plumage. Two-and-a-half to three-pound birds are recommended for roasting and braising. Some prefer waiting till the bird decomposes (six to twelve days) and develops a high gamey flavor and smell. I frankly find it too overpowering.

Partridge *(pernice)* is a form of quail or grouse, and the question of hanging is one of personal preference. The Italians usually hang for only a day, while Americans tend to go three or four days, as is the case with most game.

Quail, however, is somewhat smaller and has a delightful, gamey white meat that lends itself to all forms of cooking—sautéing, spit roasting, char-grilling, grilling, braising, and roasting, although since they are under one and a half pounds, usually everything has to be done carefully and quickly. Unlike most game birds, quail should not be ripened (hung) and are best eaten within twenty-four hours after being killed.

Snipe *(beccaccino)* are very small, and similar to woodcock, and therefore particularly delicious spit roasted or char-grilled. In spite of their small size, however, they are a game bird that is improved by three or four days of hanging. Another predilection among connoisseurs concerning these birds is that they prefer to leave the entrails in. When they get down to thrushes they eat "bones and all."

Guinea hen *(faraona)* is a fairly dry white meat bird that is usually marketed at about two pounds (enough for two people) and requires considerable larding with pork fat or bacon while cooking to ensure it having a decent moistness. Braising and roasting are best for these birds. They used to be a part of wild fowl, but are now raised domestically.

While large turkeys *(tacchino)* are impressive (sixteen to twenty-five pounds), the female hens at ten to twelve pounds are considered to provide the most tender and delicately flavored meat. Although roasting is the traditional method of cooking, there are other wonderful treatments from Emilia Romagna, the Piedmont, and elsewhere in Italy, such as *filetti di tacchino con tartufi*—sautéed turkey breasts that are then placed in a casserole with cream, white truffles, and parmigiano and baked in the oven; or *filetti di tacchino alla bolognese,* which is the same thing with a slice of prosciutto added.

Of course the amount of love you put into your cooking methods also has a great deal to do with the final result. So, when you cook birds of any kind think lovingly of what you're after—crisp crackling skin, deep rich meat falling off the bones—whatever it is, there are methods to achieve it.

For instance, the finest way to roast a bird and get that wonderful crispness outside while retaining the natural juices is to seal them in by fast-roasting at high heats of 450° to 500°F for twenty to thirty minutes, depending on the weight, and then slow cooking with continual basting at 250° to 300°F. I maintain this preference as a matter of taste in spite of the recognition of the fallacy as a chemical matter. Technically, you're probably not "sealing in" the juices, but it sure does make the bird taste good. The alternative is roasting the bird breast down at low heat (300°F) and then finishing the browning at high heat, breast up. This also works wonders.

The same principle applies to browning birds on a very high flame in a pan—even if it's necessary to use more than one pot, which it usually is—so that they are browned deeply and darkly;

then after deglazing with wine or other spirits (Cognac, Madeira, Marsala, port) cook at the back of the stove over low, low heat till the meat is practically falling off the bone.

If charcoal grilling, place the pieces in aluminum foil with some butter, a bacon or ham slice, an orange slice, and whatever herbs you prefer, and seal the package. Cook it on the grill for twenty minutes (in the case of one and one-half or two and one-half pounds of chicken for example), remove the pieces of bird from the aluminum foil and grill them directly on the fire, basting with the juices from the marinade, till beautifully golden brown.

If you're trying to make a stewed or fricasseed chicken, never let it boil—just letting it gently, gently bubble and then slow steaming it with tender loving care is the trick.

Another tip that I've probably mentioned elsewhere, but feel is worth repeating, is that the quality of the dish is seriously impaired by the introduction of poor, cheap wines and spirits. When you reach to deglaze, or to add wine, Cognac, port, sherry, Madeira, or Marsala, never use anything but the best. The acid test is to taste the product directly before using. If it's not good enough to drink, find something better, or omit the additive altogether and settle for a wonderfully simple grilled, roasted, braised, or steamed bird without the ersatz product. And please never ever use so-called cooking sherry. A simple comparison with a real sherry will tell you why. Naturally this applies to all aspects of cooking as well as birds.

Pollo Arrosto della Casa

ROAST CHICKEN OF THE HOUSE

Roast chicken is universally popular and has been savored by the Italians since ancient times. In fact, roasting was the preferred method since chickens were prized for laying eggs and only the oldest who had stopped laying were sacrificed to the pot. These older birds were good for roasting, stewing, and braising since long cooking was the key to making them tender. Washing with lemons and marinating with fruit and port are methods dating back to Apicius and brought to new heights during the Renaissance.

One 4- to 5-pound roasting hen or
  capon
2 lemons
1 cup best available port
½ cup best available Cognac
  Salt and pepper to taste
1 each apple, pear, and orange,
  roughly chopped
2 cups Brodo di Pollo (see page 89)
1 whole truffle, peeled
1 carrot, roughly chopped
2 ribs celery, roughly chopped
1 small onion, roughly chopped
2 tablespoons unsalted butter
1 cup aromatic white wine
2 jumbo egg whites
1 tablespoon arrowroot
  (optional)
½ cup water (optional)

1. Rinse the chicken and rub the outside and the cavity with the lemon juice.

2. Pour the port and Cognac over the chicken and season with salt and pepper.

3. Stuff the bird loosely with the cut fruit, squeezing the juice from the orange over the outside and the cavity. Place the bird in a covered bowl and allow to marinate for 3 to 4 hours or overnight in the refrigerator.

4. Lift the bird from the marinade and discard the fruit. Add 1 cup of chicken stock to the marinade and set it aside for basting. Set the chicken on a rack in a roasting pan with the carrot, celery, and onion underneath. Put the truffle and butter in the cavity and close with toothpicks or sew the cavity shut.

5. Roast the bird breast side in a 475°F oven for 15 to 20 minutes, until the breast is browned. Turn it on its side and for another 10 to 15 minutes brown it. Repeat on the other side. Baste frequently with the reserved marinade.

6. Turn the oven down to 300°F and roast very slowly for approximately 1 hour until a meat thermometer in the thigh reads 140°F or/and the juices are no longer pink when you pierce the meat at the joints. Baste every 15 or 20 minutes. If the breast is well browned you can prevent its drying out by placing a damp cloth on top of it and wetting the cloth very lightly with water when needed.

7. Ten to 15 minutes before the bird is done, transfer it to another pan and leave it in the 300°F oven.

8. Strain the pan juices and marinade through cheesecloth into a saucepan. Degrease this liquid and then add the remaining 1 cup of chicken stock. Reduce by a third and correct the seasoning with salt and pepper. Clarify with the egg whites and strain again. Keep warm.

9. If you feel the sauce is too thin, add the arrowroot mixed with the water and bring to a boil.

10. Remove the chicken from the oven and set it aside for 5 minutes to settle before carving. Open the cavity and slice the truffle into as many thin pieces as you can. Serve a truffle slice with each serving along with the sauce, which should be brought to the table piping hot.

NOTE: There are many variations on this theme. For example, you preslice the truffle and insert it under the skin all over the bird by making incisions in the skin with a sharp knife. Capon works beautifully this way and, to enhance it further, stuff it with a prune, apricot, and pine nut risotto. And of course a garlic clove never hurt anyone. If you're so minded by all means put a garlic clove or two (bled, naturally) into the cavity along with the butter and the truffle.

YIELD: *4 servings*

Filetto di Pollo della Casa

BREAST OF CHICKEN OF THE HOUSE

This is our own variation of two classic chicken breast treatments. The first is Bologna's celebrated *cotoletta alla bolognese.* This is traditionally done with filets of chicken, turkey, or veal, which are neutral foils for the sweet, aged parmigiano cheese and Parma ham. White truffles are the *sine qua non.*

We felt, however, one day when we found ourselves without truffles, that the basic idea of the dish was too good to give up. We created an interesting uplift by contrasting sage with the Parma ham and a pinch of nutmeg and mace in the mornay sauce, which was based on a chicken vellutata. We used the sauce to coat over and under the breasts.

In both of the recipes cited above, the breast is first sautéed, the ham and mozzarella are added and then it is baked in the oven. We have made the dish a little more delicate by gently poaching the rolled breasts in white wine and chicken stock before adding the mornay sauce. We then cut down on the baking time and finish glazing the breasts under a very hot broiler with whipped cream and parmigiano cheese.

A nouvelle approach, which can be equally as successful, is to eliminate the mornay sauce by substituting a natural reduction of heavy cream and parmigiano, although I must caution you that a mornay based on a chicken vellutata is very hard to beat.

1 *lemon*
Four *6- to 8-ounce chicken breasts, boned and skinned*
 Salt and pepper to taste
1 *teaspoon dried sage*
Four *½-ounce slices prosciutto*
Four *1-ounce slices mozzarella, ⅛ inch thick*
1 *tablespoon unsalted butter*
½ *cup Brodo di Pollo (see page 89)*
¼ *cup aromatic white wine*
2 to 3 *cups chicken-based Mornaia (see page 116)*
1 *cup heavy cream, whipped*
¼ *cup freshly grated parmigiano*
1 *teaspoon Hungarian paprika*
4 *sprigs fresh watercress or parsley*

1. Squeeze the lemon over the chicken breasts and marinate for at least 1 hour. (Do not wash with water.) Butterfly the breasts, cover with wax paper, and pound thin with the flat side of a cleaver.
2. Season with salt and black pepper and dust with crumpled sage. Lay a slice of prosciutto and a slice of mozzarella in the center of each breast. Roll up and secure with toothpicks. Wrap in aluminum foil and pierce the foil in several places.
3. Place the breasts in a buttered pan with the chicken stock and white wine. Cover the pan with foil and poach over medium heat or in a 375°F oven for 5 to 7 minutes. Remove the breasts from the foil wrappers and set aside to drain. The breasts will look pink and uncooked at this point.
4. Coat a baking dish with *mornaia* and arrange the breasts in the dish comfortably. Separate. Pour the remaining sauce over the breasts and bake in a 375°F oven for approximately 10 minutes, or until done.
5. Add the whipped cream and parmigiano. Dust with paprika, and glaze under a hot broiler until bubbling and golden brown. Place on warmed plates and serve with a watercress or parsley sprig garnish.

YIELD: *4 servings*

Spezzatini di Pollo alla Campagnola

CHICKEN PIECES COUNTRY STYLE

In this case we're cutting a small chicken into small pieces *(spezzatini)* for a quick sauté. The addition of sausages, peppers, potatoes, and onions makes it a hearty country meal in itself and when served with crusty loaves of bread washed down with good strong Barbera from Alba you know you're eating rustic Italian food. I usually start this meal with figs or melon and prosciutto and finish it with a light ricotta cheesecake.

One 2- to 2½-pound young broiler or fryer (or two 1½-pound broilers or fryers)

2 lemons, cut into large chunks

2 tablespoons olive oil

2 tablespoons unsalted fresh butter

2 cups 1½-inch cubed potatoes, peeled and blanched

Salt and pepper to taste

4 cloves garlic, bled (scored)

4 sweet Italian sausages, cut into 3 or 4 pieces each

1 large green bell pepper, cut into 1-inch pieces

1 teaspoon each dried thyme, basil, and chervil

½ teaspoon crushed red pepper

2 tablespoons finely diced white onion

1 tablespoon chopped garlic

2 tablespoons finely chopped fresh parsley

1 tablespoon white wine (Gewürztraminer preferred)

1. After cleaning the chicken, cut it into 12 pieces. Toss the pieces with the lemon chunks.

2. Heat 1 tablespoon of oil and about 1 teaspoon of butter in a heavy-bottomed sauté pan and add the potatoes to it, tossing and coating them. Season with the salt and pepper and cook over a low heat for about 30 minutes, or until well browned and cooked through. This should be done 20 to 25 minutes before beginning to sauté the chicken. An alternate method, albeit not as good, is to cook the potatoes through instead of blanching them and then introduce them into the sauté with the chicken. Not as crispy crunchy, however.

3. Heat the remaining oil and the garlic cloves over medium-high heat in a sauté pan large enough to accommodate all the ingredients, or two pans if you don't have one large enough.

Turn the heat down to medium and slightly brown the cloves; remove and set aside.

4. Place the chicken pieces in the pan, skin side down, and turn the heat up slightly. Do not, I repeat, do not touch the chicken pieces for at least 3 to 5 minutes You'll only tear the skin if you try to move them before they're well set. Test by prodding them with a spoon. If they do not free up immediately, wait a little longer. When properly browned, turn them over and brown the other side. Remove the chicken from the pan while you brown the sausage. Add the green pepper and cook slightly, leaving them al dente. Add the potatoes to the pan. Return the chicken and stir all together. Quickly add the thyme, basil, chervil, crushed red pepper, diced onions, chopped garlic, and 1 tablespoon of parsley. Return the garlic cloves to the pan. Season with salt and pepper and toss all together lightly. Cook for 1 or 2 minutes over moderate heat.

5. Quickly deglaze with the white wine, turning the heat up even slightly higher, shaking, turning, and swirling all vigorously. Tilt the pan forward. Bring the chicken pieces and other ingredients up toward the handle, stacking them if necessary and placing the bottom of the pan directly in the flame so that the liquid bubbles and reduces.

6. Add the remaining butter, melting it into the liquid and reducing all by a third to a half, depending on how much liquid you want for a sauce. Moving quickly again, place the pan horizontally. Shake, turn, and swirl to amalgamate all.

7. Serve directly on warm plates, seeing that each person gets some sausage, peppers, potatoes, and chicken. Garnish each plate with the remaining parsley.

YIELD: *4 servings*

Pollo alla Cacciatora

CHICKEN HUNTER STYLE

I can't think of chicken *campagnola* without immediately conjuring up images of its cousin with tomatoes—chicken *cacciatora.* If you'd rather do a long stewing version just change the marinara to tomatoes, get a bigger chicken and let it cook longer . . . and a little chicken stock wouldn't hurt.

One 2- to 2½-pound broiler or fryer (or
    two 1½-pound broilers or fryers)
  2 lemons, cut into large chunks
  2 tablespoons olive oil
  4 cloves garlic, bled (scored)
6 to 8 mushrooms, quartered or cut smaller,
    depending on size
  1 large onion, roughly chopped
    Salt and pepper to taste
  1 teaspoon each dried thyme, basil, and
    chervil
  ½ teaspoon crushed red pepper or to
    taste
  1 tablespoon chopped garlic
  2 tablespoons chopped fresh parsley
  1 cup Florio sweet Marsala
  1 cup best available red wine
  2 cups Marinara (see page 100)
  1 cup Fondo Bruno or 2 tablespoons
    beef glaze (page 85 or 93)
  2 tablespoons unsalted butter

1. After cleaning the chicken, cut it into 12 pieces. Toss the pieces with the lemon chunks.
2. Heat the oil and garlic cloves over medium-high heat in a sauté pan and place the chicken pieces in it, skin side down. Remove the cloves of garlic when they are brown and reserve for later use.
3. Do not touch or try to move the chicken until it is well set. Test by trying to move one piece with a spoon. If it doesn't free up easily, let the chicken cook further before trying again. When properly browned on one side turn the chicken pieces over and brown the other side.
4. Move the chicken pieces to one side and add the mushrooms, browning them slightly. Move them aside and cook the onion pieces till slightly more than translucent. Return the garlic cloves to the pan. Shake, stir, and mix all, swirling the pan. Season with salt, pepper, thyme, basil, chervil, crushed red pepper, chopped garlic, and 1 tablespoon of parsley.
5. Deglaze quickly with the Marsala and reduce the liquid to a syrup, coating and caramelizing all.
6. Add the red wine and stock. Or add the beef glaze instead of the stock, increasing the wine by ½ cup. Tilt the pan and push the solid ingredients toward the handle so that the liquid is at the bottom and therefore directly over the heat. Reduce over medium-high heat by half.
7. Add the butter to the liquid and stir to incorporate.
8. When the liquids have reduced sufficiently, level the pan horizontally again and shake, mix, and stir, swirling the whole. Plate on hot plates and garnish with the remaining parsley.

YIELD: *4 servings*

Pollo alla Romana

CHICKEN ROMAN STYLE

Here is a long braise version of chicken *cacciatora* with a different combination of ingredients.

One 2½- to 3½-pound chicken
1 lemon
½ to ¾ cup extra virgin olive oil
4 cloves garlic, bled (scored)
6 large mushrooms, quartered
¼ cup diced pancetta
1 thin slice prosciutto, diced
1 large red bell pepper, seeded and roughly chopped
1 medium-size onion, roughly chopped
½ teaspoon each dried thyme, basil, and chervil
1 teaspoon finely chopped fresh parsley
Crushed red pepper to taste
Salt and pepper to taste
½ cup Marsala
1 cup dry red wine
3 cups canned Italian plum tomatoes
1 cup Brodo di Pollo or Fondo Bruno, or a combination (see pages 89 or 85)
1 teaspoon diced garlic
2 tablespoons tomato paste

1. Rinse the chicken; squeeze the lemon over it.
2. Cut up the chicken *pezzicato*—at each joint—and then cut each piece in half so that both thigh and drumstick combination yields 3 pieces.
3. Heat the oil in a sauté pan and add 2 cloves of garlic. Brown the garlic lightly. Remove and set aside. Sauté the chicken pieces in the same pan over high heat, browning them thoroughly. Don't be afraid to darken and perhaps burn the bottom of the pan. This is a different technique to darken in the sauté because of the long braise to follow. You lose the original glaze but gain extra depth through extra browning.
4. When browned, remove the pieces from the pan and either wash the pan or use a clean one and start all over again with oil and the other 2 cloves of garlic on a medium heat. Sauté the mushrooms till lightly browned. Add the pancetta and prosciutto, sauté lightly and stir. Add the pepper, sauté lightly and stir. Add the onion, sauté lightly and stir.
5. Add the reserved chicken pieces and reserved cloves of garlic to the pan and toss all together. Quickly add the thyme, basil, chervil, parsley, crushed red pepper, salt, and pepper.
6. Quickly, so the herbs do not burn, deglaze with the Marsala. Shake and stir and let the Marsala evaporate slightly until it becomes syrupy and caramelizes the chicken.
7. Add ½ cup of the red wine and let that also evaporate slightly on a high heat. Stir! Add the tomatoes and stir thoroughly. Add the last ½ cup of red wine and stir. Add the stock and stir. Add the diced garlic and stir.
8. Reduce the heat to medium-low, stir in the tomato paste and let simmer, covered, over low heat for approximately 1 hour, until the meat is practically falling off the bone. Adjust the seasoning and serve on warm plates.

YIELD: *4 servings*

Pollo al Tetrazzini

CHICKEN TETRAZZINI

There's a lovely story in connection with this leftover special. It seems that a Madame Tetrazzini, a famous opera singer in the early 1900s, came wheeling into the Hotel St. George in Brooklyn after a rehearsal at the Brooklyn Academy of Music at about 3:30 in the afternoon just as the dining room closed. She and her entourage were famished and she exclaimed, *"Muoio di fame"* (I am dying of hunger). *"Dammi da mangiare qualche cosa per piacere"* (Give me something to eat—anything—please).

Well, the maître d' ran to the kitchen and stated the case diplomatically to the famous chef Pavani, who said, "Everything's closed. I put everything in the refrigerator. But wait. The water is still hot for pasta and there is a little *balsamella* and chicken and a few pieces of mushroom. Out! Finished! Tell Madame Tetrazzini I will make something and don't worry about it."

And the great chef went to work sautéing a few diced onions to add to the mushrooms and, after heating the *balsamella*, he combined some leftover pieces of chicken and tossed it all together with some good fresh grated parmigiano. Then he cooked spaghetti or *linguine* very *al dente* and tossed half the mixture with the pasta. Now he lined a casserole with more *balsamella*, which because of the addition of white wine and cheese had now become a mornay, and spread the spaghetti that was coated with the mixture in the casserole. Making a well in the center, he placed the remaining chicken-mushroom mixture in the well and coated the whole top with more mornay. A sprinkling of parmigiano and into the oven it went for 15 to 20 minutes at 375° and then it was finish browned under the broiler.

He followed the waiters to the table and proudly proclaimed *pollo al Tetrazzini* (chicken Tetrazzini).

Whether true or not it makes my mouth water for this dish every time I relate the story.

1 *pound cooked chicken, boned and cut into 2-inch pieces*
8 *ounces mushrooms, finely sliced and roughly cut*
2 *tablespoons diced white onion*
2 *tablespoons unsalted butter*
6 *cups Mornaia (see page 116)*
2 *cups freshly grated parmigiano*
1 *pound linguine or spaghetti*
  Salt and pepper to taste

1. Pick over the chicken pieces to make sure there aren't any bones. Shred half and leave the rest in 1½-inch cubes. The shredding can be done with a knife.
2. Cook the mushrooms in the butter in a sauté pan over medium-high heat. Add the onion toward the end of the sauté. Toss half the mushrooms, half the onions, and the shredded chicken with 1 cup of the *mornaia* and mix in some parmigiano. In a separate bowl, toss the chicken cubes with the remaining mushrooms and onions and 1 cup or so of *mornaia*.
3. Cook the pasta very al dente, drain well, and toss with the shredded chicken mixture. Add 1 cup of *mornaia*. Season with salt and pepper.
4. Line 4 individual ramekins with *mornaia* and lay the pasta mixture in each. Make a well in the center of each and put the cubed chicken mixture in each well. Evenly spoon *mornaia* over each ramekin to cover completely and sprinkle parmigiano on top.
5. Bake in a 375°F oven for 15 to 20 minutes and then brown for 1 to 2 minutes under a broiler. Serve directly.

YIELD: *4 servings*

Anatra all'Arancia

DUCK L'ORANGE

The use of fruit with birds of all kinds, and certain meats, is neither *nouvelle* nor *minceur* in origin, since many recipes are found in the cooking of Rome before the fall as recorded in Apicius, and were brought to their highest level of sophistication during the Renaissance. And so it is with the famous duck l'orange.

The key to our recipe is the use of a good duck stock to make the sauce more flavorful. Of all the presentations of festive birds, aside from *fagiano in salmis,* this is perhaps our favorite.

Three 3½- to 4½-pound ducks

   1 lemon

   Salt and pepper to taste

   4 cups roughly chopped pear, apple, and orange

   ½ cup Cognac

   ½ cup ruby port

   4 cups Brodo di Pollo or Fondo Bianco (see pages 89 and 86)

   2 cups combined roughly chopped carrot, celery, and onion

   1 head of garlic

   1 bay leaf

   ½ cup Calvados brandy or Cognac

   ¼ cup sugar

   ½ cup apple cider vinegar

   ¼ cup lemon juice

   Rind from 4 oranges, blanched and julienned

   1 tablespoon arrowroot, dissolved in ¼ cup cold water

1. Clean the ducks and reserve the gizzards and hearts. Rub inside with the lemon. Season liberally with salt and pepper. Stuff the ducks with the cut up fruit, squeezing the orange pieces, and place the ducks into a pan. Soak them well with the Cognac and port, cover, and marinate 4 to 6 hours.

2. Prick the fatty breasts and thighs with a sharp fork at ⅛-inch intervals and roast the ducks in a 450°F oven or higher for about 25 minutes, or until well browned on all sides. Save the fat in the pan.

3. Remove the ducks to a board and cut each duck into 4 serving pieces, reserving the backs, necks, wing tips and scraps for the duck stock. Set the serving pieces, still rare, meat side down in a casserole or pan with some chicken stock and set aside for finishing later.

4. Finely chop the reserved backs, necks, wing tips, bones, gizzards, and hearts. Sauté them over high heat in the fat to color nicely. Add the chopped vegetables to the pan and continue cooking to brown them. Add the head of garlic, sliced in half, and the bay leaf. Some parsley sprigs may also be added.

5. Once well browned, pour in the Calvados and ignite. When the flames subside, stir the duck and vegetables over high heat until the liquid evaporates. Pour in 1 cup of chicken stock, stirring to glaze the contents as the liquid reduces.

6. When nearly evaporated, add the remaining stock, bring to a gentle boil over medium-low heat and begin skimming and cooking the duck stock. Taste frequently for the point, after about 30 minutes, when the stock has a good duck flavor and is nicely reduced. Strain and reserve the stock.

7. Caramelize the sugar to an amber brown in a heavy-bottomed saucepan over medium heat. Stir in the vinegar and then the orange juice. Add 3 cups of duck stock, stir, and taste. Adjust the tartness with sugar and lemon. Add half the orange rind and reduce while skimming, until the sauce starts to come clear and the flavor is well pronounced. Adjust the seasonings with salt and pepper and a little port, if desired.

8. Finally, thicken as desired with a little arrowroot mixed with cold water.

9. Roast the reserved duck pieces for about 5 minutes in a 450°F oven until tender. Brown under a broiler to nicely crisp the skin. Place some sauce on each warm plate and set the duck pieces for each serving in it. Spoon more sauce over each and garnish with the remaining julienne of orange rind.

YIELD: *6 large servings*

Anatra Brasata con Piselli e Prosciutto

BRAISED DUCK WITH PEAS AND PROSCIUTTO

One *6-pound Long Island duckling (female if available), cleaned, rubbed with lemon, seasoned, stuffed, and marinated with Cognac, port, and fruit as described on page 215*

1 *cup best available Cognac*
   Salt and pepper to taste

2 *cups Fondo Bruno (see page 85)*

1 *cup best available dry red wine*

2 *cups Italian plum tomatoes, pureed*

2 *cloves garlic, bled (scored)*

1/8 *teaspoon each dried thyme, basil, and chervil*

4 *slices prosciutto, roughly diced*

1 *pound baby sweet peas (frozen acceptable)*

1. Thoroughly prick the skin of the duckling with a sharp knife and roast it on a rack in a 450° to 500°F oven for about 15 minutes on its back and then 15 minutes on its breast (or vice versa) until it is well browned but still rare. Baste with the marinade juices as it roasts.

2. Remove the duckling from the oven and discard the fruit.

3. Skim approximately 2 tablespoons of fat from the roasting pan and heat in a casserole. Place the duckling in the casserole and cook over medium heat for 2 to 3 minutes. Add and warm the Cognac, and ignite it. Let the Cognac flambé the bird till the alcohol burns out.

4. Reseason the bird with salt and pepper and add the stock, red wine, pureed tomatoes, garlic cloves, thyme, basil, chervil, and prosciutto in that order.

5. Cover tightly and cook in a 375°F oven for 40 to 50 minutes or until almost done. Add the peas and cook, uncovered, for an additional 10 to 15 minutes, stirring occasionally. Serve on warm plates with the sauce and peas liberally distributed.

YIELD: *4 servings*

Anatra Brasata con Olive Verdi

BRAISED DUCK WITH GREEN OLIVES

One *6-pound Long Island duckling (female if available), cleaned, rubbed with lemon, seasoned, stuffed, and marinated with Cognac, port, and fruit as described on page 215*

1 *cup best available Cognac*

2 *cups Brodo di Pollo (see page 89)*

2 *cups best available aromatic white wine*

2 *teaspoons dried sage*

1 *bay leaf*

18 to 24 *large green olives (pitted optional)*

3 *sprigs fresh parsley*

2 *sprigs fresh thyme or 1 teaspoon dried*

Salt and pepper to taste

2 *tablespoons arrowroot, dissolved in ½ cup water*

1. Thoroughly prick the skin of the duckling with a sharp knife and roast it on a rack in a 450° to 500°F oven for about 15 minutes breast down and then 15 minutes back down, until it is browned but still rare. Baste with the marinade juices as it roasts.

2. Remove the duckling from the oven and discard the fruit. Skim approximately 2 tablespoons of fat from the roasting pan and heat in a casserole. Place the duck in the casserole and cook over medium heat for 2 to 3 minutes. Add and warm the Cognac, then ignite it. Let the Cognac flambé the bird until the alcohol burns out.

3. Reseason the bird with salt and pepper and add the chicken stock, white wine, sage, bay leaf, green olives, parsley and thyme sprigs.

4. Cover tightly and cook in a 375°F oven for 45 minutes to an hour or until done. Remove the duck and olives to a warm plate and keep warm in the oven.

5. Strain the liquids from the casserole through a cheesecloth set in a china cap over a saucepan. Reduce slightly and skim fat and impurities carefully. Add the dissolved arrowroot to give the sauce a proper thickness.

6. Disjoint the bird and cut it into serving pieces.

Place some sauce on each warm plate and put the pieces of duckling in it, surrounded by the green olives. Top with more sauce and serve.

YIELD: *4 servings*

Filetti di Tachino alla Piemontese

TURKEY BREASTS IN THE PIEMONTESE MANNER

1 *lemon*

4 *medium-size turkey breasts, skinned, boned, and slightly flattened with a* **batta carne** *(meat pounder)*

Salt and pepper to taste

2 *cups flour, seasoned with salt and pepper*

6 *tablespoons (¾ stick) unsalted butter*

1 *cup Florio Marsala dolce (or equivalent)*

½ *cup meat glaze (see page 93), meat stock, or canned consommé, in that order of preference*

1 *ounce white truffles, sliced (optional)*

1. Squeeze the lemon over the breasts, season with salt and pepper, and dip lightly in the seasoned flour.

2. Heat 4 tablespoons of the butter over medium-high heat until foaming in a large sauté pan. Add the turkey breasts and cook gently over medium heat for 3 to 5 minutes on each side, or until done. Remove the breasts to a warm plate and hold in a warm 175° to 200°F oven.

3. Deglaze the pan with the Marsala over medium-high heat and whisk in the remaining 2 tablespoons of butter, reducing the sauce by a third. Correct the seasoning.

4. Place a bit of sauce on warm plates and lay the breasts in it. Top with the sliced truffles and the remaining sauce and serve.

YIELD: *4 servings*

Filetti di Tachino alla Bolognese

TURKEY BREAST IN THE BOLOGNESE MANNER

1 *lemon*

Four *6-ounce turkey breasts, skinned, boned, and flattened slightly with a* **batta carne** *(meat pounder)*

Salt and pepper to taste

2 *cups flour, seasoned with salt and pepper*

2 *eggs, beaten with 1 tablespoon parmigiano and seasoned with salt and pepper*

2 *cups fresh finely ground bread crumbs*

4 *tablespoons (½ stick) unsalted butter*

1 *cup meat glaze (see page 93) or meat stock, brown sauce, or canned consommé, in that order of preference*

4 *slices imported Fontina or Gruyère*

4 *thin slices imported prosciutto*

1. Squeeze the lemons over the breasts, and season lightly with salt and pepper, then dip them first in the flour, then the egg, and then the bread crumbs.

2. Heat the butter over medium-high heat in a large sauté pan until foaming. Add the crumbed turkey breasts, browning them for 3 to 4 minutes on each side, or until done.

3. Place a bit of the meat glaze on warm oven-proof plates and set the breasts in the glaze. Cover the breasts with the cheese and put under a hot broiler. When the cheese begins to melt in 1 to 2 minutes, add the prosciutto as a further topping and broil for an additional 1 to 2 minutes. Remove from the broiler and serve with a spoonful of the remaining glaze, sauce, or consommé on top.

YIELD: *4 servings*

Fricassea di Oco con Salsicce e Castagne

FRICASSEE OF GOOSE WITH SAUSAGES AND CHESTNUTS

One *6-pound goose, cleaned, rubbed with lemon, seasoned, stuffed, and marinated with fruit, Cognac, and port as described for ducks on page 215*

2 *cloves garlic, bled (scored)*

1 *medium-size carrot, peeled and sliced on the diagonal*

2 *ribs celery, sliced on the diagonal*

1 *medium-size white onion, thinly sliced*

12 *small round white onions (one step up from pearl)*

Salt and pepper to taste

    ⅛ *teaspoon each dried thyme,*
        marjoram, and crushed red pepper
    1 *cup best available Cognac*
    2 *cups Brodo di Pollo (see page 89)*
    1 *cup dry white wine*
    2 *cups Italian plum tomatoes, pureed*
6 to 8 *medium-size sweet Italian*
        sausages, cut in half
16 to 24 *chestnuts (poached in white wine)*
        Cayenne pepper to taste

1. Thoroughly prick the skin of the goose with a sharp knife and roast it on a rack in a 450° to 500°F oven for about 15 minutes on its back and then 15 minutes on its breast until it is well browned but still rare. Baste with the marinade juices as it roasts. Remove the goose from the oven and discard the fruit.

2. Skim approximately 2 to 3 tablespoons of goose fat from the roasting pan and heat it in a casserole.

3. Disjoint and cut the goose into serving pieces. Add them to the warm goose fat in the casserole. Add the garlic, carrot, celery, sliced onion, and round onions to the casserole. Season with salt, pepper, thyme, marjoram, and crushed red pepper. Add and warm the Cognac, then ignite it. Let the Cognac flambé the bird till the alcohol burns out. Add the chicken stock, white wine, and pureed tomatoes and season with salt and pepper.

4. Separately sauté the sausages till nicely browned over medium-high heat. Drain them well and add them to the goose in the casserole.

5. Tightly cover the casserole and bake in a 375°F oven for 1 hour to 1 hour and 30 minutes. Approximately 15 minutes before the goose is finished cooking, add the chestnuts and continue cooking uncovered. Plate on warm plates, evenly distributing the round onions and the chestnuts.

YIELD: *4 servings*

WILD FOWL AND GAME

Game conjures up rich exotic roasts that are perfect foils for an autumn or winter chill and roaring fires. Here in Umbria that's the time to bring out those big Sagrantinos, Barbarescos, or Barolos we've been saving to wash down the dark, gamey flavors of wild boar *(cinghiale)*, hare *(lepre)*, and deer steaks. These are special winter treats that are more readily found in Europe than in America. Wild rabbit, although slightly gamier than a domestically raised version, is basically a light, white meat animal and more like chicken than its dark meat cousin, the hare. Still it, like all game, benefits greatly from marination with oil, garlic, lemon, wine, vinegar, bay leaf, juniper berry, and the aromatics of carrot, celery, onion, and parsley. This marination is a happy marriage for all types of game and smooths out the flavors markedly whether very gamey or not.

    The basic cooking procedures are simple enough. If you want to play it safe, sear the meat till well browned, deglaze with wine and/or stock, and braise it in wine and/or stock until done. But in all cases marinate it first for at least eight to twelve hours. If the animal is old and gamier, marinate for twenty-four hours or more. This would be equally true if you were going to eat steaks from the animal, or other parts that you wanted to broil instead of braise. Use the marinade for basting.

    This basic procedure that I've outlined above is for those who come from the "falling off the bone" school of cooking as I do. I remember an episode one winter weekend with a wild duck that my then partner in a ski area that I owned in Massachusetts (Bousquet Ski Area 1955–1969) brought for me to cook. He also brought a book on cooking wild fowl and game written by a hunter-guide type from the wilds of Ontario. This gentleman—whose book and name I've lost—was very emphatic about the fact that the only way (in his opinion) to cook wild duck was to bathe it in gin and sear it on the outside on a wood fire, leaving it blood rare "6 to 8 minutes— not a second more . . ." I remember that distinctly.

As a chef I objected and cautioned my partner that we'd be better off playing it safe with a nice long braise.

"Play it safe? Long braise? We'll do no such thing, my boy."

(He was seventy-six and I was twenty-six.)

"Where's your nerve? Do like he says! He's the game expert!"

And so I did. To the minute. Now, to begin with, these birds must have been feeding on dead fish and other garbage—so putrid did they smell. And without proper marination there was nothing to tone them down. The gin certainly didn't. If anything, it aggravated the flavor by adding the odor of a sick martini to the whole mess. Needless to say, they were terrible . . . tough, bloody, putrid, inedible! My partner wasn't going to admit it till I handed a piece to the dog (who would normally eat anything) and he ran away yelping.

The question of dressing and hanging game is important if you want to avoid those wild high flavors. First of all, any animal that you shoot in the wild must be gutted and cleaned of its entrails immediately. If left in they will aggravate the gaminess to the point where no amount of marination will help. If you're getting game from a friend it would be well to emphasize this point. Secondly, beyond the twelve to twenty-four hours (two days for beef) period necessary for the enzymes to soften the meat from its rigor mortis stiffness, the question of hanging is somewhat personal. Venison, boar, and hare all seem to improve in flavor, within three to five days, depending on the size and age of the animal. Beyond that, in my opinion, putrefaction is setting in and not the development of a better flavor. But then I feel that way about game birds as well and won't wait till I smell them "going high."

As I said about poultry, water is a no-no!

Clean all kinds of game with lemons and wash what dirt or blood coagulations are necessary with water, but no more. Store well chilled with lemons and good air circulation, or covered if you're marinating. If storing unmarinated, don't hold for more than two days. Everything is downhill from there on.

As to freezing and frozen game, avoid it if you can. You're better off with a fresh chicken or fresh well aged beef than frozen pheasant, boar, or deer. Wait for the right thing and enjoy it at its best.

Pernice o Quaglia alla Perugina

PARTRIDGE OR QUAIL IN THE MANNER OF PERUGIA

I say partridge or quail, but actually, as in most cases, this recipe can be used for all kinds of birds and most meats. The barding of the breasts is done because they have a tendency to dry out and the fat helps to keep them juicy. It's not necessary with pheasant, chicken, or duck, but essential with guinea hen.

You can either brown the birds first and then bard them, or bard them and then brown them, losing some of the fat in the process. In the case of guinea hens I've found it necessary to maximize the fat on the breast and therefore I will brown them first and bard them before roasting; whereas with quail and partridge I've found that barding them first works okay as long as I don't burn off all the fat totally in the browning.

Since this recipe is highly dependent on wine for its liquid the quality of the wine used becomes even more important. Reach for the best and you won't regret it.

    1 lemon
 Four 4- to 5-ounce quail
    1 cup fruit marinade (see page 215)
       Salt and pepper to taste
 Four 2-inch strips thick bacon
    2 tablespoons extra virgin olive oil
    2 cloves garlic, bled (scored)
   ½ cup best available Cognac
   ½ bottle best available dry red wine
   ½ teaspoon dried sage or 4 to 6 fresh
       sage leaves
 6 to 8 canned black olives (not pickled)
   ½ cup Fondo Bruno or Fondo Bianco
       (see page 85 or 86), or consommé
       (see page 88)
   ½ cup port
    1 tablespoon arrowroot, dissolved in
       ¼ cup cold water
    1 tablespoon finely chopped fresh
       parsley

1. Squeeze the lemon over the quail. Follow the instructions for marinating the quail as explained for the duck on page 215, using the fruit marinade and seasoning with salt and pepper.
2. Bard the breasts by laying a slice of fat on each. Truss the birds tightly with cord. Pat them dry and, leaving the fruit inside, sauté them in the oil and garlic over medium-high heat till well browned. If you can accomplish this without burning the bottom of the pan, you will be able to flambé the birds in the same pan. You can also save the garlic cloves by removing them when they're brown and not allowing them to burn. If everything does burn up, however, in this browning process, not to worry—just get a new casserole (pan), add a bit of oil and fresh garlic cloves and begin again. Sometimes this is inevitable in browning something thoroughly. It depends on the pan and the flame of the gas.
3. Pour the Cognac over the birds, heat it, then ignite it. Let the Cognac flambé the birds till the alcohol burns off. Add the red wine, sage, olives, and stock.
4. Tightly cover the pot and braise in a 375°F oven for approximately 45 minutes, or until done. Discard the string, fruit, and fat (if any) and place the birds and olives in another pan and keep warm in a 275°F oven.
5. Strain the remaining liquids through cheesecloth set in a china cap or strainer into a saucepan. Add the port to the sauce and reduce all by half.
6. Add the dissolved arrowroot to the bubbling, boiling, reducing sauce. Whisk thoroughly till the arrowroot thickens the sauce. Correct the seasoning with salt and pepper and serve the birds on warm plates with sauce under and over, surrounded by the olives and garnished with parsley.

YIELD: *4 servings*

Quaglie alla Marosticane

QUAIL WITH CHERRIES FROM THE TOWN
OF MAROSTICANE

8 slices ⅛-inch thick bacon for
    barding (approximately 2 inches
    long)
1 cup extra virgin olive oil
2 cloves garlic, bled (scored)
8 quail, cleaned, rubbed with lemon,
    stuffed, and marinated in port and
    Cognac as found in recipe on page
    215, but instead of the mixed
    fruits use sour cherries. Bard the
    breasts and truss the birds
2 tablespoons finely diced carrots
2 tablespoons finely diced white
    onions
   Salt and pepper to taste
1 tablespoon arrowroot, dissolved in
    3 tablespoons of cold water
1 cup best available dark heavy red
    wine
½ cup sweet Florio Marsala
2 cups Fondo Bruno (see page 85)
16 to 20 sour-sweet cherries
1 vanilla bean
½ white onion stuck with 2 cloves

1. Heat the oil in a large casserole and add the
garlic cloves. Remove the garlic when browned
and set aside. Brown the birds on all sides in the
oil over medium heat. Return the garlic. Add the
carrots and onions and cook until the onion begins to brown. Season with salt and pepper.
2. Deglaze with the wine. Add the Marsala, the

stock, cherries, vanilla, and the cloves set in the
white onion.
3. Cover and cook in a 375°F oven for approximately 45 minutes or until done. Remove the
birds to a warm plate and keep warm in the
turned-off oven.
4. Strain the sauce through a cheesecloth set in a
china cap or strainer into a saucepan. Reserve the
cherries and then add them back to the sauce.
5. Bring to the boil and add the dissolved arrowroot and whisk thoroughly until it thickens the
sauce. Correct the seasoning. Place the quail on
warm plates with the sauce over and surrounded
by cherries.

YIELD: 4 servings

Quaglie alla Boscaiola

QUAIL UMBRIAN WOODSMAN STYLE

1 lemon
8 quail, cleaned
Eight 2-inch thick pieces of bacon or
       fatback
1 cup extra virgin olive oil
2 cloves garlic, bled (scored)
   Salt and pepper to taste
4 slices prosciutto, roughly chopped
½ medium-size white onion, diced
¼ teaspoon dried sage
1 cup Marsala secco (dry)
1 cup best available dry white wine

1 cup Brodo di Pollo (see page 89)
Bread crumbs
Freshly grated parmigiano

1. Squeeze the lemon over the quail. Lay a piece of bacon on the breast of each quail and truss them securely.
2. Heat the oil in a large casserole and brown the garlic cloves in it over a medium heat. Remove the garlic and set aside. Brown the birds on all sides over the same medium heat. Return the garlic to the pan and season with salt and pepper. Add the prosciutto and onion and cook briefly until the onion begins to take on color. Add the sage and deglaze with the Marsala, allowing it to evaporate slightly. Add the white wine and chicken stock and cook, uncovered, on top of the stove for 30 to 40 minutes over medium heat until the birds are tender.
3. Correct the seasoning and adjust the thickness of the sauce with bread crumbs and parmigiano if too thin, or a bit of white wine and chicken stock if too thick. Untruss the birds and serve on warm plates with the sauce under and over the birds.

YIELD: *4 servings*

Faraona alla Trevisana

GUINEA HEN FROM LAKE TREVISANO
(UMBRIA)

One 2⅓- to 3-pound guinea hen, cleaned, barded with fatback and trussed (fruit marinade optional, see page 215)

FOR THE STUFFING:

    4 tablespoons (½ stick) unsalted butter
    2 slices bacon, cut into cubes
    1 sweet Italian sausage, sautéed and diced
    1 medium-size carrot, peeled and finely diced
    2 medium-size ribs celery, finely diced
    ½ medium-size white onion, finely diced
    ½ pound radicchio rosso (other lettuces can be substituted if not available)
    2 slices white bread, soaked in milk, drained, and crumbled
    ⅛ teaspoon dried sage
    ⅛ teaspoon ground ginger
    1 cup freshly grated parmigiano
    ½ cup raisins, plumped in a bit of Marsala
    2 tablespoons finely chopped fresh parsley
       Salt and pepper to taste
    ½ cup port
    1 egg, well beaten

TO ROAST THE BIRD:

    1 large carrot, unpeeled and roughly chopped
3 to 4 ribs celery, with leaves
    1 large yellow onion, unpeeled and roughly chopped
    2 whole heads of garlic, unpeeled and cut in half
    2 bay leaves
4 to 6 juniper berries
6 to 8 whole black peppercorns
    1 cup Brodo di Pollo (see page 89)—to baste

1. For the stuffing, heat the butter in a sauté pan over medium-high heat. Add the bacon and sausage and cook until partially brown. Add the carrot, celery, and onion, in that order, and cook until the onion takes on color.

2. Add the radicchio and cook until it softens. Add the crumbled bread, the sage, ginger, parmigiano, raisins, and parsley and mix well. Season with salt and pepper and moisten with the port and beaten egg, mixing well.

3. Stuff the cavity of the bird with the stuffing. Sew the cavity closed or secure it with toothpicks and bard the breast with slices of pork fat and truss it.

4. To roast the bird, place the carrot, celery, and onion in a roasting pan. Place the garlic cut side down in the pan. Add the bay leaves, juniper berries, and peppercorns.

5. Place a rack above the vegetables and set the bird on its side on the rack in the roasting pan. Roast the bird for 15 minutes on each side in a 450°F oven until nicely browned. Turn the heat down to 300°F and continue roasting the bird on its back for 1 hour, basting occasionally with the chicken stock. During the last 20 minutes of roasting, remove the fatback so the breast skin can brown. Test the joints for doneness with a fork after 1 hour and roast longer if needed.

6. Keep the bird warm in the oven while you degrease the roasting pan and make a pan gravy from the juices and remaining chicken stock. Allow the bird to rest for 5 minutes before carving. Serve on warm plates with some of the stuffing for each person and top with a bit of pan gravy for each.

YIELD: *4 servings*

Faraona alla Paesana

GUINEA HEN COUNTRY STYLE

Two 2-pound guinea hens, cleaned, seasoned, stuffed, trussed, and marinated with fruit, Cognac, and port as described for duck on page 215 and trussed and barded with pork fat as described for quail above

4 *tablespoons (½ stick) unsalted butter*

2 *cloves garlic, bled (scored)*

1 *pound mushrooms, quartered with stems on*

2 *slices lean salt pork, cubed*
 Salt and pepper to taste

1 *cup best available Cognac*

2 *cups best available red wine*

1 *cup Fondo Bruno (see page 85)*

1 *cup canned Italian plum tomatoes, passed through a food mill*

½ *cup red wine vinegar*
 Garlic croutons (optional)

1. Roast the birds in a high heat, 450°F oven for 15 minutes on each side, basting frequently with the marinade.

2. Remove the birds from the oven, disjoint, and cut into serving pieces.

3. Melt the butter in a casserole large enough for the birds. Lightly brown the garlic cloves, mushrooms, and salt pork. Add the guinea hen pieces and season with salt and pepper. Add and warm the Cognac over medium heat, then ignite it. Let the Cognac flambé the birds till the alcohol burns out. Add the red wine, stock, tomatoes, and vinegar and season again with salt and pepper.

Tightly cover the casserole and bake it in a 375°F oven for 40 to 50 minutes, or until done. Serve on warm plates with or without a garlic crouton garnish.

YIELD: *4 servings*

Polombacci Umbriana

SQUAB UMBRIAN STYLE

1 cup extra virgin olive oil

2 cloves garlic, bled (scored)

Four 6- to 8-ounce squab, cleaned, rubbed with lemons, and cut into serving pieces; livers reserved

1 cup best available dry white wine

½ teaspoon dried sage

½ white onion stuck with 2 cloves

2 to 3 slices lemon rind

½ cup red wine vinegar

6 anchovy fillets, pounded into a paste in a mortar

Salt and pepper to taste

1 cup bread crumbs, tossed with a bit of grated parmigiano

1. Heat the oil over medium-high heat and lightly brown the garlic cloves. Remove and reserve the garlic. Sauté the squab pieces in the oil until nicely browned. Return the garlic to the pan.
2. Deglaze with white wine. Allow it to evaporate for 1 minute and then add the sage, onion stuck with cloves, the lemon rind, red wine vinegar,

and anchovy paste. Stir well and season to taste with salt and pepper.
3. Cook over medium heat, covered, for 10 to 15 minutes. Uncover and cook for another 15 to 20 minutes, or until the squab is tender.
4. Separately, sauté the livers in olive oil. Season with salt and pepper and pass through a food mill directly into the casserole, or sauté pan with the birds and their sauce.
5. If the sauce is too thin, add the bread crumbs to thicken it. If too thick, thin out with some chicken stock and white wine. Serve on warm plates with sauce over and under.

YIELD: *4 servings*

Coniglio al Barbaresco—Angelo Gaja

ANGELO GAJA'S RABBIT IN BARBARESCO

The difference between rabbit *(coniglio)* and hare *(lepre)* is like night and day. The meat of a hare is so dark and gamey that it's more like boar than it is similar to rabbit. Sweet, young rabbits are the chicken of the game world and yet the flavor goes beyond chicken to a richer meat that is recognizably different.

All the methods of cooking chicken and other birds and meats are appropriate for rabbit. If you're going to get wild rabbits from friends or a specialty house make sure they were gutted immediately upon killing. Leaving the entrails in a rabbit will give the meat a strong, unpleasant flavor.

The name of this dish came about from Angelo

Gaja's love of rabbit. Signor Gaja is one of the finest wine producers in the world and the maker of the finest Barbaresco in Italy. He is legendary because of his contributions to oenology here in Italy and because he dared to beat the great French Château Estate bottlers at their own game with his Sori Tildin '78 Riserva. It is truly one of the greatest wines in the world.

It wasn't a far jump for us to reach for his Sori Tildin '78 and prepare him a rabbit in his famous Barbaresco. The result, of course was outstanding. How could it be otherwise?

Incidentally, if you want an inexpensive, fruity red, slightly *frizzante* (fizzy) wine for a change, try his Freisa. But if you want to make the rabbit of your life, use his Sori Tildin.

> *1 lemon*
> *2 rabbits (wild or domestic), cut into 6 to 8 pieces each*
> *1 large carrot, roughly chopped*
> *2 ribs celery, roughly chopped*
> *1 medium-size white onion, roughly chopped*
> *4 to 6 cloves garlic, bled (scored)*
> *2 bay leaves*
> *2 tablespoons extra virgin olive oil*
> *2 lemons, cut up*
> *2 cups red wine (Sori Tildin preferred)*
> *6 to 8 juniper berries*
> *4 to 6 mushrooms, thickly sliced*
> *Pinch of freshly grated nutmeg*
> *Salt and pepper to taste*
> *2 teaspoons Milanese Spice (see page 236)*

1. Squeeze the lemon over the rabbits. Place the rabbit pieces in a bowl and add the carrot, celery, onion, garlic, bay leaves, olive oil, cut up lemons, 1 cup of the wine, and the juniper berries. Cover and marinate for 3 to 5 hours, or overnight in the refrigerator.

2. Pat the rabbits dry. Reserve the vegetables from the marinade as well as the liquid. Heat the oil in a large casserole and add the garlic cloves. When the garlic is slightly brown, remove and set aside. Lay the rabbit pieces in the casserole and brown over moderate heat. As with chicken, don't touch until the meat is well seared. Turn over and brown the other side. Remove the rabbit pieces and set aside. Add the mushrooms. Add the reserved carrot, celery, and onion when the mushrooms are brown.

3. When the onion is translucent, return the rabbit pieces and garlic to the pot and add the bay leaf and nutmeg. Season all with salt and pepper and deglaze with the remaining wine, stirring and allowing it to reduce slightly.

4. Add the marinade, minus the lemon pieces, and, stirring again, allow it to cook briefly. Add the Milanese spice, stirring again.

5. Cover the casserole and place in a 300°F oven for 1 hour to 1 hour and 30 minutes, until the meat is tender and moist and practically falling off the bone. Check regularly to see that it's simmering properly and turn the pieces over from time to time.

6. If, during the last half hour, the sauce is too liquid, remove the cover and allow it to reduce slightly. Serve the braise straight from the pot for a rustic and delicious presentation.

NOTES: In browning the rabbits remember you have a choice of using high heat in a separate pan or browning the rabbits over moderate heat in the casserole you're going to use, but being careful not to burn anything. In this way you get a better deglaze. I opted for this latter method in this recipe.

The Italians are very fond of adding the livers that have been sautéed and passed through a food mill to the sauce at the end. I'm not. I don't like the flavor or texture it imparts to the sauce and I think it would take away from the wonderful Barbaresco. But by all means add them if you like.

YIELD: *4 to 6 servings*

Lepri in Salmi

HARE IN SALMI

Here is a totally different approach to cooking rabbit that I think you'll find worthwhile. The same principle could be applied to other game and game birds as well. This recipe was given to me by the very well established chef-owner of Ristorante Falchetto, here in Perugia. I was impressed with the dish and asked for the recipe. It was a surprise to me to see that nothing is sautéed. The hare is boiled in its marinade, which is then strained to become the sauce.

1 **hare, approximately 4 to 4½ pounds**
4 **cups dry red wine**
½ **cup vinegar**
¼ **pound bacon**
2 **tablespoons capers**
1 **cup green olives, pitted**
3 **juniper berries**
½ **lemon**
2 **anchovy fillets**
1 **carrot**
1 **rib celery**
1 **sprig fresh rosemary**
5 **fresh sage leaves**
1 **bay leaf**
  Salt and pepper to taste

1. Cut the hare into pieces and place in a pan. Add the remaining ingredients. The wine and vinegar should cover the hare. Cover and marinate, refrigerated, for 24 hours.
2. Turn the mixture into a pan and set over medium-high heat. Allow to boil for about 1 hour. Remove the hare pieces to a platter.
3. Pass the remaining ingredients through a food mill or puree in a food processor and pour over the hare. This dish is also good cold.

YIELD: *8 servings*

CARNE

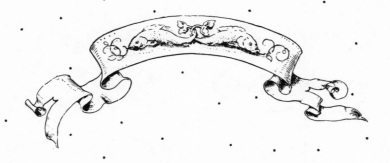

Meat

MEAT

CARNE · MEAT

Early Etruscan society (around 800 B.C.) was largely vegetarian, living mostly on grains and vegetables with occasional roasted meats or game birds for some special festival. In spite of these original meatless beginnings, however, the Italians, and more particularly the Romans, were serious meat eaters as early as 300 B.C. The Roman Emperor Maximus was said to consume forty pounds of meat each day and wash it down with as many quarts of wine. Whether true or not, meat eating was considered important enough for the Emperor Trajan (102 A.D.) to build a multilevel market next to the Forum with special meat stalls. By centralizing the butchering processes his squads of meat inspectors were better able to protect the public. In actuality, though, most of the population was not rich enough to afford meat and the poorer people of Italy were forced by economy to exist on grains, cereals, and vegetables with an occasional chicken thrown in. This forced abstention from meat existed throughout Italy till fairly recently and it is really only since the 1960s that meat of all kinds in all seasons has become prevalent and available to everyone.

The meat eating nobility and the general populace developed great recipes for meat for holiday festivities. As a result Italian cuisine is rich with recipes for all the known treatments of meat— roasting, grilling, broiling, frying, sautéing, boiling, braising, and stewing—and has contributed a great many meat dishes that have become international favorites.

The grading and butchering of meats in Italy is not the same as in America. The Italians and Europeans in general tend to butcher along the natural muscle separation line whereas American butchers cut across the grain. Thus all kinds of American meat cuts are generally different than Italian cuts.

In Italy there is no grading system as we know it in America and you must rely on your own ability to judge the quality of meat; or on the local butcher, which system I've never found satisfactory here. Supposed milkfed veal is never white and heavy aged beef (dark red) is never more than *vitelloni* (pink aged veal). You have to seek out specialty shops that feature the heavier beef of the Val di Chiana or have a special source for sucking calves, which is really what milkfed veal is all about. Unfortunately, even if you're able to find such sources, the prices are very, very expensive. Things are a bit easier in the big cities but throughout the rest of Italy getting the best quality meats is a chore, except when it comes to pork, where the quality seems so consistent that you'd think there wasn't a bad pig in Italy. Lamb and goat are also more reliable but not immune from problems and require a good source and careful shopping.

MANZO BUE • BEEF

Since earliest times the best beef in Italy has come from the Val di Chiana some thirty to forty miles south of Florence near Arezzo. The Razza Chianina breed is one of the oldest in the world (three thousand years) and the heaviest at an average of a ton and a half or more. The cattle are quite handsome, in a very large way, and resemble water buffalo with their humped backs and swinging dewlaps. Their mottled white skin and long spindly legs contribute to an overall appearance of sad gentility and a herd of white Chianina grazing in the marshy grasslands of the valley has the quality of an ancient still life.

Their meat is prized not only in Italy but throughout Europe. The most famous use it's put to is in making the internationally popular *bistecca alla Fiorentina*—a giant (3½-inch thick) porterhouse steak that is charcoal broiled "black and blue," or *ben crostato* (well crusted), with a bit of oil and lemon and served blood rare. I doubt if you can get a well done steak anywhere in Tuscany.

Tuscany, however, is not the only area that raises these prized cattle. Umbria and the Marche, which both border Tuscany, have also been raising Chianina herds for centuries. Unfortunately for those of us who live in Umbria the herds are rather small and there are only two specialty shops that I know of in the whole region that feature Chianina beef. I won't mention names, but neither of them ever has anything but Chianina beef—so they claim. In fact, a knowledgeable food buyer friend here is adamant in stating, "Not over 30 percent, I tell you . . . if that! If over 30 percent of their beef is Chianina, I'll give up smoking!"

American consumers don't have to come as far as the Val di Chiana or Umbria to get good beef, however. The U.S. government has been kind enough to help you further by breaking up the major categories of prime, choice, and good into top, middle, and low levels of each. If you have an honest butcher these differentiations—middle prime, top choice, whatever—will be reflected in his prices to you. Thus with the government's help you can zero in on value in meat.

The government has also been conscientious enough to institute a numbered system of yield grading from 1 to 5 with #1 indicating a meat with the most yield. Now you have the additional option of selecting meat on the basis of how much you're getting for what you pay as well as the quality level you want to pay for. Therefore, you might prefer a top choice yield, grade #1 over a top good product with a yield of #4, since although the top choice price will be higher its higher yield might make it more economical and yet give you meat with better flavor. It certainly wouldn't hurt to let your butcher know that you're aware of these classifications. If he's uncooperative, I'd change butchers.

As I was growing up as a chef in America, our well aged prime beef was a standard for the rest of the world. It was even considered finer than Japanese Kobi, Scotch Black Angus, or the famous *bistecca Fiorentina* of the Val di Chiana. The reasons were obvious. The grading system then (1945–1970) required prime to come from a steer that was at least four years old, range fed (not force-grain fed), and a minimum of 1400 pounds. The beautiful marbelization that was to be found is the epitome of quality beef, for it is marbled fat (not gristle) that makes meat tender and rich. When this prime beef was coupled with four to six weeks of dry aging the result was far and away the best to be had.

Unfortunately things are not quite the same anymore. The greed of the meat lobbies in America was able to force legislation about twelve years ago that reduced the standards considerably. What used to be "top choice," a lesser grade than prime, was moved up into "prime" and the need for being range fed was eliminated along with the three- to four-year-old requirement. Now prime beef is from one- to two-year-old steers and weighs approximately 1,000 pounds. The result is that by force feeding, hormonal injections, and special breeding, they are able to very rapidly produce steer with appropriate weight and yield and in so doing have given up a great deal of quality. There's no comparison between prime aged beef then and now. Unlike a goose, that if force fed and not allowed to move around produces a richer, fatter liver that is totally desirable, the just fame of American beef was based on the combination of fat and exercised muscle development only to be found in range-grazed steers. Yes, there's more beef of uniform quality today. But it just ain't as good—ever!

Aside from the essential use of the government's grading system, however, you should be aware of other considerations. They are freshness, aging, storing, and freezing.

Freshness

Although fresh-cut meat is not desirable since the aging process results in tenderization and flavor development, nonetheless if the meat has not been properly stored (dry air cooled) and handled, it will lack quality in spite of any government stamp as to prime or top choice, etc. The stamp is placed on the carcass by U.S. government inspectors when the animal is slaughtered. What happens thereafter, although subject to health inspections, is not a guarantee of continuing quality. You should develop a visual conception of what the meat should look like. For example, the outside fat should be white and creamy, not yellow, slimy, or dried out. Its color should be a good deep red with an unmistakable bright aliveness. Prime steaks should be flecked with marbled fat. The joints of ribs and roasts should have bright color and the bones should look healthy and fresh in spite of aging. All fresh meats have a pleasant, fresh, unspoiled odor and the nose test is an important one.

Aging

Meat that has just been slaughtered is tough and tasteless. Controlled aging allows the enzymes in the meat to act on the proteins and carbohydrates and to break down the connective tissue between the muscle fibers, thus making the meat tender and flavorful.

All meats, however, are highly perishable. Impeccable sanitation and dry air cooling with good circulation around each piece of meat is essential for proper aging. Moisture breeds bacteria. Therefore professional dry air coolers are the only safe way to age meat. Your home refrigerator is not a dry cooler and stacking meat in such wet coolers is dangerous. After 24 hours the bacteria counts will multiply rapidly, and the meat will spoil and become rancid anytime thereafter. Proper dry air cooling at 35° to 45°F will cause the fat and muscles to harden and permit slow aging to improve tenderness and flavor without spoilage for up to six weeks. The miracle, or should we say "cook's alchemy," of this situation is that the meat, if properly aged, will appear alive and "fresh" in spite of the fact that it has been aged . . . although admittedly you will have to scrape the green mold that has developed from aging to get this alive, fresh look.

Storing

Whether the meat you buy has been well aged or is "fresh," and regardless of type (beef, pork, veal, and grade (prime, choice, good), it is essential that you wipe the meat clean and dry, removing all excess dirt, blood, or discolored fat, and store it on a shelf in your refrigerator unwrapped, by itself, to allow circulation of air at all times around it. Check the temperature of your refrigerator and bring it to within 35° to 45°F. Do not store anything on top of the meat or do anything else that will cut off circulation or create moisture. Better yet, if you marinate whatever meat it is in a bit of oil, lemon, wine, and aromatics you will not only safeguard against spoilage but improve the final flavor of the product.

Freezing

Freezing has a tenderizing effect but also removes flavor. If you choose to freeze, the correct method is to prepare the meat in whatever portions you think you'll eventually use. Clean, trim, and dress the meat so that everything is ready for later cooking. You should then wrap the meat with both butcher's wrap (or any other plastic wrap)

and tinfoil. If meat is not wrapped properly it will become dry and hard and develop "freezer burn." Once cleaned, trimmed, dressed, and wrapped, it should be frozen at 0°F and stored at that temperature. It is a good practice to date and identify each package, since the normal storage life of beef is six to twelve months at 0°F and three to six months at 15°F.

The best method for cooking frozen meat is to thaw it out in the refrigerator first for 36 to 48 hours, depending on the size and type of meat, although it can also be thawed at room temperature (70°F) in 16 to 24 hours. It is also possible to cook meat directly from the freezer. Cooking times, however, will be approximately half again longer. Once unthawed, however, the meat must be used directly. Refreezing meat not only ruins the flavor but is also quite dangerous. Unthawed meat spoils very rapidly because of the excess moisture contained in the ice crystals that were formed in the original freezing process.

General Cooking Techniques

As mentioned previously, the cooking techniques for meat are much the same here in Italy as in America. Spit roasting, roasting, baking, broiling, charcoal broiling, frying, panfrying, sautéing, braising, stewing, or boiling are all used with various cuts of meat to good effect. The common denominator, however, in all cases except boiling, is an initial searing to brown the meat on the outside, which imparts that universally desirable rich, dark, crusty flavor preliminary to finishing cooking as a roast, braise, or stew.

Here, for your convenience and reference, is a list of American cuts of beef and the cooking methods best suited to them.

NECK *(braise)*

Ground meat	Stew meat

FOREQUARTERS *(broil, panfry, roast, braise)*

Shoulder clod	Chuck short ribs
Triangle	Cubed steak
Boneless inside chuck	Blade steak
Chuck tender	Stew meat
Chuck steak	Ground chuck
Chuck roast (usually rolled)	Arm pot roast

BRISKET *(braise, boil)*

Shoulder cut brisket	Boned rolled brisket
Corned beef brisket	

SHANK *(braise, stew)*

Shank	Stew meat

RIBS *(roast, broil, panfry)*

Rib roast	Short rib
Rib steak	Rib eye roast

PLATE *(roast, braise, boil)*

Short rib	Plate
Rolled plate	

SIRLOIN *(broil, panfry)*

Boned rolled sirloin	Pin bone sirloin steak
Sirloin roast	Full tenderloin
Sirloin steak	Fillet steak

SHORT LOIN *(broil, panfry)*

Porterhouse steak	Club steak
T-bone steak	

FLANK *(broil, braise)*

Flank steak	Flank skirt
Flank steak fillet	Thin skirt

RUMP *(braise, roast)*

Rump pot roast	Rolled rump
Rump steak	

ROUND *(roast, broil, panfry, braise)*

Hind shank	Silverside
Heel of round	Ground beef
Round steak	Knuckle (sirloin tip)
Top round	Rolled topside
Bottom round	

LEG *(braise, boil, panfry)*

Stew meat	Ground beef

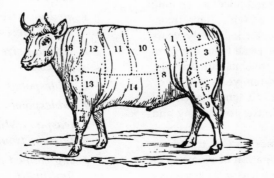

The question of doneness can be learned very rapidly through trial and error as I'm sure most backyard cooks have learned with grilling. Roasts and braises can easily be tested with a standard meat thermometer which will show you ranges of doneness from rare to well done. Your butcher can also tell you how many minutes per pound you should cook the piece of meat he's selling. The final test, however, should lie within your own instincts and ability to learn exactly how you would like your meat cooked. My advice as a professional is to use the minute per pound formula along with a meat thermometer and at the same time train yourself to second guess what is happening. By and by you'll be able to consistently cook meat exactly as you like it—which is after all the only object of the lesson.

Brasato di Bue al Barolo

BRAISED BEEF IN BAROLO

One of the most popular meat dishes when I was growing up was a wonderful long-braised pot roast. Brown and succulent braised beef develops aromatic sauces from its natural juices when long cooked with a good bottle of wine. This treatment of beef was very prevalent in Italy years ago, when most of the beef came from old farm animals that had outlived their usefulness. Six, seven, sometimes eight or ten years old, they weren't exactly what we'd call tender cuts, and therefore lent themselves better to braising and long stewing.

One of my favorite recipes for this treatment of beef comes from a combination of Piemontese and Lombardian recipes. The use of Barolo and a

flambé of Cognac are particularly Piemontese, while the addition of the special spice mixture (equal amounts of ground cinnamon, cloves, nutmeg, bay leaf, and white pepper) is from Lombardy, being a Milanese specialty.

1 cup combined diced carrot, celery, and onion

3 to 4 cloves garlic, bled (scored)

3 tablespoons olive oil

1 bottle Barolo wine (Prunotto Riserva preferred)

2 bay leaves

Pinch each dried thyme, basil, and chervil

1 medium-size white onion, peeled and cut into 4 pieces

6 whole black peppercorns

½ cup finely chopped fresh parsley

2 to 2½ pounds top or bottom round beef (well aged and top choice preferred)

Salt and pepper to taste

Pinch of freshly grated nutmeg

½ cup best available Cognac

1 cup sweet Florio Marsala

2 cups Fondo Bruno (see page 85) or consommé (see page 89)

1 medium-size carrot, peeled and cut into 4 pieces

1 medium-size rib celery, cut into 4 pieces

2 tablespoons tomato paste

1 tablespoon chopped garlic

1 teaspoon Milanese Spice (see recipe introduction)

1 cup canned plum tomatoes (optional)

1. Make a marinade with diced carrot, celery, and onion, the garlic cloves, 1½ tablespoons oil, cup wine, the bay leaves, thyme, basil, chervil, onion pieces, peppercorns, and parsley.

2. Set the meat in the marinade, coating it well on all sides, and allow to marinate for 6 to 8 hours at room temperature (assuming it's not August) or refrigerate overnight for 12 to 16 hours.

3. When ready, pat the meat dry, wipe it clean and reserve the marinade. In a heavy-bottomed casserole, heat some oil with the whole cloves of garlic from the marinade. Sear the outside of the roast over medium-high heat, browning the outside on all sides without burning it. Be sure the heat is not too high. If need be, set the garlic cloves aside so they don't burn.

4. When properly browned, season with salt, pepper, and nutmeg. Immediately pour Cognac over the meat, heat it, then ignite it. Let the Cognac flambé the meat till the alcohol burns out. Add the Marsala and reduce it, turning the meat over in it till the meat starts to caramelize. There should be some liquid remaining, however.

5. Add the stock and reduce it by a third over medium heat. Add the remaining Barolo and the pieces of carrot and celery. Strain the marinade; either incorporate the "juices" from the marinade or leave them out. I prefer to leave them out to make the final sauce leaner. Add the strained vegetables from the marinade to the casserole. Add the tomato paste, the chopped garlic, and the Milanese spice and stir all together.

6. Cover tightly and braise in a 375°F oven for approximately 20 minutes without opening it.

7. Open, stir, and add the tomatoes, if you like a more tomatolike sauce. Put the lid back on tightly and braise at 350°F for approximately 1 hour, or until the meat is very tender. Check occasionally to see nothing is sticking and to turn the meat over.

8. Remove the meat and keep warm in a 200°F oven or on top of the stove.

9. Now pass the remaining liquid and vegetables through a food mill. Return the strained vegetables and liquid to the casserole. Skim or blot any excess grease. Correct the seasoning and heat the sauce. Serve immediately with the pot roast on warm plates.

NOTE: If you'd prefer, the pieces of carrot and celery can be reserved and served the with the meat. If you do that you might want to make a few more carrots and celery so everyone has a piece or two. The reason for the two types of carrot is the same as the use of whole cloves of garlic and diced garlic. It's not a mistake—nor essential—but creates interesting taste sensations.

YIELD: *4 to 6 portions*

Involtina alla Fiorentina

FLORENTINE STEAK ROLLS

This recipe comes from a Tuscan chef I hired to replace myself at the Potting Shed, a Northern Italian supper club in Lenox, Massachusetts, in 1958 or 1959; as does the name, about which he patiently explained, "Alla Fiorentina does not mean with spinach. We prefer artichokes!"

There are two ways to approach this recipe: either as a sauté of steak with a reduced *espagnole* called "Candy Glaze" (see page 96), or as a long stewing braise made with top round. In either case the filling is the same and the stock and wines used in either saucing are the same.

The steak recipe is more expensive but more elegant. The braise is cheaper and more rustic. In both cases *gnocchi* (potato dumplings) are the perfect accompaniment.

Two 3½- to 4-ounce prime aged beef
    strip, thinly sliced
    Salt and pepper to taste
    Pinch each dried thyme, basil,
    chervil, marjoram, and oregano,
    mixed together
    2 *thin slices Genoa salami*
    1 *tablespoon raisins*
    1 *tablespoon pine nuts*
    1 *tablespoon diced citron*
   ¼ *teaspoon grated orange rind*
    1 *tablespoon freshly grated*
    parmigiano
½ to ¾ *cup Espagnole (see page 96)*
   ½ *cup Fondo Bruno or consommé (see*
    page 85 or 89), reduced by half
    1 *cup Marsala (Florio sweet*
    preferred)
   ½ *cup sweet vermouth (Cinzano*
    preferred)
    1 *tablespoon oil or clarified butter*
24 to 30 *Gnocchi (see page 64)*
    2 *tablespoons chopped fresh parsley*
    to garnish

1. Lay the slices of beef between two sheets of plastic wrap and pound lightly to tenderize and flatten slightly. Do not make holes in the meat. Remove the plastic wrap and set the slices side by side. Dust with salt, pepper, and the dried herb mixture. Divide the salami, raisins, pine nuts, citron, orange rind, and parmigiano evenly between the slices of steak.

2. Roll the steaks up by tucking in the outside edges and rolling forward. Secure each with toothpicks and set aside.

3. Mix the *espagnole,* reduced stock, ½ cup Marsala, and the vermouth together in a saucepan.

Whisk while reducing to half the volume over medium-high heat. You should have 1 cup of thick syrupy liquid; this is the candy glaze. Reserve.

4. Sauté the steak rolls in the oil over medium-high heat for 2 to 3 minutes, allowing them to brown well without burning and without overcooking them.

5. Deglaze with ½ cup Marsala, add 1 tablespoon of the candy glaze and season with salt and pepper. Allow these liquids to practically evaporate and caramelize the meat.

6. In another saucepan, carefully heat the remaining sauce just enough for it to thicken a bit. Watch closely as it may evaporate quickly.

7. Plate the steak rolls, removing the toothpicks, on a warm round plate with the *gnocchi* surrounding them. Pour the thickened candy glaze over the meat and the *gnocchi,* drizzling slowly to distribute evenly. Garnish with the remaining chopped parsley and serve immediately.

YIELD: *1 serving, 2 rolls*

Braised Steak Rolls

  8 *Steak Rolls (see page 237)*
  4 *cups (approximately) Florio sweet*
    Marsala
    Salt and pepper to taste
  2 *cups (approximately) Espagnole (see page*
    96)
  3 *cups Fondo Bruno or consommé (see page*
    85 or 89)

3 cups (approximately) sweet
    vermouth (Cinzano)
72 to 100 (as you wish) 1-inch Gnocchi (see
    page 64)
2 tablespoons chopped fresh parsley

1. Sauté the toothpicked beef rolls and deglaze
with a bit of Marsala (1 cup), reducing and caramelizing the meat. Season with salt and pepper.
2. If your rolls are in a large braising pot, just add
the Marsala, *espagnole*, stock, and vermouth, and
reduce by a quarter on a medium-high heat for 5
to 7 minutes, uncovered. (If you've sautéed in a
separate pan, place the rolls in a large braising pot
and proceed as above.) Reduce the heat to lowest
possible and diffuse it with several diffusers.
Cook on very low heat, uncovered, for at least 1
hour and really for as long as you'd like. If the
sauce reduces too much just add more of all four
liquids in equal proportion—or just stock if that's
all you have.
3. To serve, remove the toothpicks from each and
plate on round plates (warm). Surround the rolls
(two to a portion) with *gnocchi*. Spoon the sauce
over the top and garnish with chopped parsley.
Serve directly.

YIELD: *4 servings*

Bistecca alla Pizzaiola

STEAK PIZZAIOLA

This is a favorite Neapolitan presentation of a
quick steak sauté with tomatoes. The peppers
and onions are probably an American innovation.

You could very well use Marsala or a red wine (or
both) to deglaze, and mushrooms also work well
in this dish, but "freshness," or should I say
"lightness" in this case, is best achieved without
either.
    This dish is best when the meat is well crusted
on the outside, but rare inside, and the vegetables
still crunchy. Hence the speedy sauté. Be careful
not to burn the herbs and diced garlic before adding the tomatoes.

2 to 4 cloves garlic, bled (scored)
1 small green and/or red bell pepper,
    cut into strips
½ cup coarsely chopped onion
3 tablespoons extra virgin olive oil
10 to 12 ounces boneless New York strip or
    fillet, sliced into wide strips
    Salt and freshly ground black
    pepper to taste
    Pinch each dried thyme, basil, and
    chervil, mixed together
1 sprig fresh thyme, if available
    Crushed red pepper to taste
1 teaspoon chopped garlic
1 tablespoon chopped fresh parsley
1 cup canned Italian plum tomatoes
    (or Marinara, see page 100)

1. Sauté the garlic cloves, pepper strips, and onion
in the oil over high heat to brown and crisp. Remove and set aside.
2. Add the meat slices and brown. Season with
salt, pepper, the herbs, and diced garlic. Add the
reserved onions, peppers, and garlic cloves.
3. Add half the parsley, and toss the contents,
turning the meat while maintaining a brisk heat.
Add the tomatoes, breaking them up and amal-

gamating the whole. Cook another 1 to 2 minutes to reduce the sauce. Garnish with the remaining parsley. Serve immediately on warm plates.

YIELD: *2 servings*

Filetto di Bue Sorpresa

STEAK FILET SURPRISE

This recipe is from a trattoria with an open display kitchen that I created at One Grandview in Pittsburgh, Pennsylvania, in 1974. The design was rather unique in that it not only served for open display cooking but also was so constructed as to allow the customers to select their lobster or trout from live tanks, or have their steak cut by the ounce, and then hand their selection to the chef, who would demonstrate the dish while explaining the recipe. In other words, they actually walked into the kitchen and watched some very interesting island cooking. Great fun!

The surprise is that we use white wine and chicken stock in this beef dish, rather than red wine and beef stock, to create an unusual flavor. Could you use red wine and beef stock? Of course . . . as long as you cook with love, knowledge and devotion . . . anything's possible.

Four 6-ounce filet mignon (prime aged beef)
    Salt and pepper to taste
Four 1-ounce slices mozzarella
Four ½-ounce slices prosciutto
6 to 8 medium-size mushrooms, sliced and sautéed
    2 cups all-purpose flour, seasoned with salt and pepper
2 to 3 eggs, lightly beaten with 2 tablespoons water and 1 tablespoon grated parmigiano
2 to 3 cups bread crumbs
    2 tablespoons pure olive oil
4 to 6 cloves garlic, bled (scored)
    1 cup Gerwürztraminer (or best available aromatic white wine)
    2 cups Brodo di Pollo (see page 89)
    2 teaspoons fresh lemon juice
    2 tablespoons finely chopped fresh parsley
    1 tablespoon chopped garlic

1. Butterfly, or have your butcher butterfly, the filets and season the open halves with salt and pepper.
2. Place a slice of mozzarella, a slice of prosciutto, and a quarter of the mushrooms in each and close the two halves by pressing them together firmly.
3. Dredge the filets, one at a time, with the flour, egg wash, and bread crumb breading. Shake off the excess crumbs and set each aside.
4. Heat the oil with the garlic cloves in an ovenproof sauté pan and sauté the steaks over medium-high heat on both sides till golden brown but not cooked inside. Season with salt and pepper.
5. Deglaze with the white wine and allow it to reduce slightly. Add the chicken stock, lemon juice, 1 tablespoon parsley, and the diced garlic and reduce again slightly.
6. Still in the same pan, cook in a 375°F oven for 5 to 7 minutes, uncovered. Turn each filet out on a warm plate and spoon the remaining sauce over them. Garnish with the remaining chopped parsley.

NOTE: If you want rare steak omit the oven procedure, but this is one of those situations where the dish doesn't have to be rare to be good.

YIELD: *4 servings*

Spezzatini di Bue allo Spiedo

BEEF KEBABS

I'm not going to bother to teach you how to broil a steak since most Americans have years of back-yard experience. But there is a recipe for an Italian shish kebab that is best on a charcoal grill, even though it could be done in the oven, that I'd like to share with you. The simple marinade of oil, garlic, rosemary, and red wine is what makes the final product so delicious. Remember to have sautéed the mushrooms slightly first. Or if you really want to play it safe, precook all the veggies in a hot oven. In this manner you can leave the steak very rare without the vegetables being undercooked.

1½ *pounds (trimmed weight) prime aged beef, strip or filet mignon, cut into 1½- to 2-inch cubes*

3 *tablespoons extra virgin olive oil*

4 to 6 *cloves garlic, bled (scored)*

2 *sprigs fresh rosemary*

2 *cups best available red wine*

Salt and pepper to taste

8 *green, yellow, or red bell peppers, cut into 2-inch pieces*

4 *large mushroom caps, quartered and sautéed lightly*

Eight *2-inch pieces white onion*

Crushed red pepper to taste

1. Place the meat and vegetables in a large pot or bowl. Add the oil, garlic, rosemary, red wine, salt, and pepper and marinate for 4 to 6 hours in a cool place or overnight in a refrigerator.

2. Thread the beef (3 to 4 cubes per kebab) and vegetables on skewers in whatever fashion you prefer—normally meat, onion, meat, mushroom, meat, pepper.

3. Cook the skewered meat on a hot charcoal fire and baste continually with the marinade. Serve directly on warm plates.

YIELD: *4 servings*

VITELLO · VEAL

Veal in a real sense is baby beef. It comes from calves that are anywhere from three months to a year in age. After that, here in Italy, it is called *vitellone* till the age of three and one half, or after it has been used as a work animal; then it becomes *manzo*. In America, the government grades veal prime, choice, and good, which is fine, but nowhere do they guarantee milk fed veal. White veal—milk fed veal—has always been very difficult to find in America. The surprise to me has been that it's equally hard to find here in Italy. There are good reasons why.

Certain basic principles must be understood before you start paying $18 to $22 (last I checked it was $28) a pound for supposed "milkfed white veal." To begin with, the calf must be a nursing infant. It should never have eaten anything but milk—no grass, no feed—and should have barely moved around. No wonder the flesh is so white and the meat extraordinarily delicate. This rare delicacy is certainly worth a bonus price for those willing to pay for it. And the high price is understandable since the yield is extremely low because the animal is so small. How small? Ah! Well there's the rub.

A leg from a baby milk fed calf weighs 12 to 18 pounds, and the animal has been slaughtered at, or under, three months of age. Yet show me the butcher that has legs of that weight. As a chef, a consultant, and now at the Cooking School of Umbria for the past five years, I've been unable to find any commercial butchers (Italy or America) with legs weighing less than 48 pounds. Two things have happened to make the legs weigh this much. First, the animal is far older than three months—more like eight months to a year and a half—and secondly, the calf is no longer nursing. The calf has been fed grass and feed and the meat no longer bears any resemblance to white veal. The flesh is now rosy pink to bright red and should be sold at normal prices. Yet all the butchers and wholesalers I've encountered will look you straight in the eye and say: "Whadda you crazy? Fifty pounds is what they all weigh! It's stamped 'Plum de Veau,' what more do you want!"

Now "Plum de Veau" happens to be a brand name, but if you remonstrate him with the fact that a leg from a nursing calf is under 20 pounds, the answer is: "What I said! You're crazy! Who can sell little stuff like that? Never heard of it."

This conversation surprisingly enough has taken place innumerable times here in Italy as well as in America. On both sides of the Atlantic I've been unable to find baby milk fed veal on any commercial level. For myself, my own restaurants, or for clients, over the last twenty years I've had to rely on local farmers where I could contract for the whole animal to be slaughtered at

two and one half to three months old. Of course the difference in quality is obvious. When I make veal *piccata* with thin scallops from this veal everyone says I'm a magician. Magic, no! Real baby white milk fed veal, yes! And the price ends up at $7 per pound because I'm able to use all the different parts—calf's brains, liver, feet, leg, loin, rib, breast, shoulder, and shank for special dishes, roasts, chops, stocks, sauces, braises, and stews.

When it comes to scaloppine, *medaglione,* or loin chops, nothing is as good as baby milkfed veal. But for many other uses regular U.S. prime or good will serve as well if not better in some cases. Roasts, braises, and stews that require long cooking will all be better from a somewhat larger animal. Here the 50-pound legs serve very well. In that case, the coloration to look for is bright pink (not white) and the fat should be creamy white.

The same principles for butchering, handling, storing, and freezing that apply to beef apply to veal as well and I refer you to those particular comments in the section on beef. The question of aging, however, is altogether different. Whereas good beef requires four to six weeks to develop maximum flavor, veal is too delicate to benefit from this process. As stated earlier, all meat (pork and lamb included) is tough and tasteless when first slaughtered. From experience I've found that veal (even baby milk fed veal) improves in taste and tenderness for a few days thereafter. The redder the meat, as opposed to white, the longer it will continue to improve by aging, up to a maximum of ten days.

Cooking methods

Veal is very different from beef in that it has very little fat content. It is naturally tender and quite lean. It is essential therefore to cook it very rapidly in small, thin pieces since it will otherwise toughen; or in the case of larger cuts for roasts, braises, and stews, it is important to lard or bard it to provide supplemental fat so that it doesn't dry out and toughen. Methods for sautéing scaloppine or *medaglione* will be given in detail in specific recipes as will all other pertinent techniques, but generally it is important to remember that veal, like fish, has very little connective tissue and therefore requires careful attention when cooking. A minute is a long time when sautéing veal and it is one of the prime areas where less is more!

Here are the American cuts of veal and the methods of cooking best suited to them, with special notations as to when baby milk fed veal is worth the extra money.

NECK *(braise, stew)*

Roast neck	Stew meat
Stuffed neck	

SHOULDER *(braise, panfry)*

Blade roast	Blade steak
Arm roast	Arm steak
Boneless shoulder	Shoulder scaloppine
roast	Ground veal

FORESHANK *(braise, stew)*

Osso buco	Stew meat

BREAST *(roast, braise, stew)*

Roast breast of veal	Mock chicken legs
Stuffed breast of veal	Veal loaf
Riblets (for stew)	Stew meat

RIB *(roast, braise, panfry)*

Rib roast	Rib chops
Crown roast	Rib cutlets

FLANK *(patties, panfry)*

Ground meat can come from every section, but flank is always included.

From the Hindsaddle:

*LOIN *(roast, broil, panfry, braise)*

Loin veal chops	Boneless sirloin roast
Veal steaks (top loin)	Cube steaks
Single kidney veal	Sirloin chops
chops	Stuffed double veal
Loin roast	chops
Sirloin roast	Veal kebabs

*LEG RUMP AND ROUND *(roast, braise, stew)*

Rump roast	Scaloppine
Round roast	Eye round roast
Stuffed roast and	Medallions (from the
boneless	eye of the round)
Pinbone or hipbone	Cutlets
veal chops	Round steak

HINDSHANK *(braise, stew, panfry patties)*

Osso buco	Ground veal
Stew meat	

*Baby milkfed preferred

Piccata di Vitello della Casa

VEAL SCALOPPINE WITH LEMON

Della casa, meaning of the house, lets people know that it's your own recipe. In this case we have taken the liberty of expanding the classic combination of veal *medaglioni* or scaloppine with lemon with the addition of aromatic wine, sauterne, mushrooms, onion, and truffle to make the dish more interesting without overpowering the delicacy of the veal. Of all the wonderfully delicate veal presentations possible I think *piccata* is the most elegant.

The technical aspect of the sauté presented here is an important method for all quick sautés where you want to add other ingredients without overcooking the main ingredients.

Ten *¾- to 1-ounce veal medallions (cut from the eye of the loin)*

2 to 3 *tablespoons all-purpose flour, seasoned with salt and pepper*

2 *tablespoons unsalted butter*

4 *medium-size champignon mushrooms, thinly sliced (approximately 1 cup)*

1 *tablespoon finely minced shallots or onion*

Salt and pepper to taste

2 *teaspoons chopped fresh parsley*

Fresh lemon juice

1 *teaspoon diced black truffle*

¼ *cup Gewürztraminer or other spicy, dry white wine*

1 *tablespoon sauterne*

1. Pound the veal medallions between plastic wrap until paper thin. Lightly flour them, dusting off the excess, then lay on a plate, well spaced.
2. Heat the oil and 1 tablespoon of butter over low heat and gently sauté the veal for 30 seconds to 1 minute on one side until set but not browned. Turn the medallions over and sauté for another 30 seconds.
3. Push the veal to the top of the pan near the handle and tilt the pan downward. Add the mushrooms and shallots to the lower portion of the pan with a little more butter and cook briefly for about 1 minute.
4. Flatten the pan, season the meat and vegetables with salt and pepper, 1 teaspoon of parsley, the lemon juice, and the truffles and combine the ingredients by swirling the pot by the handle with both hands. Turn up the heat and add the Gewürztraminer and sauterne, tossing the veal in the liquid to coat evenly. Work quickly to avoid overcooking the veal.
5. Bring the meat, mushrooms, and shallots back up toward the handle and tilt the pan again to allow the liquids to reduce without cooking the other ingredients. Reduce for 1 minute (or more) over a high heat. Melt a bit of butter into the reduction and reduce by half. Flatten the pan again and swirl all together. Arrange the medallions on hot plates and spoon the sauce with the vegetables on top. Garnish with the remaining chopped parsley and serve immediately.

NOTE: The combination of the dry Alsatian Gewürztraminer and rich sauternes is a very special balancing act, the high aromas of one balancing the honeyed sweetness of the other. Substitute a good German Auslese or other world-class dessert wine for the sauterne, but only in conjunction with the Gewürztraminer. Or, use a soft, well-made Californian "Gewürz" in place of both . . . but remember, it's not the same.

Variation

•

To make *medaglioni alla marsala,* substitute an equal amount of the best quality sweet Marsala for the white wines. A few drops of beef or dark veal glaze is also good in this version.

YIELD: *2 servings*

Saltimbocca alla Romana

VEAL CUTLETS WITH PROSCIUTTO, MOZZARELLA, AND SAGE

The normal presentation of this dish in Rome, Bologna, or Milan is a combination of veal, sage, mozzarella, and prosciutto cooked in the manner of an open-faced sandwich with the mozzarella and prosciutto changing position from final topping to middle part of the sandwich. It is also done as a sauté and finished under the broiler to melt the cheese, or baked in the oven. Many of the recipes call for chicken stock; a few for veal stock; all a touch of Marsala or white wine; and some require a bit of lemon juice. I've been pleased with all of these variations except when the stock used is obviously from bouillon cubes thickened with flour and butter and not properly cooked out.

The term *saltimbocca*—to jump *(saltare)* from the pan to the mouth *(bocca)*—seems not to have any literal application since it's hardly that quick a sauté by the time you melt the cheese. Of course it may be that the original recipe didn't call for cheese, and as Waverley Root points out in *The Food of Italy*:

"Saltimbocca is composed of thin slices of veal seasoned with sage, 'married' (maritati) by means of wooden toothpick skewers to slices of prosciutto ham, the whole sautéed in butter and braised with Marsala wine. The name means 'jump into the mouth,' the idea being that saltimbocca is so delicious that it prompts you almost by its own volition to pop a piece of it in without hesitating for an instant."

My own version of this dish was given to me years ago by Chef Gatti, the executive chef at the Plaza Hotel in New York, who proclaimed its authenticity, although it's unlike any other version I've seen anywhere else, which leads me to believe it was his own creation. I've used it ever since and it has proven so popular that, for example, at my restaurant One Grandview, my son and I had to make a concerted effort in the dining room to steer the customers into other dishes, since better than 50 percent of the orders from an eighty-five-item menu suddenly were for *saltimbocca*.

Two 2-ounce veal cutlets
    Salt and pepper to taste
    Pinch of dried sage or 1 to 2 fresh leaves
  1 *thin slice prosciutto*
  1 *ounce mozzarella, sliced*
  ½ *cup all-purpose flour, seasoned with salt and pepper*
  2 *large eggs, lightly beaten and seasoned with parsley, parmigiano, nutmeg, salt, and pepper*
  ½ *cup bread crumbs, seasoned with salt, pepper, and parmigiano*
  1 *tablespoon extra virgin olive oil*
  1 *tablespoon unsalted butter*
  ½ *cup Fondo Bruno or consommé (see page 85 or 88)*
  ¼ *cup Marsala*
  ¼ *cup sweet vermouth*
  1 *tablespoon tomato paste*
  1 *mushroom cap, sautéed golden brown in 1 teaspoon of oil*
  1 *teaspoon finely chopped fresh parsley*
  1 *sprig fresh parsley*

1. Pound the veal between two sheets of plastic wrap with the flat side of a cleaver. They should be wafer thin and will double in size.
2. Lay the cutlets on a work surface and lightly sprinkle 1 cutlet with salt, pepper and crumbled

sage. Lay the slice of mozzarella and the prosciutto on the cutlet and cover with the second
one. Seal the edges by pressing with your fingers.
3. Flour the pocket lightly, dip it in the egg wash,
and then into the bread crumbs. Pat firmly and
shape the double cutlet with your hand, covering
it liberally with bread crumbs and pressing hard
so that it stays together.
4. Heat the butter and oil over a medium heat.
Reduce the heat to low and sauté the *saltimbocca*
slowly on both sides until golden brown and
done, about 5 to 8 minutes.
5. Meanwhile, combine the stock, Marsala, vermouth, and tomato paste. Heat over medium-
high heat and reduce by half.
6. Place a bit of the sauce on a warm plate and
place the *saltimbocca* in the sauce. Top with a bit
more of the sauce and garnish with the sautéed
mushroom cap, the chopped parsley and the
whole parsley sprig. Serve immediately.

YIELD: *1 serving*

Costollete di Vitello alla Milanese

VEAL CUTLETS MILANESE

It seems as if everyone in the world loves a
breaded veal cutlet. General Radetzky of the
Austrian Imperial Army back in the 1800s
thought so highly of it that he brought the recipe
back with him from Milan to Vienna and thereby
created the famous "Vienna Schnitzels" of Germany. The difference between a *Weinerschnitzel*

and a *costolette* (or *cotolette*) *di vitello* is that the Italians use a bone-in rib chop while their Austrian
cousins use a boneless cut from the loin or the
round.

Two 2- to 3-inch-thick veal rib chops (6 to 8
    ounces each)
  1 cup flour, seasoned with salt and
    pepper
  1 egg, lightly beaten with 2 tablespoons
    water and seasoned with salt and
    pepper
  1 cup bread crumbs (2/3 toasted, 1/3
    plain)
  1 tablespoon extra virgin olive oil
  1 tablespoon unsalted butter
  2 mushroom caps
  2 wedges lemon

1. Pound the chops and their bones between two
sheets of plastic wrap with a meat pounder.
2. Set out the seasoned flour, beaten egg, and
bread crumbs in three dishes. Pass the chops first
through the flour, then the egg wash, and then
the bread crumbs, shaping and pressing the
crumbs tightly on the chops.
3. Heat the oil and butter over medium heat and
sauté the chops, turning them over occasionally.
4. In the meantime, and in a separate pan, sauté
the mushroom caps till they are golden brown.
5. When the chops are thoroughly brown crusted,
turn them out onto paper towels to drain. Plate
on warm plates and serve with a lemon wedge.

YIELD: *2 servings*

Osso Buco di Vitello

VEAL SHANKS

I don't know of any other recipe more typically Northern Italian than this one and although there are several variations from Bologna, Novara, and Genoa, the basic ingredients all seem to be the same: veal shanks (preferably with the marrow in), *battuto*, stock, tomatoes and tomato concentrate, lemon rind and/or orange rind, Marsala and white wine. Some recipes such as the ones from Genoa and Novara (Piedmont) omit the tomatoes. Our research indicates that the classic Milanese recipe has our favorite Milanese spice mixture (see page 236) in addition to a basic thyme and garlic flavoring.

The essence of the dish, however, is the meat falling off the bone effect of long slow braising, what the Milanese call *stracotto*. The addition of *gremolata* (a mixture of anchovy, garlic, lemon rind, and parsley) at the end of cooking is traditional, although there are many places in Milan that leave it out of the cooking and serve it as a relish on top of the marrow—a procedure I prefer.

Osso buco with Risotto alla Milanese (see page 130) is one of those essential gastronomic marriages "made in heaven" that combine to make the quintessential dish for cold wintry days. I must admit, however, that in testing this dish again for this book on a hot July day I was no less able to enjoy it. *Buon appetito!*

2 tablespoons extra virgin olive oil

4 cloves garlic, bled (scored)

2 veal shanks with the edges (nerves) cut, tied and lightly floured

Salt and pepper to taste

Pinch each dried thyme, basil, chervil, and oregano

Few grains crushed red pepper

1 teaspoon each finely chopped carrot, celery, and onion

½ cup Florio Marsala

½ cup best available dry white wine

2 cups Fondo Bruno (see page 85)

1 tablespoon tomato paste

1 teaspoon chopped garlic

1 tablespoon finely chopped fresh parsley

½ teaspoon Milanese Spice (see page 236)

½ cup canned Italian plum tomatoes

1 tablespoon tomato paste

1 teaspoon lemon rind

½ teaspoon orange rind

2 teaspoons Gremolata (see note below)

Crushed red pepper to taste

1 tablespoon chopped fresh parsley

1. Heat oil and garlic in a sauté pan over medium-high heat.

2. Brown the veal shanks, seasoning with salt and pepper. It helps prevent curling if you cut the tendons in the meat of the shanks. Usually a scissors is the best tool for this job.

3. Add the thyme, basil, chervil, oregano, and red pepper flakes. Add the celery, carrots, and onion and cook on low heat, mixing the ingredients but not browning the onion.

4. Deglaze with Marsala. Reduce the liquid to caramelize the shanks. Add the white wine and a bit of the stock and reduce by a third.

5. Swirl in the tomato paste. Add the minced garlic, 1 teaspoon of parsley, and the Milanese spice.

6. Add in the tomatoes, breaking them up with a spoon, and turn up the heat slightly. Add the remaining stock, cover the pan, and braise in a

370°F oven for approximately 1 hour, or until done.

7. Fifteen minutes before finishing, add in the lemon peel and orange rind and stir. Serve with a teaspoon of *gremolata* on each shank as a garnish after saucing.

NOTE: To make *gremolata,* combine 1 clove diced garlic, ¼ teaspoon diced lemon rind, 1 anchovy fillet, 1 tablespoon chopped parsley, and 1 tablespoon extra virgin olive oil.

YIELD: *2 servings*

Involtini di Vitello alla Modenese

VEAL ROLLS IN THE MODENESE STYLE

Involtini are made of pieces of rolled meat, fish or poultry which are stuffed with a variety of forcemeats bound together with eggs, cheese, and/or *balsamella.* They can be sautéed in a pan with wine and aromatics or braised in the oven after an initial browning. Either way you're best served if they're cooked through and soft and tender to the touch.

This particular recipe is a variation on one given me by a chef in Modena. The variation consists of the addition of the Milanese spice (see page 236) to the filling. Unusual is the use of scamorza instead of mozzarella in the stuffing.

The whole slices of carrot are a sweetener that works along with the Milanese spice to produce a deliciously different sauce. Serve the carrots around the rolls for an attractive presentation.

These tender little rolls braise rather quickly; therefore it is good to use a heavy bottomed pot to cook them.

2 *pounds veal, sliced across the grain into eight 4-ounce slices (you may use pink veal in this recipe)*
  Salt and pepper to taste

4 *sweet Italian sausages, about 8 ounces, casing removed and broken up*

1 *cup diced scamorza or mozzarella*

½ *cup diced prosciutto*

2 *tablespoons pine nuts*

½ *cup grated freshly parmigiano*

1 *teaspoon Milanese Spice (see page 236)*

4 *slices crustless white bread*
  Milk (to moisten bread)

2 *jumbo eggs*

2 *tablespoons extra virgin olive oil*

1 *tablespoon unsalted butter*

4 *cloves garlic, bled (scored)*

2 *cups flour, seasoned with salt and pepper*

½ *cup Marsala (sweet Florio preferred)*

3 *cups Fondo Bianco or Brodo di Pollo (see pages 86 and 89)*

3 *medium-size or 2 large carrots, peeled, halved, and quartered lengthwise*

½ *cup best available white wine, aromatic preferred*

2 *tablespoons finely chopped fresh parsley*

1 *tablespoon arrowroot, dissolved in ½ cup water (optional)*

1. Place the veal slices between sheets of plastic wrap and pound thin with a meat mallet and without tearing the veal. Place the slices on a plate and sprinkle lightly with salt and pepper. Set aside.

2. In a large bowl, mix together thoroughly the sausage, *scamorza,* prosciutto, pine nuts, and parmigiano. Season with salt, pepper, and the Milanese spice.

3. Put the bread slices in a shallow dish and add enough milk to moisten but not soak them. Squeeze the milk from the bread, discard it, and add the torn bread and the eggs to the bowl, mixing and amalgamating thoroughly. If the mix is too wet, add a bit of dry, crustless bread. If too dry, add a bit of milk. It's good, but not necessary, to make this stuffing a few hours ahead of time and allow it to marinate in the refrigerator.

4. To make the rolls, place a slice of veal on a firm surface in front of you and spread the mixture on it, leaving a ¼-inch border around the edges for rolling. Roll up the veal, tucking in the sides. Secure the roll with two or three toothpicks. Set aside and repeat with the remaining 7 pieces of veal.

5. Heat the oil, butter, and garlic cloves over medium-high heat in a thick-bottomed braising pot that will hold the 8 rolls comfortably though snugly.

6. Dust the rolls with the seasoned flour and shake off the excess. Place them seam down in the oil. Adjust the heat to avoid burning and cook for about 5 minutes, turning them as necessary until evenly browned. Season with salt and pepper. Deglaze with Marsala and reduce the liquid so that it caramelizes on the rolls but there is a bit of liquid remaining in the pot.

7. Add 1½ cups of stock and reduce it by a third.

8. Add the rest of the stock, the carrots, and the white wine, mix, cover, and braise in a 375°F oven for 15 or 20 minutes until tender. If the stock reduces too fast, add a little more. Remove the rolls and carrots to a warm plate and reserve in a 175°F oven.

9. Reduce the sauce if necessary to the consistency of a velouté. If you're afraid of losing the volume, strain the sauce through cheesecloth and then bring it to a boil with a bit of arrowroot dissolved in water. This will quickly give you the desired thickness.

10. Plate 2 rolls and pieces of carrots on each warm plate with a bit of sauce under and over and sprinkle with the parsley garnish. Serve immediately.

YIELD: *4 servings*

AGNELLO • LAMB

The history of sheep (and goats) seems as old as that of man himself, since the ancients were always pictured as sheep or goat herders. I say seems because actually their recorded history goes back only to 8000 or 9000 B.C.

Lamb, of course, has played a significant role throughout the ages, serving both as an essential food and a sacrificial offering. Eventually it became an enduring metaphor for the guiltless, meek, oppressed peoples of the world; and to this day is the symbol of innocence.

The implication of course of that innocence for cooks is that the younger the animal the better. As with baby milk fed veal, baby lamb is prized in most of the Western world—France, Italy, Germany; only in England and the Moslem countries of the Middle East is the more mature, and much more flavorful, mutton preferred. America doesn't seem to think too much of either. Lamb sales are behind those of beef, pork and chicken by at least 50 percent according to recent buying surveys, and mutton is rarely sold. The reason could well be that the American public has not had the benefit of eating the best lamb. As with beef and veal, the highest quality lamb is either a baby suckling animal (four to six weeks old) or one that has been allowed to mature to one and

one half to two years or more. The American grading system merely stamps animals under one year as lamb and over one year as mutton, and it is precisely this middle ground age of the animal that is the least flavorful.

Baby lamb—*abbacchio* in Roman dialect—is a much prized meat here in Italy that is generally available; even the lamb that is beyond the suckling stage and no longer *abbacchio* is better than its American cousins because the animal is smaller and slaughtered between three and six months and not six and nine months as is the case in America. One way to tell baby lamb is by the weight of a leg. The real thing is never more than six to eight pounds and usually three to five pounds.

Mutton is called *montone* here and comes from animals that are close to two years old and are rich with fat. Mutton from animals over a year and a half is best hung in a dry air cooler for one to two weeks.

There are specialty butchers in most of the major cities that are able to provide baby lamb or mutton, but if you wish to avoid that premium price your best bet is to seek out the nearest farm where you can specify your needs and get the right lamb or mutton.

As in the case of beef and veal, certain cooking methods are best suited to certain cuts; below are the various American cuts of lamb and the suggested methods of preparation.

NECK (*braise, broil, panfry patties*)

Neck slices	patties
Ground meat for	

SHOULDER (*roast, broil, panfry, braise, patties*)

Rolled shoulder	Shoulder blade chops
Boneless shoulder	Arm chops
chops or roast	Stew meat
Cushion shoulder	Square cut shoulder

BREAST (*roast, broil, panfry, bake, braise*)

Breast	Riblets
Rolled breast	Stew meat
Stuffed breast	Ground lamb

SHANK (*roast, bake, braise*)

Lamb shanks	Ground meat

RACK (*roast, broil*)

Lamb rib roast	Crown roast
Hotel rack roast	Frenched rib chops
Rack of lamb	Kebabs
Rib chops	

LOIN (*roast, broil, panfry, braise*)

Loin roast	English chops (double
Saddle of loin	chops)
Laced saddle of lamb	Rolled loin roast
Loin chops	

SIRLOIN (*broil, pan fry*)

Lamb steaks	Boneless loin roast
Double loin chops	Double loin roast

LEG (*roast, braise, stew*)

American leg	Lamb butt
(haunch)	Butterflied leg
French leg (full with	Kebabs
shank)	Stew meat
Boneless sirloin roast	Ground meat

Legs and Racks of Lamb

I can't think of lamb without conjuring up images of a well crusted leg, the meat still pink and the juices running; or a rack with the chops joined to give you crunchy crisped bones to gnaw on after the delicate meat is finished. The key for both these presentations, in my opinion, is to have the meat pink and juicy—medium rare, if you will. And of course the outside crust seems absolutely essential. The question of marination has more latitude, although I must admit that the Italian use of lemon, extra virgin olive oil, garlic, wine, and fresh rosemary is hard to beat. Should you marinate a rack as well as a leg? Why not!

Casciotto di Agnello al Rosmarino

LEG OF LAMB WITH ROSEMARY

One 4- to 6-pound leg of lamb, bone in, shank removed
1 cup extra virgin olive oil
4 cloves garlic, slivered
2 tablespoons thinly sliced prosciutto
2 tablespoons thinly sliced pancetta
1 tablespoon fresh lemon juice
1 cup best available aromatic white wine
2 bay leaves
1 medium-size onion, roughly chopped
3 or 4 sprigs fresh rosemary
Salt and pepper to taste

1. Place the leg of lamb in a large bowl with the rest of the ingredients and set in a cool place for 3 to 4 hours. If you need to refrigerate, because of hot weather, marinate for 4 to 6 hours.
2. After marinating, remove the lamb from the bowl and reserve the marinade. Make incisions with the point of a sharp knife all over the meat. Insert the garlic slivers, prosciutto, pancetta, and rosemary sprigs into the incisions and rub oil and wine all over the meat. Season with salt and pepper.
3. Place the leg of lamb on a rack in a roasting pan and roast in a 450°F oven for 15 to 20 minutes or until browned.
4. Turn the heat down to 275° to 300°F and roast slowly for approximately 1 hour, or till the juices run pink. (Lamb generally roasts at 20 minutes per pound.) Baste every 5 or 10 minutes while roasting with the liquid from the marinade.
5. Allow the lamb to rest for 3 to 5 minutes in a warm spot before carving.
6. You can deglaze the roasting pan with a bit of white wine and serve the lamb au jus; or, if you have lamb, veal, or beef stock, deglaze the pan juices into the stock and make a more formal sauce. In either event serve directly on warm plates.

NOTE: I should point out that baby or spring lamb (*abbacchio* in Roman dialect) is the absolute best lamb to roast. If you can find a nursing calf by all means substitute it. Just takes less time to cook for *abbacchio alla romana* and you might need two.

YIELD: *4 to 6 servings*

Carré d'Agnello

RACK OF LAMB

A rack of lamb comes from the front rib section and should have the outside fat, top of the rib and chine bone removed. If you don't know how to do this, it's a simple matter for your butcher and while he's at it tell him to French the bones as well. This removes more of the top fat, exposing the bones like little handles. These are fine as is, but if you want to get fancy you can buy different colored paper panties or frills to put on each bone for a final presentation. Don't do as one student did, calling me to say "They all burnt up!" because he put them in the oven with the roast. They are merely a decorative touch that is applied after roasting or broiling.

Actually, the best way to prepare a rack is to broil it. The broiler will better give you that most desirable outside crustiness while allowing the meat to remain pink and moist inside.

A normal quarter rack is enough for two people, yielding at least four chops. It will weigh about two to two and a half pounds with the bones in and comes from a normal prime lamb, which is about nine months old. If you were to use baby spring lamb you'd need a whole rack for two portions.

One 2- to 2½-pound rack of lamb (prime ¼ rack)

2 tablespoons extra virgin olive oil

2 cloves garlic, bled (scored)

1 teaspoon fresh lemon juice

2 tablespoons best available aromatic white wine

2 tablespoons finely chopped fresh parsley
Salt and pepper to taste

1. Set the rack of lamb in a bowl in a marinade made with all the other ingredients, preserving 1 tablespoon of parsley for garnish. Allow to marinate for 1 to 2 hours.

2. Rub the marinade all over the rack and season with salt and pepper. Place on a "sizzler" (a thick steel plate used for broiling) or a heavy pan. Broil at high heat for 5 to 10 minutes or until done, basting frequently with the marinade and turning on all sides.

3. Place paper panties (frills, ruffs) on each exposed bone, if you desire, and serve directly, garnished with the remaining parsley.

Yield: *2 servings*

Agnello in Fricassea con Carciofi

FRICASSEE OF LAMB WITH ARTICHOKES

While we're talking about baby spring lamb, here is a recipe from Liguria that my Uncle Frank, the baker, used to make for Easter; and always with *abbacchio,* baby spring lamb.

One 2½- to 3-pound leg of baby milk-fed lamb (or meat from other parts)

2 cups Olive Marinade (optional—recipe follows)

2 tablespoons extra virgin olive oil

2 cloves garlic, bled (scored)

4 to 6 medium artichokes, cleaned, choked, parboiled, and cut into 2-inch pieces

1 tablespoon diced garlic

Pinch each dried thyme, basil, and chervil

1 tablespoon finely chopped fresh parsley

Salt and pepper to taste

1 cup best available aromatic white wine

1 cup Brodo di Pollo or Fondo Bianco (see pages 89 or 86)

2 extra large eggs, well beaten

Juice of 1 lemon

1. Bone the meat from the leg or other parts that you're using into approximately 2-inch pieces or ask the butcher to do it for you. Trim any fat and gristle.

2. Marinate for 2 to 3 hours if you have the time and inclination, or go directly to sautéing.

3. Heat the oil and garlic cloves over medium-high heat and add the meat cubes, being careful not to crowd them in the sauté pan. Brown them for 2 to 3 minutes and then add the artichokes and brown them slightly with the lamb. Add the diced garlic. Season with thyme, basil, chervil, 1½ tablespoons of chopped parsley, salt, and pepper. Stir.

4. Deglaze with white wine and allow to reduce till practically evaporated, constantly turning the meat and artichokes over to coat them.

5. Add the stock and continue cooking, again allowing it to reduce by half. Stir a little of the hot sauce into the beaten eggs, then add them along with the lemon juice to the sauce. Remove from the stove and mix well. Season with salt and pepper, garnish with the remaining chopped parsley, and serve directly on warm plates.

YIELD: *4 servings*

Olive Marinade

4 cups mixed olives

2 cups red wine vinegar (homemade preferred)

2 heads garlic, peeled and bled (scored)

2 teaspoons each dried thyme, basil, and chervil, mixed together

2 to 4 whole dried red peppers, cracked

2 sprigs fresh rosemary

4 large bay leaves, torn

2 cups extra virgin olive oil

Rind and juice of 1 lemon

Salt, in generous quantity

Freshly ground black pepper to taste

Place all the ingredients in a large crock and mix well. Use immediately, or you can store, covered, in a cool, dark place for up to 6 months.

Agnello con Finocchietto

LAMB WITH FENNEL

The use of sundried tomatoes and fennel in this recipe, also known as *agnello da Sardegna* or lamb from Sardinia, is a specialty of the town of Nuoro, the home of *malloreddus,* those wonderful little *gnocchetti* made with saffron.

Although I see sundried tomatoes being sold throughout Italy—or at least on display in the stores—I rarely find a recipe in Italian cookbooks that calls for them, nor do any of my Italian friends and chef acquaintances ever seem to use them. Most Italians dry the tomatoes themselves. Be that as it may, their smoky flavor works well here with the fennel to make a most unusual tasting lamb dish.

1 to 1½ pounds 2-inch lamb cubes (preferably from leg)

2 cups Olive Marinade (optional) (see page 253)

2 tablespoons extra virgin olive oil

2 cloves garlic, bled (scored)

1 medium-size fresh fennel bulb with a few leaves, sliced and parboiled

½ medium-size onion, roughly chopped

1 cup chopped sundried tomatoes

1 tablespoon finely chopped fresh parsley

Salt and pepper to taste

1 cup best available aromatic white wine

1 cup Brodo di Pollo or Fondo Bianco (see page 86 or 89)

1. Either marinate the lamb in the olive marinade for 2 to 3 hours or proceed directly.

2. Heat the oil and garlic cloves in a heavy-bottomed sauté pan over high heat and sauté the lamb browning it on the outside but leaving it rare. Do not crowd the pan; saute the lamb in batches, if necessary. If need be, remove the garlic cloves while you're doing this so they don't burn.

3. Add the precooked fennel slices, the onion, sundried tomatoes, and ½ tablespoon of chopped parsley and stir. Cook briefly over medium-high heat. Season with salt and pepper and return the garlic cloves to the pan.

4. Deglaze with the white wine, evaporating it by half.

5. Remove the meat and set aside. Add the stock and reduce by half. Return the meat to the pan, cover, and braise in a preheated 350°F oven for approximately 40 minutes, or until done. Plate on warm plates and garnish with the remaining chopped parsley.

NOTE: The question of removing the meat or not during the second reduction is always optional. The meat is going to be cooked further anyway and therefore there is no "rare" to be preserved. However, it depends on how the sauté has gone and what the meat looks like at the point of this second reduction. In other words, it is an intuitive judgment that determines whether you want to subject the lamb cubes to the high boil necessary for the reduction. Another way around the problem is to cook the dish on low heat, uncovered, for a longer period, thus allowing a natural slow reduction.

YIELD: *4 portions*

Stufatino d'Agnello alla Romana

ROMAN LAMB STEW

Here's another lovely lamb stew and once again the recipe calls for baby milk-fed lamb. It certainly is the best meat for these dishes, but if you are unable to get that quality lamb, do not despair, just cook whatever lamb you do get longer. If you like, you can marinate the lamb in 2 cups Olive Marinade (see page 253) for 2 or 3 hours before you start.

      2 *tablespoons extra virgin olive oil*

4 to 6 *cloves garlic, bled (scored)*

      1 *to 1½ pounds cleaned 2-inch lamb cubes (from leg or other)*

        Salt and freshly ground black pepper to taste

   ⅛ *teaspoon dried thyme*

   ⅛ *teaspoon dried rosemary*

      1 *cup Marsala, preferably sweet Florio*

      1 *cup Brodo di Pollo (see page 89)*

      1 *cup Fondo Bruno (see page 85)*

      1 *cup Salsa di Pomodoro (see page 103)*

      2 *cups fresh or frozen peas*

      1 *tablespoon diced garlic*

      1 *teaspoon grated lemon rind*

      2 *cups dry fresh bread crumbs*

      1 *tablespoon chopped fresh parsley*

1. Heat the oil and garlic cloves in a large saucepan over high heat, then sauté the lamb, just browning it but leaving it rare. Season with salt, pepper, thyme, and rosemary, and deglaze the pan with the Marsala, allowing it to evaporate and caramelize the meat.

2. Add the chicken and beef stocks and *salsa di pomodoro,* then remove the meat, and reduce the liquid by half on high heat.

3. Return the meat to the pan and add the peas, diced garlic, and lemon rind. Cook for 2 or 3 minutes over medium-high heat.

4. Pour into a casserole dish, top all with the bread crumbs, and place, uncovered, in a preheated 375°F oven for about 20 minutes.

5. Spoon the lamb and sauce out on warm plates, giving each person some of the crusty bread crumb topping. Garnish with the chopped parsley.

YIELD: *4 servings*

Polpettone di Agnello e Salsicce

LAMB AND SAUSAGE MEATLOAF

Since I'm always afraid there won't be enough when I serve lamb, I usually buy a bit too much. It's a pleasant failing since I'm very fond of lamb hash and more particularly this lamb and sausage meatloaf. It's a wonderful use of leftover lamb and will even please those who turn up their noses at the very thought of meatloaf of any kind. The combination of lamb and sausage provides an unusual enough taste sensation to make them forget they're eating meatloaf. Personally, I think it's smashing and consider it among my most favorite meat dishes.

2 sweet Italian sausages (approximately ½ pound)
2 tablespoons extra virgin olive oil
2 garlic cloves, bled (scored)
½ cup best available dry red wine
Salt and freshly ground black pepper to taste
1 tablespoon chopped fresh parsley
Sprig fresh rosemary
4 slices white bread
1 cup milk
2 ounces roughly chopped mushrooms (2 to 3 tablespoons)
1 tablespoon unsalted butter
2 tablespoons Marsala
2 ounces roughly chopped zucchini (2 to 3 tablespoons)
Pinch of dried thyme
Pinch of dried basil
Pinch of dried chervil
4 to 6 ounces lamb, diced, per serving (2 pounds total)
2 extra large eggs
2 tablespoons freshly grated parmigiano
1 tablespoon freshly grated pecorino Romano
2 cups Salsa di Pomodoro (see page 103)

1. Marinate the sausages in 1 tablespoon of the oil, garlic, wine, salt, pepper, parsley, and rosemary for at least 2 hours.
2. Soak the bread slices in the milk for at least 5 minutes.

3. In a small saucepan over medium-high heat, sauté the mushrooms in ½ tablespoon of the butter and ½ tablespoon of the oil. Season with salt and pepper and deglaze with the Marsala.
4. In another small saucepan over medium-high heat, sauté the zucchini in ½ tablespoon of the oil and the remaining butter until tender. Season with the thyme, basil, chervil, salt, and pepper.
5. Now pass the lamb and sausage through a meat grinder, mixing well together. Add the wine from the marinade to the mix.
6. Remove the bread slices from the milk and squeeze them together with the meat with your hands, mixing and totally amalgamating everything. Season with salt and pepper, and add the mushrooms and zucchini with their juices, as well as the eggs, and mix thoroughly again. Add the cheeses and mix again.
7. Shape the mixture into a loaf. Coat the bottom of a baking pan with half the *salsa di pomodoro* and lay the meat in the pan. Pour the remaining *salsa di pomodoro* over the top and bake in a preheated 375°F oven for approximately 1 hour.
8. Allow to rest for 3 or 4 minutes before slicing onto warm plates to serve.

YIELD: *4 to 6 servings*

MAIALE • PORK

I love the definition of pork in the *New Larousse Gastronomique*:

Pork.porc—Domestic pachyderm which is not usually referred to by this name until after slaughter. The male is called pig or stag and the young animal is called piglet, porker or sucking pig.

Seems strange that an animal with such noble sounding names, so many derogatory associations. Pork has had such an infamous history over the last 2,000 years, what with its propensity toward trichinosis and the religious prohibitions surrounding it, that it's a wonder we eat it at all. But eat it we do; and have over the years eaten "every part of the pig except the oink."

Of course the fact that it is so easily domesticated, almost self-sufficient, and highly regenerative has had a great deal to do with its popularity. As they say down on the farm, "All you need is a strong boar, a good sow, and a pail for the slops, and you'll have yourself a pig farm with a hundred head in jig time."

Many years ago pork's negative reputation was probably well earned, but fortunately the United States Wholesome Meat Act of 1951 has changed all that.

Standard rules and regulations for the growing, processing, and distributing of meat in America have effectively eliminated the danger of spoilage and disease in all meats, including pork. In fact, by law government inspectors are provided with an office at meat packing plants and slaughterhouses to ensure continual inspection of the sanitary and temperature conditions of the premises. In addition to this, all animals raised for consumption are inoculated against a full spectrum of diseases, including trichinosis, thus eliminating totally the problem that existed with pork.

With the advent of meat thermometers, we are able to enjoy normally cooked, and even medium-rare, pork. Pork products have to be cooked only until the internal temperature reaches 138°F in order to destroy the properly feared parasitic bacteria *trichinae*; not to 152°F, which has been the common practice for so many years.

How many times have we heard:

"Well, I'll eat pork once in a while . . . but only if it's done well . . . and I mean *well done!*"

That kind of caution is no longer necessary. Actually, cooking pork until it is well done is the worst way to treat this kind of meat. Although pork has a great deal of fat, those parts are made into bacon, sausage, and salami, while the leaner parts such as a loin of pork have little or no mar-

belization and therefore get tough from prolonged cooking.

So the good news is that pork can now safely be cooked to juicy, tender succulence without fear, thus opening up a multitude of preparations for this sweet and delicious meat.

For example, have you ever had a baby roast sucking pig, spit roasted over hot embers, and served with sauerkraut that caught the drippings as it slowly cooked underneath the meat?

Or, wild boar braised in the Renaissance manner in a sauce composed of cinnamon and chocolate, among other things? Or, grilled pork chops that are then braised in white wine with cabbage, raisins, pine nuts, tomatoes, vinegar, and sugar to make a very special *costolette di maiale con cavolo agrodolce*?

Large pigs are used mainly to make hams, bacon, sausage, and salami. But there is a smaller, leaner pig being raised here in Umbria that is highly preferable for roasting. This is the type of pork roast that is so popular here in Todi and Perugia, sold at little roadside stands with the simple black and white sign *Porchetta*. A slice of this with its ¼-inch-thick brown outer crust on a good coarse country bread with extra salt and pepper makes as tasty a sandwich as can be found in Italy.

There is also no question that the Italians love *salumi* and sausages. You'll find prosciutto, salami, and sausages on practically every restaurant menu in Italy . . . North or South. But it's from the North Central towns of Parma, Modena, and Bologna that prosciutto, mortadella, cotechino, and zampone have been brought to such perfection that they are not only shipped all over Italy, but now worldwide as well. The well deserved fame of these Italian products has been occasioned by local insistence on the highest quality ingredients and an almost religious respect for the ancient, well-proven methods of aging, curing, and smoking.

In central Umbria and particularly Norcia and its surrounding areas, *salume* of all kinds is so popular as to be rivaled only by truffles. In fact, the pork products of Norcia are so famous that throughout Italy a very fine butcher is called a *norcino* instead of a *macellaio*.

Since every part of the pig is usable, including the bristles that go into brushes and upholstery, the pig is considered the most economical animal we have. Its popularity is also due to the fact that it's the easiest meat to preserve. It is delicious smoked, salted, or air dry cured. Prior to refrigeration, this was a boon to the meat eaters of the world and salt pork fed many an army in ancient times.

As with all types of meats, certain cuts are best suited to certain methods of preparation. Here is a list of cuts with the suggested cooking techniques.

JOWL *(broil, panfry, braise)*

Bacon square

PICNIC
(SHOULDER) *roast, broil, panfry, braise, bake)*

Fresh picnic shoulder	Cushion picnic
Smoked picnic	shoulder
shoulder	Shoulder hocks
Rolled fresh picnic	Arm steak
shoulder	Ground pork

TOP SHANK AND PIGS' FEET *(boil and/or pickle)*

BOSTON BUTT
roast, bake, broil, panfry, braise, boil)

Butt steak	Lard
Smoke daisy	Ground pork (sausage
Rolled Boston butt	meat)
Fatback	

SIDE *(sauté, bard, lard, broil, roast, braise)*

Bacon belly	Spareribs
Salt pork	

LOIN *(roast, broil, panfry, braise)*

Loin roast center	Tenderloin
Crown roast	Loin chops
Sirloin roast	Rib chops
Blade loin roast	Country style ribs
Boneless loin roast	Canadian bacon

HAM *(roast, sauté, panfry)*

Ham shank half	Fresh ham roast
Ham butt half	Rolled fresh ham
Center slice steak	roast
Butt slice steak	

Buying Tips

The U.S. government has such confidence in the uniformity of the quality of pork that it doesn't bother to grade it as it does with beef, veal, and lamb. All commercially sold pork is inspected for conditions of health and sanitation and the government does provide a yield grading system of from 1 to 4.

It is, therefore, important to know what to look for when buying pork. The flesh should be pale pink and the fat creamy white and firm. The meat should look and smell healthy. The skin will be smooth, free of wrinkles, and firm and tight to the touch. The bones should have some red blood in them. Don't buy any pork that is discolored or even slightly "off-smelling."

Once again, the "delicacy" comes from baby sucking pigs that weigh from 3 to 5 pounds and are still nursing. At fourteen to eighteen weeks and about 110 to 120 pounds they're called "porkers." After a year they are referred to as hogs. Next to baby sucking pigs, young hogs at 60 to 75 pounds and six months to a year are the best, providing much sweeter meat than larger animals. Unlike beef, pork is better at the baby stage or the middle ground from six months to a year. It is also important to note that pork does not improve by aging and should therefore be eaten fresh. By that I mean of course after the rigor mortis (stiffening of the muscles) has had a chance to relax and the meat becomes softer. With pork this takes one to two days only and then you should be counting each day against its freshness.

Arista di Maiale

ROAST PORK

The derivation of the term *arista* is attributed to some Greek ambassadors who were attending a Florentine banquet in the 1400s. When the pork roast was served one of them exclaimed *"Arista,"* which in Greek means "the best"—and so it has been called ever since.

It's traditionally done with a boned pork loin but I prefer leaving the bone in and roasting it all in one piece. The marinade is the standard olive oil, garlic, and rosemary, and should also be used to baste the roast. Obviously this same recipe

could be used for other cuts such as leg (ham), hock, and shoulder, but the loin is without doubt the best for this treatment.

> One 3- to 4-pound loin of pork, bone in
> 2 tablespoons extra virgin olive oil
> 4 garlic cloves, bled, (scored)
> 2 to 3 fresh sprigs rosemary
> 1 bay leaf
> 1 cup aromatic white wine
> Salt and pepper to taste

1. Marinate the pork loin in the oil, garlic, rosemary, bay leaf, white wine, salt, and pepper for 2 to 3 hours.
2. Place the loin on a rack in a roasting pan, season with more salt and pepper, and baste it with the marinade. Roast in a 450° oven for 15 to 20 minutes, until browned. Turn the heat down to 300°F and roast for another 45 minutes to 1 hour till it's medium rare: the meat is pink and the juices run freely. (The internal temperature should be 135°F on the meat thermometer.) Baste with the marinade frequently during roasting. Serve directly on warm plates.

NOTE: Cooking times are hard to reduce to charts by weight since they depend equally on thickness as they do on weight. And the fat layer will affect the time as do particularly uninsulated, or conversely, insulated ovens. For example, a half loin of pork of the same thickness as a whole loin will take just as long to cook in spite of the fact that it's only half the weight. Best to look, feel, see, touch, and smell, and use a meat thermometer.

It works very well to put sauerkraut, or potatoes, or both in the pan under the rack so that they are cooked in the pork juices.

YIELD: *6 to 8 servings*

Arista di Maiale
A'Latte ed Aglio

ROAST PORK WITH MILK AND GARLIC

The surprising thing about this pork roast is that the 40 garlic cloves all melt into the milk sauce and become very sweet—a most unusual treat and one of the surprise Italian presentations of pork loin. I first encountered this recipe at a friend's house here in Umbria some five years ago. Since then I also had this dish in a restaurant outside of Venice, except they weren't brave enough to use the 40 cloves of garlic. Nor was another restaurant in Reggio Emilia that limited the garlic to three cloves. In any event I suggest you try it with the garlic cloves. Everyone I know who's had it this way loves it.

> One 2- to 2½-pounds boneless loin of pork, tied securely
> ¼ cup extra virgin olive oil
> 40 cloves garlic
> Salt and pepper to taste
> 2 sprigs fresh rosemary
> 3 to 4 tablespoons best available Cognac or brandy
> 8 cups (approximately) milk

1. Sauté the loin in oil over medium-high heat until well crusted on all sides. Use the same, tight-fitting casserole or pot you'll braise it in. Set the loin aside.
2. In the remaining oil, brown the garlic cloves. Replace the loin, season it heavily with salt and pepper, add the rosemary sprigs, then add and warm the Cognac and ignite it. Let the Cognac flambé the meat till the alcohol burns out.

3. Add enough milk to cover the loin and braise slowly, partially covered, in a 375°F oven for about 1 to 1½ hours, or until an internal temperature of 135° to 140°F is reached. Remove the loin and keep warm. Remove the rosemary.
4. Pass the pan juices and garlic through a food mill or puree in a food processor. You should have about 2 cups. If you need more volume add milk. If necessary, reduce the sauce over medium heat to thicken it. Carve the meat and serve with the sauce.

YIELD: *8 to 10 servings*

Costolette di Maiale con
Cavolo in Agrodolce

SWEET AND SOUR PORK CHOPS WITH CABBAGE

Sweet and sour, cabbage and raisins, sugar and vinegar, tomatoes and white wine, sage and thyme, basil and chervil spiced with crushed red pepper: this is a treatment that can be used for all kinds of meat, fish, poultry, game, and vegetables. In Italian they call it *agrodolce* and it is a trademark of Sicilian cooking. I've been making this dish for thirty-five years and can't remember where it came from, except that it must have been a family recipe. Various recipes I've seen increase the sugar and others rub the herbs into the pork, all of which work well, I suppose, but I've been so satisfied with this presentation that I'm hardly tempted to change it by anything I've read.

2 cloves garlic, bled (scored)

2 tablespoons extra virgin olive oil

Two 8- to 10-ounce center-cut pork chops

¼ (approximately) medium-size head cabbage, thickly shredded

½ cup raisins

¼ cup pine nuts

Salt and freshly ground black pepper to taste

Crushed red pepper to taste

Pinch of ground sage

Pinch each dried thyme, basil, and chervil, mixed together

½ cup aromatic white wine

½ cup white wine vinegar

1 cup Marinara (see page 100)

1 tablespoon finely chopped fresh parsley

1. Sauté the garlic in oil over medium-low heat till browned. Set aside. Add the chops, raise the heat, and sear them on both sides. Remove and set aside.

2. Add the cabbage and sauté, tossing, until it begins to wilt. Add raisins and pine nuts, stir, and then add seasonings.

3. Add the wine and stir to deglaze and combine. Simmer for 2 to 3 minutes to soften the cabbage and plump the raisins.

4. Stir in the vinegar and marinara sauce. Return the chops and garlic to the pan, burying them in the cabbage.

5. Gently braise, covered, in a 350°F oven for about 20 minutes until the chops are done and tender. Garnish with parsley and serve.

YIELD: *2 servings*

Costolette di Maiale con Menta e Arance

PORK CHOPS WITH MINT AND ORANGES

I had this dish in Sicily many years ago and remember well the pleasant combination of mint and oranges in a light tomato sauce flavored with lemon and orange juice. The chef and I got to talking and he said that he wasn't sure this was a traditional Sicilian dish but he and his family had been making it for a number of years. The use of lemon in the tomato sauce reminds me of the recipe for *Sfinciuni* (see page 302) that is an old traditional Sicilian pizza.

1 tablespoon extra virgin olive oil

2 cloves garlic, bled (scored)

Two 6- to 8-ounce center-cut pork chops (bone in preferred)

1 medium-size white onion, finely sliced

Pinch of ground sage

1 tablespoon finely chopped fresh parsley

Salt and pepper to taste

Crushed red pepper to taste

½ cup dry, aromatic white wine

1 cup Marinara (see page 100)

4 to 6 orange slices

1 teaspoon fresh orange juice

1 teaspoon fresh lemon juice

½ teaspoon grated lemon rind

1. Heat the oil and garlic in a sauté pan over medium-high heat and add the pork chops, browning them on both sides. If need be, remove the garlic and put it back later to keep it from burning. Add the onions and continue the sauté. Sprinkle with sage, ½ tablespoon of parsley, salt, pepper, and crushed red pepper. Deglaze with the white wine and reduce it, turning the chops over so that the liquid permeates the meat.

2. Add the marinara sauce, orange slices, orange juice, lemon juice, and lemon rind. Stir, cover the pot, and cook on a very low heat for 15 to 20 minutes. Remove the cover and cook for another 10 minutes on medium heat.

3. Serve directly on warm plates, spooning the sauce on top and garnishing with the remaining chopped parsley.

NOTE: Could you have braised it in the oven? Of course! I'm merely presenting alternative methods.

YIELD: *2 servings*

Salsicce con Uva

SAUSAGES WITH GRAPES

Sausages are popular the world over and Italy is no exception. While perhaps they don't eat as many as their German neighbors, the Italians are prolific sausage makers and consumers. I first saw this dish in a restaurant in Terni (here in Umbria) four or five years ago and haven't stopped using it since. It's part of our regular Friday night pizza parties during course weeks and has never failed to win high praise—if oohs and aahs can be counted as praise.

8 *pork sausages, best sweet or hot Italian available (about 2 pounds)*

2 *tablespoons extra virgin olive oil*

4 *cloves garlic, cut into pieces*

1 *cup dry aromatic white wine*

2 *sprigs fresh rosemary*

  Salt and pepper to taste

  Crushed red pepper to taste

  White grapes, whole, stemmed, unseeded

1. Put all the ingredients in a large casserole except half the grapes. Marinate in a cool place for 6 to 8 hours.

2. Bake, uncovered, in a 400° to 500°F oven for 15 to 20 minutes, basting and turning occasionally. The sausages should be well browned.

3. Add the remaining grapes and cook for another 5 to 10 minutes. Serve directly on warm plates, spooning the juices on top of each serving.

YIELD: *4 servings*

FRATTAGLIE • VARIETY MEATS

Lambs' tongues, peacocks' brains, pork jowels, veal testicles, pigs' feet, oxtails, calves' heads, chicken hearts and livers, beef kidneys, cows' udders, thymus glands of veal (sweetbreads), pigs' lungs, sheeps' intestines, and the double stomachs of a cow (tripe) are some of the better known variety meats, otherwise known as utility meats or "offal," that were used extensively by the Romans and are still popular today.

For some of us it takes a bit of honest hypocrisy to consider these delicious morsels for what they really are. At a very tender age (thirteen or fourteen) I was a very big fan of sweetbreads. At that point I had never seen them before they were cooked and had no idea of where they came from. I only knew from the tone of my mother's voice that when Grandpa Rheil, her German butcher father, brought home sweetbreads we were in for a special treat. My first experience with them was deep fried in a beer batter served with a lemon wedge, salt, and pepper for garniture. And were they ever delicious. I remember crying out, "They're just like fried oysters only different."

They all fell about laughing, which became even more intense when my grandmother mock seriously intoned, "Different part of the animal, dear boy. Different part."

Of course I didn't know about mountain oysters or prairie oysters—beef and veal testicles. As a result the double entendre went right over my head.

When I finally saw them uncooked, in a gelatinous state and looking like something you'd find in a jar in the laboratory of a mad scientist, I thought, "Okay, so that's what they look like, but my God they are delicious."

And that was the end of that and the beginning of my acceptance of all the parts of the animal as being equally edible as a rib or a leg, although to this day I'll be damned if I can entertain the thought of nibbling on a goat's eyeball as the Italians are wont to do.

The Italians are also very fond of calves' brains, sweetbreads, tripe, and braided sheeps' intestines, which they call *treccia di pecora*. The Romans, ancient and present, were and are very fond of oxtail and make a delicious *coda di bue* as well as a dish with cows' udders, or a special part of the intestine that contains a creamy substance in it which is long stewed with tomatoes to make a sauce for big macaroni, usually *rigatoni*. It's called *pagliata* and is surprisingly sweet and delicious.

I suppose the most internationally famous Italian use of *interiore* (innards) is calves' liver in the Venetian style called *fegato alla Veneziana*. This is a quick sauté of baby calves' liver with onions.

And what *fritto misto* would be complete without *cervelle* (brains), *animelle* (sweetbreads), *fegato* (liver) and *rognoni* (kidneys)? Whether stewed, braised, sautéed, or fried, the Italians make good use of all the parts of all the animals.

If you're one of those whose hypocrisy gets the better of you and you're unable to tolerate the thought of calves' brains, for example, in spite of the fact that you're fond of prime steak, blood rare, then I suggest you seriously consider sautéing calves' brains in browned butter with capers and lemon juice, fresh milled pepper, and a sprinkling of fine chopped parsley. The slightly crisped outer skin that comes from the sauté marries with the brown butter, which the lemon and capers then make tart. This leaves the wonderfully soft brains inside the outer crust as the perfect contrast to the rest of the sauté. I'm not quite sure how any serious gourmet could not find this dish exquisite unless those deep-seated hypocritical energies were still so dominant as to preclude any kind of objectivity.

In other words, if you like and eat meat generally, these other parts are more tender and succulent than the main haunches and are an important part of Italian, French and international cooking.

And America? Well, most Americans don't like beets or calves' liver, either.

Unfortunately, I don't have time or space to treat all the variety meats in detail. But what recipes I will now provide are mostly interchangeable among the variety meats and when you understand the basic principles involved in sautéing, broiling, braising, and boiling, you shouldn't have any trouble handling them all.

Trippa alla Genovese

TRIPE IN THE GENOVESE STYLE

I think it's safe to say tripe is not the most favored meat in the world. Many people won't even consider eating it and when I put it on the menu at One Grandview ('73) it was a hard sell all the way except for a few diehard lovers who couldn't have been happier.

When you taste tripe, however, without your hypocritical prejudices intervening, if such a thing is possible, it is certainly sweet and delicious and tastes like a soft cross between chicken and pork. It's surprisingly good simply charcoal grilled (after boiling to tenderize) with a *diavolo* sauce made with mustard. For this type of un-stewed presentation you want the tripe from the second stomach of a cow, known as the honey-comb. It is much more tender and, after being washed, cleaned of fat, and soaked in acidulated water for several hours, and then lightly boiled with aromatics for 40 minutes or so till tender, it is ready for broiling or braising.

The recipe here presumes the prepreparation just outlined and does assume you'll have honey-comb tripe. If only plain tripe from the first stomach is available (the rumen), increase the cooking times of both the parboiling and the braise by 30 minutes each.

> 2 to 2½ pounds honeycomb tripe
> 3 cups combind finely diced carrot, celery, and onion
> 1 bay leaf
> 5 to 6 juniper berries
> 6 whole black peppercorns
> 3 tablespoons extra virgin olive oil
> 4 cloves garlic, bled (scored)
> ¼ cup finely diced salt pork (about 2 ounces)
> 1 tablespoon chopped garlic
> 1 teaspoon dried thyme
> 1 tablespoon each dried basil, oregano, chervil, and rosemary
> Salt and pepper to taste
> 1 teaspoon crushed red pepper
> 1 cup Marsala, Florio Sweet, or best available
> ½ cup dry aromatic white wine
> 2 cups Fondo Bianco or Brodo di Pollo (see pages 89 and 86)
> 1 cup Marinara (see page 100)
> 2 cups freshly grated parmigiano
> 1 tablespoon finely chopped fresh parsley
> 4 to 8 sprigs fresh parsley

1. Soak, wash, clean, and parboil the tripe for 30 to 40 minutes with 2 cups of the combined carrot, celery, and onion, the bay leaf, juniper berries, and peppercorns. Drain, and pat dry, and cut the tripe into strips about ½ inch by 3 inches (or whatever size you'd like).

2. Heat the oil with the garlic cloves in an oven-proof casserole and sauté the tripe on medium-high heat. Add the salt pork and lightly brown it for 3 to 5 minutes. Add the remaining cup of combined vegetables. When the onions are trans-lucent and the carrot and celery are lightly sweated, add all of the herbs and spice and season with salt and pepper.

3. Deglaze with the Marsala, turning the tripe and vegetables, and reduce the Marsala to a syruplike consistency to coat or caramelize the tripe. Add the white wine and reduce by half. Add the stock, the marinara sauce, 1 cup of the parmigiano, and a bit of chopped parsley.

4. Cover and braise in a 400°F oven for 45 minutes

to 1 hour, or until soft and tender. Serve in warm bowls and garnish with the remaining parmigiano, chopped parsley, and parsley sprigs.

YIELD: *4 servings*

Animelle Brasate con Tartufi

BRAISED SWEETBREADS WITH TRUFFLES

Unlike tripe, which I'm only moderately fond of, sweetbreads remain a special culinary treat that I savor as much in the anticipation as in the eating. Like calves' brains, they're wonderful sautéed in browned butter with capers and lemon, or poached in a court bouillon with white wine and served with a delicate velouté of veal laced with truffles. This recipe is similar in treatment except that the sweetbreads are braised after being partially poached in the court bouillon and the sauce is a simple reduction of the braising liquid (veal stock) thickened by a puréed *battuto*. Beautiful to look at and exquisite to taste.

1½ *pounds sweetbreads, soaked, cleaned, and parboiled*

 Salt and pepper to taste

2 *cups flour, seasoned with salt and pepper*

1 *tablespoon extra virgin olive oil*

1 *tablespoon unsalted butter*

4 *cloves garlic, bled (scored)*

1 *cup Marsala, Florio Sweet preferred*

2 *cups combined finely diced carrot, celery, and onion*

1 *large truffle*

 Freshly grated nutmeg to taste

2 *cups Fondo Bianco, reduced by a third (see page 86)*

1 *cup aromatic white wine*

1. Rinse and clean the sweetbreads in several changes of water and finally soak them for 10 to 15 minutes in acidulated (lemon) water.
2. Remove the membrane and weight the sweetbreads down with plates for 5 to 10 minutes to shape them. Season with salt and pepper and dust with seasoned flour.
3. Heat the oil and butter with the garlic in a casserole over medium-high heat and lightly brown the sweetbreads. Deglaze with the Marsala and reduce it to a syrup, caramelizing the sweetbreads.
4. Remove the sweetbreads, set aside, and add the combined vegetables. Dice enough of the truffle to measure 1 teaspoon and add to the pan. Cook over medium heat till the vegetables are sweated (not browned; the onion just translucent).
5. Lay the sweetbreads back in the pan on top of the vegetables and season all with salt and pepper and a few gratings of fresh nutmeg. Add the reduced stock and the white wine and cover the pot. The sweetbreads should be just barely covered with liquid. Braise in 350°F oven for 20 to 30 minutes, or until almost done.
6. Remove the sweetbreads and set aside. Pass all the vegetables and liquid through a food mill. Return this thickened liquid to the stove, and reduce by a third and degrease it. Return the sweetbreads to the pan and coat thoroughly with the sauce.
7. Slice the remaining truffle and place the slices on top of the sweetbreads, spooning some of the sauce on each. Cover the casserole tightly to seal in the truffle aroma and braise all in a 425°F oven for 5 to 10 minutes till everything is nicely glazed. Serve directly on warm plates.

YIELDS: *4 servings*

Coda alla Vaccinara alla Romana

OXTAIL IN THE MANNER OF ROMAN BUTCHERS

The meat yards and butchers' shops of Rome go back to the early Roman Empire, when the butchers were called *vaccinari,* hence the origin of this recipe's name.

If you're going to eat oxtail, this Roman recipe is about as good a recipe as can be found. The celery and tomatoes work well in the braise to complement the darker-than-beef flavor of the oxtail. The Marsala and red wine compound these flavors into a pleasing whole that is subtly sweetened by the carrot, onion, and celery. The garlic—well, we all know what garlic does—it makes it unmistakably Italian.

The question of larding is optional. Some chefs swear it's essential while others refuse to consider the idea. I think the larding helps make a better dish and so I included it in this recipe.

- 2 to 2½ pounds oxtail, cut into pieces at the joint
- ½ pound lardoons (2- by ¼-inch strips pork fat)
- 2 cups Olive Marinade (see page 253)
- 2 tablespoons extra virgin olive oil
- 4 cloves garlic, bled (scored)
- 1 cup roughly chopped carrots
- 2 cups celery cut into 2-inch slices
- 1 cup Marsala, Florio Sweet preferred
  Salt and frshly ground pepper to taste
- 1 cup best available dry red wine
- 1 cup Consommé (see page 88)
- 2 tablespoons tomato paste
- 2 cups canned Italian plum tomatoes
- 1 bay leaf
- 1 tablespoon diced garlic

1. Marinate the oxtail and the lardoons in the marinade for 2 to 3 hours.
2. Remove the oxtail pieces and the lardoons. Pat dry and lard the oxtail by making incisions in the meat and inserting the marinated strips of pork fat into them.
3. Heat the oil and the garlic over medium-high heat in an ovenproof casserole and brown the oxtails on all sides. Remove and set aside. Sauté the carrot and celery till they are sweated but not browned.
4. Return the meat to the casserole and deglaze with the Marsala, reducing it till it becomes syrupy and caramelizes the meat. Season with salt and pepper and add the red wine and consommé. Reduce the liquid by a third and add the tomato paste, amalgamating well by stirring. Add the tomatoes and the bay leaf, torn in two, and the diced garlic.
5. Cover tightly and braise it in a 375°F oven for 30 to 40 minutes until the meat is tender. Serve directly from the pot, spooning the sauce on top of the tails. Naturally, warm plates are essential.

YIELD: *4 servings*

Fegato di Vitello alla Veneziana

CALVES' LIVER VENETIAN STYLE

The basics of this internationally famous dish are not agreed upon by chefs I have spoken with in Venice. There are those who insist that the liver be paper thin and others who prefer more substance to the slices. The paper thin group argue that the onions are sweated in oil first and then the liver added without browning, while the other group insists on sautéing the liver, slightly browning it, and then adding the separately sweated onions and cooking it all together for a few minutes. I personally prefer the second method and even dare break with tradition further by adding a bit of lemon juice, nutmeg, and white wine.

Whichever way you prefer it, everyone seems to be in agreement that you must search out liver from a baby milk-fed calf. For those of you who don't "like" liver, this recipe may be the antidote. It's possible you've been accustomed to strong beef liver, which is at best rather unpleasant. Try baby calves' liver with onions and see if that doesn't change your mind.

> 2 *cups finely sliced white onion (about 3 or 4 onions)*
> 2 *tablespoons extra virgin olive oil*
> 2 *tablespoons unsalted butter*
> 1 *cup aromatic white wine*
> *Juice of 1 lemon*
> *Freshly grated nutmeg to taste*
> *Salt and pepper to taste*
> 1½ to 2 *pounds cleaned and sliced baby calves' liver*

1. In a sauté pan, sweat the onions on a low heat with 1 tablespoon of oil and 1 tablespoon of butter. When transluscent, add the wine, lemon juice, nutmeg, salt, and pepper and cook for about 20 minutes, stirring occasionally.
2. Heat the remaining oil and butter over medium-high heat in another sauté pan and add the liver, rapidly searing on both sides and browning lightly. Season with salt and pepper.
3. Combine the onions and liver and amalgamate all by stirring. Cook briefly for 2 or 3 minutes and plate on warm plates with the liver sitting on top of the onions. Serve directly.

YIELD: *4 servings*

Cervelle al Burro Nero

BRAINS IN BLACK BUTTER

Calves' brains are preferred in the North and are an intrinsic part of *fritto misto Milanese.* In the South and particularly Rome, however, lambs' brains are preferred and are served in a caper butter sauce or deep fried in a light batter.

With either calves' or lambs' brains, the younger the animal the better. Brains from nursing calves are far more delicate than those of older animals and the very nature of this dish is "delicacy." It's therefore foolish to try to use pork brains or beef brains as a substitute, and whatever savings might accrue is not worth the change in texture that will occur. Whether bread crumbed and fried, batter fried, poached, braised, or sautéed in butter, as is done here, freshness is essential with this delicate meat.

1 to 1½   pounds baby calves' brains
8 to 12   tablespoons (1 to 1½ sticks) unsalted butter
2   tablespoons capers
    Juice of 2 lemons
1   teaspoon white wine vinegar
    Salt and pepper to taste
1   tablespoon finely chopped fresh parsley

1. Wash and clean the brains, removing the membrane. Rinse in several changes of cold, clear water. Soak them in acidulated water for at least 1 hour. Pat dry with paper towels.

2. Heat the butter in a sauté pan over medium-high heat till foaming and add the brains. Cook quickly, turning them frequently. Do not brown. Add the capers.

3. Allow the butter to brown and then add the lemon juice and vinegar. Stir, mixing well. Season with salt and pepper and serve directly on warm plates with the chopped parsley garnish.

YIELD: *4 servings*

PANE
E
PIZZA

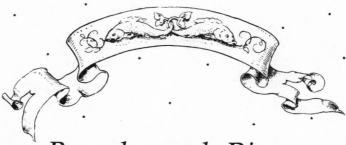

Breads and Pizza

BREADS AND PIZZA

Italian chefs are individualistic and nowhere is this individualism put to better use than in the making of bread. While the French have codified their breadmaking, as they have their saucemaking, thus limiting variety, the Italians make as many different breads as there are bakers—35,000 at least, according to Carol Field in her wonderful book, *The Italian Baker.* Hundreds of shapes, sizes, and textures are available as you travel from region to region, town to town within each region, baker to baker within each town, and then further differentiations according to the type and condition of the flour, yeast, air, temperature, and humidity. Considering all these factors, you'd think no two loaves could ever be alike. While this is only partially true, the miracle of breadmaking is that it doesn't matter. You can set out to make a *ciabatta* (slipper) from the North, around Lake Como, and find that you neither have a slipper nor the porosity you remember from the *ciabatta* you sampled on your trip to the lake district. But, accurate or not, by God, it's good! And even if it isn't good enough for guests, it's easily converted to bread crumbs or toast points for small antipasti. Breadmaking is a forgiving art all right.

For a period of about twelve years, from the early 1950s to the mid-sixties, mechanized breadmaking took over Italy and made packaged cotton white bread supreme. The Italian manufacturers were trying to ape the soporific packaged bread of America. Fortunately, the Italians didn't go for it. Artisan bakers remained true to their trade and because of this serious threat to breadmaking, they dug in their heels and dug out even more ancient recipes to produce what you have now in Italy—the most interesting variety of rustic, rich, crusty and chewy breads in the world.

Unfortunately the subject is too large to teach comprehensively in this book on basic Italian cooking, but I do intend to give you the basics of Italian breadmaking which you can expand on in future studies.

INGREDIENTI · INGREDIENTS

Unless otherwise specified, all-purpose, cake, and regular whole wheat flours are fine for all our recipes that require flour. We do not use self rising flours, as they contain baking soda, which evaporates if the prepared item is not used immediately. Also, because a predetermined amount of baking soda has already been added, its use may be good for one recipe and not another.

I do, however, want to give you an overview of the primary flours used in Italian bread making.

Hard wheat *(Grano duro).* This wheat is grown in winter and, because of its higher protein count (14 to 16 percent), it forms gluten strands well, making it a "strong" flour which is excellent for making breads. It is also called bread flour.

Semolina flour *(Semolina di grano duro).* This is milled from the endosperm (inner core) of the kernel of the hardest winter wheats. Canada and certain mountainous regions of America and Italy grow this grain best. It is the key to quality in the manufacture of *pasta secca* (dry boxed pasta). Although it is much harder to knead because of the higher gluten content, it will make a very fine bread with, or without, the addition of all-purpose flour.

All-purpose flour ("0" and "00" in Italy). All-purpose flour in America is a combination of hard winter wheat and soft summer wheat, having a protein count of between 10 and 13 percent, depending on who made it. It is slightly stronger than its Italian counterpart "0" and "00" flours, which are roughly between 9 and 12 percent. The distinction in Italy between "0" and "00" is a question of the amount of fiber remaining from the grain and not the strength of the protein or gluten; "00," therefore, is simply whiter and finer milled than "0." The equivalents in America would be all-purpose flour for "0" and cake or pastry flour for "00."

Whole wheat flour *(Farina integrale).* In regular hard and soft wheat flours the bran *(crusca)* or coat of the seed or kernel is removed. In milling whole wheat flour, the bran, germ, and endosperm—the "whole" thing—is milled; thus we have whole wheat, which must be stored in the refrigerator or it will become rancid.

Fortunately for home cooks, all-purpose flours and regular cake flours will make very acceptable products in all forms of baking.

Corn flour *(Farina di mais, granoturco).* Corn bread is not just American. They've been making it in Italy for centuries, particularly in the North, where polenta is so popular. Corn flour is actually a finer grind of cornmeal and comes in various degrees of silkiness. Rough or smooth, its ancient uses include the making of breads, cakes, cookies, puddings, and, of course, polenta.

Cornmeal, a coarse grain of corn flour, is essential in baking breads. It allows you to slide wet doughs on and off surfaces and into the oven without sticking. It is also very useful as an addition to other flours in making coarse rustic breads.

Soy flour *(Farina di soia).* This flour comes from soybeans and, when finely ground, makes a wonderful flour for Italian bread. It's very popular here in Umbria, and the bakers usually add wheat berries to give their bread a crunchier effect. It is also good to mix in with your regular breads, at a ratio of about 25 percent, to add nutritive elements as well as flavor.

Barley flour *(Farina di orzo).* Barley was one of the first grains cultivated in ancient Egypt, and quite frequently is found in soups in the Veneto and Umbria. It also makes good flour, although it is very low in gluten content. It's usually a part of grain breads here in Italy.

Bran flour *(Farina di crusca).* I've seen this used in breads called *cereali,* where a multiplicity of grains are employed. Although good for you, bran flour is not commonly used in Italy, as it is in America, to make bran muffins. Caution—low gluten content.

Rice flour *(Farina di riso).* I was surprised at a lunch in Genoa by some very delicate *fritti* (fries) of fish and cheese. When I asked the chef why the batter was so delicate, he said it was because he used rice flour. I knew this to be the practice in oriental cooking, but was unaware of Italian chefs using it. It's also very popular today as part of the seven-grain or *cereali* breads. This also has a low gluten.

Rye flour *(Farina di segale)* The use of rye flour

to make bread goes back to the Middle Ages, and is a specialty of the northernmost part of Lombardy in the Valtellina valley. The flour is made of whole rye grains and as a result is darker and richer in flavor and nutrients, since the bran is not removed in milling. Sourdough rye starters *(biga)* are used to good effect here. However, because of its low gluten content and resultant lack of rising capability, you'll need some wheat flour to help it along.

LIEVITO · LEAVENING AGENTS

The flours we described above all contain varying amounts of starch and protein, or gluten; wheat flour, having a high gluten content, makes well-structured products. But the gluten needs two things to be activated properly in making bread: liquid and a leavening agent, most often yeast. The liquid coagulates the gluten strands, and subsequent kneading, as in the case of breadmaking, stretches these strands and makes them elastic. The yeast ferments when the liquid is added, producing carbon dioxide gas and alcohol. The gas is trapped between the long elastic gluten strands and, as it expands, causes the dough to rise. The alcohol then evaporates in the baking and if all has been done reasonably correctly, you have a well-risen, properly structured bread. Starches have also contributed to this "structure" by absorbing moisture and then expanding, or "gelatinizing," to, in the case of bread, make a firmer loaf.

I should mention at this point, however, that the first breads known to man were made without any leaveners whatsoever. They were, and are, called flat breads, or unleavened breads, and were cooked on hot stones. They are known in Italy as *torta sul testo,* the *torta* signifying "cake" rather than a loaf, and to this day they sell a griddle called a *testo* that, when put over a gas burner, simulates the ancient method of cooking these flat breads on hot stones in an open fire.

Yeast, being a living organism, is sensitive to variations in temperature and won't begin to ferment till warmed to about 60°F. From there to 75°F the fermenting action is rather slow. Between 75° and 90°F fermentation is at its best. Above 100°F the process begins to reverse, and by the time you reach 140°F, fermentation is dead and the yeast is killed.

I find the little 2-ounce packages of fresh yeast to work best for me, although active dry yeast is equally usable. Dry active yeast is more potent, however, and therefore requires much less than fresh compressed yeast. You need about 40 percent of dry yeast to equal a fresh yeast quantity. On the other hand, dry yeast requires about four times its weight in warm water to activate, whereas fresh compressed yeast requires less. In both cases the water should be about 110°F.

In addition to acting as a leavener, yeast also adds flavor to what it's used in. In the case of breads, it is therefore desirable to use starters *(biga)*—where yeast, water, and a bit of flour are left to ferment at room temperature for a day or more—which, when added to the regular bread dough recipe, will provide a much richer flavor. **Starter (Biga).** As I mentioned earlier, in the comments about yeast, a starter, or a *biga,* is simply a preparation of yeast and water with a bit of flour that is left to stand at room temperature for a day or more. After four or five days, these starters become "sour," thus giving the name to the sourdough breads so popular in San Francisco. They can be changed in flavor by using *verjuice* (green grape juice), malt, and other flavoring agents. These starters, or biga, are also called sponges. You can slow down or retard their fermentation action by storing them in the refrigerator.

The most ancient starter, of course, and one that is used today throughout Italy, is simply a piece of dough that's left over from yesterday's breadmaking. Is it possible that the dough I get from my local *fornaio* is coming down to me through centuries of yesterday's doughs that became starters? Hardly! But then nostalgia sometimes reigns supreme.

Water *(Acqua)*. There is no question that water contributes flavor, good or bad. You need good, clean, relatively pure fresh water, without any "off" flavors, to cook with. Here in Italy, if a baker finds his water too hard, he'll have it softened. If there is too much chlorine, he'll have it purified. It is my considered opinion that whereas we can relax the stringency of our specifications when it comes to flour, the quality of the water used in cooking is a different matter. Preferably, one should have the purest, sweetest, freshest spring water in the world to cook with at all times. Failing that, fix what you have the best you can.

Milk *(Latte)*. Many bread recipes call for whole milk instead of water. If so, it must be scalded and then cooled before using, otherwise it will weaken the dough.

Salt *(Sale)*. Salt is another ingredient I had to think long and hard about. There is no question that sea salt is more flavorful than iodized salt. Fortunately for us here in Italy it's readily available in two consistencies—coarse ground and rock, crystal size. The latter is great for topping focaccia and other types of rustic breads and regular coarse ground sea salt is marvelous to cook with. Unfortunately, in America sea salt is very expensive. What to do? Is it necessary to use sea salt? Some Italian bakers will say yes, and certainly it contributes better flavor. But on balance, I think not. Like all-purpose flour, regular iodized salt is satisfactory to cook with, and works well enough in baking also. When baking with yeast, be careful of the amount of salt you use; too much will cut back dramatically on the yeast expansion and will result in, for example, a very small loaf of bread. Too little and the bread will be weak, poorly constructed, and generally oversized.

ABOUT SWEET BREADS

Making sweet breads is not really different from making regular breads except for the addition of eggs, butter, sugar, and, most often, dried or candied fruits of various kinds. Their effect on baked products is as follows:

EGGS

Eggs impart flavor and, when coagulated, give structure to cake or bread. Their high protein content offsets the weakening effect that sugar and butter (or other fats) have on the gluten strands of the flour. They also contribute to the smoothness of a batter and thereby produce finer texture and increased volume. Eggs do tend to "toughen" the strands when used in quantity and need to be counteracted by the use of fats and sugar. Eggs also serve as a leavener.

BUTTER

Always use unsalted butter in cooking and baking. It, in my opinion, allows you to salt to taste and has better flavor than salted butter. The great advantage of using butter as a shortening is its wonderful flavor. The disadvantage is that it is hard to handle. Some bakeries will use half butter and half shortening to try to glean the best of both worlds. I prefer to work with 100 percent sweet butter and suffer the inconveniences to gain the wonderful texture and flavor that butter imparts.

But whether butter, or other shortenings, are used, their purpose is to tenderize the product. Whereas flour, or eggs, can become tough and excessively chewy, butter or other shortenings make the gluten strands softer, more tender, and marry everything together in a rich, savory manner.

SUGAR

Satisfying your sweet tooth is not the only function sugar has. It provides food for yeast, thereby activating it, contributes to tenderness by softening gluten strands, in bread and pasta prevents staling by retaining moisture, and also, in baked goods, gives a product a browner crust. Regular granulated sugar is fine for our purposes here, except when a particular recipe calls for confectioners' sugar.

EQUIPMENT FOR BREADMAKING

The equipment necessary to make a loaf of bread is minimal. You really need only a bowl to mix and let it rise in, a surface to knead it on, and an oven to bake it in. If you wish to pursue the subject further, however, here is a small list of equipment that you will find useful.

Mixing bowls. Pyrex, stainless steel, or ceramic all work well.

Rising bowls. Same thing goes as for mixing bowls, only here the size is essential. Most breads have to double in size when they rise, thus requiring bowls large enough to accommodate the process. High, straight-sided bowls are best.

Work surface. Almost any smooth flat surface will suffice, although marble's coolness tends to inhibit the gluten expansion—not to say you can't make bread on marble. I've done it many times, but wood or even Formica are better surfaces for kneading. Here in Italy, they use a bread or pasta board, made with a tongue in groove joining that provides a very smooth even surface that doesn't warp. They also have a two-inch lip on them to prevent slipping and sliding by fitting snugly against your regular tabletop. They are usually 30 by 36 inches but can be made in any size you'd like at your local lumberyard. I'm told

some gourmet equipment stores in America now carry them ready-made.

Dough scraper. A dough scraper is a wonderful tool for keeping kitchen tables clean, and is quite necessary for scraping flour and bits of dough that have stuck to the table, unless you want to dull your knives.

Baking stone. There are two ideal ovens for baking breads—a wood-burning oven for flavor and a gas convection steam oven for getting the perfect crust. Failing these two, you can buy a baking stone from your local brickyard, cut to measure to fit the floor of your oven. These stones are specially fired at high heat, and improve the crustiness of your bread. It needs to be dusted with cornmeal liberally before each use.

Baking pans. Once again, failing the two ovens mentioned above, and the baking stone, the next best thing is to have good heavy baking pans and/or loaf pans for baking bread. The heavy black metal type are good, as are aluminum, as long as you avoid those thin-bottomed types that are not stable.

Water sprayer. There are very good, inexpensive plastic water sprayers for plants on the market that are suitable to spray the oven on top of and around the bread to create some steam, which will help make a better crust. It's also good practice to put a small pan of water in the oven to aid in crusting.

Peel. A peel is usually a 14- by 18-inch piece of wood or steel with a handle that is used like a shovel to place the risen bread dough in the oven. The back of a baking pan, or any pan, will do, however. Just remember in all cases to dust it well with cornmeal to avoid the dough sticking.

Parchment paper. Some sticky doughs like the *ciabatta* are difficult to handle, and will stick to a peel or inverted pan in spite of the cornmeal. Parchment paper will work wonders in sliding these doughs on and off their supporting surfaces.

Bread knife. A large well-sharpened serrated

bread knife is the proper tool for cutting bread and various cakes that might call for butterflying (cutting in half horizontally).

Regular knife or razor. A good sharp kitchen knife will do the job of "scoring" (making deep incisions in the top of the bread) adequately, but if you happen to have a single-edged razor cutter in a handle of some sort, they work even better. You want the incisions to be very deep (for example, 2 inches for a 3- to 4-inch-thick loaf) since they tend to close up again as the dough expands.

Oil can. Oil cans are not only pretty and give your kitchen a certain note of professionalism, but are also very functional in oiling pizza and other products in a controlled manner. They come in stainless aluminum, tin, and copper; if you want the best effect, the copper oil cans are worth the extra money.

Pizza wheel. These rolling-round cutters with serrated edges (usually) are very useful in cutting pizza of all types, as well as ravioli and agnolotti. They will outperform a knife in this regard by a comfortable margin.

Rolling pin. I use a small (10-inch) wood pin to flatten out pizza before working the dough with the tips of my fingers. This is the only pin I feel is necessary for making breads, *focacce,* and pizza. Naturally, we have an assorted variety of rolling pins for making pasta, pie crusts, and other specialties.

You may have noticed that our equipment schedule does not include a mixer or processor. The omission is deliberate since I prefer to knead all doughs by hand. In my opinion, the product is different when done by hand rather than by machine, whether it be rolls, pizza, or pasta. Further, it is not only different, but far better if you prefer the homely "goodness" of handmade products. But there are still other reasons. We are concerned here with basic cooking skills, not quantity cooking, and if you learn properly to make these products by hand, all the labor-saving devices will later be at your disposal. Last, but in no

way least, a very important part of cooking with love, knowledge, and devotion is the touching, smelling, seeing, and tasting process that goes on when you are really involved, physically and spiritually. Kneading and mixing by hand brings you into that process directly, and with an immediacy that is invaluable.

For the same reasons, the instructions that I am about to impart concerning breadmaking and baking are kept to basic essentials. The purpose is to teach you to make bread, not to make a professional baker out of you at this point.

METHODS AND TECHNIQUES

MEASURING

Fortunately, in basic breadmaking, precise measurements are not important. Anyone who tells you to use $22\frac{1}{8}$ ounces or 864 grams or $1\frac{1}{8}$ cups or $5\frac{1}{4}$ tablespoons of flour is assuming factors that are virtually uncontrollable at home. First of all the amount of flour necessary to a cup of water (for example) depends on the type of flour being used to begin with. Then how lightly is the cup packed? What is the temperature, the humidity, both of the ingredients and the room? How hard is the water? All of these things will affect absorption.

The general ratio I use is about 1 cup of water to about 3 cups of flour. Put the yeast and water, or starter and yeast and water, in a bowl and add a generous amount of flour (2 cups), but not so much as to dry the dough out, and mix with a wooden spoon.

Keep adding flour until you can knead the dough into a loose ball with one hand in the bowl. Bring the loose ball of dough out onto a floured surface and knead till you have a smooth elastic ball. Knead without adding any more flour for five or more minutes. If the dough is too sticky, open it up and add more flour as you knead. In this way, you provide the dough with the right amount of flour regardless of the type or weather.

PREPARING THE YEAST

Yeast *(Lievito, fermento).* The good news today is that yeast is alive and well. Thirty-five years ago, when I first began this unending romance with nature through cooking, we had to proof the yeast, that is, put the yeast with a pinch of sugar in some warm water and let it set for about ten minutes at room temperature to see if it foamed. If it did, the yeast was good. Today, commercial yeast, fresh in a package or dry, is so reliable that proofing has become totally academic. Technically speaking, the water that is needed to activate yeast should be between 90° and 100°F. But from my experience, I've found that warm "to the touch" water, similar to the temperature of a baby's bottle, is fine for the rustic Italian breads we are concerned with in this basic course. Add the yeast to it and stir well, mixing with a wooden spoon. It's ready to use as soon as it's dissolved. Since salt retards the fermentation of the yeast, it's better to add the salt after the flour, while the dough is still wet but before kneading—that's assuming there is salt in the recipe.

MAKE THE DOUGH

Now that the yeast has been dissolved, add it to the other liquid ingredients, mix well with a wooden spoon, and begin adding the flour. Mix and knead the dough as described above under "Measuring." If you are using a starter, mix the dough in the same way. You can use the starter as the sole leavener, using it in place of the yeast dissolved in water; as an addition to the yeast where the starter acts as part leavener and part flavoring agent; or as a small addition to a yeast fermentation for flavor only.

KNEADING

Take the ball of dough out of the bowl and place it in front of you on a floured surface. Hold, or brace, the dough with your left hand, curling the tips of your fingers lightly under it. Sprinkle the dough with flour and press the palm of your right hand (left-handed people are out of luck here— just kidding) down into the dough and away from you, moving the fingers of your left hand out of the way. Now turn the dough over by a quarter and repeat the process—putting the fingers of your left hand under, lifting the dough, and then kneading again with the palm and fingers of your right hand slightly cupped. Now comes the most important part. Put one foot in front of the other; I prefer the left foot forward. Now lean into the kneading as you turn the dough over and press down, and then rock back as you release before beginning again. Start slowly, deliberately, till you get the rhythm going smoothly. The goal is to create a steady rhythmic motion so that the gluten strands will stretch and then relax, stretch and relax, till you give it "structure." Don't let anyone tell you that there's only one way to knead. Whatever makes you comfortable, whether one foot is in front of the other, both are flat, rocking or not, if you stretch and relax the gluten strands rhythmically, you'll be kneading well. Knead less and your bread will have a coarser, more rustic crumb. Knead it more and you'll smooth out the texture of the bread, creating a finer textured loaf. Some *focacce,* pizza, and other breads are hardly kneaded at all.

How much flour to add while kneading? Very little or none. If your original ball was elastic enough you should be able to knead without flour and without sticking. If, when you're kneading, you find the dough too sticky, break down the ball, open it up, and put in a bit more flour. That should do it.

How do I know when the dough has been kneaded enough? Aside from experience, which comes faster than you might think—four or five loaves and you're experienced—the goal is to have a sleek elastic oval that is as silky as a baby's bottom, as they say. It should spring back if you indent it with your fingers. Generally it requires five to ten minutes of kneading.

Can a dough be overkneaded? Yes; the gluten strands can only stretch so far and, if they will break, there will be no structure. But, actually, by hand you'd be hard pressed to overknead; it would require considerably more pressure than the average person can put into it by hand. The danger is more real when kneading by machine.

RISING

Professional bakers call this proofing (not to be mixed up with the proofing of yeast). Most of the breads in this book will be risen twice, although in special recipes some may be risen three times.

The procedure is quite simple. Lightly oil an oversized bowl (use about one teaspoon) and turn the ball of dough over in it several times, till coated lightly. Since flavor develops and is imparted by every step in making bread, I use good extra virgin olive oil for added richness. It is also true that more flavor develops by slow rising. A little warm corner and a bit of sun (not the blazing suns of August) in your kitchen will produce the slow room temperature rising that is the most desirable. The dough will need 1½ to 2½ hours to double in size in this circumstance. If you're in a hurry use the bottom part of your oven (if you have a gas oven) with just the pilot light on. The temperature will be about 90° to 100°F and will rise the dough in 45 minutes to an hour and a half. If you don't even have that much time available to you, make one of the *focacce* (flat breads) that can be risen in 15 to 20 minutes.

Getting back to the bowl, once the dough is oiled, place it seam side down in the bowl and cover it tightly with plastic wrap. Allow it to rise till double in size. If you have trouble judging the "doubling," there are plastic, see-through containers with covers that allow you to actually

measure the progress, and the ultimate size, of the risen dough. Another test is indenting the dough with your fingertips. If it springs back rapidly, it is still unproofed, unrisen, too elastic. If it springs back slowly, and not completely, it is properly risen. If it is so lacking in structure that it won't spring back at all, and your fingers hardly leave an impression, the dough is over-risen. But not to worry. Knead a bit of flour into it, shape it into a ball again, replace in an oiled bowl and cover it, then let it rise again. Fortunately bread is virtually indestructible.

Here are some general rules:

- less kneading and less rising give you a coarser texture
- extra thorough kneading and a third rising will give a much finer texture
- slow rising imparts more flavor
- under-rising will produce a bread that's too "dense"—hard—or even doughy at the center
- over-rising will produce a bread that lacks structure and flavor—too "airy"
- properly kneaded and risen breads will have good texture (also known as crumb) and structure and be properly "chewy."

The fermentation of dough can be suspended or retarded by putting it in the refrigerator. This is very useful if you start a bread and are suddenly called away. Just remove the dough from the bowl and lay it out on an oiled pan so that it is about 2 inches thick. This is done so the dough will chill down rapidly and uniformly; otherwise the center will continue to ferment before the cold reaches it. Cover the dough with plastic wrap and refrigerate. When you return home, or the next day for that matter, remove the pan of dough from the refrigerator and allow it to come to room temperature—this will take 1 to 2 hours, depending on the size of the dough and the weather. Then reshape it into a ball, kneading it lightly, and begin the rising process again.

SHAPING FOR THE SECOND RISING

After the first rising, "punch down" the dough in the bowl and remove it to a lightly floured surface. The punching down is done with your knuckles and your hand. You will see that the risen dough immediately collapses as the air is released. Knead the dough on the floured surface lightly and begin to shape it. We're not using loaf pans here, so it is important to shape the dough firmly. The trick is to "grab" pieces of the dough and work them into the shape you're after. If you wanted a long cylindrical loaf, you would flatten out the ball and then roll it up again into a cylinder shape, tucking and folding the ends of the dough into itself. Don't be timid. Take the pieces of dough and force them into the shape you want. If you're shaping a round loaf, keep stretching and pulling the top down over and tuck the ends into the center of the bottom. This becomes the bottom seam and should be on the bottom for the second rising as well as the baking. There are hundreds of shapes possible, braids and horses, angels and rabbits, birds and flowers—whatever imagination dictates is possible to make with a good elastic dough. It's really no different than shaping putty or clay. Once you have a well-risen loaf that has been properly shaped you then want to set it out for a second rising. Put the shaped loaf on a peel, or the back of a pan that has been well dusted with cornmeal. The second rising takes much less time than the first and requires considerably less than a doubling in size. Of course we're assuming here that the recipe does not call for a third rising, in which case the second rising would be identical to the first rising and the shaping would take place after the second rising. But back to our once risen, well-shaped loaf: Place it in a warm spot and let it increase in size, anywhere from half to two-thirds depending on the type of bread.

SCORING

Once the second or third rising has taken place, you can, if you wish, score or "slash" the top of the bread with a very sharp knife or a razor. For cylindrical loaves, I like to to make four or five well-spaced "slashes" on an angle. They should be substantially deep (2 inches) so that the dough doesn't close back over them. In the case of a round loaf, I'm very fond of slicing into it horizontally, three quarters of the way up the side, resulting in somewhat of a mushroom effect. It's an attractive, rustic looking loaf, especially if dusted liberally with flour.

"WASHING" THE LOAF

Washes are used to produce different kinds of crust—lighter, darker, thinner, thicker. They're brushed on the loaf right before baking with a pastry brush, paintbrush, or any smooth-haired brush you happen to have reserved for this purpose. Milk, milk with sugar, whole eggs, egg yolks, egg whites, with or without water, all will contribute to a more attractive crust. The lightest wash is made from slightly beaten egg whites. The darkest wash is made from using beaten egg yolks with nothing added, although they would be difficult to spread; usually some water is beaten in. I generally use a whole egg with ½ cup of water, well beaten, as an all-purpose wash. But by all means do experiment and use what suits you.

BAKING THE BREAD

If you don't have a stone (or fire brick) to bake your bread on, the back of a heavy duty pan will do nicely. Either way, dust the surface with cornmeal and set the loaf on it. Heat activates the dough, so that when you first put your bread into a preheated (350° to 400°F for egg breads and those enriched with milk, 400° to 450°F for those that are eggless and milkless) oven, the expansion of the carbon dioxide gases is very rapid. The gluten strands will expand with the gases, but will also trap them at the same time, thus rising the dough again into a well structured loaf. Moisture in the form of steam also acts as a leavener, so it is extremely helpful to provide just that during the first few minutes of baking. You can accomplish this by putting a pan of water in the oven 10 to 15 minutes before you put in the bread, at which time the pan should be taken out, and/or you can spray water all around the loaf in the oven. This should be done three or four times during the first 10 to 15 minutes of baking. I always start my loaf on the bottom stone floor of my oven to give the bottom a browner crust. Since heat rises, after 30 to 40 minutes I move the loaf to the upper rack and allow it to finish baking there, so that the top crust is crisper and browner.

TESTING FOR DONENESS

Depending on the size of the loaf, the normal breads we are making here are done in an hour to an hour and a half, more or less. Test the bread by removing it from the oven and "knocking" on the bottom. It will take five or six loaves to get to know the timbre of that hollow base sound, but once you do you'll never forget it. It's a very reliable system for testing doneness in spite of its highly subjective nature. After all, who's to say when the sound of "thumping" is hollow enough? You, the baker, that's who! The one thing you can't do is open it up to see if it's done.

COOLING

It is important to cool breads before cutting into them. Once taken out of the oven, they continue to bake and also release moisture, both of which processes are necessary for proper texture. Wire racks are best for this purpose, since they allow air to circulate freely all around the loaf. In normal sized loaves, cooling takes 30 to 45 minutes.

STALING

Fresh homemade breads without preservatives go stale quickly . . . sometimes within several hours. Those made with fats (butter, oil, lard) do better, but not much. They all can be wrapped in moisture-proof bags after they've totally cooked and kept fairly well. Bread dough freezes well and can be baked directly from the freezer. You can also refresh stale bread by wrapping it in damp paper towels, then aluminum foil, and placing it in a hot (400°F) oven. Allow the bread to heat through for about 10 minutes or so, then remove the paper, replace the foil loosely, and return to the oven to crisp. Of course you don't need fresh bread to make bread crumbs, toast points, toast, and dozens of recipes that actually work better with stale bread.

Before I move on to the recipes, I'd like to suggest to those of you who've never baked before that you start with a simple, crusty, crunchy, chewy, country loaf and make the same recipe over again—five, six, seven times—watching all the processes change, kneading, shaping, rising, scoring, crusting, with each new loaf you make. Keep at it till you get a "feel" for the ever-changing reactions you get from your efforts. When your "feel" gives you the confidence to control the variations you have witnessed in your first attempts, then move on to more complicated breads. By and by . . .

Biga

STARTER

As explained previously, a *biga*, or starter, is a little flour, water, and yeast that has been left to ferment for a day or more. It adds taste to the breads and has levitating capabilities. If refrigerated you will retard the yeast fermentation process; therefore, if you won't be using it for 3 or 4 days, refrigerate it.

> *1/8 cake fresh or 1/2 teaspoon dried yeast*
> *1 cup water, at about 100°F*
> *2 cups all-purpose flour*

1. Stir the yeast in the warm water till dissolved. Add the flour and mix well with a wooden spoon.
2. Cover with plastic wrap and set aside for 24 hours before using.

NOTE: Malt can also be added to a *biga* and the flour changed from all-purpose to wheat, rye, or whatever, for different flavors.

Torta sul testo

ORIGINAL UNLEAVENED SALT BREAD

Before we even get to use the *biga*, however, let's back up in time and reproduce the original unleavened bread, or a reasonable facsimile, made to this day throughout Italy. *Torta* means cake, or flat bread, and a *testo* is a flat griddle, usually round with two handles, that is a modern (50 years) replacement for the ancient stone or hearth of a fireplace that this unleavened flat bread was originally baked on. Frankly there's no comparison between the ancient method and a *testo*, and here at the school we still make this bread in the fireplace under a bed of ashes covered with hot glowing wood embers. It is always a distinct pleasure to make this bread in a manner that you know has existed since the very beginning of bread making. The delightful surprise is that the finished product can't be improved upon. It's like a pizza toasted on both sides and when sliced (horizontally) open and stuffed with a piece of prosciutto, cheese, vegetable, or sausage, and returned to a grill over hot embers, one has the original sandwich of mankind. And best of all, there isn't a simpler recipe I know of.

> *2 cups all-purpose flour*
> *1 teaspoon salt*
> *1/4 cup extra virgin olive oil*
> *1 1/2 cups water, at about 100°F*
> *Cornmeal, for dusting*

1. Place the flour in a bowl and mix in the salt. Add the oil and mix again. Add 1 cup water and mix. Add another cup and mix. Watch the consistency carefully before adding the last 1/2 cup. The dough should be loose but together. Depending on humidity and temperature, all doughs require more, or less, water.

2. Lightly knead the dough with your knuckles in the bowl, and when it holds together, turn it out on a floured board. Lightly knead the dough for 3 or 4 minutes. Immediately shape it into a round similar to a pizza, pressing the dough out with the tips of your fingers. Place on a peel liberally dusted with cornmeal. There is no rising necessary at all.

3. Have a fire going well in your fireplace for 1 hour before baking. Use cardboard and paper in the fire so that there is some buildup of ashes and not just cinders. Pull some hot glowing embers (coals) a foot or two from the fire to heat the stone base. Sweep the stone free of the embers and place the *torta* on the hot stone base. Immediately cover it with ashes from the fire and then place more hot embers on top of the ashes. The ashes will protect the dough from burning from the hot embers.

4. Let the *torta* bake for approximately 15 minutes in the above manner and then sweep off all ashes and embers with a clean, rough brush.

5. Using a very fine brush, clean the bread thoroughly and toast it further on a grill over more hot embers, if necessary.

6. When done, slice open horizontally with a bread knife and fill the sandwich with a bit of cooked sausage, greens, cheese, or whatever. Return to the grill to cook further till the cheese melts, or the ingredients are warmed, and serve.

YIELD: *1 loaf*

Basic Bread Dough

Here is the recipe for a basic bread dough without a starter. It is a versatile recipe that will make bread, rolls, pizza, *focacce,* and *grissini* (breadsticks), although all of these can be improved upon by the addition of oil or malt, and by kneading more or less. Pizza, for example, works better if it has oil in the dough and is kneaded less. It is a base recipe that can be changed very simply by changing the flours to whole wheat, corn, or rye. Bear in mind our comments about the imprecision of measurements due to variations in climatic conditions. Although this recipe normally requires three cups of flour, it required four yesterday because it was raining.

> *1 cup water, at about 100°F*
> *½ cake fresh or 1¾ teaspoons dried yeast*
>   *About 3 cups all-purpose flour*
>   *About ½ teaspoon salt*
>   *About 1 teaspoon vegetable oil*

1. Stir 2 tablespoons of water with the yeast in a large bowl till smooth. Add the remaining water.

2. Begin adding the flour, 1 cup at a time, while stirring and mixing with a large, sturdy kitchen spoon. Now add the salt into this loose mixture. Incorporate as much flour as you can with the spoon, forming a dough, and absorbing the flour from the sides of the bowl. Use your knuckles to continue forming the dough in the bowl while adding the remaining flour. This should take about 2 to 3 minutes.

3. Turn out the dough onto a lightly floured surface and knead for about 10 minutes until smooth, bouncy, and not sticky. If you want a more rustic loaf, knead less.

4. Place the dough in a clean, large, oiled bowl, cover tightly, and let it rise as required for a specific recipe (see below).

Variations

•

FOR PIZZA

1. Let the dough rise for about 45 minutes in a very warm place (about 90°F) until barely doubled in bulk.
2. Cut the dough in half and knead each half into a smooth ball, dusting minimally with flour.
3. Either roll or finger-press the dough into the shape and size desired.
4. Place in an oiled baking pan, or on an inverted pan bottom, pizza peel, or other flat sturdy object (I've used cardboard) that has been dusted with fine cornmeal or flour.
5. Top as desired and bake immediately in as hot an oven as possible, 450° to 500°F.

FOR FOCACCIA

1. Let the dough rise as for pizza and then knead into a smooth ball, without cutting in half.
2. Shape as for pizza but twice as thick.
3. Place in a similarily oiled and dusted pan or a dusted peel, cover loosely, and allow to rise again until nearly doubled.
4. Top as desired and bake immediately as for pizza.

Whole Wheat: Use up to 2 cups whole wheat flour instead of the all-purpose flour.
Pane al mais (Italian Corn Bread): Substitute 1 cup cornmeal for the all-purpose flour. After the first rising, shape the dough into a long loaf and roll in cornmeal before the second rise. Bake as instructed

YIELD: *1 loaf*

Basic Bread Dough with a Starter

- 1 *cup water, at about 100°F*
- ¼ *cake fresh or 1 teaspoon dried yeast*
- 2 *heaping tablespoons starter (biga), aged 24 hours (see page 281)*
  About 3 cups all-purpose flour
- 1 *teaspoon salt*
- 1 *teaspoon vegetable oil*

1. Combine 2 tablespoons of warm water with the yeast and stir to dissolve.
2. Add 2 tablespoons of starter to the water-yeast solution and a bit more water and mix well.
3. Now continue with all the other bread making steps using the above ingredients.

Variation

•

Pane all'olio (Bread with Oil): Follow the above recipe, using 4 to 6 tablespoons of starter and 2 tablespoons of extra virgin olive oil.

YIELD: *1 loaf*

Pane Toscana

TUSCAN BREAD

1 cup water, at about 100°F

3 to 4 cups all-purpose flour

½ cake fresh or 1¾ teaspoons dried yeast

4 to 6 tablespoons starter (biga), aged 24 hours (see page 281)

1. The same as other breads. (See page 282.)

Pizza al Formaggio

CHEESE BREAD

This is really a bread and not a pizza, but here in Umbria they always refer to it as *pizza al formaggio*.

About 1 pound all-purpose flour

1 cake fresh or or 3½ teaspoons dried yeast

¾ cup water

½ teaspoon salt

1 tablespoon extra virgin olive oil

2 large eggs

1 cup freshly grated pecorino Romano

1 cup freshly grated parmigiano

Freshly ground black pepper to taste (optional)

1. Make a bread dough with ¾ of the pound of flour, the yeast, water, and salt. Knead well and let rise once until doubled, as clearly described on page 278.

2. Punch down the risen dough, turn it out onto a floured surface, and knead in the oil until incorporated.

3. Mix 1 egg and the cheeses and thicken the mixture with the remaining flour. Knead the cheese dough with the bread dough until thoroughly combined. Use as much flour as needed to keep the dough from sticking.

4. Form the dough into a long cylinder and then a ring, joining the ends securely. Let the ring rise by 50 percent.

5. Lightly beat the remaining egg and brush it on the ring. Bake in a 375°F oven till crusty, glazed, and cooked through.

YIELD: *1 loaf*

Pane Integrale con Noci

WHEAT BREAD WITH WALNUTS

This is really the same as *pane scuro toscano* except that cornmeal is worked into the dough, along with walnuts and parmigiano. To get a good rise and richer flavor from the lower gluten whole wheat flour you will need more starter. Malt in the starter will also provide a richer flavor. I sometimes make this a little lighter by using 50 percent wheat and 50 percent white flour.

½ cake fresh or 1¾ teaspoons dried yeast

1 cup water, at about 100°F

4 to 6 *tablespoons starter (biga), aged for 24 hours (see page 281)*
     1 *cup all-purpose flour*
   ½ *teaspoon salt*
     2 *tablespoons cornmeal*
     2 *cups broken walnuts*
     1 *cup freshly grated parmigiano*

1. Dissolve the yeast with the warm water and add the starter.
2. Add the flour, a third at a time, and turn it out onto a floured board to knead, having added the salt in the middle. Add the cornmeal and knead for 5 to 7 minutes till elastic and springy. Set to rise in the normal manner as described on page 278.
3. Punch down and add the walnuts and parmigiano while the dough is still in the rising bowl.
4. Turn the dough out onto a floured board and knead it to incorporate the nuts and cheese. Shape and set to rise again as normal as described on page 279.
5. Slash, wash, bake, and rack to cool, as normal, as described on page 279.

YIELD: *1 loaf*

Pane con Olive

BREAD WITH OLIVES

You can use just regular white bread dough or wheat bread dough to create this really rustic country loaf, but I prefer a dark wheat bread with some oil from the olive marinade and an enriched two- or three-day-old *biga*.

1½ *cups black olives*
1 ½ *cups Olive Marinade, olives omitted (see page 253)*
   ½ *cake fresh or 1¾ teaspoons dried yeast*
4 to 6 *tablespoons starter (biga), aged 2-3 days (see page 281)*
     1 *cup water, at about 100°F*
     2 *teaspoons olive oil*
     2 *cups whole wheat flour*
     1 *cup all-purpose flour*
   ½ *teaspoon salt*

1. Marinate the olives for several days. Cut 1 cup of the olives into quarters and leave ½ cup in large pieces (halves).
2. Mix the yeast, starter and water as described on page 276. Add the oil.
3. Add the flours and salt and knead as described on page 277.
4. Let the dough rise to double in size as described on page 278.
5. Punch down the dough and add the olives, kneading them into the dough in the rising bowl.
6. Turn the dough out onto a floured board and knead further until the olives are thoroughly incorporated.
7. Shape, slash, and set to rise 50 percent.
8. Proceed with the rest as normal, as described on page 279.

YIELD: *1 loaf*

Crescente

BACON BREAD

1 batch Basic Bread Dough (see page 282), made with 1 cup warm milk instead of water

8 ounces smoked or unsmoked pancetta or bacon, diced and fried with a pinch of sugar till crisp

1 egg

1. Allow the dough to rise once. Before punching down, pour the cooked, diced pancetta with its fat onto the dough, mixing as much as possible with a spoon and then kneading on a floured surface to incorporate thoroughly.
2. Roll the dough out into a circle about 1-inch thick. Place the circle on an oiled pan. Score the top with criss-cross lines to form 1-inch squares. Cover loosely and allow to rise by 50 percent.
3. Make an eggwash with the egg and a few drops of water. Glaze the dough lightly with it.
4. Bake in a 375°F oven till hollow sounding when the bottom is tapped, about 50 minutes. Cool on a rack for 20 minutes or so before serving.

YIELD: *1 loaf*

Pizza Sfogliata

LAYERED PIZZA

Here's another bread that's called a pizza. The *sfogliata* part means puff pastry, and is so used here because the sheets of bread dough are layered over the cheese. It's a very special bread that never fails to bring out the "oohs" and "aahs" from the hungry people. Since it is a flat bread with a cheese filling, you also don't have to rack and cool it before eating. It can be served hot, which adds to its popularity.

1 cup water, at about 100°F

3 to 4 cups all-purpose flour

¼ cake fresh or ¾ teaspoon dried yeast

2 tablespoons oil

1 teaspoon salt

2 cups freshly grated parmigiano

1 cup shredded mozzarella

1 cup shredded Gruyère

1 cup diced gorgonzola

1 cup diced taleggio cheese

1 egg
   Salt and freshly ground black pepper to taste

¼ teaspoon freshly grated nutmeg

1. Make a basic bread dough with the first 5 ingredients, following the instructions on page 282.
2. Knead lightly and let rise by 50 percent.
3. Punch down the dough and roll it into a ball, kneading slightly on a floured board.
4. Mix the cheeses together, reserving ½ cup of parmigiano for topping.

5. Make the egg wash by shaking an egg with a few drops of water in a small covered jar.

6. Cut the bread ball into thirds and roll each out to about 1/8-inch-thick sheets the size of a small cookie pan.

7. Lay a sheet of dough on a pan well dusted with cornmeal and brush the edges with the egg wash.

8. Place half the cheeses on the sheet of dough, distributing thoroughly but mounding slightly in the center. Season the cheese with salt, pepper, and nutmeg to taste.

9. Lay the next sheet of dough over the cheese and press down, sealing the edges to the egg-washed first sheet.

10. Repeat the procedure and braid the edges, sealing the whole well.

11. Brush the top with egg wash and sprinkle with the remaining parmigiano.

12. Bake in a 375°F oven for approximately 30 minutes, or until done through and golden brown.

YIELD: *1 pizza*

Ciabatta

SLIPPER BREAD

As I mentioned in the introduction to breadmaking, *ciabatta* is a slipper-shaped bread, and can be very formal in presentation—a completely designed slipper replete with braiding, or a very loose representation that might more resemble a flat boat. The recipe that we've found to work the best comes from Carol Field's very fine book *The Italian Baker,* with some modifications.

1/8 *cake fresh or* 1/2 *teaspoon dried yeast*

1/2 *cup water, at about 100°F*

1/2 *cup milk, at about 100°F*

3 to 4 *cups all-purpose flour*

2 *teaspoons extra virgin olive oil*

1 *cup starter (biga), aged 24 hours (see page 281)*

1 *teaspoon salt*

1. Mix the yeast, water, and milk in a bowl till the yeast has dissolved.

2. Add two-thirds of the flour and the oil and mix well. Add the next third of the flour with the salt and mix well again. Start to knead with your knuckles in the bowl.

3. Form a loose dough. Turn it out onto a floured board and knead rhythmically for 8 to 10 minutes till very elastic.

4. Set to rise in a plastic-covered bowl for about 1 hour till doubled in size. It will be very loose and sticky.

5. Cut the dough in half and shape and roll each piece of dough into a rectangle.

6. Make indentations with your fingertips as you would to press out pizza dough (see page 279).

7. Cover loosely with damp towels and set to rise till doubled again, for 1 to 1 1/2 hours.

8. Do not expect the rectangles to look well risen and don't let their flatness upset you. Since the dough is very sticky, you must use double care with flour and cornmeal underneath to guard against sticking to your pan or peel during baking.

9. Bake in a 450°F oven for 20 to 30 minutes, employing the spraying technique explained on page 280 during the first 10 minutes.

YIELD: *2 loaves*

Panettone

CHRISTMAS BREAD

This famous Christmas bread from Milan is not exactly the easiest sweet bread to make and this recipe required considerable research and experimentation with the Italian ladies who help at the school. The final recipe is slightly denser than a commercially made product but far richer and better tasting in my opinion. The key to this *casareccia* effect is the inclusion of a whole mashed potato in the dough. It's a bit of work, and time-consuming, and therefore probably better suited for a more advanced cook. However, it seems to me that I couldn't have a chapter on Italian breads without it, and its cousin, the equally rich Easter bread called *colomba*.

The quantities used here will make a very tall (10 to 12 inches) domed cake that can be baked in a ceramic bowl or other form. I used a pot-shaped glazed ceramic bowl that is 7 inches high and 7 ½ inches in diameter. If you don't have anything similar you can make a form out of cardboard, in which case you must grease it and flour it extra heavily.

The rising times here were calculated on the dough being risen in a gas oven with the pilot light on. The temperature was about 110°F. The first rising is a doubling, at about 3½ hours. The second rising, another doubling, took 4½ hours. In both cases, the ladies insisted on putting a pan of boiling water in the oven to create steam and additional heat. Although I'm not sure this duplicates the conditions of a professional baker's proof box, where humidity speeds up the rising, the principle is certainly sound, and with a dough that takes 6 to 8 hours for rising in a humidified oven, is obviously a help.

Baking at 375°F for 10 minutes and then reduc-

ing the heat to 350°F is an important part of the process and not a casual indication.

Finally, the use of two *filone* (bread seams) may seem strange at first but it's really only a bread dough made with another bread dough as a starter. In other words it's a double yeasty bread.

FOR THE FIRST DOUGH OR FILONA I:

1 cup all-purpose flour
¼ cup water, at about 100°F
2 tablespoons starter (biga), aged 24 hours (see page 281)
¼ cake fresh or ¾ teaspoon dried yeast (preferably beer yeast)
Pinch of salt

FOR THE SECOND DOUGH, OR FILONA II:

½ cake fresh or 1¾ teaspoons dried yeast
½ cup water, at about 100°F
¾ to 1 cup all-purpose flour
1 batch filona I

1. To make the first dough, combine the ingredients in the normal manner (see pages 276 to 278) and allow to rise for 1½ hours, or until doubled in size in a warm, draft-free place.
2. Punch it down and use it as the starter for the second dough.
3. To make the second dough, mix the yeast and water. Add it and the flour to the *filona* in a bowl and knead with your knuckles till this dough forms a ball.
4. Turn the dough out onto a floured board and knead lightly for 3 to 5 minutes. Set to rise and allow to double.
5. Punch down and use in the sweet dough as follows.

FOR THE PANETTONE DOUGH:

8 to 9   *cups all-purpose flour*
   1   *teaspoon salt*
      Filona dough (see page 288)
   1   *egg, at room temperature*
   6   *egg yolks, at room temperature*
   1   *cup sugar, dissolved in 1 cup hot water*
  10   *tablespoons (1¼ sticks) unsalted butter, melted and slightly cooled*
   ½   *cup raisins, soaked in water for 30 minutes and drained*
   2   *tablespoons candied fruits, soaked in warm water to cover*
   2   *tablespoons finely minced orange rind*
   1   *teaspoon orange-flower water*
   1   *medium-size potato, peeled, boiled until tender, and mashed*
  1½   *tablespoons unsalted butter, softened but not melted*
   2   *tablespoons hot water, mixed with 1 tablespoon sugar, for glaze*

1. Put the flour in a large bowl and make a well in the center. Sprinkle the salt around the edges of the well. Place the punched down *filona* in the well.
2. Heat water in the bottom of a double boiler and remove from the stove.
3. Place the egg and egg yolks in the top of the double boiler set over the hot water and add the dissolved sugar, the butter, raisins, candied fruits, orange rind, orange flower water, and mashed potato.
4. Add this somewhat liquid mixture gradually—in thirds or less—to the flour and *filona*, amalgamating all together. Knead with your knuckles in the bowl till it takes form. It should be somewhat more wet and sticky than a normal dough, but firm enough to handle. Add flour if needed.
5. Coat the board, or other kneading surface, lightly with vegetable oil. Turn out the *panettone* dough, knead it for about 5 minutes until smooth and unsticky.
6. Place the dough in an oiled bowl covered with plastic wrap and set to rise for 3 to 4 hours in a pilot-lit oven (110° to 120°F) till doubled. Put two pans of boiling water in the oven for humidity. Reheat the water twice during the rising.
7. Turn the dough out onto an oiled board, punch down, and knead lightly for 1 to 2 minutes.
8. Place the dough in whatever container or form you're going to use. Cut a deep cross in the top of the dough and slice under each point of the cross, lifting a piece of the dough back slightly. This is done so that you can place some butter in the cross and under these flaps when half through baking.
9. Return to the rising oven with the two pans of boiling water and let the dough rise again till double in size. Reboil the water twice as before. This rising will take 3 to 5 hours, depending on climatic conditions.
10. After removing the dough from the oven, preheat it to 375°F. Put the *panettone* in the oven for 10 minutes and then reduce the heat to 350°F.
11. Bake for approximately 1 hour until done. Test by inserting a toothpick or skewer. When it comes out clean the bread is done. Halfway through the baking, put the softened butter in the center of the cross and under the flaps. When it's finished baking, brush the top of the bread with the glaze.
12. Wrap to cool and serve when cool.

YIELD: *1 panettone*

Colomba Pasquale

EASTER BREAD

It's interesting to note that the two most important festival breads in Italy both come from Lombardy, and more particularly, Milan. *Panettone* at Christmas and *colomba* at Easter are displayed and sold everywhere. Bars, supermarkets, small grocers, gourmet shops, and of course all the *pasticcerie* are stocked with what seems like endless tons of these festive packages. It seems that there aren't enough people in Italy to consume half of the breads on display. And of course they don't disappear. Just after the holiday, the piles get smaller and after a month or two, dwindle to one little minor display . . . but never disappear completely. You can buy *panettone* and *colomba* year round in some places.

The recipe we're using here is from a great regional Italian book (in Italian) by Sosetti with of course the inevitable confirmations and changes insisted upon by the Italian ladies who help me here at the school.

The use of a bread dough and a mashed potato for levitation and texture gives this cake its characteristic texture. The crossed form that is used for *colomba* is readily available in Italy, but if you have difficulty in finding one in America, use a large loaf pan that takes a 2.2-pound dough. Remember it rises about double as it bakes.

FOR THE BREAD DOUGH:

- 1½ cakes fresh yeast or 4½ teaspoons dried yeast
- ¼ cup water, at about 100°F
- 1 cup cake or pastry flour
  Pinch of salt
- 12 cups water

FOR THE COLOMBA:

- 3 to 3½ cups cake or pastry flour
- 3 egg yolks
  Pinch of salt
- ½ cups sugar
- ¼ teaspoon orange flower water
  Grated rind of 1 lemon
- 12 tablespoons (1½ sticks) unsalted butter, melted
- ½ cup cooked mashed potatoes
- ¼ cup milk, scalded
- 1 tablespoon diced candied orange peel
- 1 tablespoon diced citron
- 4 to 6 candied cherries, chopped

FOR THE TOPPING:

- 1 large egg, lightly beaten
- ¼ cup blanched almonds
- 5 or 6 candied red maraschino cherries
- 2 tablespoons sugar for garnish

1. For the bread dough, dissolve the yeast in the water. Stir in the flour with a pinch of salt and form a very firm dough, firmer than normal bread dough.

2. Turn the dough out onto a board and knead it well for about 10 minutes till firm and elastic. Form a ball and cut a deep cross in the top.

3. Heat the water to about 110°F in a pot and put the ball in it. Cover the pot. When the ball pops to the surface, turn it periodically for 15 minutes or so, keeping all the surfaces moist.

4. For the *colomba*, place the flour on a board and form a well. In the center of the well place the egg yolks, salt, sugar, orange flower water, and lemon rind. With an electric hand beater on medium speed, mix these ingredients thoroughly on the bottom of the well, incorporating a bit of flour as you go.

5. Add the melted butter, the potato, and the milk, and beat again, incorporating a bit more flour.

6. Add the bread dough ball, which by this time is wet and falling apart, to the other ingredients in the well and mix all together with your fingers, incorporating all the remaining flour.

7. Turn the dough out onto a work surface and knead for approximately 10 minutes. It should be soft and almost sticky. If you have trouble handling it, oil the board and continue kneading. If it's too stiff, add a little more scalded milk. The finished dough should be wrinkled, blistered, very soft, and wet.

8. Set the dough in a warm, oiled bowl, covered with plastic, in an oven with the pilot on (90° to 100°F) and let it rise till doubled, about 1½ hours. Punch the dough down and knead briefly on an oiled board with oiled hands. Don't let the stickiness throw you. Add the candied orange peel and citron and knead them into the dough.

9. Place the dough in an oiled *colomba* form (or loaf pan) and set in a warm (90° to 100°F) oven to rise again till it comes level with the form (or the edge of the loaf pan)

10. When ready for the topping, brush the beaten egg onto the top and partially insert the blanched almonds and maraschino cherries in whatever decorative manner you'd like. Sprinkle with sugar.

11. Bake in a preheated 350°F oven for 1 hour. Turn off the oven and leave the colomba in it to dry out for another 30 minutes. Of course, apply the toothpick test as well.

YIELD: *One 2.2-pound cake*

PANINI · ROLLS

Although there are special doughs that can be used for various types of rolls, I'll limit the recipes to those using basic bread dough, with some added ingredients.

There is very little comment necessary as to the particulars of making rolls. Use whatever bread dough you like—with oil or lard, with cheese, with walnuts, with olives, whole wheat, or white, cornmeal or grain bread dough—and knead it till properly elastic. Now shape it into a long flat sausage and slice it into 2-inch-thick rounds. Roll the rounds into balls and stretch each top down over into itself so that the seam is on the bottom. I also further knead them by squeezing the little ball between my palms very hard in a rapid circular motion, pressing down and releasing the pressure as I complete several turns. The rolls become nice and springy in this manner. Place them in oiled muffin tins if you want them formed, or simply set them on a heavy duty sheet pan that has been oiled. Leave enough space for them to double in size and cover them with plastic wrap, or damp towels. Let them double the same as you would for bread, punch down each roll, knead them again, and then let rise a second time before baking.

Panini al Pomodoro

TOMATO ROLLS

1 batch Basic Bread Dough (see page 282)
¼ cup finely chopped onion
1 tablespoon olive oil
2 tablespoons all-purpose flour
6 tablespoons tomato paste
1 tablespoon cornmeal for dusting

1. Work the dough as usual through the first rising (see page 277).
2. While it rises, gently sauté the onion in the oil. Set aside to cool.
3. Flatten the risen dough out in front of you. Lay the onions over it and spread the tomato paste over the onions. Sprinkle with the flour, fold up the dough into a package, and begin to knead. Don't be concerned with the pink mess that ensues as you continue to knead. Keep going until the dough is smooth again. Cut the dough into twelve equal parts. Mash each part between the palms of your hands, rotating them vigorously to form the rolls. Place on a pan dusted with cornmeal and set to rise by about 50 percent.
4. Bake in a 375°F oven for 20 to 30 minutes until crusted and hollow sounding when tapped. Spray as usual (see page 280) three times during the first 10 minutes of baking.

Variations

•

Panini al basilico (Basil Rolls): Work a full cup of finely chopped fresh basil and a tablespoon of oil, seasoned as desired, into the Basic Bread Dough and proceed as normal. *Panini al pesto* (Pesto Rolls): Work a cup of pesto into the dough and proceed as normal. *Panini trifolati* (Truffle rolls): Work a cup of mushroom and truffle paste into the dough and proceed as normal.

YIELD: *about 12 rolls*

Panini con Mandorle

ALMOND ROLLS

This recipe was developed for a restaurant called the Five Reasons Steak and Ale House, which I operated in Lenox, Massachusetts, many years ago (1956 to 1959). It's simple enough to make and has a round twist.

½ cake fresh or 1½ teaspoons dried yeast
1 cup water, at about 100°F
2 tablespoons milk
¼ teaspoon almond extract
2 tablespoons almond paste
3 to 4 cups all-purpose flour
½ cup sugar
1 teaspoon salt
½ cup finely ground almonds
½ cup broken almonds
1 egg

1. Place the yeast in the warm water with 1 tablespoon of milk and the almond extract, reserving 1 tablespoon milk for an egg wash. Mix until the yeast is dissolved. Add the almond paste and dissolve it.

2. Add 1 cup of flour and mix all into a paste. Sprinkle in the sugar and salt and mix. Add another cup of flour and begin to form the dough. Add the rest of the flour and knead with your knuckles in the bowl.

3. Turn the dough out onto a floured board and knead for 10 minutes until smooth and elastic.

4. Set to rise in an oiled bowl covered with plastic wrap for 1 to 1½ hours or till doubled in size.

5. Turn it out, punch it down, and roll it into a rectangle on a floured board. Place the finely ground almonds and almond pieces on the rectangle, folding up the sides to shape. Knead again into a ball. Knead for 1 or 2 minutes till the almonds are well amalgamated.

6. Cut the dough into 14 to 16 pieces and roll each piece out into a cylinder about 5 inches long. Picking one end of each cylinder up, wrap it over and around the other end, forming a circular braided round roll.

7. Set the rolls on an oiled pan to rise again by 50 percent. Combine the egg with the remaining tablespoon of milk and brush this over the rolls.

8. Bake in a 400°F oven for 10 minutes, spraying the while, and then finish baking for approximately another 15 to 20 minutes at 375°F. Cool on a rack before serving.

YIELD: *14 to 16 rolls*

Panini all'Uva

RAISIN ROLLS

This is another recipe we owe in inspiration to *The Italian Baker* by Carol Field. She calls them *maritozzi* or Roman sweet buns.

2 tablespoons starter (biga), aged 6 to 12 hours (see page 281)

1 cake fresh or 1 tablespoon dried yeast

½ to 1 cup all-purpose flour

3 to 4 cups all-purpose flour

½ cup sugar

1 egg

1 egg yolk

1 teaspoon salt

1 tablespoon grated lemon rind

1 tablespoon grated orange rind

½ cup milk, scalded

8 tablespoons (1 stick) unsalted butter, melted

2 cups raisins, soaked in 1 cup water for 30 minutes

¼ teaspoon vanilla extract

1. Put the starter in a bowl and add the flour, sugar, egg, egg yolk, salt, orange and lemon rinds, and milk. Mix well and then add the melted butter. Stir and mix well with a wooden spoon.

2. Begin kneading in the bowl with the knuckles of your hand.

3. Turn the dough out and knead on a floured board for 10 minutes until very elastic.

4. Set the dough to rise in a vegetable oiled or buttered bowl, covered with a plastic wrap for 1 to 1½ hours, or until doubled.

5. Punch the dough down and turn it out onto a floured board. Roll it out into a flat rectangle. Place the water-soaked raisins tossed in a bit of flour on top of the bread rectangle and fold it up on all sides, shaping it into a ball.

6. Knead it lightly for 1 or 2 minutes, amalgamating the raisins thoroughly. Cut the dough into 14 to 16 pieces and knead with the palms of your hands, as explained on page 277.

7. Place the rolls on buttered parchment paper and set to rise by 50 percent.

8. Bake in a 400°F oven for approximately 20 minutes.

NOTE: You could also use an egg wash of any kind to give the top a more finished look.

YIELD: *14 to 16 rolls*

GRISSINI · BREADSTICKS

Our regular basic bread dough, when rolled into long thin strands, will make very acceptable breadsticks, but they are usually better if the dough is enriched by the addition of olive oil and/or malt. Taking these additions further, my favorite of favorites is *grissini con anice* (breadsticks with anise). I use a combination of anise and fennel seeds to make these wonderfully fragrant licorice bread crusts. Cheese is also a very popular addition today, as are garlic, oil, and a variety of herbs. Generally, however, the Italians prefer a plain, well-made breadstick to all the different flavored kinds. I prefer the rough variegated sizes of homemade *grissini* to the uniform appearance of packaged breadsticks, and encourage you to make all different sizes.

Basic Breadsticks

1 batch Basic Bread Dough (see page 282)
Cornmeal for dusting

1. Work dough as usual through the first rising.
2. Pat out into a rough rectangle, about three times as long as it is wide, and about ½ inch thick.
3. Cut across the dough to form the *grissini*. Finish each one by gently stretching it. Place on a well-dusted pan and bake immediately in a 400°F oven until browned and cooked through, about 20 minutes. Turn the oven off and let the breadsticks dry in the oven another 10 to 15 minutes. Cool on racks before serving.

Variations

•

All'anice (Anise Breadsticks): Work 2 tablespoons fennel seed and 1 tablespoon anise seed into the dough after the first rising.
Al formaggio (Cheese Breadsticks): Work in a good cup full of preferred cheese or cheeses after the first rising.

Grissini al Malto

MALT BREADSTICKS

Malt and oil are traditional ingredients in commercially made breadsticks. This recipe is basically the same as our regular bread recipes except that there is a little more yeast, oil, and, of course, malt. You could also enrich them further by the use of a *biga* as we've seen in so many other recipes.

1 cup water, at about 100°F
½ cake fresh or 1¼ teaspoons dried yeast

2 tablespoons starter (biga), aged 6 to 12 hours (see page 281)
1 tablespoon malt
1 tablespoon extra virgin olive oil
3 to 4 cups all-purpose flour
1 teaspoon salt
Cornmeal for dusting

1. Make a bread dough in the normal manner, following the instructions on page 277, adding the malt to the yeast, biga, and water solution before the addition of the flour.
2. Let the dough rise till it doubles in bulk, 1 to 1½ hours.
3. Punch the dough down in the bowl and turn it out onto a floured surface. Knead lightly and shape into a 1½- to 2-inch-thick rectangle. Cut off strips of dough and stretch and roll them on the floured board to the shapes you desire.
4. Place in a cornmeal-dusted pan and bake in a 400°F oven for approximately 20 minutes. Turn the oven off and let the breadsticks dry out for 10 minutes.

YIELD: *20 to 24 breadsticks*

FOCACCE · PIZZA

Both of these are flat breads. *Focaccia* actually means cake, and the main difference between it and a pizza is the thickness. Pizza in Italy is generally wafer thin, and when they make thicker (1 to 2 inches) they are called *focacce.* The dough for both is the same and is only slightly different from our basic bread dough in that it has oil, less yeast, is kneaded less, and is allowed to rise less. Throughout Italy, "pizza" is generally called pizza, but *focacce* have many different names, de-

pending on the region you're in. In Tuscany, they're called *schiacciata,* and in Emilia Romagna, *piadino.* But regardless of these differences these are the flat breads that go back to ancient Egyptian civilizations and were originally unleavened. The ingredients used to top them are endless—although I must caution that I don't think pineapple and peanut butter heat well, or are good toppings for a bread laced with garlic and oil . . . not that I'm against peanut butter sandwiches, mind you, but not on the pizza, please. Here's a small list of more frequently used ingredients for toppings that you'll encounter in Italy:

Anchovies	Gorgonzola	Prosciutto
Artichokes	Green olives	Provolone
Basil	Mozzarella	Rosemary
Black olives	Oil	Sage
Boragine	Onions	Sardines
Brown olives	Pancetta	Sausage
Capperi	Parmigiano	Spinach
Eggs	Pecorino	Taleggio
Fontina	Peperoncini	Thyme
Garlic	Peppers	Tomatoes

It is important to realize that, unlike American pizza makers, the Italians use toppings very sparingly. A little oil, onion, and salt for a *pizza bianca*; very little tomatoes and some mozzarella for a *pizza margherita*; add a few capers and anchovies for a *pizza napoletana*—and I do mean a few—using 4 pieces of anchovy and 6 or 8 capers for the whole thing. The thinness of the crust, which is much preferred here in Italy, will not support a lot of topping and will end up being soggy—which is a big no-no in the Italian world of pizza.

Of course, wood-burning ovens, with their 1,200°F magic heat, work best for these thinner breads. A gas oven with a stone floor, however, will produce a very suitable product.

Bruschetta

4 large, ¾-inch-thick slices coarse
  fresh country bread
6 large cloves garlic
¾ to 1 cup extra virgin olive oil
  Salt and freshly ground black
  pepper to taste

1. Roast the bread slices over a wood fire till
charred.
2. Rub with garlic and then with oil. Season to
taste with generous amounts of salt and pepper.

NOTES: This being such a simple recipe, any sub-
stitution will radically change the dish. For example, don't try to roast a finely textured bread such
as French or sourdough; make a garlic butter and
grill it instead. Likewise, the whole beauty of this
dish is the underlying charred flavor from the
coals, which are a common cooking medium in
Italian restaurants. You may have to plan a coal-
grilled entree to justify the fire.

In Umbria, *bruschette* are served hot as an appetizer course, either alone or with a plate of anchovies or marinated eggplant. It's delicious as a
salad accompaniment or as part of a large antipasto. The rustic flavors beg for a robust red wine.

All sorts of additions are possible here. The
more traditional Italian ones are chicken liver
paste, mushroom and truffle paste, and diced
tomatoes.

YIELD: *4 servings*

Pizza Dough

Although you can use our basic bread dough recipe to make pizza and all its brothers, sisters, and
cousins, here is the proper recipe for this simple
bread dough.

⅛ cake fresh or ¾ teaspoon dried yeast
1 cup water, at about 100°F
2 tablespoons extra virgin olive oil
3 to 4 cups all-purpose flour
1 scant teaspoon salt

1. Mix the yeast in the water till dissolved. Add
the oil and 1 cup of flour and mix to a paste. Add
the salt to the paste, mix, and add another cup of
flour. Mix well.
2. Add more flour and shape into a loose form,
kneading with your knuckles.
3. Turn the dough out onto a floured board and
knead for 3 to 5 minutes. Set to rise in an oiled
bowl covered with plastic wrap for about 30 minutes to rise by 50 percent.
4. Punch down, turn out onto a floured board,
and knead lightly for 1 minute into a ball. Cut the
ball in half and flatten half out with the palm of
your hand into a round disk. Roll the disk out
lightly once or twice with a small pizza pin.
5. Flour the board under the pizza excessively.
This is necessary to finger-stretch the pizza out
into a very thin disk. There can't be too much
flour. Lock the fingers of your right hand (left
handers—reverse) in between, and on top of, the
fingers of your left hand, so that you can knead-
press the dough out from the center to the outer
rim with the tips of your eight fingers. (The
thumbs are not involved.) Starting from the center, press down and out with the tips of your

eight fingers, tapping the dough rhythmically in rapid succession. Repeat 10 to 12 times. The dough will expand to 3 times its size, making a 10- to 12-inch disk.

6. Place the enlarged disk on a peel (or back of a pan) liberally dusted with cornmeal. Dress it in any way you want, to make a variety of pizzas.

7. Bake the pizza in a 450° to 500°F oven for 2 to 3 minutes on the floor of the oven and then bring it to the top rack for another 2 to 3 minutes depending on the density and moisture of the toppings.

YIELD: *2 pizzas*

Variations

•

Pizza bianca (White Pizza): Using an oil can, drizzle some of your best olive oil in a circular motion very lightly, making rings of oil on the pizza disk. Sprinkle lightly with salt and pepper. Lay in randomly, or in a ring pattern, enough sliced onions to cover the disk lightly, about ½ to 1 cup. Drizzle more oil lightly across the onions, then season with salt, pepper, and crushed red pepper. Bake in a hot oven as described and serve immediately.

Pizza margherita: Using an oil can, drizzle some of your best olive oil in a circular motion very lightly, making rings of oil on the pizza disk. Sprinkle lightly with salt and pepper. With the back of a spoon, spread 1 cup of canned Italian plum tomatoes to cover the disk lightly. Then add shredded mozzarella, lightly around, but not completely covering, the tomatoes. Now, top with oil, salt, pepper, crushed red pepper, and fresh basil leaves. Bake in a hot oven as described and serve immediately.

Pizza frutti di mare (Seafood Pizza): This one is only available on Thursdays and Fridays here in Umbria, when fresh seafood makes its appearance. The procedure is exactly the same as for *pizza margherita,* except that now you add a few clams, mussels, squid, and shrimp to the oiled, seasoned, tomato disk. Once again, I can't emphasize too strongly how thin the pizza should be and how light the topping is. Try it this way, and if it doesn't make a convert of you, then go back to whatever toppings you like, naturally.

Pizza ai quattro formaggi (Pizza with Four Cheeses): Proceed as for *pizza bianca* without the onions and then add whatever cheeses you like. The ones I prefer are parmigiano, taleggio, gorgonzola, and Gruyère. Reseason with salt, pepper, and crushed red pepper, if you like, and omit the second oiling, since the cheeses have their own fat.

Pizza ai tartufi (Truffle Pizza): This is really an extension of *pizza ai quattro formaggi,* only use less cheese and sprinkle on, or spoon on, a mixture of mushroom and truffle paste. Another way this is done is to shave truffles on top after it's baked, before serving. Yet another way I've had it served is as a *pizza bianca* without the onions and then truffles shaved on top after baking and before serving.

Pizza alle Cipolle

ONION PIZZA

There is a little story in connection with this one, which might serve as an example as to how recipes develop.

My son, Dino, who is a very fine chef, culinarian, wine expert, and teacher in his own right, was asked by some friends in the wine business to prepare something Italian that would go with a German wine tasting. It was to be an appetizer-type dish, not an entree, and would be served after the traditional cheese and bread palate cleansers, at the end of the wine tasting as a special sort of bonus that would enable the tasters to drink a little more wine without being ravenous. After much racking of the brain (I'm told) and considerable research into dishes of Valtellina, Trento, and Friuli–Venezia Giulia, he came across a reference to an onion pie that was German in origin called *Zwiebelkuchen*. It wasn't a far step to convert this idea into a pizza. From there came the ideas to use whole wheat flour, and since the original was a pie, to build up the pizza dough into a thick *focaccia* to support, as he said, "A ton of onions. The key is three kinds of onions, white, red, and yellow, sweated in butter and oil, nutmeg, salt, pepper, and crushed red pepper, and then tossed with taleggio, parmigiano, gorgonzola, mozzarella, and Gruyère. Bake the *focaccia* first so the bread is cooked and firm enough to support all the topping. Then top it lavishly (2 to 3 inches thick) with the onion-cheese mix. Garnish with more grated parmigiano and bake till the cheeses have melted and the top of the onions are golden brown."

1/8 *cake fresh or* 3/4 *teaspoon dried yeast*

1/2 *cup water, at about 100°F*

1 *tablespoon malt (optional)*

3 *tablespoons extra virgin olive oil*

1/2 *cup all-purpose flour*

1 *cup whole wheat flour*

  Salt

  Cornmeal for dusting

  Freshly ground black pepper to taste

2 *cups chopped white onions*

2 *cups chopped red onions*

2 *cups chopped yellow onions*

2 *tablespoons unsalted butter*

  Freshly grated nutmeg to taste

  Crushed red pepper to taste

  Water or white wine (optional)

2 *cups freshly grated parmigiano*

1 *cup shredded taleggio*

1 *cup shredded mozzarella*

1 *cup shredded gorgonzola*

1 *cup shredded Gruyère*

1. Dissolve the yeast in the water and add the malt and 2 tablespoons of oil.

2. Add enough flour to make a paste. Add 1/2 teaspoon salt to the paste. Add the rest of the flour and proceed as in making regular pizza (see page 296).

3. After punching down and kneading a second time, cut the dough in half to make 2 pizzas. Roll the dough out into disks approximately 8 inches in diameter and 2 to 3 inches thick.

4. Place on a peel, or inverted pan, liberally dusted with cornmeal. Season with salt, pepper, and a few drops of oil.

5. Bake in 450°F oven for 5 to 7 minutes, or until the disks are well set up but not cooked through. Bring them out of the oven and set aside.

6. Meanwhile prepare the onions by sweating them in the butter and remaining tablespoon of oil in a covered pan. Season the onions liberally with salt, pepper, nutmeg, red pepper. Add a bit of water, if needed. Cook the onions for 15 to 20 minutes or longer until they start to brown lightly. Remove the cover for the last 5 minutes if they're too wet.

7. Mix the cheeses with the onions, reserving 1/2 cup of parmigiano for topping both pizzas. Mound the onion-cheese mixture on top of the baked pizza disks and top with the remaining parmigiano.

8. Bake in a 450°F oven for 5 to 10 minutes, or until the top is browned nicely and everything is cooked through. Serve immediately.

NOTE: You could also cook the onions in successive stages for different textures if you'd like by staggering the cooking times: yellow onions first, then 5 minutes later red onions, and 5 minutes after that the white onions. It's not essential for this recipe, however.

YIELD: *two 8-inch pizzas*

Schiacciata

SANDWICH PIZZA

The *schiacciatas* of Umbria and Tuscany are simply flavored breads. Unlike the *torta sul testo,* where you bake the bread first, then slice it open and stuff it lightly with greens or ham and retoast it, the *schiacciata* dough is mixed with the particular ingredient and then baked in a pan.

> ½ cup water, at about 100°F
>
> ⅛ cake fresh or ¾ teaspoon dried yeast
>
> 1½ to 2 cups all-purpose flour
>
> ½ teaspoon salt
>
> 1 tablespoon extra virgin olive oil
>
> 1 cup diced prosciutto

1. Make the dough in the normal manner, following instructions on page 296, and set to rise for approximately 45 minutes till doubled in size.
2. Punch it down and add the prosciutto.
3. Roll out the dough to a 1½- to 2-inch-thick rectangle and place it in a well-oiled sheet pan. Set to rise for 10 to 15 minutes.
4. Bake it in a 400°F oven for 10 to 15 minutes or until done. Serve directly.

YIELD: *6 to 8 servings*

CALZONE

Whether stuffed with prosciutto and mozzarella or artichokes, olives, or eggs, this oversized, sealed envelope sandwich is made with basic pizza dough stretched out, stuffed, and folded in half. It's interesting to note that even though a *schiacciata* or *torta sul testo* is similar, you'll never see a calzone stuffed with greens nor the *torta sul testo* with artichokes, although it might seem that there's no serious reason why it couldn't be so done. But these customs that have developed over the centuries in Italy are not without reason.

If you put cooked greens in a calzone that is then sealed and baked, the moisture from the greens is liable to make the whole thing soggy, whereas since the *torta sul testo* is already cooking and then sliced open before stuffing, the greens don't get a chance to steam in their own juices, so to speak.

Once again, it's important to exercise restraint in the stuffing of a calzone. No point in loading it up with so much stuff that it can't bake properly. This world of Italian pizza and *focaccia* is not the same as the "Dagwood Bumstead" syndrome in America . . . not to imply that under the right circumstances, one of his architectural wonders wouldn't be tempting.

Focaccia Rustica con Salvia e Cipolle

FOCACCIA WITH SAGE AND ONIONS

½ cup water, at about 100°F

⅛ cake fresh or ¾ teaspoon dried yeast

½ cup whole wheat flour

½ cup all-purpose flour

1 teaspoon salt

1 tablespoon extra virgin olive oil

Salt and freshly ground black pepper to taste

Crushed red pepper to taste

1 cup thinly sliced onions

About 12 fresh sage leaves

1 to 2 teaspoons coarse salt

1. Pour water over the crumbled yeast in a large bowl and stir to dissolve.

2. Mix in the wheat flour and half the all-purpose flour and add salt. Mix in as much of the remaining flour as needed to make a fairly firm dough.

3. Turn the dough out onto a lightly floured surface and knead steadily until smooth. Put the dough in an oiled bowl, cover, and let rise until doubled in bulk.

4. Punch down the dough, divide in half, knead briefly, and shape into round pizzas about 2 inches thick.

5. Drizzle the oil over the pizzas. Sprinkle with the salt, pepper, and crushed red pepper. Spread the onions evenly over the pizzas and arrange the sage leaves decoratively. Sprinkle with coarse salt.

6. Bake in a preheated 450°F oven until bronzed and cooked through.

YIELD: *1 pizza*

Focaccia all'Aglio Arrosto

FOCACCIA WITH ROASTED GARLIC

1 batch Basic Bread or Pizza Dough (see page 282 or 296)

15 cloves garlic, unpeeled

1 tablespoon extra virgin olive oil

Salt and freshly ground black pepper to taste

2 tablespoons aromatic white wine, like Gewurztraminer

Cornmeal for dusting

Crushed red pepper to taste

1. Work the dough as usual through the first rising.

2. Sauté the garlic cloves in their skins in the oil, crusting on all sides. Season with salt and pepper. Deglaze with white wine and remove to a plate to cool.

3. Form the risen dough into a *focaccia* on a peel or pan dusted with cornmeal. Make the indentations in the *focaccia* with your fingertips, peel the garlic cloves and place a clove in each dent.

4. Let the *focaccia* rise about 25 percent. Then drizzle more oil on top, season with crushed red pepper, and bake in about a 400°F oven until crusty and cooked through.

Pizza alla Romana Con Cipolle e Rosmarino

PIZZA WITH ONIONS AND ROSEMARY

How many of you have been to Rome and had a slice of semi-thick pizza from a large black sheet pan that is unmistakably good? My favorite is with potatoes, onions, and rosemary. The surprise is that while the dough is thicker than normal Italian pizza, the cakier texture gives it an equal lightness, and the understatement of thin sliced potatoes and onions barely covering, not smothering, the pizza, carries out further this delightful exercise in restraint. I've found the combination so subtle that I had to ask the pizza maker if the dough was made with potato flour. He laughingly said, in wonderful broken English: "Itsa no different. Justa la pizza!"

For the cakier dough we will use a little more yeast and knead and rise it a little longer. You can also put mashed potatoes (!) in the dough, regardless of what my friend the pizza maker said.

- ¼ cake fresh yeast or 1½ teaspoons dried yeast
- ½ cup water, at about 100°F
- 1 to 2 tablespoons extra virgin olive oil
- 1 small potato, boiled and mashed (optional)
- 1½ to 2 cups all-purpose flour
- ½ teaspoon salt
- Freshly ground pepper to taste
- 2 medium-size potatoes, very thinly sliced and blanched
- Sprigs fresh rosemary to taste
- Thinly sliced onions to taste

1. Dissolve the yeast in the water.

2. Add 1 tablespoon of oil and the mashed potato. Add some flour and stir into a paste, seasoning with the salt. Knead in the bowl with your knuckles.

3. Turn the dough out onto a floured board, and knead rhythmically for 5 to 7 minutes.

4. Set to rise in an oiled bowl covered with plastic wrap for 45 minutes to 1 hour, until just under doubled in size.

5. Punch down and roll out into a long rectangle, shaping the dough with your eight fingers, again as in making regular pizza on page 296. It should be about 1 inch thick.

6. Place in a well-oiled 16- by-12-inch pan and set to rise again by half.

7. Once risen, top with a little oil, salt and pepper, and the sliced, blanched potatoes. Season again with salt and pepper and liberally top with the rosemary, broken into pieces.

8. Bake in a 400°F oven for approximately 5 minutes or until three quarters of the way cooked. Add the thinly sliced onions, season with salt and pepper and a few drops of oil, and finish baking for another 3 to 5 minutes, or until done. Don't brown the top excessively. It will spoil the potato flavor.

Pizza alla Marinara con Uova

PIZZA WITH TOMATO SAUCE AND EGGS

When I first came to live in Italy, I stayed with a friend who had introduced me to Todi, and his mother was forever coming up with dishes to entice us to stay home rather than go to a restaurant. One night we were all set to go out for a wood-burning oven pizza, when she said enticingly, "Have you ever had a *pizza marinara* with an egg?"

My curiosity being instantly aroused, I turned to my friend and asked, "What's that?"

"She makes a fried pizza dough in a pan on top of the stove with tomatoes and fried eggs on top. Quite bloody good." (His father was an English soldier.)

I watched her make a quick pizza dough and shape it (without rising) into a three-inch cake bread. She then heated some olive oil—quite a bit—in a black skillet and proceeded to fry the dough, first on one side and then the other. In the meantime, with a little garlic and oil she made a quick marinara by searing a small can of tomatoes. At the same time she was frying three eggs in a bit of oil—one for each of us. When everything was cooked (a matter of 10 minutes), she took out the fried pizza, dripping with oil, put the tomatoes on top, and the eggs on top of that, liberally sprinkled the whole with salt and pepper and quickly served it in pie-shaped servings (a third for each) with an egg on top. Absolutely delicious. Not only that, my friend said it was "Bloody well good!" Do we need any more recipe than that? I'll repeat.

1. Make an unrisen pizza dough (or rise it if you have time).
2. Fry it in oil (liberal).
3. Make a marinara (see sauce recipe).
4. Fry some eggs, sunnyside up.
5. Put some sauce on the fried pizza.
6. Top with the fried eggs.
7. Serve seasoned as you will.

Sfinciuni

SICILIAN PIZZA

The thick pan-cooked pizza of Sicily is very popular in America. *Sfinciuni* is the best I know of that genre. It is unique in that it has lemon juice in the dough and the long-stewed onion and tomato sauce with anchovy pieces on top is finished with fine ground toasted bread crumbs in oil. This extra thick topping serves the cakey dough well.

FOR THE DOUGH:

   ¾ *cake fresh yeast or 3¾ teaspoons dried yeast*
   ½ *cup water, at about 100°F*
   2 *tablespoons extra virgin olive oil*
   2 *tablespoons fresh lemon juice*
 2½ *cups all-purpose flour*
   ½ *teaspoon salt*
   ½ *teaspoon freshly ground black pepper*
   ½ *cup freshly grated parmigiano*

FOR THE SAUCE:

   4 to 5 *tablespoons extra virgin olive oil*
   1 *small white onion, finely sliced*
   2 to 2½ *cups canned or fresh peeled, seeded, and chopped Italian plum tomatoes*
     Salt and freshly ground black pepper to taste
   2 *tablespoons finely chopped fresh parsley*
   5 to 6 *anchovy fillets, halved*
   3 *tablespoons finely diced parmigiano*
   3 *tablespoons finely diced pecorino Romano*

3 tablespoons finely diced Gruyère

3 tablespoons finely ground, toasted bread crumbs

1. For the dough, mix the yeast in the warm water in a bowl till dissolved.

2. Heat the oil and lemon juice to approximately 110°F and add to the yeast.

3. In a separate bowl, mix together the flour, salt, pepper, and parmigiano. Add the yeast, lemon, and oil mixture.

4. Knead in the bowl with your knuckles and form the dough into a ball.

5. Turn the dough out onto an oiled board and knead lightly for 3 to 5 minutes until smooth and elastic. Place in an oiled bowl, cover with plastic wrap, and let rise for about 1 hour or until doubled in size.

6. While it is rising, make the sauce. Pour 4 to 5 tablespoons of olive oil in a sauté pan over very low heat. Cook the onion for 2 to 3 minutes till they start to take on color. Add the tomatoes and break up with a spoon.

7. Season with salt and pepper and cook over low heat for 30 to 40 minutes, stirring occasionally. Add the parsley, anchovy fillets, and the cheeses. Cook for another 10 minutes on the same low heat.

8. Punch down the risen bread dough, turn it out onto an oiled board and knead lightly.

9. Shape the dough into a rectangle approximately 7- by 10-inches and indent the top with your fingertips.

10. Oil a 7- by 10-inch pan and set the dough in it for a second rise of about 30 to 40 minutes—somewhat less than doubling.

11. Oil the top very very lightly with a brush and

bake in a preheated 375°F oven for 10 to 15 minutes. Remove from the oven and spread three fourths of the tomato sauce on top, leaving a 1-inch border of crust.

12. Return the pizza to the oven and bake for another 20 to 30 minutes.

13. Take it from the oven again and coat with the rest of the tomato sauce and then the finely ground toasted bread crumbs, which have been reserved in oil. Bake for another 10 to 15 minutes until the toppings and the bread have married into an unmistakably unified whole. Serve immediately.

YIELD: *6 to 8 slices/2 to 2½ cups sauce*

INDEX